The Pronunciation
of Placenames

The Pronunciation of Placenames

A Worldwide Dictionary

ADRIAN ROOM

McFarland & Company, Inc., Publishers
Jefferson, North Carolina, and London

LIBRARY OF CONGRESS CATALOGUING-IN-PUBLICATION DATA

Room, Adrian.
   The pronunciation of placenames : a worldwide dictionary /
Adrian Room.
     p.   cm.
   Includes bibliographical references.

   ISBN-13: 978-0-7864-2941-7
   softcover : 50# alkaline paper ∞

   1. Names, Geograhical — Pronunciation. I. Title.
G105.R67 2007
910.3 — dc22   2007012670

British Library cataloguing data are available

Cover image © 2007 Comstock

Manufactured in the United States of America

McFarland & Company, Inc., Publishers
  Box 611, Jefferson, North Carolina 28640
   www.mcfarlandpub.com

Contents

Contents

Introduction

This new dictionary aims to give the pronunciations of over 12,000 of the world's placenames. It also aims to be reader-friendly, and to this end employs a transcription system which uses only the regular letters of the English alphabet rather than the International Phonetic Alphabet or similar specialized characters. (Details of the system are set out below.)

The names chosen for inclusion are mainly those that are familiar, although some names of less well-known places are here because of their awkward or unusual pronunciation.

The best-known placenames of the world, such as those of countries and their capital cities, are often familiar in a form differing from the original, depending on the language of the speaker. What English speakers call *Spain* is *Espagne* to the French, *Spanien* to Germans, *Spagna* to the Italians, and *España* to the Spanish themselves. Most readers of this book will be English speakers, so will expect to find *Austria*, *Copenhagen*, and *Lisbon*, not French *Autriche*, *Copenhague*, and *Lisbonne*. (As a lure for linguists, however, the *native* names of well-known places are entered, with their pronunciations, in the Appendix, so that German *Österreich*, Danish *København*, and Portuguese *Lisboa* will be found there.)

Many placenames have a single standard form of pronunciation, and this is naturally the one chosen for entry. Even so, there may well be alternate forms, and this is particularly the case in the distinctive British and American ways of pronouncing a name. Two of the most common differences are an American flat *a* where the British pronunciation would have a broad one, and the sounding of *r* where British speech would omit it. By way of example, Americans would pronounce the name of the English city of *Bath* to rhyme with *math*, but in a British pronunciation it has the *a* of *father*. An identical disparity in fact occurs within Britain itself, with northerners favoring the flat *a* and southerners the broad one. Similarly, Americans sound the *r* in a name such as *Burgundy*, but speakers of British English omit it. Again,

1

in American English the vowel *o* in names such as *Oxford* is pronounced *ah*, whereas in British English it is an open vowel, pronounced with rounded lips. (Compare the respective pronunciations of *hot*.) Sometimes a name's pronunciation combines one of these three main differences with an altered vowel, as in the famous American *Berkeley* (with first *e* as in *burn* and sounded *r*) and British *Berkeley* (with first *e* as in *barn* and no *r* sound).

Many placenames have a formal and an informal pronunciation, the latter often adopted by local residents or by those who know a place well. As Bill Bryson points out in *Mother Tongue* (1990), the informal pronunciation is often simply a slurred form of the formal. He offers some examples:

> Australians will tell you they come from "'stralia," while Torontoans will tell you they come from "Tronna." In Iowa it's "Iwa" and in Ohio it's "Hia." People from Milwaukee say they're from "Mwawkee." In Louisville it's "Loovul," in Newark it's "Nerk," and in Indianapolis it's "Naplus." People in Philadelphia don't come from there; they come from "Fuhluffia." The amount of slurring depends on the degree of familiarity and frequency with which the word is spoken [p. 81].

American speech may well embrace such elisions more readily than British English. What is certain is that many places have both an American and a British pronunciation. In the present book, where well-known names are involved, both such pronunciations are usually given, the American first, the British (indicated by UK) following in brackets. Where identically spelled names in the UK and USA have different pronunciations, they are given separate entries, as for England's *Birmingham* and its Alabama namesake (which was adopted from it). Britons referring to the American city may well pronounce its name in the British way, of course, and conversely Americans pronounce the British name in the American way, enunciating the final *-ham*. But often an accommodation will be made, so that Americans referring to *Derby*, England, may well pronounce it in the British way, even if sounding the *r*, while Britons speaking of the Connecticut or Kansas town may take care to pronounce the *e* as in *herb*, even if *not* sounding the *r*. Such accommodations are helpful, if only for sake of clarity and courtesy.

Other alternate forms of placename pronunciation exist, sometimes as a variant stress (accent). For example, most people pronounce the name of *Montevideo* with the stress on the final *e* (-vid*e*o) but others prefer to accent the *i* (-v*i*deo). There are also local or regional variants, as represented in written form by the well-known "Noo Yoik" for *New York*.

The English pronunciation of foreign placenames is a more complex issue. There are basically three options. Either (1) the name is pronounced in a manner as close to the native form as possible, or (2) a more or less successful stab is made at the foreign pronunciation, or (3) the name is pronounced in a way that conforms to English-language norms, meaning those of American English or British English. This last usually involves a so-called spelling pronunciation, where the name is articulated according to its letters or syllables as seen through English-seeing eyes and heard through English-hearing ears. Thus when an English speaker refers to *Paris*, the capital of France, the resulting pronunciation may reproduce the French, which properly involves a broadish *a*, a French "throaty" *r* (technically known as a voiced uvular fricative), a "tight" vowel *i*, and omission of the *s* sound, the outcome being stressed on the second syllable. But in practice no English speakers would do this, unless of course actually speaking French. An approximation is represented by the written form "Paree." A conformity to English-language norms is the regular form, so that the name rhymes with *embarrass*. (*Paris* is one of the major European city names that has not acquired an altered English form, unlike *Athens, Brussels, Cologne, Milan, Moscow, Naples, Prague, Rome, Vienna*, or *Warsaw*, among others. Some such names have gained their standard English forms via the medium of other languages, as *Cologne* through French. It is also worth recalling that names of this type adopted for places in another country, as notably in the USA, will often have a quite different pronunciation from that in their native land. See, for example, the dual entries for *Cairo, Lima, Milan, Montevideo, Versailles*, and *Vienna*.)

The general principle in this dictionary is that where a foreign place is sufficiently important or well enough known to have a name with an anglicized pronunciation, that pronunciation will be given, in both American and British forms if necessary, along with the indigenous form. An example is Denmark's seaport city of *Esbjerg*, with a name usually pronounced by Americans as Esbyuhrg (sounding the *r*) and by the British as Esbyuhg (not sounding it), but by the native Danes as Esbyer (not sounding the written *g*). Another example is Germany's *Magdeburg*, with a name pronounced by Americans as Magdabuhrg and by Britons as Magdabuhg, but by Germans as Mahgdaboork. All three forms are given.

Places that are less important, or less familiar, will mostly have their native pronunciation and none other, even where an anglicized form is possible or even likely. An example here is the Argentine town of *Casilda*. Obviously, this name could be (and probably is) pronounced by many English speakers to rhyme with "Matilda," but its Spanish-speaking residents will enunciate the name distinctively with broad vowels (*a* as *ah*, *i* as *ee*), and this is the pronunciation given. Similarly, the small Italian town of *Palestrina* is given solely its Italian pronunciation, despite the English spelling pronunciation familiar from that of the composer of the same name. When referring to a foreign place, English speakers who are aware of the name's indigenous pronunciation may well adopt a dual approach, saying the name in an English manner among fellow English speakers but in the native way, or an approximation of it, when speaking with a resident of the place or when actually visiting it. This highlights a practical feature of the present dictionary, in that it provides the native pronunciation of a place's name for use when appropriate.

For places in the former Soviet Union, the native Russian pronunciation is often given, even when the place in question may now well be in an independent state and not in Russia proper, such as *Andizhan*, Uzbekistan, or *Ashkhabad*, Turkmenistan. This is because the name's "native" pronunciation is historically its Russian one, especially where its spelling has remained in its transliterated Russian form. And although Andizhan is more correctly *Andijon* in its native land, and Ashkhabad similarly *Ashgabat*, these names and certain others of this type are not entered under their local forms. In many cases, however, both the historic transliterated form and the local one are given, as for *Nikolayev* and *Mykolayiv* in Ukraine and *Mogilev* and *Mahilyow* in Belarus. For the former, either the conventional English (and sometimes Russian) or the local pronunciation will be given, depending on the importance or familiarity of the place, while the latter will have its local pronunciation only. For example, *Kharkov*, Ukraine, has both its English (US and UK) and Russian pronunciations, while *Kharkiv*, its local form, has just the Ukrainian.

As well as pronouncing a name's vowels, consonants, and syllables correctly, in either anglicized or native version, it is also necessary to observe the right stress or accent. Russia's *Vladimir* is an ancient and beautiful city, popular among tourists. But it is Vlad*ee*mir, with the stress on the second syllable, not *Vlad*imir, and a native Russian will pronounce the name thus, even when speaking English.

Arrangement of the Entries

The placenames run in alphabetical order, A through Z, with spellings based on those in the works listed in the Select Bibliography. Some of the names are historical, as *Neapolis* or *Tanganyika*, and some are current alternate forms, as *Calcutta* and *Kolkata*. No indication is given as to the nature of the place bearing the name (the dictionary is not a gazetteer), although a geographical identifier is provided, usually the name of the country or continent where the place is located. Generic words that normally precede a name, such as *Lake* or *Mount*, are usually omitted, giving *Superior* (not *Lake Superior*), *Tacoma* (not *Mount Tacoma*), although (with the sole exception of *River*) generic words that follow a name are often added in brackets, as *Danakil (Desert)*, *Pacific (Ocean)*. An exception is made for foreign names where the generic word is inseparable from the whole, such as *Mont Blanc* and *Rio Grande*, and in certain cases to show where the stress falls, as in *Coney Island* (where *Island* is stressed, not *Coney*). In fact there are many territorial areas or population centers named for natural features, as the city of *Superior* or state of *Colorado*, and the transcription can be taken as applying to them as readily as to the respective lake and river that gave these two names. The same principle also applies to names of administrative areas formed by the addition of a generic element to an existing name, as notably with the *-shire* in English county names. Where such an addition has resulted in an altered form of the original name, however, it qualifies for entry. Thus *Cheshire* (based on *Chester*) and *Wiltshire* (based on *Wilton*) are in, but not, for example, *Bedfordshire*, *Lincolnshire*, or *Yorkshire*. (For a consideration of the different pronunciations of *-shire* in such names, see the entry for *Berkshire*.) The same principle generally applies to placenames with a geographical "compass" addition such as *North* or *West*. Some names of this type are entered, however, in order to indicate the position of the stress. Names prefixed *East*, *North*, *South*, or *West* are rarely stressed on this word, although there are exceptions, as for *South Island* and *West Point*. (In cases where a phrase is formed by the addition of a generic word to a placename, the stress usually falls on that word, or on its stressed syllable, as with Boston *beans*, or New Hampshire *primary*.)

Historical places are set in their present geographical locations, so that *Troy* and *Ephesus*, for example, are sited in modern Turkey, although primarily associated with ancient Greece. Just as no physical descriptive is given for a place, so no indication is given of any relationship between one name and another. Thus no cross reference is made between Danish *Godthåb* and Greenlandic *Nuuk*, or between German *Marienbad* and Czech *Mariánské Lázně*, although each pair of words describes a single place. Both names have their entries, however. (Historical *Marienbad* justifies its inclusion by its continuing familiarity, if only from the classic 1961 movie *Last Year at Marienbad*. To most English speakers, it is also more memorable and readily pronounceable than *Mariánské Lázně*.)

The somewhat bald listing of names and pronunciations is interspersed with comments on noteworthy individual names or quotations regarding the actual pronunciation. Such comments (enclosed in square brackets) may involve an etymology, as for the English town of *Haltwhistle*, or an alternate recommended pronunciation, as for Spain's *Majorca*. England's town of

Cirencester has a long-disputed pronunciation, and a selection of quotations centers on this dispute. Where such additions are made, the entry also usually offers a descriptive (as town or river) and in many instances a more precise geographical location. A good example of such complementary material is that provided for *Derby*. (For reasons already explained, there are separate entries for this name, referring respectively to the American and English cities. As such, they are labeled ¹**Derby** and ²**Derby**, as are similar doublets throughout the dictionary.)

The alphabetical principle of arrangement is applied not only to the headwords of the entries but to the geographical locations of two or more identically named places. Thus there are places named *Newcastle* in Australia, Canada, England, South Africa, and the USA, and their country locations are named in this alphabetical order. Similarly, the entry for *Cairo*, Egypt, precedes that for *Cairo*, USA, not because the city is better known or more important but because alphabetically "Egypt" comes before "USA." (Sometimes this principle results in the reverse, so that Canada's *Delhi* precedes the famous Indian city of this name.)

Transcription System

As stated, each placename has a phonetic transcription using only the standard letters of the English alphabet. The transcription is effectively a rewriting of the name and as such begins with a capital letter, like the name itself. If the name consists of more than one word, each beginning with a capital letter, the transcription does the same, although in a very few cases it may be necessary to omit a second or subsequent capital for practical reasons.

If the name consists of more than one syllable, so does its transcription, but with the syllables spaced out for ease of reading. The stressed (accented) syllable is printed in *italics*. (It will be noticed that only a single syllable is stressed, even in names comprising more than one word. This is done for sake of simplicity and practicality. In fact even a lengthy name such as *Jerez de la Frontera* will sound acceptable if stressed solely on the second syllable of the last word, with the first part of the name spoken evenly or with a natural emphasis.)

Where both American and British pronunciations are given for names comprising two or more words, identically pronounced parts of the name in the British pronunciation are not repeated but represented by ellipses points (...), as Kah dur *Id* ris (UK Kad ur...) for *Cader Idris*. The transcriptions of non–English forms are usually spelled out in full, however, as Ree oh *Grand* (Spanish Ree oh *Grahn* day) for *Rio Grande*.

As can be seen from these last examples, letters used in a transcription often correspond to some extent to those in the spelling of the name. In a few cases they correspond fully, as with *Nablus*, transcribed *Nab* lus. Either way, the transcription is usually readily recognizable as that of a particular name. It is not hard to see that *Bawl* ta mawr is *Baltimore*, or even that Puhr pee *nyahn* is *Perpignan*. But in this text the letters also play a more detailed role as phonetic representatives, either singly or in combination.

The following consonants, *used singly*, represent their usual English sound: *b* as in *box*, *d* as in *dog*, *f* as in *fog*, *h* as in *how*, *j* as in *jug*, *k* as in *kite*, *l* as in *log*, *m* as in *mug*, *n* as in *nod*, *p* as in *pot*, *r* as in *rat*, *s* as in *sit*, *t* as in *top*, *v* as in *vat*, *w* as in *wag*, *y* as in *yap*, *z* as in *zone*. Note that a final *s* must not be taken for a *z*. Thus *Nees* as the transcription of the French city of *Nice* rhymes with *niece*, not *knees*.

The consonant *c* is not used singly but only in the combination *ch* to represent *ch* as in *chop*. The consonant *s* may be used either singly or in the combination *sh* to represent *sh* as in *shop*. The consonant *k* is used in the combination *kh* to represent the sound of *ch* in German *nach* and Scottish *loch* (respectively in placenames such as *Eisenach* and *Pitlochry*).

The distinctive Spanish *b* sound properly voiced by the *v* in *Ávila* and the *b* in *Fray Bentos* is transcribed by *v* or *b* according to the name's usual spelling, although really it is not quite either. It occurs between vowels and is technically known as a voiced bilabial fricative. It is produced not by placing the lower lip in contact with the upper teeth, as for English *v*, but by placing the lips almost together, as for English *w*, but with the lips held back, not protruded. The International Phonetic Alphabet represents it by the Greek letter beta (β).

The combination *th* represents unvoiced *th* (*thin*), but *dh* represents voiced *th* (*that*). This use of *dh* is logical, as *d* is the voiced equivalent of *t*. Moreover, the digraph *dh* is used by some authorities to represent the letter *ð* (a barred *d* known as *eth* or *edh*) in spellings of Icelandic placenames, as in *Seydhisfjördhur* rather than *Seyðisfjörður*. The combinations *th* and *dh* are similarly used in the transcription of Spanish placenames, as for *Badajoz*, where the *d* is represented by *dh* and the *z* by *th*, i.e. as Bah dhah *hawth*.

The combination *zh* represents the sound of *s* in English *leisure* or French *j* in *jeu*. Its use in this way is already familiar in the English transliteration of Russian placenames, as *Nizhny Novgorod* and *Voronezh*. (It also occurs in family names, such as *Zhukov* and *Brezhnev*.)

The combination *hl* is used in Welsh names to represent the distinctive *ll*, as in Bed *wehl* ti (*Bedwellty*) and Hlan *ber* is (*Llanberis*). (The entry for the latter has more detail on this.)

The consonants *q* and *x* are not used at all.

The consonant *y* is used either before or after a vowel. Before a vowel, the vowel itself will have one of the values indicated below. After a vowel, the resulting diphthong will be as also shown below. Thus, *ya* sounds as in *yam*, but *ay* as in *may*.

The vowels *a, e, i, o*, and *u* are used in transcriptions either singly or in combination as follows, with an example of a name containing the vowel in parentheses.

A single *a* denotes either the stressed vowel sound in *bad* (*Abington*) or the unstressed vowel sound in *about* (*Dakota*). (As a stressed vowel it is italicized except in names of one syllable, such as *Chad*.) The combination *ah* denotes the vowel sound in *far* (*Fano*). It also represents the sound of *u* in words such as *cut* (*Muncie*). At one time there would have been a clear distinction between the spoken forms of *calm* and *come*, but the former vowel, sounded further back in the mouth, has now moved further forward, so that there is effectively little if any difference, especially when unstressed. The combination *aw* denotes the vowel sound in *paw* (*Caldwell*). The combination *ay* denotes the vowel sound in *day* (*Cambridge*).

A single *e* denotes the vowel sound in *bed* (*Delhi*). The combination *ee* denotes the vowel sound in *see* (*Eastbourne*). It is also used to represent the sound of French *u* in *tu* (*Cluny*) and German *ü* in *über* (*Düsseldorf*). French *sur*, "on," in names such as *Chalon-sur-Saône* is thus transcribed *seer*.

A single *i* denotes the vowel sound in *tip* (*Pitcairn*). The combination *iy* denotes the vowel sound in *cry* (*Heidelberg*).

A single *o* denotes the vowel sound, not encountered in American English, in British English *hot* (*Conway*). The equivalent American vowel sound is usually *ah* or *aw*. The combination *oh* denotes the vowel sound in *boat* (*Togo*). The combination *oo* denotes the (short) vowel sound in *book* (*Woodbridge*). The combination *ooh* denotes the (long) vowel sound in *goose* (*Tooting*). The combination *ow* denotes the vowel sound in *how* (*Slough*). The name of the island republic of *Palau*, transcribed *Pah* low, thus has a second syllable rhyming with *cow*, not *low*. The combination *oy* denotes the vowel sound in *boy* (*Boise*).

A single *u* is used to denote the sound of unstressed *a* within a syllable. As such it commonly occurs in the placename ending *-ton*, so that *Aston* is *As* tun. In a name such as *Pendleton* it represents both unstressed syllables, i.e. as *Pen* dul tun. As mentioned above, where the sound of unstressed *a* is not within a syllable it is represented by *a*, so that *Dakota* is transcribed Da *koh* ta. In such cases it often corresponds to an *a* in the original. The combination *uh* denotes the long vowel sound in *turn* (*Wirksworth*).

Although as stated the distinction between the American and British pronunciation of a name is usually represented, some differences are ignored. For example, in certain cases most Americans voice the unvoiced consonant *t* so that it sounds more like *d*. The word *atom* in American speech thus sounds almost identical to the name *Adam*. But no allowance is made for this disparity in the transcription of a placename such as *Matterhorn*. The same goes for *t* after the consonant *n*, when the *t* is silent, so that *banter* sounds like *banner*. This occurs in names such as *Canterbury*.

One distinction that *is* indicated is the British tendency to "swallow" the vowel sound in an unstressed syllable, whereas in American speech it is audible. This is noticeable in names such as *Newbury*, where the *u* is usually omitted in British speech, as if the name were "Newbry." This particular name also contains the distinctive American *ooh* for the usual British *yooh*. (Hence the spelling "Noo Yoik" already cited above.) Finally, there is normally a difference between the pronunciation of *ar* in names such as *Caria*, readily evident in the personal name *Mary*, which in American speech is more like British English *merry*. Under the present transcription system, the American *ar* is rendered *er*, but the British equivalent as *ay* a (with stressed *ay*). *Maryland* is a good example of this distinction.

The attention focused here and above on American and British English must not detract from the transcriptions of many non–English names. Unless one is pedantically particular, it is impossible to represent the exact sound or stress of a foreign name, even with the use of specially devised phonetic symbols. Mention has already been made of the Spanish *b* and *v*, French *u*, and German *ü*. These are only individual letters, however, and of relatively rare occurrence. A more general speech phenomenon that needs special treatment is the distinctive French nasal sound in words such as *grand*, *vin*, and *bon*. These are in fact quite easy for an English speaker to pronounce but not so easy to convey by means of a modified transcription system such as the one employed here. Even so, the rendering of names such as *Caen*, *Melun*, and *Boulogne* offers a fairly faithful reproduction of the native sound.

Spanish and Italian placenames are on the whole much easier to handle, with broad vowel sounds such as *ah* and *oh* used to represent the indigenous equivalent in names such as *Tarragona* and *Altamura*. It will be noticed that the transcriptions of Spanish *Tarragona* and Italian *Barletta*, among others, include the doubled consonant (respectively *rr* and *tt*) of the original. This reflects the pronunciation, in which the speaker "lingers" on the letter without actually sounding it twice. No attempt, however, is made to represent the distinctive "trill" of Spanish *rr* or the "throaty" French *r* referred to above with regard to the name of *Paris*.

The dictionary concludes with the Appendix and Select Bibliography mentioned above, each of which has its own preamble.

Finally, with regard to the main entries, it is suggested that reading the pronunciations out loud may aid familiarization with the (user-friendly!) transcription system.

THE DICTIONARY

Aachen, Germany : *Ah* kun (German *Ah* khun)

Aalborg, Denmark : *Awl* bawrg (UK *Awl* bawg) (Danish *Awl* bawr)

Aalen, Germany : *Ah* lun

Aalsmeer, Netherlands : *Ahls* mayr

Aalst, Belgium : Ahlst

Aalto, Finland : *Ahl* toh

Aarau, Switzerland : *Ah* row

Aargau, Switzerland : *Ahr* gow

Aarhus, Denmark : *Ahr* hoohs (UK *Aw* hoohs) (Danish *Awr* hoohs)

Aasiaat, Greenland : *Ah* see aht

Aba, Nigeria : *Ah* bah

Abadan, Iran : A ba *dahn*

Abaetetuba, Brazil : A biy te *tooh* ba

Abakan, Russia : A ba *kahn*

¹Abbeville, France : Ab *veel* (UK *Ab* vil) (French Ahb *veel*)

²Abbeville, USA : *A* bi vil

Abbottabad, Pakistan : *A* ba ta bahd

Abéché, Chad : A bay *shay*

Åbenrå, Denmark : *Aw* bun raw

Abeokuta, Nigeria : Ah *bay* oh kooh tah

Aberaeron, Wales : A ba *riy* run (Welsh Ah ber *iy* ron)

Aberdare, Wales : A bur *der* (UK A ba *day* a) [No Welsh pronunciation is given for the town's name, or for those of **Aberdovey**, **Abergavenny**, or **Abertillery** below, as the spellings have been "anglicized" from the Welsh original.]

¹Aberdeen, Scotland : A bur *deen* (UK A ba *deen*)

²Aberdeen, USA : *A* bur deen (UK A ba *deen*)

Aberdour, Scotland : A bur *dow* ur (UK A ba *dow* a)

Aberdovey, Wales : A bur *dah* vi (UK A ba *dah* vi)

Aberfeldy, Scotland : A bur *fel* di (UK A ba *fel* di)

Aberffraw, Wales : A *ber* frow (UK A *bay* a frow)

Aberfoyle, Scotland : A bur *foyl* (UK A ba *foyl*)

Abergavenny, Wales : A bur ga *ven* i (UK A ba ga *ven* i)

Abergele, Wales : A bur *gel* i (UK A ba *gel* i) (Welsh Ah ber *gel* ay)

Abernethy, Scotland : A bur *neth* i (UK A ba *neth* i)

Aberporth, Wales : A bur *pawrth* (UK A ba *pawth*)

Abersoch, Wales : A bur *sohk* (UK A ba *sohk*) (Welsh Ah ber *sawkh*)

Abersychan, Wales : A bur *sik* un (UK A ba *sik* un) (Welsh Ah ber *suh* khan)

Abertillery, Wales : A bur ta *ler* i (UK A ba ti *lay* a ri)

Aberystwyth, Wales : A ba *ris* twith (Welsh Ah ber *uhs* doo ith)

Abidjan, Côte d'Ivoire : A bi *jahn*

Abilene, USA : *A* ba leen

Abingdon, England; USA : *A* bing dun

Abington, USA : *A* bing tun

Abkhazia, Georgia : Ab *kah* zha (UK Ab *kah* zi a)

Åbo, Finland : *Aw* booh

11

Abomey, Benin : A boh *may*
Abram, England : *Ab* rum
Abridge, England : *Ay* bridj
Abruzzi, Italy : A *broot* si (Italian Ah *brooht* see)
Abu Dhabi, United Arab Emirates : Ah boo *Dah* bi (UK A boo...)
Abuja, Nigeria : A *booh* ja
Abu Qir, Egypt : Ah booh *Keer*
Abu Simbel, Egypt : Ah booh *Sim* bul (UK A booh...)
Abydos, Egypt; Turkey : A *biy* dus
Abyssinia, Africa : A bi *sin* i a
Acadia, Canada : A *kay* di a
Acajutla, El Salvador : Ah kah *hooht* lah
Acapulco, Mexico : Ah ka *poohl* koh (UK A ka *pool* koh) (Spanish Ah kah *pool* koh)
Acarigua, Venezuela : Ah kah *ree* gwah
Acayucán, Mexico : Ah kah *yooh* kahn
Accomac, USA : *Ak* a mak
Accra, Ghana : A *krah*
Accrington, England : *Ak* ring tun
Acerra, Italy : Ah *cher* rah
Achaea, Greece : A *kee* a
Achill, Ireland : *A* kil
Achinsk, Russia : *Ah* chinsk
Achnasheen, Scotland : Ak na *sheen*
Acklins (Island), Bahamas : *A* klinz
Acle, England : *Ay* kul [The Norfolk town's name formerly had a varied local pronunciation, as noted in the quote below.]

> The villagers of the present day call the place ACLEY and OAKLEY [George Munford, *An Attempt to Ascertain the True Derivation of the Names of Towns and Villages, and of Rivers, and of other Great Natural Features of the County of Norfolk*, 1870].

Acoma, USA : A *koh* ma
Aconcagua, Chile : A kun *kah* gwa (UK A kun *kag* wa) (Spanish Ah kohn *kah* gwah)
Acqui Terme, Italy : Ah kwee *Ter* may
¹**Acre**, Brazil : *Ah* kree
²**Acre**, Israel : *Ay* kur (UK *Ay* ka)
Actium, Greece : *Ak* tee um
Acton, England; USA : *Ak* tun

Ada, USA : *Ay* da
Adamawa, Africa : Ah dah *mah* wah
Adana, Turkey : A *dah* na (Turkish Ah dah *nah*)
Adapazari, Turkey : Ah da pah zah *ruh*
Ad Dammam, Saudi Arabia : Ad Dam *mahm*
Addis Ababa, Ethiopia : A dis *A* ba ba [The name of the capital city was long traditionally pronounced A dis A *bah* ba by English speakers.]

> There never was any danger of *Addis Ababa* not being recognized when it was called "Addis a Barber"; whether it became more instantaneously recognizable when it was called "Addis Abbaber" is an open question [Lloyd James 1937, p. 3].

Addison, USA : *Ad* a sun (UK *Ad* i sun)
Adelaide, Australia : *A* da layd
Adélie (Land), Antarctica : A *day* li
Aden, Yemen : *Ay* dun
Adirondack (Mountains), USA : A da *rahn* dak (UK A da *ron* dak)
Adiyaman, Turkey : Ah di yah *mahn*
Adlestrop, England : *A* dul strahp (UK *A* dul strop)
Admiralty (Islands), Papua New Guinea : *Ad* mrul ti
Adoni, India : A *doh* nee
Adra, Spain : *Ah* dhrah
Adrar, Africa : Ah *drahr* (UK Ah *drah*)
Adria, Italy : *Ah* dree ah
Adrian, USA : *Ay* dri un
Adriatic (Sea), Italy : Ay dri *a* tik
Adur, England : *Ay* dur (UK *Ay* da)
Adwa, Ethiopia : *Ah* dwah
Adwalton, England : Ad *wawl* tun. [The name of the district near Morley, Yorkshire, has or had a local pronunciation US *Adh* ur tun, UK *Adh* a tun. According to Pointon, p. 3, this derives from *Heather Town*, "an old name for the area." But it is more likely that the reverse is true, and that this old name evolved as a written form of the local pronunciation, itself from an original form recorded in an

early 14th-century document as *Athelwaldon*.]

Adwick le Street, England : Ad wik li *Street*

Adygeya, Russia : Ah di *gay* a

Aegean (Sea), Greece : I *jee* un

Aegina, Greece : I *jiy* na

Aetolia, Greece : I *toh* li a

Afghanistan, Asia : Af *gan* a stan (UK Af *gan* i stahn)

Afragola, Italy : Ah frah *goh* lah

Africa : *Af* ri ka

Afyon, Turkey : Ah *fyohn*

Agadez, Niger : Ah gah *dez*

Agadir, Morocco : Ah gah *dir* (UK A ga *di* a)

Agana, Guam : Ah *gahn* yah

Agartala, India : A *gur* ta la

Agawam, USA : *A* ga wahm

Agde, France : Ahgd

Agedabya, Libya : Ah je *dah* bi a

Agen, France : A *zhahn*

Agincourt, France : *A* jin kawrt (UK *A* jin kaw)

Aginskoye, Russia : A *geen* ska ya

Agra, India : *Ah* gra

Agrigento, Italy : Ag ri *jen* toh (Italian Ah gree *jen* toh)

Aguadilla, Puerto Rico : Ah gwah *dhee* yah

Aguascalientes, Mexico : Ah gwahs kah *lyen* tays

Agulhas, Africa : A *gah* lus

Ahlen, Germany : *Ah* lun

Ahmadabad, India : *Ah* ma da bahd

Ahmadnagar, India : Ah mud *nah* gur

Ahome, Mexico : Ah *oh* may

Ahuachapán, El Salvador : Ah wah chah *pahn*

Ahvaz, Iran : Ah *vahz*

Aigues-Mortes, France : Eg *Mawrt*

Aiken, USA : *Ay* kun

Ailsa Craig, Scotland : Ayl sa *Krayg*

Ain, France : En

Aïn Beïda, Algeria : Iyn *Bay* dah

Aïn Sefra, Algeria : Iyn Sef *rah*

Aïn Témouchent, Algeria : Iyn Tay mooh *shent*

Aintree, England : *Ayn* tree

Airdrie, Scotland : *Er* dri (UK *Ay* a dri)

Aire, England : Er (UK *Ay* a)

Aislaby, England : *Ayz* la bi [The name of the North Yorkshire village is locally pronounced *Ay* zul bi, as for **Aslackby**.]

Aisne, France : En

Aix-en-Provence, France : Ayks ahn Praw *vahns*

Aix-la-Chapelle, Germany : Ayks lah Shah *pel*

Aix-les-Bains, France : Ayks lay *Bahn*

Aíyion, Greece : *Ee* yee awn

Aizawl, India : Iy *zowl*

Ajaccio, Corsica : Ah *yah* choh (UK A *jas* i oh) (French A zhak *syoh*)

Ajaria, Georgia : A *jah* ri a

Ajax, Canada : *Ay* jaks

'Ajman, United Arab Emirates : Aj *man*

Ajmer, India : Ahj *mir*

Akhisar, Turkey : Ahk hi *sahr*

Akita, Japan : Ah *kee* tah

Akkad, Asia : *A* kad

Akmola, Kazakhstan : Ahk *maw* la

Akmolinsk, Kazakhstan : Ahk *maw* linsk

Akola, India : A *koh* la

Akron, USA : *Ak* run (UK *Ak* ron)

Akrotiri, Cyprus : Ah kroh *tir* i (UK Ak roh *ti* a ri)

Aksum, Ethiopia : *Ahk* soohm

Aktyubinsk, Kazakhstan : Ak *tyooh* binsk

Akure, Nigeria : Ah *kooh* ray

Akureyri, Iceland : *Ah* keer ay ree

Alabama, USA : A la *bam* a [A UK pronunciation A la *bah* ma is sometimes heard for the state's name and was recommended by Lloyd James 1937.]

Alabaster, USA : *A* la bas tur (UK *A* la bas ta)

Alagoas, Brazil : A la *goh* us

Alagoinhas, Brazil : A la *goy* nyus

Al Ahmadi, Kuwait : Ahl *Ah* mah di

Alajuela, Costa Rica : Ah lah *hway* lah

Alalakeiki, USA : Ah lah lah *kay* kee

¹Alameda, Spain : Ah lah *may* dhah

²Alameda, USA : A la *mee* da

Alamo, USA : *A* la moh

Álamo, Mexico : *Ah* lah moh
Alamogordo, USA : A la ma *gawr* doh
  (UK A la ma *gaw* doh)
Alamosa, USA : A la *moh* sa
Åland, Finland : *Aw* lund (Swedish *Oh* lahn)
Al 'Arish, Egypt : Ahl A *reesh*
Alaska, USA : A *las* ka
Al 'Ayn, United Arab Emirates : Ahl *Iyn*
Alba, Italy : *Ahl* bah
Albacete, Spain : Ahl bah *say* tay
Alba Iulia, Romania : Ahl ba *Yooh* lya
Alba Longa, Italy : Ahl ba *Lawng* ga
Albania, Europe : Al *bay* ni a
¹**Albany**, Australia : *Al* ba ni [The name of the Western Australia town and port was originally pronounced as ²**Albany**, but subsequently settled to its present pronunciation.]
²**Albany**, USA : *Awl* ba ni [Albany, Georgia, is alternately known as Al *bay* ni.]
Al Bayda, Libya : Al *Biy* dah
Albemarle, USA : *Al* ba mahrl (UK *Al* ba mahl)
Albens, France : Ahl *bahn*
Alberta, Canada : Al *buhr* ta (UK Al *buh* ta)
¹**Albertville**, France : Ahl ber *veel*
²**Albertville**, USA : *Al* burt vil (UK *Al* but vil)
Albi, France : Ahl *bee*
Albion, USA : *Al* bi un
Ålborg, Denmark : *Awl* bawrg (UK *Awl* bawg) (Danish *Awl* bawr)
Albuquerque, USA : *Al* ba kuhr ki (UK *Al* ba kuh ki) [The name of the New Mexico city is of Spanish origin. *Cp.* Alburquerque.]
  Albuquerque, N. Mex., is *Al-bu-ker-ky*, with the accent on the first syllable, the *a* of which is American, not Spanish [Mencken, p. 541].
Alburquerque, Spain : Ahl boor *ker* kay
Albury, Australia : *Awl* ber i (UK *Awl* bri)
Alcácer do Sal, Portugal : Al kah sayr dooh *Sahl*

Alcalá de Henares, Spain : Ahl kah lah dhay Ay *nah* rays
Alcamo, Italy : *Ahl* kah moh
Alcántara, Spain : Al *kan* ta ra (Spanish Ahl *kahn* tah rah)
Alcatraz, USA : *Al* ka traz
Alcázar de San Juan, Spain : Ahl kah thahr dhay Sahn *Hwahn*
Alcester, England : *Awl* stur (UK *Awl* sta)
Alchevsk, Ukraine : *Al* chefsk
Alcira, Spain : Ahl *thee* rah
Alcoa, USA : Al *koh* a
Alconbury, England : *Awl* kun ber i (UK *Awl* kun bri)
Aldabra (Islands), Seychelles : Ahl *dah* bra
Aldan, Russia : Al *dahn*
Aldeburgh, England : *Awld* buhr oh (UK *Awld* bra)
Alderley Edge, England : Awl dur li *Ej* (UK Awl da li...) [The Cheshire town's name was at one time pronounced *Aw* dhur li, as noted in the quote below.]
  [This pronunciation is] not often heard now, but [was] frequent forty years since [Robert Holland, *A Glossary of Words Used in the County of Chester*, 1886].
Aldermaston, England : *Awl* dur mas tun (UK *Awl* da mahs tun)
Alderney, Channel Islands, Europe : *Awl* dur ni (UK *Awl* da ni)
Aldershot, England : *Awl* dur shaht (UK *Awl* da shot)
Aldington, England : *Awl* ding tun
Aldridge, England : *Awld* rij
Alegrete, Brazil : A le *gray* tee
Aleksandriya, Ukraine : A lik sun *dree* yah
Alençon, France : A lahn *sohn*
Alentejo, Portugal : A layn *tay* zhooh
Alenuihaha, USA : Ah lay nooh ee *hah* hah
Aleppo, Syria : A *lep* oh
Aleria, Corsica : A *lir* i a
Alès, France : Ah *les*
Alessandria, Italy : Ah les *sahn* dree ah

Ålesund, Norway : *Aw* la soon
Aleutian (Islands), USA : A *looh* shun
Alexander (Archipelago), USA : A lig
  zan dur (UK A lig *zahn* da)
Alexandretta, Turkey : A lig zan *dret* a
  (UK A lig zahn *dret* a)
Alexandria, Egypt; USA : A lig *zan* dri
  a (UK A lig *zahn* dri a)
Alexandroúpolis, Greece : Ah lek sahn
  dhrooh poh lees
Al Faw, Iraq : Ahl *Fow*
Alföld, Hungary : *Awl* fuhld
Alford, England : *Awl* furd (UK *Awl*
  fud)
Alfreton, England : *Awl* fra tun (UK
  Awl fri tun)
Algarve, Portugal : Ahl *gahr* va (UK Al
  gahv) (Portuguese Ahl *gahr* vee)
Algeciras, Spain : Al ji *sir* us (UK Al ji
  see a rus) (Spanish Ahl hay *thee* rahs)
Algeria, Africa : Al *jir* i a (UK Al *ji* a ri
  a)
Al Ghurdaqah, Egypt : Ahl *Goohr* dah
  ka
Algiers, Algeria : Al *jirz* (UK Al *ji* uz)
Algoa (Bay), South Africa : Al *goh* a
Algonac, USA : *Al* ga nak
Al Hillah, Iraq : Ahl *Hil* a
Alhucemas, Morocco : Ah looh *say*
  mahs
Al Hudaydah, Yemen : Ahl Hoh *day*
  dah
Al Hufuf, Saudi Arabia : Ahl Hoh *foohf*
Alicante, Spain : A li *kan* ti (Spanish Ah
  lee *kahn* tay)
Alice, USA : *A* lis
Alice Springs, Australia : A lis *Springz*
Alingsås, Sweden : *Ah* ling sohs
Aliwal (North), South Africa : *A* li
  wawl
Al Kharijah, Egypt : Ahl Khah *ree* ja
Alkmaar, Netherlands : *Ahlk* mahr
Al Kufrah, Libya : Ahl *Kooh* fra
Allahabad, India : A la ha *bahd*
Allauch, France : Ah *loh*
Allegheny (Mountains), USA : A la *gay*
  ni
Allendale Town, England : A lun dayl
  Town

Allentown, USA : *A* lun town
Allier, France : Ahl *yay*
Alloa, Scotland : *A* loh a
Alloway, Scotland : *A* la way
Alma, Canada; Ukraine; USA : *Al* ma
Alma-Ata, Kazakhstan : Al mah A *tah*
Almadén, Spain : Ahl ma *dayn* (Spanish
  Ahl mah *dhayn*)
Almalyk, Uzbekistan : Al ma *lik*
Al Marj, Libya : Ahl *Mahrj*
Almaty, Kazakhstan : Al *mah* tee
Al Mawsil, Iraq : Ahl Mow *seel*
Almeida, Portugal : Awl *may* da
Almería, Spain : Al ma *ree* a (Spanish
  Ahl mah *ree* ah)
Almetyevsk, Russia : Al mi *tyefsk*
Almirante Brown, Argentina : Ahl mee
  rahn tay *Brown*
Almondbury, England : *Ah* mund ber i
  (UK *Ah* mund bri) [Other pronunci-
  ations were formerly recorded for the
  district of Huddersfield, Yorkshire, as
  noted in the quote below.]
  [Almondbury] is called by the polite
  Aimbury; by the genuine Yorkshire-
  man, Aumbury, or, better still, Oam-
  bury [Alfred Easther, *A Glossary of the
  Dialect of Almondbury and
  Huddersfield*, 1883].
Almondsbury, England : *Ah* mundz ber
  i (UK *Ah* mundz bri) [The name of
  the Gloucestershire village is locally
  also pronounced *Aymz* bri.]
Almora, India : Ahl *moh* ra
Al Muharraq, Bahrain : Ahl Maw *hah*
  ruk
Al Mukalla, Yemen : Ahl Maw *kah* la
Alnmouth, England : *Aln* mowth [The
  name of the Northumberland coastal
  resort is also locally pronounced *Ayl*
  muth.]
Alnwick, England : *A* nik
Alofi, Cook Islands : Ah *loh* fee
Alor, Indonesia : A *lawr* (UK A *law*)
Alor Setar, Malaysia : A lawr Sa *tahr*
Alpena, USA : Al *pee* na
Alps, Europe : Alps
Al Qasr, Egypt : Ahl *Ka* sur
Al Qatif, Saudi Arabia : Ahl Kah *teef*

Alresford, England : *Ahlz* furd (UK *Ahlz* fud) [An alternate local pronunciation of the Essex village's name is *Ayls* fud. *Cp.* **New Alresford**.]

Alrewas, England : *Awl* rus [The name of the Staffordshire village] is pronounced to rhyme with *walrus* [John Hadfield, ed., *The Shell Book of English Villages*, 1980].

Als, Denmark : Ahls

Alsace, France : Al *sas* (French Ahl *zahs*)

Alsager, England : *Awl* sa jur (UK *Awl* sa ja)

Alsdorf, Germany : *Ahls* dawrf

Altadena, USA : Al ta *dee* na

Alta Gracia, Argentina : Ahl tah *Grah* see ah

Altamura, Italy : Ahl tah *mooh* rah

Altay, Russia : Ahl *tiy*

Altdorf, Switzerland : *Ahlt* dawrf

Altenburg, Germany : *Ahl* tun boork

Althorp, England : *Awl* thawrp (UK *Awl* thawp) [The name of the Northamptonshire village, site of the ancestral home of Diana, Princess of Wales, is locally also pronounced *Awl* trup, as regularly is the aristocratic title. (The observation below is thus not quite true.)]

> Viscount Althorp pronounces his name "awltrop," while the rather more sensible people of Althorp, the Northamptonshire village next to the viscount's ancestral home, say "allthorp" [Bill Bryson, *Mother Tongue*, 1990].

Altiplano, Bolivia : Ahl tee *plah* noh

Alton, England; USA : *Awl* tun

Altoona, USA : Al *tooh* na

Altrincham, England : *Awl* tring um [The former Cheshire town's name could have evolved with a written form *Altringham*, but the putative *g* is pronounced soft and is represented by the *ch* of the present spelling.]

Alturas, USA : Al *too* rus

Alvescot, England : *Al* vi skut [The name of the Oxfordshire village is locally pronounced *Awl* skut.]

Alvin, USA : *Al* vin

Amadora, Portugal : A ma *doh* ra

Amagasaki, Japan : Ah mah gah *sah* kee

Amalfi, Italy : Ah *mahl* fee

Amapá, Brazil : A ma *pah*

Amaravati, India : A ma *rah* va tee

Amarillo, USA : A ma *ri* loh

Amasya, Turkey : Ah mah *syah*

Amazon, South America : *A* ma zun

Amazonas, Brazil; Colombia : A ma *zoh* nus

Amazonia, South America : A ma *zoh* ni a

Ambato, Ecuador : Ahm *bay* toh

Amberg, Germany : *Ahm* berk

Ambleside, England : *Am* bul siyd

Amboina, Indonesia : Am *boy* na

Amboise, France : Ahn *bwahz*

Ambon, Indonesia : Am *bahn* (UK Am *bon*)

America : A *mer* i ka

Americana, Brazil : A mi ree *kah* na

Americus, USA : A *mer* i kus

Amersfoort, Netherlands : *Ah* murs fohrt

Amersham, England : *A* mur shum (UK *A* ma shum)

Amery (Ice Shelf), Antarctica : *Ay* ma ri

Ames, USA : Aymz

Amesbury, England; USA : *Aymz* ber i (UK *Aymz* bri)

Amherst, Canada; USA : *A* murst (UK *A* must)

Amiens, France : *Am* i on (French Ah *myahn*)

Amirante (Islands), Seychelles : *A* mi rant

Amityville, USA : *A* ma ti vil

Amlwch, Wales : *Am* look (Welsh *Ahm* lookh)

Amman, Jordan : A *mahn*

Ammanford, Wales : *Am* un furd (UK *Am* un fud)

Amos, Canada : *Ay* mus (UK *Ay* mos)

Amoy, China : A *moy*

Ampleforth, England : *Am* pul fawrth (UK *Am* pul fawth)

Ampthill, England : *Amt* hil

Amravati, India : Ahm *rah* va ti

Amritsar, India : Am *rit* sur (UK Am *rit* sa)

Amstelveen, Netherlands : *Ahm* stul vayn

Amsterdam, Netherlands; USA : *Am* stur dam (UK *Am* sta dam) (Dutch *Ahm* stur dahm)

Amu Darya, Asia : Ah mooh *Dah* ri a

Amundsen (Gulf), Canada : *Ah* mun sun

Amur, Russia : Ah *moor* (UK A *moo* a)

Anaconda, USA : A na *kahn* da (UK A na *kon* da)

Anacortes, USA : A na *kawr* tus (UK A na *kaw* tus)

Anadyr, Russia : A na *dir*

Anaheim, USA : *A* na hiym

Anambas (Islands), Indonesia : Ah *nahm* bahs

Anapa, Russia : A *nah* pa

Anápolis, Brazil : A *nah* pooh lees

Anatolia, Turkey : A na *toh* li a

Anchorage, USA : *Ang* ka rij

Ancona, Italy : Ang *koh* na (Italian Ahng *koh* nah)

Andalusia, Spain : An da *looh* zha (UK An da *looh* si a)

Andaman (Islands), Indian Ocean : *An* da mun

Andenne, Belgium : Ahn *den*

Anderlecht, Belgium : *Ahn* dur lekht

Andernach, Germany : *Ahn* dur nahkh

Anderson, USA : *An* dur sun (UK *An* da sun)

Andes, South America : *An* deez

Andhra Pradesh, India : Ahn dra Pra *daysh*

Andizhan, Uzbekistan : An di *zhan* (Russian An dyi *zhahn*)

Andorra, Europe : An *daw* ra

Andorra la Vella, Andorra : An daw ra la *Vel* ya

Andover, England; USA : *An* doh vur (UK *An* doh va)

Andreanof (Islands), USA : An dree *an* awf

Andria, Italy : *Ahn* dree ah

Andros, Greece : *An* drus (UK *An* dros)

Anegada (Passage), West Indies : A na *gah* da

Aného, Togo : Ah *nay* hoh

Angara, Russia : An ga *rah*

Angarsk, Russia : An *gahrsk*

Angeles, Philippines : *Ahng* gay lays

Angers, France : Ahn *zhay*

Angkor, Cambodia : *Ang* kawr (UK *Ang* kaw)

Anglesey, Wales : *Ang* gul si

Angmering, England : *Ang* mur ing

Angola, Africa : Ang *goh* la

Angoulême, France : Ahn gooh *lem*

Angren, Uzbekistan : An *gryen*

Angri, Italy : *Ahn* gree

Anguilla, West Indies : Ang *gwil* a

Angus, Scotland : *Ang* gus [A Scots pronunciation *Ang* gis also exists.]

Anhui, China : Ahn *hway* (UK An *hway*)

Anjou, France : Ahn *zhooh*

Anju, North Korea : Ahn *jooh*

Ankara, Turkey : *Ang* ka ra (Turkish *Ahng* ka ra)

Anklam, Germany : *Ahng* klahm

Annaba, Algeria : An *nah* ba

An Nabatiya, Lebanon : An Na ba *tee* ya

Annaberg-Buchholz, Germany : Ah na berk *Boohkh* hohlts

An Nafud, Saudi Arabia : An Na *foohd*

An Najaf, Iraq : An Na *jaf*

Annam, Vietnam : A *nam*

Annan, Scotland : *A* nun

Annapolis, USA : A *nap* a lis

Annapurna, Nepal : A na *poor* na (UK A na *puh* na)

Ann Arbor, USA : An *Ahr* bur (UK ... *Ah* ba)

Anne Arundel, USA : An A *rahn* dul [The name of Lady Anne Arundel, wife of the second Lord Baltimore, has a rather perfunctory pronunciation in the Maryland county name.]

Annecy, France : Ahn *see*

Annfield Plain, England : An feeld *Playn*

Anniston, USA : *An* is tun

Anqing, China : Ahn *ching*

Ansbach, Germany : *Ahns* bahkh

Anshan, China : Ahn *shahn* (UK An *shan*)

Ansongo, Mali : Ahn *song* goh

Ansonia, USA : An *soh* ni a

Anstruther, Scotland : *An* strah dhur (UK *An* strah dha) [The Fife resort and port has a name with a traditional local pronunciation *Aynst* a. Hence its nickname of "Auld Ainster."]

Antakya, Turkey : Ahn *tah* kya (UK An *tak* ya) (Turkish Ahn tah *kyah*)

Antalya, Turkey : Ahn *tah* lya (UK An *tal* ya) (Turkish Ahn tah *lyah*)

Antananarivo, Madagascar : An ta na na *ree* voh

Antarctica : An *tahrk* ti ka (UK An *tahk* ti ka) [An illiterate or at best casual pronunciation also exists as US An *tahr* ti ka, UK An *tah* ti ka, omitting the middle *c*.]

Antequera, Spain : Ahn tay *kay* rah

Antibes, France : Ahn *teeb* (UK On *teeb*)

Anticosti (Island), Canada : An ta *kah* sti (UK An ti *kos* ti)

Antietam, USA : An *tee* tum

Antigua, West Indies : An *tee* ga [The island's name is sometimes pronounced An *teeg* wa or, especially in the UK, An *tig* yoo a, as in the anonymous limerick beginning : "There was a young bride of Antigua / Whose husband said 'Dear me, how big you are.'"]

Antilles, West Indies : An *ti* leez

Antioch, Turkey; USA : *An* ti ahk (UK *An* ti ok)

Antioquia, Colombia : Ahn *tyoh* kyah

Antofagasta, Chile : An ta fa *gas* ta (Spanish Ahn toh fah *gahs* tah)

Antrim, Northern Ireland : *An* trim

Antsirabe, Madagascar : Ahnt si *rah* bay

Antsiranana, Madagascar : Ahnt si *rah* na na

Antwerp, Belgium : *Ant* wuhrp (UK *Ant* wuhp)

Anuradhapura, Sri Lanka : A *noor* a da poor a

Anyang, China; South Korea : Ahn *yahng* (UK An *yang*)

Anzhero-Sudzhensk, Russia : An zher a Sooh *jensk*

Anzin, France : Ahn *zang*

Anzio, Italy : *An* zi oh (Italian *An* tsyo)

Aomori, Japan : Ah *oh* moh ree

Aosta, Italy : Ah *aws* tah

Apalachee (Bay), USA : A pa *la* chi

Apalachicola, USA : A pa la chi *koh* la

Apeldoorn, Netherlands : *Ah* pul dohrn

Apennines, Italy : *A* pa niynz

Apia, Samoa : *Ah* pi a

Apolda, Germany : Ah *pawl* da

Appalachia, USA : A pa *lay* cha

Appenzell, Switzerland : *A* pun zel (German *Ah* pun tsel)

Appleby, England : *A* pul bi

Appledore, England : *A* pul dawr (UK *A* pul daw)

Appleton, USA : *A* pul tun

Apple Valley, USA : A pul *Val* i

Appomattox, USA : A pa *mat* uks

Aprilia, Italy : Ah *pree* lyah

Apsheron, Azerbaijan : Ap shi *rawn*

Apucarana, Brazil : A pooh ka *rah* na

Apulia, Italy : A *pyooh* li a

Aqaba, Jordan : *Ah* ka bah (UK *A* ka ba)

Aqmola, Kazakhstan : Ahk *maw* la

Aqtöbe, Kazakhstan : Ak *tuh* be

Aquitaine, France : Ak wi *tayn* (French Ah kee *tayn*)

Aquitania, France : A kwa *tay* ni a

Ara, India : *Ah* ra

Arabia, Asia : A *ray* bi a

Aracaju, Brazil : Ar a ka *zhooh*

Aracati, Brazil : Ar a ka *tee*

Araçatuba, Brazil : Ar a sa *tooh* ba

Arad, Romania : Ah *rahd*

Arafura (Sea), East Indies : Ahr a *foor* a (UK A ra *foo* a ra) [The sea bounds the northern coast of Australia, where the name is often pronounced A ra *fyoo* a ra.]

Aragats, Armenia : Ar a *gahts*

Aragon, Spain : *Ar* a gahn (UK *Ar* a gun)

Aragona, Italy : Ah rah *goh* nah

Araguaia, Brazil : Ar a *gwiy* a
Araguari, Brazil : Ar a gwa *ree*
Arak, Iran : Aw *rahk*
Aral (Sea), Asia : *Ar* ul
Aram, Asia : *Ar* um
Aran (Islands), Ireland : *Ar* un
Aranjuez, Spain : Ah rahng *khwayth*
Arapaho, USA : A *rap* a hoh
Arapiraca, Brazil : Ar a pi *ra* ka
Araraquara, Brazil : Ar a ra *kwah* ra
Ararat, Turkey : *Ar* a rat
Arauca, Colombia : Ah *row* kah
Araucanía, Chile : Ah row *kah* nyah
Arauco, Chile : Ah *row* koh
Arayat, Philippines : Ah *riy* aht
Arba Minch, Ethiopia : Ahr bah *Minch* (UK Ah bah...)
Arbela, Iraq : Ahr *bee* la (UK Ah *bee* la)
Arbil, Iraq : Ahr *beel* (UK Ah *beel*)
Arboga, Sweden : Ahr *booh* ga
Arborfield, England : *Ahr* ba feeld (UK *Ah* ba feeld)
Arbresle, France : Ahr *brel*
Arbroath, Scotland : Ahr *brohth* (UK Ah *brohth*)
Arcadia, Greece; USA : Ahr *kay* di a (UK Ah *kay* di a)
Arcata, USA : Ahr *kay* ta (UK Ah *kay* ta)
Archangel, Russia : *Ahr* kayn jul (UK *Ah* kayn jul)
Arcos de la Frontera, Spain : Ahr kohs dhay lah Frohn *tah* rah
Arcot, India : *Ahr* kaht (UK *Ah* kot)
Arctic (Ocean) : *Ahrk* tik (UK *Ahk* tik) [As with **Antarctica**, the sound of the middle *c* may be omitted in casual speech, giving US *Ahr* tik, UK *Ah* tik.]
Ardabil, Iran : Ahr da *beel*
Ardèche, France : Ahr *desh*
Ardee, Ireland : Ahr *dee* (UK Ah *dee*)
Arden, England : *Ahr* dun (UK *Ah* dun)
Ardennes, Belgium : Ahr *den* (UK Ah *den*)
Ardfert, Ireland : *Ahrd* furt (UK *Ahd* fut)
Ardingly, England : *Ahr* ding liy (UK *Ah* ding liy)

Ardmore, USA : *Ahrd* mawr (UK *Ahd* maw)
Ardnamurchan, Scotland : Ahrd na *muhr* kun (UK Ahd na *muh* kun)
Ardrishaig, Scotland : Ahrd *rish* ig (UK Ahd *rish* ig)
Ardrossan, Scotland : Ahrd *rah* sun (UK Ahd *ros* un)
Ards, Northern Ireland : Ahrdz (UK Ahdz)
Arecibo, Puerto Rico : Ah rah *see* boh
Arendal, Norway : *Ah* run dahl
Arenig Fawr, Wales : A ren ig *Vow* ur (UK ... *Vow* a)
Arequipa, Peru : Ah ray *kee* pah
Arezzo, Italy : Ah *ret* soh
Arfon, Wales : *Ahr* vun (UK *Ah* vun) (Welsh *Ahr* von)
Argentan, France : Ahr zhahn *tahn*
Argenteuil, France : Ahr zhun *tuh* i
Argentina, South America : Ahr jen *tee* na (UK Ah jen *tee* na)
Argolis, Greece : *Ahr* ga lis (UK *Ah* ga lis)
Argonne, France : Ar *gawn*
Argos, Greece : *Ahr* gahs (UK *Ah* gos)
Argyll, Scotland : Ahr *giyl* (UK Ah *giyl*)
Århus, Denmark : *Ahr* hoohs (UK *Aw* hoohs)
Ariana, Tunisia : Ahr yah *nah*
Arica, Chile : A *ree* ka
Ariège, France : Ahr *yezh*
Arima, Trinidad and Tobago : A *ree* ma
Aristazabal (Island), Canada : A ra *staz* a bal
Arizona, USA : A ri *zoh* na
Arkansas, USA : *Ahr* kun saw (UK *Ah* kun saw) [Thus the river and state, but in Kansas and Colorado the river is also known as Ahr *kan* zus, and this is the regular pronunciation for **Arkansas City**, Kansas, located on the river. The name's spelling and pronunciation have been more controversial than those of any other US state. Initially, the pronunciation approximated the French spelling (usually *Arkansa*) of the Native American tribal name. In 1819, an

Act of Congress formally established the Territory of *Arkansaw*, spelling the name thus eight times. Subsequently, the written form settled as *Arkansas* but locally the pronunciation remained *Ahr* kun saw. When the name became more widely known, however, it was generally pronounced Ahr *kan* zus, following the official spelling. Despite this, the local pronunciation of the state's name eventually prevailed, and the Legislature of the State in an act approved March 15, 1881, decided that the name "should be pronounced in three syllables, with the final *s* silent, the *a* in every syllable with the Italian sound, and the accent on the first and last syllable" (quoted in Mencken, p. 641). The second *a* has now been reduced, however. An acount of the dispute is given in George R. Stewart, *Names on the Land*, 1967, pp. 335–7.]

Arkansas City, USA : Ahr kan zus *Si* ti. [See comment on **Arkansas** above.]

Arkhangelsk, Russia : Ahr *kan* gelsk (UK Ah *kan* gelsk) (Russian Ar *khan* gilsk)

Arkle, Scotland : *Ahr* kul (UK *Ah* kul)

Arklow, Ireland : *Ahrk* loh (UK *Ahk* loh)

Arlanc, France : Ahr *lahn*

Arles, France : Ahrl

Arlington, USA : *Ahr* ling tun (UK *Ah* ling tun)

Arlon, Belgium : Ar *lawn*

Armadale, Scotland : *Ahr* ma dayl (UK *Ah* ma dayl)

Armagh, Northern Ireland : Ahr *mah* (UK Ah *mah*)

Armagnac, France : Ar ma *nyak* (UK Ah mun *yak*) (French Ahr mah *nyahk*)

Armavir, Russia : Ar ma *veer* (UK Ah ma *vee* a)

¹**Armenia**, Asia : Ahr *meen* i a (UK Ah *meen* i a)

²**Armenia**, Colombia : Ahr *mayn* yah

Armentières, France : Ahr mun *tirz* (UK *Ah* mun ti uz) (French Ahr

mahn *tyer*) [The name became familiar in World War I under the phonetic rendering *Armenteers*, as in the lines of the popular song : "Mademoiselle from Armenteers, / Not been kissed for forty years."]

Armidale, Australia : *Ahr* mi dayl (UK *Ah* mi dayl) [In Australia itself, the New South Wales town's name is often pronounced as **Armadale**, in fact its original spelling.]

Armorica, France : Ahr *maw* ri ka (UK Ah *mor* i ka)

Arnhem, Netherlands : *Ahr* num (UK *Ah* num) (Dutch *Ahrn* hem)

Arnhem Land, Australia : *Ahr* num Land (UK *Ah* num...)

Arno, Italy : *Ahr* noh (UK *Ah* noh)

Arnold, England : *Ahr* nuld (UK *Ah* nuld)

Arnsberg, Germany : *Ahrns* berk

Arnstadt, Germany : *Ahrn* shtaht

Arraiján, Panama : Ahr riy *khahn*

Arran, Scotland : *Ar* un

Arras, France : *Ar* us (French Ah *rahs*)

Arrecife, Canary Islands : Ah ra *see* fay (UK A ra *see* fay) (Spanish Ah ray *see* fay)

Arrochar, Scotland : *Ar* a kur (UK *Ar* a ka)

Arsenyev, Russia : Ar *syen* yif

Arsinoë, Egypt; Libya : Ahr *sin* oh ee (UK Ah *sin* oh ee)

Artem, Russia : Ar *tyawm*

Artemisa, Cuba : Ahr *tay* mee sah

Artemovsk, Russia; Ukraine : Ar *tyaw* mufsk

Artigas, Uruguay : Ahr *tee* gahs

Artois, France : Ahr *twah* (UK Ah *twah*)

Aruba, West Indies : A *rooh* ba

Arunachal Pradesh, India : Ah roo nah chul Pra *daysh*

Arundel, England : *Ar* un dul [The name of the West Sussex town is sometimes misaccented A *rahn* dul by those unfamiliar with the correct form.]

Arusha, Tanzania : Ah *rooh* shah

Arvada, USA : Ahr *vad* a
Arzamas, Russia : Ar za *mahs*
Arzano, Italy : Ahr *dzah* noh
Arzew, Algeria : Ahr *zuh*
Asab, Eritrea : *Ah* sub
Asaba, Nigeria : Ah sah *bah*
Asahikawa, Japan : Ah sah *hee* kah wa
Asansol, India : As un *sohl*
Asbest, Russia : Az *best* (Russian Ahz *byest*)
Asbury Park, USA : Az ber i *Pahrk* (UK Az bri *Pahk*)
Ascension (Island), Atlantic Ocean : A *sen* chun
Aschaffenburg, Germany : Ah *shah* fun boork
Aschersleben, Germany : *Ah* shurs lay bun
Ascoli Piceno, Italy : Ahs koh lee Pee *chay* noh
Ascona, Switzerland : A *skoh* na (Italian Ah *skoh* nah)
Ascot, England : *As* kut [This is generally reckoned to be the "correct" pronunciation of the Berkshire village's name, especially among those attending the fashionable races here (Royal Ascot), although US *As* kaht, UK *As* kot are also widely heard.]
  Ascot is pronounced as Ascut, with the emphasis on the first syllable [Guy Egmont, *The Art of Egmontese*, 1961].
Asela, Ethiopia : Ah *say* la
Asenovgrad, Bulgaria : A *sen* uf grahd
Ashanti, Ghana : A *shan* ti
Ashbourne, England : *Ash* bawrn (UK *Ash* bawn)
Ashburton, England : *Ash* buhr tun (UK Ash *buh* tun)
Ashby-de-la-Zouch, England : Ash bi di la *Zoohsh* [According to Ross, p. 37, the last word of the Leicestershire town's name should be pronounced Zoohch, although it rarely is.]
Ashdod, Israel : *Ash* dahd (UK *Ash* dod)
Asheville, USA : *Ash* vil
Ashfield, Australia : *Ash* feeld
Ashford, England : *Ash* furd (UK *Ash* fud)

Ashgabat, Turkmenistan : *Ahsh* gah baht
Ashikaga, Japan : Ah shee *kah* gah
Ashington, England : *Ash* ing tun
Ashkhabad, Turkmenistan : Ahsh ka *bahd* (UK *Ash* ka bad) (Russian Uhsh kha *baht*)
Ashland, USA : *Ash* lund
Ash Shariqah, United Arab Emirates : Ahsh *Shah* ree ka
Ashtabula, USA : Ash ta *byooh* la
Ashtaroth, Syria : *Ash* ta rawth (UK *Ash* ta roth)
Ashton-in-Makerfield, England : Ash tun in *May* kur feeld (UK ... *May* ka feeld)
Ashton-under-Lyne, England : Ash tun ahn dur *Liyn* (UK ... ahn da...)
Ashwaubenon, USA : Ash *wah* ba nun
Asia : *Ay* zha (UK *Ay* sha)
Asiago, Italy : Ah si *ah* goh (UK A zi *ah* goh) (Italian Ahz *yah* goh)
Asir, Saudi Arabia : A *sir*
Askham, England : *As* kum
Askrigg, England : *Ask* rig
Aslackby, England : *Ay* zul bi [The name of the Lincolnshire village is pronounced identically with the local pronunciation of **Aislaby**.]
Asmara, Eritrea : Az *mah* ra
Asnières, France : Ahn *yer*
Aspatria, England : As *pay* tri a [According to Johnston, p. 114, the name of the Cumbria town is locally pronounced *Spat* ri.]
Aspen, USA : *As* pun
Assam, India : A *sam*
As Samawah, Iraq : Ahs Sa *mah* wa
Asseb, Eritrea : *Ah* sub
Assen, Netherlands : *Ah* sun
Assiniboine, Canada : A *si* ni boyn
Assisi, Italy : A *see* si (Italian A *see* zi)
Assiz, Brazil : A *sees*
As Sulaymaniyah, Iraq : Ahs Sooh liy *mah* nee ya
Assyria, Asia : A *si* ri a
Astana, Kazakhstan : A *stah* na
Asti, Italy : *Ah* sti (UK *As* ti) (Italian *Ahs* tee)

Aston, England; USA : *As* tun
Astorga, Spain : Ah *stawr* ga
Astoria, USA : A *staw* ri a
Astrakhan, Russia : As tra *kan* (Russian *As* tra khun)
Asturias, Spain : As *toor* i as (UK As *too* a ri as) (Spanish As *toor* yas)
Asunción, Paraguay : Ah soohn *syohn*
Aswan, Egypt : As *wahn*
Asyut, Egypt : Ahs *yooht*
Atacama (Desert), Chile : Ah tah *kah* mah
Atakpamé, Togo : Ah tahk *pah* may
Atar, Mauritania : Ah *tahr* (UK Ah *tah*)
Atbara, Sudan : *At* ba ra
Atchafalaya, USA : A cha fa *liy* a
Athabasca, Canada : A tha *bas* ka
Athenry, Ireland : A thun *riy* [The name of the Co. Galway town (in origin Irish *Baile Átha an Rí*, "town of the ford of the king") is liable to be mangled as At *hen* ri by English speakers unaware of the true pronunciation, as recorded in the anecdote below.]
    In July 1905 he was cycling with a cousin in County Galway when overtaken by a car — a rare sight at the time — the driver of which was seeking directions. "Kindly tell me," said he, "am I on the right road for At-Henry?" [Bernard Share, *Naming Names*, 2001, quoting from Edward MacLysaght in Sharon Gmelch, *Irish Life and Traditions*, 1986].
Athens, Greece; USA : A thunz (UK A thinz) [The name of Athens, New York, is also pronounced *Ay* thunz.]
Atherton, England : A dhur tun (UK A dha tun)
Athis-Mons, France : Ah tees *Mawns*
Athlone, Ireland : Ath *lohn*
Athol, USA : A thawl (UK *Ath* ol)
Atholl, Scotland : A thul
Athos, Greece : A thahs (UK A thos) (Greek *Ah* thaws)
Athy, Ireland : A *thiy*
Atlanta, USA : At *lan* ta
Atlantic City, USA : At lan tik *Si* ti
Atlantic (Ocean) : At *lan* tik

Atlas (Mountains), Morocco : *At* lus
Atlixco, Mexico : Aht *lees* koh
Attica, Greece; USA : A ti ka
Attleboro, USA : A tul buhr oh
Attleborough, England : A tul buhr oh (UK A tul bra)
Attu, USA : A tooh
Atyrau, Kazakhstan : *Ah* tee row
Aubagne, France : Oh *biyn*
Aube, France : Ohb
Aubenas, France : Ohb *nah*
Aubervilliers, France : Oh bur veel *yay*
Auburn, Australia; USA : *Aw* burn (UK *Aw* bun)
Aubusson, France : Oh bee *sawn*
Auch, France : Ohsh
Auchterarder, Scotland : Awk ta *rahr* dur (UK Awk ta *rah* da)
Auchtermuchty, Scotland : Awk tur *mahk* ti (UK Awk ta *mahk* ti)
Auckland, New Zealand : *Awk* lund
Aude, France : Ohd
Audenshaw, England : *Aw* dun shaw
Aue, Germany : *Ow* a
Auerbach, Germany : *Ow* ur bahkh
Aughrim, Ireland : *Aw* grim
Aughton, England : *Aw* tun [There are several villages of the name, and that near Lancaster, Lancashire, is pronounced *Af* tun.]
Augrabies (Falls), South Africa : Oh *khrah* bees
Augsburg, Germany : *Owgz* buhrg (UK *Owgz* buhg) (German *Owks* boork)
Augusta, Italy; USA : Aw *gahs* ta (Italian Ow *goohs* ta)
Augustów, Poland : Ow *goohs* toohf
Aulis, Greece : *Aw* lis
Aulnay-sous-Bois, France : Oh nay sooh *Bwah*
Aulne, France : Ohn
Aulnoye-Aymeries, France : Ohn wah Aym *ree*
Ault, France : Ohlt
Aunis, France : Oh *nees*
Aurangabad, India : Ow *rahng* gah bahd
Auray, France : Oh *ray*
Aurillac, France : Oh ree *yahk*

Aurora, Canada; USA : A *roh* ra

Auschwitz, Poland : *Owsh* wits (German *Owsh* vits)

Austerlitz, Czech Republic : *Aw* stur lits (UK *Aw* sta lits)

Austin, USA : *Aw* stun (UK *Os* tin)

Australasia : Aw stra *lay* zha (UK Os tra *lay* zha)

Australia, Oceania : Aw *stray* li a (UK Os *tray* li a)

Austria, Europe : *Aw* stri a (UK *Os* tri a)

Auteuil, France : Oh *tuh* i

Autrans, France : Oh *trahn*

Autun, France : Oh *tuhn*

Auvergne, France : Oh *vern*

Auvers-sur-Oise, France : Oh ver seer *Wahz*

Aux Cayes, Haiti : Oh *kay*

Auxerre, France : Oh *ser*

Auxi-le-Château, France : Ohk seel Sha *toh*

Auxonne, France : Oh *sawn*

Ava, Myanmar : *Ah* vah

Avalon, Canada; USA : *Av* a lahn (UK *Av* a lon)

Avarua, Cook Islands : Ah vah *rooh* ah

Avebury, England : *Ayv* ber i (UK *Ayv* bri) [The name of the Wiltshire village, famous for its ancient stone circle, is locally also pronounced *Ay* bri.]

Aveiro, Portugal : A *vay* rooh

Avellaneda, Argentina : Ah vay yah *nay* dah

Avellino, Italy : Ah vay *lee* noh

Aversa, Italy : Ah *ver* sah

Avesnes, France : Ah *ven*

Avesta, Sweden : *Ah* va stah

Aveyron, France : Ah vay *rawn*

Aviemore, Scotland : A vi *mawr* (UK A vi *maw*)

Avignon, France : A vee *nyohn* (UK *A* vee nyon) (French Ah vee *nyawn*) [The UK stress on the first syllable of the town's name is familiar from the French children's song "Sur le pont / D'Avignon" as essayed by young schoolchildren, which "out of the mouths of babes and sucklings" usu-

ally sounds more like "*Sooh* la pon / *Dav* i nyon."]

Ávila, Spain : *Ah* vee lah

Avilés, Spain : Ah vee *lays*

Avoca, Ireland : A *voh* ka

¹Avon, England; Scotland : *Ay* vun [There are five rivers of this name in England, with that rising on Dartmoor, Devon, pronounced *A* vun. Scotland has at least two Avons. That flowing into the Firth of Forth east of Grangemouth is as here. The other is ²Avon. (In each case the name means simply "river," from a Celtic word that gave Welsh *afon*.)]

²Avon, Scotland : Ahn [This northern Avon joins the Spey south of Elgin.]

³Avon, USA : *Ay* vahn (UK *Ay* von) [The name of Avon, New York, is generally pronounced *A* vun.]

Avondale, USA : *A* vun dayl

Avonmore, USA : *A* vun mawr (UK *A* vun maw)

Avonmouth, England : *Ay* vun mowth

Avranches, France : Av *rahnsh*

Awasa, Ethiopia : *Ah* wah sah

Awe, Scotland : Aw

Awka, Nigeria : *Aw* kah

Axel Heiberg, Canada : Ahk sul *Hiy* buhrg (UK ... *Hiy* buhg)

Axholme, England : *Aks* hohm

Axim, Ghana : Ah *sheem*

Axminster, England : *Aks* min stur (UK *Aks* min sta)

Ayacucho, Peru : Iy ah *kooh* choh

Ayers Rock, Australia : Ayrz *Rahk* (UK Ay uz *Rok*)

Aylesbury, England : *Aylz* ber i (UK *Aylz* bri)

Aylesford, England : *Aylz* furd (UK *Aylz* fud)

Aylesham, England : *Ayl* shum

Aylmer, Canada : *Ayl* mur (UK *Ayl* ma)

Aylsham, England : *Ayl* shum [The name of the Norfolk town has an alternate local pronunciation *Ahl* sum.]

Aynho, England : *Ayn* hoh

Ayot St Lawrence, England : Ay ut Saynt *Law* runs (UK ... Sunt *Lor* uns)

Ayr, Australia; Scotland : Er (UK *Ay* a)
Ayutthaya *see* **Phra Nakhon Si Ayut-thaya**
Azay-le-Rideau, France : Ah zayl Ree *doh*
Azemmour, Morocco : A za *moohr*
Azerbaijan, Asia : Ah zur biy *jahn* (UK A za biy *jahn*)
Azogues, Ecuador : Ah *soh* ges
Azores, Atlantic Ocean : *Ay* zawrz (UK A *zawz*) [Tennyson gives the island group's name three syllables, as in the Portuguese original (see Appendix, p. 219), in the opening line of his 1878 poem "The Revenge" : "At Flores in the Azores Sir Richard Grenville lay."]
Azov, Russia : *Ay* zahv (UK *Ay* zov) (Russian *Ah* zawf)
Azua, Dominican Republic : *Ahs* wah
Azul, Argentina : Ah *soohl*
Az Zarqa', Jordan : Ahz *Zahr* ka (UK ... *Zah* ka)
Baalbek, Lebanon : *Bahl* bek
Babahoyo, Ecuador : Bah ba *hoh* yoh
Babar (Islands), Indonesia : *Bah* bahr (UK *Bah* bah)
Bab el Mandeb, Red Sea : Bab el *Man* deb
Babelsberg, Germany : *Bah* buls berk
Babuyan (Islands), Philippines : Bah boo *yahn*
Babylon, Iraq; USA : *Bab* a lun (UK *Bab* i lun)
Babylonia, Asia : Ba ba *loh* ni a
Bacabal, Brazil : Ba ca *bahl*
Bacan, Indonesia : *Bah* chahn
Bacău, Romania : Ba *kow*
Bacolod, Philippines : Bah *koh* lohd
Bactria, Asia : *Bak* tri a
Bacup, England : *Bay* kup [It is said that in World War II a German secret agent working in England inadvertently revealed his identity by referring to the Lancashire town as *Bak* up.]
Badajoz, Spain : Bah da *hohs* (UK Ba da *hoz*) (Spanish Bah dhah *hawth*)
Badalona, Spain : Bah dhah *loh* nah

Bad Dürkheim, Germany : Baht *Deerk* hiym
Bad Ems, Germany : Baht *Ems*
Baden, Austria : *Bah* dun
Baden-Baden, Germany : Bah dun *Bah* dun
Badenweiler, Germany : Bah dun *viy* lur
Baden-Württemberg, Germany : Bah dun *Wuhr* tum buhrg (UK ... *Vuh* tum buhg) (German Bah dun *Veer* tum berk)
Badgastein, Austria : Baht gah *stiyn*
Bad Godesberg, Germany : Baht *Goh* duz buhrg (UK Bad *Goh* duz buhg) (German Baht *Goh* dus berk)
Bad Harzburg, Germany : Baht *Hahrts* boork
Bad Hersfeld, Germany : Baht *Hers* felt
Bad Homburg, Germany : Bahd *Hahm* buhrg (UK Bad *Hom* buhg) (German Baht *Hawm* boork)
Bad Ischl, Austria : Baht *Ish* ul
Bad Kissingen, Germany : Baht *Kis* ing un
Bad Kreuznach, Germany : Baht *Kroyts* nahkh
Bad Reichenhall, Germany : Baht *Riy* khun hahl
Bad Salzuflen, Germany : Baht *Zahlt* sooh flun
Baena, Spain : Bah *ay* nah
Bærum, Norway : *Bar* um
Baffin, Canada : *Baf* in
Bafoulabé, Mali : Ba fooh la *bay*
Bagamoyo, Tanzania : Bah gah *moh* yoh
Bagé, Brazil : Ba *zhay*
Baghdad, Iraq : *Bag* dad (UK Bag *dad*)
Baghlan, Afghanistan : *Bahg* lahn
Bagnères-de-Bigorre, France : Bah nyerd Bi *gawr*
Bagni di Lucca, Italy : Bah nyee dee *Loohk* kah
Bagno a Ripoli, Italy : Bay nyoh ah *Ree* poh lee
Bagnolet, France : Bah nyoh *lay*
Bagnols-sur-Cèze, France : Bah nyohl seer *Sayz*
Bagrationovsk, Russia : Ba gra tee *awn* ufsk

Bagshot, England : *Bag* shaht (UK *Bag* shot)

Baguio, Philippines : *Bah* gee oh

Bahamas, West Indies : Ba *hah* muz

Bahawalpur, India : Ba *hah* wul poor

Bahia, Brazil : Bah *ee* a

Bahía Blanca, Argentina : Bah ee ah *Blahng* kah

Bahoruco, Dominican Republic : Bah oh *rooh* koh

Bahraich, India : Ba *riyk*

Bahrain, Asia : Bah *rayn*

Baia Mare, Romania : Biy a *Mah* ray

Baie-Comeau, Canada : Bay *Koh* moh (French Bay Koh *moh*)

Baikal, Russia : Biy *kal* (Russian Biy *kahl*)

Baildon, England : *Bayl* dun

Bailén, Spain : Biy *layn*

Bailleul, France : Ba *yuhl*

Baja California, USA : Bah hah Kal a *fawr* nya (UK ... Ka la *faw* ni a)

Bajram Curri, Albania : Biy rahm *Koor* ee

Baker (Island), Pacific Ocean : *Bay* kur (UK *Bay* ka)

Bakersfield, USA : *Bay* kurz feeld (UK *Bay* kuz feeld)

Bakewell, England : *Bayk* wel

Bakhchisaray, Ukraine : Bahkh chi sa *riy*

Bakhtaran, Iran : Bahkh tah *rahn*

Baki, Azerbaijan : Bah *kee*

Baku, Azerbaijan : Bah *kooh*

Bala, Wales : *Bal* a

Balaïtous, France : Bah liy *tooh*

Balaklava, Ukraine : Ba la *klah* va

Balakovo, Russia : Bul a *kaw* va

Balashikha, Russia : Bul a *shee* kha

Balaton, Hungary : *Bah* la tahn (UK *Bal* a ton) (Hungarian *Baw* law tohn)

Balboa, Panama : Bal *boh* a

Balbriggan, Ireland : Bal *brig* un

Balcarce, Argentina : Bahl *kahr* say

Balclutha, New Zealand : Bal *klooh* tha

Balcombe, England : *Bawl* kum

Baldock, England : *Bawl* dahk (UK *Bawl* dok)

Baldwin, USA : *Bawld* win

Bâle, Switzerland : Bahl

Balearic (Islands), Spain : Ba li *ar* ik

Balen, Belgium : Ba *len*

Balham, England : *Bal* um

Bali, Indonesia : *Bah* lee

Balikesir, Turkey : Bah la ki *sir*

Balikpapan, Indonesia : Bah lik *pah* pahn

Balkanabat, Turkmenistan : Bahl kahn ah *baht*

Balkans, Europe : *Bawl* kunz

Balkhash, Kazakhstan : Bahl *kahsh*

Ballachulish, Scotland : Ba la *hooh* lish

Ballantrae, Scotland : Bal un *tray*

Ballarat, Australia : *Bal* a rat

Ballater, Scotland : *Bal* a tur (UK *Bal* a ta)

Balleny (Islands), Antarctica : *Bal* a ni

Ballina, Australia : *Bal* i na

Ballinasloe, Ireland : Ba li na *sloh*

Ballwin, USA : *Bawl* wun

Ballycastle, Northern Ireland : Ba li *kas* ul (UK Ba li *kah* sul)

Ballymena, Northern Ireland : Ba li *mee* na

Ballymoney, Northern Ireland : Ba li *mah* ni

Ballynahinch, Northern Ireland : Ba li na *hinch*

Balmoral, Scotland : Bal *maw* rul (UK Bal *mor* ul)

Balqash, Kazakhstan : Bal *kash*

Balquhidder, Scotland : Bal *wid* ur (UK Bal *wid* a) [Scots would pronounce the village's name as Bal *hwid* ur.]

Bălţi, Moldova : Bults

Baltic (Sea), Europe : *Bawl* tik

Baltimore, USA : *Bawl* ta mawr (UK *Bawl* ti maw) [Various local pronunciations exist for the name of the Maryland city, such as *Bawlt* mur or *Bawl* mur. As pointed out in the first quote below, there can be a considerable disparity between a name's local pronunciation and its more widely current form.]

(1) The natives always drop the medial *i* and so reduce the name to two

syllables; in addition they substitute a neutral vowel, very short, for the *o*. The name thus becomes *Baltm'r* [Mencken, p. 540].
(2) Baltimore (pronounced by all natives Bawlamer) [Alistair Cooke, *Letter from America*, "HLM: RIP," February 3, 1956].

Baltiysk, Russia : Bul *teesk*

Baluchistan, Asia : Ba looh chi *stan* (UK Ba looh chi *stahn*)

Bam, Iran : Bahm

Bamako, Mali : *Bah* mah koh

Bambari, Central African Republic : Bahm bah *ree*

Bamberg, Germany : *Bam* buhrg (UK *Bam* buhg) (German *Bahm* berk)

Bamburgh, England : *Bam* bra

Bamian, Afghanistan : Bah mee *ahn*

Bampton, England : *Bamp* tun

Banaba, Kiribati : Bah *nah* bah

Banat, Europe : *Bah* naht

Banbridge, Northern Ireland : *Ban* brij

Banbury, England : *Ban* ber i (UK *Ban* bri)

Banchory, Scotland : *Bang* ka ri

Banda Atjeh, Indonesia : Bahn dah *Ah* chee

Banda Besar, Indonesia : Bahn dah Bay *sahr*

Bandar Abbas, Iran : Bahn dur A *bas* (UK Ban dur...)

Bandar Lampung, Indonesia : Bahn dur *Lahm* poohng (UK Ban da...)

Bandar Seri Begawan, Brunei : Bahn dur Ser i Ba *gah* wun (UK Ban da...)

Bandon, Ireland : *Ban* dun

Bandundu, Democratic Republic of the Congo : Bahn *doohn* dooh

Bandung, Indonesia : *Bahn* doong (UK *Ban* doong)

Banes, Cuba : *Bah* nays

Banff, Canada; Scotland : Bamf

Bangalore, India : Bang ga *lawr* (UK Bang ga *law*)

Banggai (Archipelago), Indonesia : *Bahng* giy

Bangil, Indonesia : *Bang* il

Bangka, Indonesia : *Bang* ka

Bangkok, Thailand : Bang *kahk* (UK Bang *kok*)

Bangladesh, Asia : Bang gla *desh*

[1]**Bangor**, Northern Ireland; Wales : *Bang* gur (UK *Bang* ga) (Welsh *Bahng* gawr)

[2]**Bangor**, USA : *Bang* gawr (UK *Bang* gaw)

Bangui, Central African Republic : Bahng *gee* (UK Bong *gee*)

Bangweulu, Zambia : Bahng gway *ooh* looh

Baní, Dominican Republic : Bah *nee*

Banja Luka, Bosnia-Herzegovina : Bahn ya *Looh* ka (UK Ban ya...)

Banjarmasin, Indonesia : *Bahn* jahr mah sin

Banjul, Gambia : *Bahn* joohl (UK *Ban* joohl)

Banks (Island), Canada : Bangks

Bankstown, Australia : *Bangks* town

Bankura, India : *Bahng* koo rah

Bannockburn, Scotland : *Ban* uk buhrn (UK *Ban* uk buhn)

Bannu, Pakistan : *Bah* nooh

Banská Bystrica, Slovakia : Bahn skah *Bis* trit sah

Banstead, England : *Ban* stid

Bantry, Ireland : *Ban* tri

Banyuls-sur-Mer, France : Bah nyool seer *Mer*

Banyumas, Indonesia : *Bahn* yooh mahs

Banyuwangi, Indonesia : Bahn yooh *wahng* gi

Baoding, China : Bow *ding*

Baotou, China : Bow *toh*

Bar, Ukraine : Bahr

Baraboo, USA : Ba ra *booh*

Baracaldo, Spain : Bah rah *kahl* doh

Baracoa, Cuba : Bah rah *koh* ah

Barahona, Dominican Republic : Bah rah *oh* nah

Baranagar, India : Ba *rah* na gur

Baranovichi, Belarus : Ba *rah* na vee chee

Barbacena, Brazil : Bahr bah *say* nah

Barbados, West Indies : Bahr *bay* dohs (UK Bah *bay* dos)

Barbuda, West Indies : Bahr *byooh* da (UK Bah *byooh* da)

Barce, Libya : *Bahr* chay

Barcelona, Spain; Venezuela : Bahr sa *loh* na (UK Bah si *loh* na) (Spanish Bahr thay *law* nah)

Barceloneta, Puerto Rico : Bahr se loh *nay* tah

Barcoo, Australia : Bahr *kooh* (UK Bah *kooh*)

Barddhaman, India : *Bahr* da mun

Bardejov, Slovakia : Bahr da *yawf*

Bardera, Somalia : Bahr *der* a (UK Bah *day* a ra)

Bardsey, Wales : *Bahrd* si (UK *Bahd* si)

Bareilly, India : Ba *ray* lee

Barents (Sea), Arctic Ocean : *Ber* unts (UK *Bar* unts)

Bargoed, Wales : *Bahr* goyd (UK *Bah* goyd)

Bari, Italy : *Bah* ri

Barinas, Venezuela : Bah *ree* nahs

Barisal, India : Bar a *sahl*

Barjols, France : Bahr *zhohl*

Barking, England : *Bahr* king (UK *Bah* king)

Barkly (Tableland), Australia : *Bahrk* li (UK *Bahk* li)

Bar-le-Duc, France : Bahrl *Deek*

Barletta, Italy : Bahr *let* tah

Barmouth, Wales : *Bahr* muth (UK *Bah* muth) [The Welsh form of the resort's name is *Y Bermo*, as represented by the statement quoted below.] Colloquially the name at times gets clipped down to "Bermo" [Johnston, p. 127].

Barnard Castle, England : Bahr nurd *Kas* ul (UK Bah nud *Kah* sul)

Barnaul, Russia : *Bahr* nowl (UK *Bah* nowl) (Russian Bur na *oohl*)

Barnegat (Bay), USA : *Bahr* ni gat (UK *Bah* ni gat)

Barnes, England : Bahrnz (UK Bahnz)

Barnet, England : *Bahr* nut (UK *Bah* nit)

Barneveld, Netherlands : *Bahr* na velt

Barnoldswick, England : Bahr *nohldz* wik (UK Bah *nohldz* wik) [An alternate local pronunciation of the Lancashire (formerly Yorkshire) town's name is *Bah* lik.]

Barnsley, England : *Bahrnz* li (UK *Bahnz* li)

Barnstable, USA : *Bahrn* sta bul (UK *Bahn* sta bul)

Barnstaple, England : *Bahrn* sta pul (UK *Bahn* sta pul)

Baroda, India : Ba *roh* da

Barotse, Zambia : Bah *roht* say

Barquerizo Moreno, Ecuador : Bahr kay ree soh Moh *ray* noh

Barquisimeto, Venezuela : Bahr kee see *may* toh

Barra, Scotland : *Ba* ra

Barrackpore, India : *Bar* uk pohr

Barra Mansa, Brazil : Bah ra *Mahn* sa

Barrancabermeja, Colombia : Bahr rahng kah ber *may* hah

Barranquilla, Colombia : Bah run *kee* ya (UK Ba run *keel* ya) (Spanish Bahr rahn *kee* yah)

Barre, USA : *Ba* ri

Barretos, Brazil : Ba *ray* toohs

Barrhead, Scotland : Bahr *hed*

Barrie, Canada : *Ba* ri

Barrington, USA : *Bar* ing tun

Barrow-in-Furness, England : Ba roh un *Fuhr* nus (UK ... in *Fuh* nis)

Barry, Wales : *Ba* ri

Barstow, USA : *Bahr* stoh (UK *Bah* stoh)

Bartle Frere, Australia : Bahr tul *Fray* ur (UK Bah tul *Fray* a)

Bartlesville, USA : *Bahr* tulz vil (UK *Bah* tulz vil)

Bartlett, USA : *Bahrt* lut (UK *Baht* lut)

Bartoszyce, Poland : Bahr taw *shit* se

Barwick, England : *Bahr* wik (UK *Ba* rik)

Barysaw, Belarus : Ba *ree* suf

Basel, Switzerland : *Bah* zul

Basford, England : *Bays* furd (UK *Bays* fud) [This is the pronunciation for the best-known Basford, a district of Nottingham. Other places of the name are usually pronounced US *Bas* furd, UK *Bas* fud.]

Bashan, Syria : *Bay* shun
Bashkiria, Russia : Bahsh *kir* i a (UK Bash *kee* a ri a)
Bashkortostan, Russia : Bahsh kawr ta *stahn* (UK Bash kaw ta *stan*)
Basilan, Philippines : Bah *see* lahn
Basildon, England : *Baz* ul dun
Basilicata, Italy : Bah zee lee *kah* tah
Basingstoke, England : *Bay* zing stohk
Basle, Switzerland : Bahl
Basque (Country), Spain : Bask
Basra, Iraq : *Bahs* ra (UK *Baz* ra)
Bassaleg, Wales : Ba *sal* eg
Bassano, Italy : Bah *sah* noh
Bassein, Myanmar : Ba *sayn*
Bassens, France : Bah *sahns*
Bassenthwaite, England : *Bas* un thwayt
Basseterre, St. Kitts & Nevis : Bas *ter* (UK Bas *tay* a)
Basse-Terre, Guadeloupe : Bas *ter* (UK Bas *tay* a)
Bassetlaw, England : *Bas* it law
Bass (Strait), Australia : Bas
Bastia, Corsica, France : Bahs *tyah*
Basutoland, Africa : Ba *sooh* toh land
Bata, Equatorial Guinea : *Bah* tah
Bataan, Philippines : Ba *tahn*
Batala, India : Ba *tah* la
Batalha, Portugal : Ba *tah* lya
Batang, Indonesia : *Bah* tahng
Batangas, Philippines : Bah *tahng* gahs
Batavia, Indonesia; USA : Ba *tay* vi a (Dutch Bah *tah* vee ah)
Bath, England; USA : Bath (UK Bahth)
Bathealton, England : *Bat* ul tun
Bathgate, Scotland : *Bath* gayt
Bathurst, Australia; Canada : *Bath* uhrst (UK *Bath* uhst)
Batley, England : *Bat* li
Batna, Algeria : *Bat* na
Baton Rouge, USA : Bat un *Roohzh* [An alternate pronunciation of the Louisiana city's name as Bat un *Roohj* is sometimes heard.]
    The *Rouge* in *Baton Rouge* gets its French value locally, but the *Baton* become *bat'n*, with the *bat* rhyming with *cat*, and the *o* reduced to a neutral vowel [Mencken, p. 542].

Battambang, Cambodia : *Baht* tahm bahng
Battenberg, Germany : *Bat* un buhrg (UK *Ba* tun buhg) (German *Bah* tun berk)
Battersea, England : *Bat* ur see (UK *Bat* a si)
Batticaloa, Sri Lanka : Ba ti ka *loh* a
Battipaglia, Italy : Baht tee *pahl* yah
Battle, England : *Bat* ul
Battle Creek, USA : *Bat* ul Kreek
Battleford, Canada : *Bat* ul furd (UK *Bat* ul fud)
Batumi, Georgia : Ba *tooh* mi
Batu Pahat, Malaysia : Bah tooh *Pah* haht
Bat Yam, Israel : Baht *Yahm*
Batz, France : Bah
Bauchi, Nigeria : *Bow* chi
Bauru, Brazil : Bow *rooh*
Bautzen, Germany : *Bowt* sun
Bavaria, Germany : Ba *ver* i a (UK Ba *vay* a ri a)
Bawean, Indonesia : *Bah* way ahn
Bawtry, England : *Baw* tri
Bayamo, Cuba : Bah *yah* moh
Bayamón, Puerto Rico : Biy ah *mohn*
Bayeux, France : Bah *yuh*
Baykonur, Russia : Biy ka *noohr*
¹**Bayonne**, France : Biy *awn* (UK Biy *on*) (French Bah *yawn*)
²**Bayonne**, USA : Bay *ohn*
Bayreuth, Germany : Biy *royt* [According to Ross, p. 44, the name of the city, famous for its operas, should be pronounced Bay *royt*, although he adds: "The name can also be pronounced in the German way." Lloyd James 1937 recommends the stress Biy royt.]
Baytown, USA : *Bay* town
Baza, Spain : *Bah* thah
Beachy Head, England : Bee chi *Hed*
¹**Beaconsfield**, Australia; Canada : *Bee* kunz feeld
²**Beaconsfield**, England : *Bek* unz feeld
Beaminster, England : *Bem* in stur (UK *Bem* in sta) [A spelling pronunciation *Bee* min sta is sometimes heard

among people unfamiliar with the name of the Dorset town.]

Béarn, France : Bay *ahrn*

Bearpark, England : *Beer* pahrk (UK *Bi* a pahk)

Bearsden, Scotland : *Berz* dun (UK *Bay* uz dun)

Beatrice, USA : Bee *at* rus [The name of the Nebraska city is also pronounced *Bee* trus, closer to the conventional pronunciation of the female forename from which it derived.]

Beattock, Scotland : *Bee* tuk

Beau Bassin, Mauritius : Boh Ba *sahn*

Beaucaire, France : Boh *ker*

Beauce, France : Bohs

¹Beaufort, Malaysia; USA (North Carolina) : *Boh* furt (UK *Boh* fut)

²Beaufort, USA (South Carolina) : *Byooh* furt (UK *Byooh* fut)

Beaufort (Sea), Arctic Ocean : *Boh* furt (UK *Boh* fut)

Beaugency, France : Boh zhahn *see*

Beaujolais, France : Boh zhaw *lay*

Beaulieu, England : *Byooh* li

Beauly, Scotland : *Byooh* li

Beaumaris, Wales : Boh *mar* is

¹Beaumont, England (Cumbria) : *Bee* munt

²Beaumont, England (Essex); USA : *Boh* mahnt (UK *Boh* munt)

Beaune, France : Bohn

Beauport, Canada : Boh *pawr* (UK Boh *paw*)

Beauvais, France : Boh *vay*

Beaverton, USA : *Bee* vur tun (UK *Bee* va tun)

Bebington, England : *Beb* ing tun

Beccles, England : *Bek* ulz

Béchar, Algeria : Bay *shahr* (UK Bay *shah*)

Bechuanaland, Africa : Bech *wah* na land

Beckenham, England : *Bek* num

Beckley, USA : *Bek* li

Beckum, Germany : *Bek* um

Becontree, England : *Bek* un tree

Bedale, England : *Bee* dul [This is correct for the North Yorkshire town,

but Bedales School, Hampshire, is *Bee* daylz.]

Beddgelert, Wales : Bedh *gel* urt (UK Bedh *gel* ut) (Welsh Baydh *gel* ert)

Bedford, England; USA : *Bed* furd (UK *Bed* fud)

Bedlington, England : *Bed* ling tun

Bedwellty, Wales : Bed *wel* ti (Welsh Bed *wehl* ti)

Beersheba, Israel : Bir *shee* ba (UK Bi a *shee* ba)

Beeston, England : *Bee* stun

Beijing, China : Bay *jing* [The Chinese capital's name is sometimes popularly (but irregularly) pronounced Bay *zhing*.]

Beira, Mozambique; Portugal : *Bay* ra (UK *Biy* ra)

Beirut, Lebanon : Bay *rooht*

Beith, Scotland : Beedh

Beja, Portugal : *Bay* zha

Béja, Tunisia : Bay *zhah*

Bejaïa, Algeria : Be *jiy* a

Bekasi, Indonesia : Bay *kah* si

Békés, Hungary : *Bay* kaysh

Békéscsaba, Hungary : *Bay* kaysh chaw baw

Bela Ckrva, Serbia : Be lah *Tsurk* vah

Belarus, Europe : Bel a *roohs*

Belawan, Indonesia : Bay *lah* wahn

Belaya Tserkov, Ukraine : Byel a ya *Tser* kuf

Belcher (Islands), Canada : *Bel* chur (UK *Bel* cha)

Belém, Brazil : Be *lem*

Belfast, Northern Ireland; USA : *Bel* fast (UK *Bel* fahst) [The name of the Northern Ireland capital is alternately accented Bel *fahst*.]

Belfort, France : Bel *fawr*

Belgaum, India : Bel *gowm*

Belgium, Europe : *Bel* jum

Belgorod, Russia : *Bel* ga rahd (UK *Bel* ga rod) (Russian *Byel* ga rut)

Belgorod-Dnestrovskiy, Ukraine : Byel ga rut Dnis *trawf* ski

Belgrade, Serbia : Bel *grayd*

Belitung, Indonesia : Bay *lee* toong

Belize, Central America : Bi *leez*

Bellaire, USA : Be *ler*
Belleek, Northern Ireland : Ba *leek*
Bellefontaine, USA : Bel *fown* tun
Belle Fourche, USA : Bel *Foohsh*
Belle Isle, Canada : Bel *Iyl*
Belleville, Canada; USA : *Bel* vil
Bellevue, USA : *Bel* vyooh
Bellflower, USA : *Bel* flow ur
[1]Bellingham, England (London) : *Bel* ing um
[2]Bellingham, England (Northumberland) : *Bel* in jum
[3]Bellingham, USA : *Bel* ing ham (UK *Bel* ing um)
Bellingshausen (Sea), Antarctica : *Bel* ingz how zun
Bellinzona, Switzerland : Bel un *dzoh* na
Bellmawr, USA : Bel *mahr* (UK Bel *maw*)
Belluno, Italy : Bel *looh* noh
Bellville, South Africa : *Bel* vil
Bell Ville, Argentina : Bel *Veel* (Spanish Bezh *Vee* zhay)
Bellwood, USA : *Bel* wood
Belmont, USA : *Bel* mahnt (UK *Bel* mont)
Belmopan, Belize : Bel moh *pahn*
Belo Horizonte, Brazil : Bel oh Haw ra *zahn* ti (UK ... Hor i *zon* ti) (Portuguese Bay loh ree *zohn* tee) [The Portuguese pronunciation of the city's name blends the -*lo* of *Belo* with the *Ho*- of *Horizonte*.]
Beloit, USA : Ba *loyt*
Belorussia, Europe : Bel oh *rah* sha
Belper, England : *Bel* pur (UK *Bel* pa)
Belsen, Germany : *Bel* sun (German *Bel* zun)
Belton, USA : *Bel* tun
Beltsy, Moldova : *Byel* tsi
Belvidere, USA : *Bel* va dir (UK *Bel* va dee a)
Belvoir, England : *Bee* vur (UK *Bee* va) [The name is best known as that of the Vale of Belvoir, Leicestershire, and for Belvoir Castle atop a hill here. In London street names it is often pronounced US Bel *voyr*, UK Bel *voy* a.]

Belz, France : Bels
Bembridge, England : *Bem* brij
Bemidji, USA : Ba *mij* i
Benares, India : Bi *nah* riz
Benbecula, Scotland : Ben *bek* yoo la
Bendery, Moldova : Ben *der* ee
Bendigo, Australia : *Ben* di goh
Bene Beraq, Israel : Ba nay Ba *rahk*
Benenden, England : *Ben* un dun
Benevento, Italy : Ben i *ven* toh (Italian Bay nay *vayn* toh)
Bengal, Asia : Ben *gawl*
Bengbu, China : Bung *booh*
Benghazi, Libya : Ben *gah* zi
Bengkulu, Indonesia : Beng *kooh* looh
Bengo, Angola : *Beng* goh
Benguela, Angola : Beng *gwel* ah
Benha, Egypt : *Ben* ha
Beni, Bolivia : *Bay* nee
Beni Abbès, Algeria : Bay ni Ah *bes*
Benicia, USA : Ba *nee* sha
Benidorm, Spain : *Ben* a dawrm (UK *Ben* i dawm)
Benin, Africa : Ba *neen*
Beni Suef, Egypt : Be nee Soo *ayf*
Ben Lomond, Australia; Scotland : Ben *Loh* mund
Ben Macdhui, Scotland : Ben Muk *dooh* i
Ben Nevis, Scotland : Ben *Nev* is
Bennington, USA : *Ben* ing tun
Benoni, South Africa : Ba *noh* ni
Bensheim, Germany : *Bens* hiym
Benson, England : *Ben* sun [The name of the Oxfordshire village was originally *Bensington*, but when this was locally pronounced as now, the spelling followed the pronunciation.]
Benton, USA : *Ben* tun
Benue, Nigeria : *Bayn* way (UK *Ben* oo ay)
Benxi, China : Ben *chee*
Bequia, West Indies : *Bek* wi
Berat, Albania : Ba *raht*
Berbera, Somalia : *Buhr* bur a (UK *Buh* bur a)
Berbérati, Central African Republic : Ber ba *rah* tee

Berbice, Guyana : Buhr *bees* (UK Buh *bees*)

Berchem-Sainte-Agathe, Belgium : Ber khem Sahnt A *gaht*

Berchtesgaden, Germany : *Berkh* tus gah dun

Berck, France : Berk

Berdichev, Ukraine : *Buhr* di chef (UK *Buh* di chef) (Russian Bir *dee* chif)

Berdyansk, Ukraine : Buhr *dyansk* (UK Buh *dyansk*) (Russian Bir *dyansk*)

Berdychiv, Ukraine : *Bir* dee chif

Berea, USA : Ba *ree* a

Berezniki, Russia : Bi riz ni *kee*

Bergamo, Italy : *Buhr* ga moh (UK *Buh* ga moh) (Italian *Ber* gah moh)

Bergen, Norway : *Buhr* gun (UK *Buh* gun) (Norwegian *Bar* gun) [Lloyd James 1937 recommended US *Ber* gun, UK *Bay* a gun for the seaport city's name and this remains an alternate today.]

Bergen op Zoom, Netherlands : Ber kha awp *Zohm*

Bergerac, France : Berzh *rahk*

Bergisch Gladbach, Germany : Ber gish *Glaht* bahkh

Bering (Sea), Pacific Ocean : *Bir* ing (UK *Bay* a ring)

¹**Berkeley**, England : *Bahr* kli (UK *Bah* kli)

²**Berkeley**, USA : *Buhr* kli (UK *Buh* kli)

Berkhamsted, England : *Buhr* kum sted (UK *Buh* kum sted) [Some residents of the Hertfordshire town favor the pronunciation *Bah* kum sted.]

Berkley, USA : *Buhr* kli (UK *Buh* kli)

Berkshire, England : *Bahrk* shur (UK *Bahk* sha) [The -*shire* that ends many English county names is usually pronounced -sha by British speakers, although some prefer -shi a or a more mannered -shiyr.]

(1) There is an old convention that the -*shire* element in county names is either glided over with hardly any stress, as in "Chesha," "Yorksha," "Worcestersha," or given more stress and pronounced "-shire" (to rhyme

with "wire")— the latter preferred by Scottish-English speakers. But the newest trend among [radio] announcers is to stress and elongate the last syllable and pronounce it "sheer" [Fritz Spiegl, *MediaSpeak*, 1989]. (2) Further pronunciation-trends to be found there [on the radio] and elsewhere include saying -*sheer* for -*shire* in names of counties (*Northamptonsheer* for old -*shuh*) [Kingsley Amis, *The King's English*, 1997].

Berkshire (Hills), USA : *Buhrk* shir (UK *Buhk* sha)

¹**Berlin**, Germany : Buhr *lin* (UK Buh *lin*) (German Ber *leen*)

²**Berlin**, USA : *Buhr* lun (UK *Buh* lun)

Bermondsey, England : *Buhr* mund zi (UK *Buh* mund zi)

Bermuda, Atlantic Ocean : Bur *myooh* da (UK Ba *myooh* da)

Bern, Switzerland : Buhrn (UK Buhn) (German Bern)

Bernburg, Germany : *Bern* boork

Bernerie-en-Retz, France : Bern ree ahn *Ray*

Bernese Oberland, Switzerland : Buhr neez *Oh* bur land (UK Buh neez *Oh* ba land)

Bernina, Switzerland : Ber *nee* na

Bernkastel-Kues, Germany : Bern kas tul *Kees*

Berry, France : Be *ree*

¹**Berwick**, Australia; England : *Ber* ik [Most English Berwicks have a name pronounced as here, although the village of Berwick, East Sussex, is or was locally known as ²**Berwick**.]

²**Berwick**, USA : *Buhr* wik (UK *Buh* wik)

Berwick-upon-Tweed, England : Ber ik a pahn *Tweed* (UK ... a pon...)

Berwyn, USA; Wales : *Buhr* win (UK *Bay* a win)

Besançon, France : Bi zahn *sawn*

Beslan, Russia : Bes *lahn*

Bessarabia, Moldova : Bes a *ray* bi a

Bessemer, USA : *Bes* i mur (UK *Bes* i ma)

Bet Guvrin, Israel : Bayt Ga *vreen*

Bethany, USA : *Beth* un i
Bethel, USA : *Beth* ul
Bethesda, USA; Wales : Bi *thez* da
Bethlehem, South Africa; USA; West
  Bank : *Beth* li hem
Bethpage, USA : Beth *payj*
Béthune, France : Bay *teen*
Bet She'an, Israel : Bayt Sha *ahn*
Bet Shemesh, Israel : Bayt *Shem* esh
Bettembourg, Luxembourg : Bay tahn
  boohr
Betws-y-coed, Wales : Bet us i *koyd*
  (Welsh Bet us a *kaw* id) [The name of
  the village and tourist center, set
  amid woods and streams, means
  "chapel in the wood," from Welsh
  betws, "oratory" (literally "bead
  house," from the English, with
  "bead" in its now obsolete sense
  "prayer"), *y*, "the," and *coed*, "wood."]
  (1) One strong tip about *y*. Whenever
  you see it between hyphens in [Welsh]
  place-names (Betws-y-coed is a well-
  known case), do not pronounce that
  particular *y* as *ee*. Pronounce it like *u*
  in English "fur" [Wynford Vaughan-
  Thomas and Alun Llewellyn, *The
  Shell Guide to Wales*, 1969].
  (2) [Most non–Welsh] look at Betws-
  y-Coed ... and can't work out what to
  do with the "w," so they leave it out
  and end up, as often as not, with that
  well-known Welsh schoolgirl, Betsy
  Co-Ed [Leaver, p. 1].
Betws-yn-Rhos, Wales : Bet us in *Rohs*
  (Welsh Bet us un *Raws*)
Beulah, USA : *Byooh* la
Beveren, Belgium : *Bay* va run
Beverley, England : *Bev* ur li (UK *Bev* a
  li)
Beverly, USA : *Bev* ur li (UK *Bev* a li)
Beverwijk, Netherlands : *Bay* vur viyk
Bewdley, England : *Byoohd* li
Bex, Switzerland : Bay
Bexar, USA : Ber (UK *Bay* a)
Bexhill, England : Beks *hil*
Bexley, England; USA : *Beks* li
Bexleyheath, England : Beks li *heeth*
Béziers, France : Bay *zyay*
Bezons, France : Bi *zawn*

Bhadreswar, India : Ba *dres* wur
Bhagalpur, India : *Bah* gul poor
Bhaktapur, India : *Bahk* ta poor
Bhamo, Myanmar : Ba *moh*
Bharatpur, India : *Bah* rut poor
Bhatpara, India : Baht *pah* ra
Bhavnagar, India : Bow *nah* gur
Bhilai, India : Bi *liy*
Bhopal, India : Boh *pahl*
Bhubaneswar, India : Booh ba *nesh* wur
Bhutan, Asia : Booh *tahn*
Biafra, Africa : Bi *af* ra
Biak, Indonesia : Bee *ahk*
Biała Podlaska, Poland : Byah wah
  Pawd *lahs* kah
Białogard, Poland : Byah *waw* gahrt
Białystok, Poland : Bi *ahl* i stahk (UK
  Bi *al* i stok) (Polish Bya *wi* stawk)
Biarritz, France : Bee a *rits* (UK Bi a
  rits) (French Byah *reets*)
Bicester, England : *Bis* tur (UK *Bis* ta)
Bida, Nigeria : *Bee* dah
Biddeford, USA : *Bid* a furd (UK *Bid* a
  fud)
Biddulph, England : *Bid* ahlf
Bideford, England : *Bid* a furd (UK *Bid*
  i fud)
Bié, Angola : Byay
Bielefeld, Germany : *Beel* felt
Bielsko-Biała, Poland : Byel skaw *Byah*
  wah
Bielsk Podlaski, Poland : Byelsk Pawd
  lah ski
Bien Hoa, Vietnam : Byen *Hwah*
Bigbury, England : *Big* bri
Bigelow (Mountain), USA : *Big* a loh
Biggar, Scotland : *Big* ur (UK *Big* a)
Biggleswade, England : *Big* ulz wayd
Big Sur, USA : Big *Suhr* (UK ... *Suh*)
Bihać, Bosnia-Herzegovina : *Bee* hahch
Bihar, India : Bi *hahr* (UK Bi *hah*)
Bijapur, India : Bi *jah* poor
Bikaner, India : Bi ka *nir*
Bikini (Atoll), Marshall Islands : Bi *kee*
  nee
Bila Tserkva, Ukraine : Bee la *Tserk* va
Bilbao, Spain : Bil *bah* oh
Bilhorod-Dnistrovskyy, Ukraine : Beel
  ha rod Dnis *trawf* ski

Billerica, USA : Bil *rik* a
Billericay, England : Bil a *rik* i [Ross, p. 47, favors the pronunciation Bil i *rik* i for the Essex town.]
Billinge, England : *Bil* inj
Billingham, England : *Bil* ing um
Billings, USA : *Bil* ingz
Billingshurst, England : *Bil* ingz huhrst (UK *Bil* ingz huhst)
Billiton, Indonesia : Bee *lee* tohn
Billom, France : Bee *yawn*
Bilma, Niger : *Bil* ma
Biloxi, USA : Bi *lahk* si
Bima, Indonesia : *Bee* mah
Bimini, Bahamas : *Bim* a ni
Bingen, Germany : *Bing* un
Bingerville, Côte d'Ivoire : Bahn zhay *veel*
Binghamton, USA : *Bing* um tun
Bingley, England : *Bing* li
Binjai, Indonesia : Bin *jiy*
Bío-Bío, Chile : Bee oh *Bee* oh
Bioko, Equatorial Guinea : Bi *oh* koh
Biratnagar, Nepal : Bi *raht* na gur
Birkenhead, England; New Zealand : *Buhr* kun hed (UK Buh kun *hed*)
Birkirkara, Malta : Bir kir *kah* rah
Bîrlad, Romania : Bir *lahd*
¹**Birmingham**, England : *Buhr* ming um (UK *Buh* ming um) [As Ross, p. 47, points out, train announcers often pronounce the city's name *Buh* ming ham, similar to US ²**Birmingham**. A former spelling *Brummagem* represented the name's local pronunciation *Brah* ma jum.]
²**Birmingham**, USA : *Buhr* ming ham (UK *Buh* ming um)
[*Birmingham*] is pronounced as spelled in the United States, and never in the clipped English manner [Mencken, p. 540].
Birnam, Scotland : *Buhr* num (UK *Buh* num)
Birnin Kebbi, Nigeria : Beer neen *Keb* bi (UK Bee a neen...)
Birobidzhan, Russia : Bir oh bi *jahn*
Birr, Ireland : Buhr (UK Buh)
Biscay, Europe : *Bis* kay

Bishkek, Kyrgyzstan : Bish *kek*
Bishnupur, India : *Bish* noo poor
Bisho, South Africa : *Bee* shoh
Bishop Auckland, England : Bish up *Awk* lund
Bishop's Stortford, England : Bish ups *Stawrt* furd (UK ... *Stawt* fud)
Biskra, Algeria : *Bis* kra
Bisley, England : *Biz* li
Bismarck, USA : *Biz* mahrk (UK *Biz* mahk)
Bismarck (Archipelago), Papua New Guinea : *Biz* mahrk (UK *Biz* mahk)
Bissagos (Islands), Guinea-Bissau : Bi *sah* gus
Bissau, Guinea-Bissau : Bi *sow*
Bistriţa, Romania : *Bees* treet sah
Bithynia, Asia : Bi *thin* i a (UK Biy *thin* i a)
Bitola, Macedonia : *Bit* o la
Bitterfeld, Germany : *Bit* ur felt
Biysk, Russia : Beesk
Bizerta, Tunisia : Ba *zuhr* ta (UK Bi *zuh* ta)
Bjelovar, Croatia : Bye law *vahr*
Blaby, England : *Blay* bi
Blackburn, England : *Blak* buhrn (UK *Blak* buhn) [An alternate local pronunciation of the Lancashire town's name is *Blag* buhn.]
Blackheath, England : Blak *heeth*
Blackley, England : *Blayk* li [The Manchester district has this unexpected pronunciation.]
Blackpool, England : *Blak* poohl
Blackrock, Ireland : *Blak* rahk (UK *Blak* rok)
Blackwood, Wales : Blak *wood*
Bladon, England : *Blay* dun
Blaenau Ffestiniog, Wales : Bliy niy Fes *tin* i og
Blaenavon, Wales : Bliy *na* vun
Blagoevgrad, Bulgaria : Blah *gaw* ev graht
Blagoveshchensk, Russia : Bla ga *vyaysh* chinsk
Blaine, USA : Blayn
Blairgowrie, Scotland : Bler *gow* ri (UK Blay a *gow* ri)

Blakely, USA : *Blayk* li
Blakeney, England : *Blayk* ni
Blanc, Mont *see* **Mont Blanc**
Blandford, England : *Bland* furd (UK *Bland* fud)
Blankenberge, Belgium : *Blahn* kun ber kha
Blankenburg, Germany : *Blahng* kun boork
Blantyre, Malawi : Blan *tiyr* (UK Blan *tiy* a)
Blarney, Ireland : *Blahr* ni (UK *Blah* ni)
Blawith, England : Blahdh [The name of the Cumbria village is so pronounced, but Blawith Road running off Station Road, Harrow, London, is *Blay* with.]
Blaydon, England : *Blay* dun
Blaye, France : Bliy
Blencathra, England : Blen *kath* ra
Blenheim, Germany; New Zealand : *Blen* im
Blennerhassett (Island), USA : Blen ur *has* it (UK Blen a *has* it)
Bletchley, England : *Blech* li
Blida, Algeria : *Blee* da
Blitar, Indonesia : *Blee* tahr
Blitta, Togo : *Bleet* tah
Bloemfontein, South Africa : *Bloohm* fahn tayn (UK *Bloohm* fun tayn)
Blois, France : Blwah
Bloomington, USA : *Blooh* ming tun
Bloomsbury, England : *Bloohmz* ber i (UK *Bloohmz* bri)
Blora, Indonesia : *Bloh* rah
Bloxham, England : *Blahk* sum (UK *Blok* sum)
Bluefields, Nicaragua : *Blooh* feeldz
Bluff, New Zealand : Blahf
Blumenau, Brazil : Blooh ma *now*
Blyth, England : Bliydh
Blythe, USA : Bliydh
Blytheville, USA : *Bliy* vil
Boaco, Nicaragua : Boh *ah* koh
Boa Vista, Brazil : Boh a *Veesh* ta
Bobbingworth, England : *Bah* bing wuhrth (UK *Bob* ing wuhth) [Although now pronounced as given here, the name of this village near

Chipping Ongar, Essex, had a former local pronunciation *Bah* ving a, today represented in the name of nearby *Bovinger*.]
Bobigny, France : Baw bee *nyee*
Bobo-Dioulasso, Burkina Faso : Baw boh Dyooh lah *soh*
Bobruysk, Belarus : Bah *brooh* isk
Boca Raton, USA : Boh ka Ra *tohn*
Bocas del Toro, Panama : Bo kahs del *Toh* roh
Bocholt, Germany : *Baw* khawlt
Bochum, Germany : *Baw* khoom
Bodaybo, Russia : Ba *diy* baw
Bodiam, England : *Boh* di um
Bodinayakkanur, India : Boh di *nah* ya ka noor
Bodmin, England : *Bahd* min (UK *Bod* min)
Bodø, Norway : *Boh* duh
Boën, France : Baw *ahn*
Boeotia, Greece : Bi *oh* sha
Bogalusa, USA : Boh ga *looh* sa
Bognor Regis, England : Bahg nur *Ree* jis (UK Bog na...)
Bogor, Indonesia : *Boh* gawr (UK *Boh* gaw)
Bogota, USA : Ba *goh* ta
Bogotá, Colombia : Boh ga *tah* (UK Bog a *tah*) (Spanish Boh goh *tah*)
Bogra, Bangladesh : *Boh* gra
Bohemia, Czech Republic : Boh *hee* mi a
Bohol, Philippines : Boh *hawl*
Boise, USA : *Boy* zi [The name of the Idaho state capital is also pronounced *Boy* si.]
Bojador, Western Sahara : Baw ja *dawr* (UK Boj a *daw*)
Bojonegoro, Indonesia : Boh joh na *goh* roh
Boké, Guinea : Boh *kay*
Bokhara, Asia : Boh *hah* ra (UK Baw *khah* ra)
Boksburg, South Africa : *Bahks* buhrg (UK *Boks* buhg)
Bolama, Guinea-Bissau : Boh *lah* mah
Bolgatanga, Ghana : Bohl gah *tahn* ga
Bolingbrook, USA : *Boh* ling brook

Bolívar, Argentina; Colombia; Ecuador :
 Boh *lee* vahr
Bolivia, South America : Ba *liv* i a
Bolligen, Switzerland : *Baw* li gun
Bologna, Italy : Ba *loh* nya (Italian Boh
 loh nyah)
Bolsover, England : *Bahl* soh vur (UK
 Bol soh va) [An alternate local pro-
 nunciation of the Derbyshire town's
 name is *Bohl* zoh va.]
Bolton, England : *Bohl* tun
Bolton-le-Sands, England : Bohl tun li
 Sandz
Bolzano, Italy : Bohl *tsah* noh
Boma, Democratic Republic of the
 Congo : *Boh* mah
Bombay, India : Bahm *bay* (UK Bom
 bay)
Bonaire, Netherlands Antilles : Ba *ner*
 (UK Bon *ay* a)
Bonao, Dominican Republic : Boh *now*
Bonavista, Canada : Bah na *vis* ta (UK
 Bon a *vis* ta)
Bondi, Australia : *Bahn* diy (UK *Bon*
 diy)
Bondoukou, Côte d'Ivoire : Bawn dooh
 kooh
Bondowoso, Indonesia : Bon doh *woh*
 soh
Bône, Algeria : Bohn
Bo'ness, Scotland : Boh *nes*
Bongabon, Philippines : Bawng *ah*
 bawn
Bongor, Chad : Bawng *gawr* (UK
 Bawng *gaw*)
Bonifacio, Corsica, France : Boh nee
 fah choh
Bonn, Germany : Bahn (UK Bon)
 (German Bawn)
Bonne Terre, USA : Bahn *Ter* (UK Bon
 Tay a)
Bonneville, USA : *Bah* na vil (UK *Bon*
 a vil)
Bonthe, Sierra Leone : Bahn *tay* (UK
 Bon *tay*)
Boom, Netherlands : Bohm
Boos, France : Boh
Boothia (Peninsula), Canada : *Booh* thi
 a

Bootle, England : *Booh* tul
Bophuthatswana, South Africa : Boh
 pooh tah *tswah* nah [The name
 means "place where the Tswana
 gather," for the people who gave the
 name of **Botswana.**]
Bopolu, Liberia : Boh *poh* looh
Bor, Russia; Serbia : Bawr
Borås, Sweden : Booh *rohs*
Bordeaux, France : Bawr *doh* (UK Baw
 doh)
Borders, Scotland : *Bawr* durz (UK
 Baw duz)
Bordighera, Italy : Bawr dee *gay* rah [A
 UK pronunciation Bawd i *gee* a ra has
 also been current for the seaport and
 winter resort.]
Bordj Bou Arreridj, Algeria : Bawrj
 Booh A ray *reej* (UK Bawj...)
Borehamwood, England : Baw rum
 wood
Borinage, Belgium : Baw ree *nahzh*
Borisoglebsk, Russia : Ba rees a *glyepsk*
Borisov, Belarus : Ba *ree* suf
Borna, Germany : *Bawr* nah
Borneo, Malay Archipelago : *Bawr* ni
 oh (UK *Baw* ni oh)
Bornholm, Denmark : *Bawrn* hohm
 (UK *Bawn* hohm) (Danish Born
 hohlm)
Borodino, Russia : Bawr a *dee* noh (UK
 Bor a *dee* noh) (Russian Bur a dee
 naw)
Borovichi, Russia : Bur a vi *chee*
Borrowash, England : *Bah* roh wahsh
 (UK *Bah* ro wosh)
Borrowdale, England : *Bawr* oh dayl
 (UK *Bor* a dayl)
Borstal, England : *Bawr* stul (UK *Baw*
 stul)
Borth, Wales : Bawrth (UK Bawth)
Borwick, England : *Baw* rik (UK *Bor*
 ik)
Boscastle, England : *Bahs* kas ul (UK
 Bos kah sul)
Boscawen, USA : *Bahs* kwin (UK *Bos*
 kwin)
Boscobel, England : *Bahs* ka bel (UK
 Bos ka bel)

Bosham, England : *Bah* zum (UK *Boz* um) [The name of the West Sussex village, a noted sailing center, is alternately pronounced *Bosh* um.]

Boskoop, Netherlands : *Baws* kohp

Bosnia, Bosnia-Herzegovina : *Bahz* ni a (UK *Boz* ni a)

Bosporus, Turkey : *Bahs* pa rus (UK *Bos* pa rus)

Boston, England; USA : *Baws* tun (UK *Bos* tun) [Some residents of the Massachusetts city pronounce the name *Bah* stun, but this is usually regarded as an affectation.]

Bosworth Field, England : Bahz wurth *Feeld* (UK Boz wuth...)

Botany Bay, Australia : Bah tun i *Bay* (UK Bot un i...)

Bothnia, Europe : *Bahth* ni a (UK *Both* ni a)

Bothwell, Scotland : *Bahth* wul (UK *Both* wul)

Botoşani, Romania : Boh toh *shahn*

Botswana, Africa : Baht*s wah* na (UK Bots *wah* na)

Bottrop, Germany : *Bawt* rawp

Bouaké, Côte d'Ivoire : Bwah *kay*

Boucherville, Canada : *Booh* shur vil (UK *Booh* sha vil)

Boufarik, Algeria : Booh fah *reek*

Bougainville, Pacific Ocean : *Booh* gan vil [In Australia the name of the largest of the Solomon Islands is pronounced *Boh* gan vil.]

Bougie, Algeria : Booh *zhee*

Bouïra, Algeria : Bwee *rah*

Boulder, USA : *Bohl* dur (UK *Bohl* da)

Boulogne, France : Boo *lohn* (UK Boo *loyn*) (French Booh *loyn*) [According to Ross, p. 50, the name of the seaport city is best pronounced Boo *lohn*, in the US way, although he adds that Boo *loyn* "can still be heard." In fact the UK pronunciation is regularly in use.]

Bourbon, USA : *Buhr* bun (UK *Buh* bun)

¹**Bourbonnais**, France : Boohr baw *nay*

²**Bourbonnais**, USA : Buhr *boh* nus

Bourg-en-Bresse, France : Boohrk ahn *Bres*

Bourges, France : Boohrzh

Bourgneuf-en-Retz, France : Boor nuhf ahn *Ray*

Bourke, Australia : Buhrk (UK Buhk)

Bourne, England; USA : Bawrn (UK Bawn)

Bournemouth, England : *Bawrn* muth (UK *Bawn* muth)

Bouxwiller, France : Books vee *ler*

Bovey Tracey, England : Bah vi *Tray* si

Bovingdon, England : *Bah* ving dun (UK *Bov* ing dun)

Bow, England : Boh

Bowdoin (Lake), USA : *Boh* dun

Bowen, Australia : *Boh* un (UK *Bow* in)

Bowie, USA : *Booh* i [This is the pronunciation of places named for frontiersman James Bowie (1796–1836), although he himself is said to have pronounced his name *Boh* i.]

Bowland (Forest), England : *Boh* lund

Bowral, Australia : *Bow* rul

Boxtel, Netherlands : *Bawks* tul

Boyacá, Colombia : Boh yah *kah*

Boyle, Ireland : Boyl

Boyne, Ireland : Boyn

Boyoma (Falls), Democratic Republic of the Congo : Boh *yoh* mah

Bozeman, USA : *Bohz* mun

Bozouls, France : Boh *zoohl*

Brabant, Belgium : Bra *bant* (Flemish *Brah* bahnt; French Bra *bahn*) [The name of the province and former duchy is still sometimes pronounced *Bra* bunt by English speakers.]

Brabourne, England : *Bray* bawrn (UK *Bray* bawn)

Bracknell, England : *Brak* nul

Bradenton, USA : *Bray* dun tun

Bradford, England : *Brad* furd (UK *Brad* fud) [The name of the Yorkshire city is locally also pronounced *Brat* furd.]

Bradley, England : *Brad* li [There are several villages of this name, a few of which are pronounced *Brayd* li.] [The name of Bradley in Staffordshire] should be pronounced Bradeley [John Hadfield, ed., *The Shell Book of English Villages*, 1980].

Bradwell-on-Sea, England : Brad wul ahn *See* (UK ... on...)

Brady, USA : *Bray* di

Braemar, Scotland : Bray *mahr* (UK *Bray* mah)

Braga, Portugal : *Brah* ga

Bragado, Argentina : Bra *gah* doh

Bragança, Brazil; Portugal : Bra *gan* sa

Braganza, Portugal : Bra *gan* za

Brahmapur, India : *Brah* ma poor

Brahmaputra, Asia : Brah ma *pooh* tra

Brăila, Romania : Bra *ee* lah

Brainerd, USA : *Bray* nurd (UK *Bray* nud)

Braintree, England; USA : *Brayn* tree

Brakpan, South Africa : *Brak* pan

Brampton, Canada; England : *Bramp* tun

Brandenburg, Germany : *Bran* dun buhrg (UK *Bran* dun buhg) (German *Brahn* dun boork)

Brandon, Canada; England; USA : *Bran* dun

Branford, USA : *Bran* furd (UK *Bran* fud)

Brantford, Canada : *Brant* furd (UK *Brant* fud)

Brasília, Brazil : Bra *zil* i a (Portuguese Brah *zee* lya)

Braşov, Romania : Brah *shohv*

Brasschaat, Belgium : *Brahs* skhaht

Brasted, England : *Bray* sted

Bratislava, Slovakia : Brah ti *slah* va (UK Brat i *slah* va) (Slovak *Brah* tyee slah vah)

Bratsk, Russia : Brahtsk

Brattleboro, USA : *Brat* ul buhr oh (UK *Brat* ul bra)

Braunston, England : *Brawn* stun

Braunton, England : *Brawn* tun

Brawley, USA : *Braw* li

Bray, England; Ireland : Bray

Brazil, South America : Bra *zil*

Brazzaville, Republic of the Congo : *Braz* a vil (French Brah za *veel*)

Brčko, Bosnia-Herzegovina : *Buhrch*

koh (UK *Buhch* koh) (Serbian *Brch* kaw)

Breadalbane, Scotland : Bra *dawl* bin

Breage, England : Breeg [The name of the Cornish village has settled to the present pronunciation, as explained in the quote below.]
  The older pronunciation is "Braig" (rhyming with "Haig"), but "Breeg" (rhyming with "league") is now common [O.J. Padel, *A Popular Dictionary of Cornish Place-Names*, 1988].

Breamore, England : *Brem* ur (UK *Brem* a)

Breaston, England : *Bree* stun

Brebes, Indonesia : *Bray* bes

Brechin, Scotland : *Bree* kin

Brecht, Belgium : Bret

Breckenridge, USA : *Brek* un rij

Breckland, England : *Brek* lund

Brecknock, Wales : *Brek* nahk (UK *Brek* nok)

Brecon, Wales : *Brek* un

Breda, Netherlands : *Bree* da (Dutch Bray *dah*)

Bredon, England : *Bree* dun

Bregenz, Austria : *Bray* gens

Breisach, Germany : *Briy* zahkh

¹**Bremen**, Germany : *Bray* mun

²**Bremen**, USA : *Bree* mun

Bremerhaven, Germany : *Bray* mur hah vun (German Bray ma *hah* fun)

Bremersdorp, Swaziland : *Bray* murs dawrp (UK *Bray* mus dawp)

Bremerton, USA : *Brem* ur tun (UK *Brem* a tun)

Brenner (Pass), Italy : *Bren* ur

Brentford, England : *Brent* furd (UK *Brent* fud)

Brentham, England : *Bren* tum

Brentwood, England; USA : *Brent* wood [The name of the Essex, England, town was at one time locally pronounced *Buhnt* wood, truer to the etymology, which is "burnt wood."]

Brescia, Italy : *Bray* shah

Bressanone, Italy : Bray sah *noh* nay

Bresse, France : Bres

Brest, Belarus; France : Brest

Brest-Litovsk, Belarus : Brest Li *tawfsk* (UK ... Li *tofsk*)

Bretton Woods, USA : Bret un *Woodz*

Briançon, France : Bree ahn *sawn*

Bridgend, Wales : Brij *end*

Bridgeport, USA : *Brij* pawrt (UK *Brij* pawt)

Bridgeton, USA : *Brij* tun

Bridgetown, Barbados : *Brij* town [A local pronunciation of the capital's name is *Brij* tahn.]

Bridgewater, Canada; USA : *Brij* waw tur (UK *Brij* waw ta)

Bridgnorth, England : *Brij* nawrth (UK *Brij* nawth)

Bridgwater, England : *Brij* waw tur (UK *Brij* waw ta)

Bridlington, England : *Brid* ling tun

Bridport, England : *Brid* pawrt (UK *Brid* pawt)

Brie, France : Bree

Brierfield, England : *Briy* ur feeld (UK *Briy* a feeld)

Brig, Switzerland : Breek

Brigham City, USA : Brig um *Si* ti

Brighouse, England : *Brig* hows

Brighstone, England : *Briy* stun [The name of the Isle of Wight village has a local pronunciation *Brik* stun, corresponding to the historic spelling *Brixton*, recorded in 1399.]
   (1) Notwithstanding the local pronunciation "Bry-stone," this charming little village began to appear on certain maps as "Brixton" [H.G. Stokes, *English Place-Names*, 1948].
   (2) The 14th-century spelling *Brixton* represents the local pronunciation of the name still heard [A.D. Mills, *The Place-Names of the Isle of Wight*, 1996].

Brightlingsea, England : *Briyt* ling see

Brighton, Australia; England; USA : *Briy* tun

Brindisi, Italy : *Brin* di zi (Italian *Breen* dee zee) [A UK pronunciation Brin *dee* zi or Brin *dee* si is also quite widely heard for the port city's name.]

Brisbane, Australia : *Briz* bun

Bristol, England; USA : *Bris* tul [The English city's name was recorded as *Bristou* in the Domesday Book (1086) so that one would have expected a modern spelling *Bristow* and a pronunciation *Bris* toh. But a local quirk of speech which adds an *l* to a final vowel sound gave the name's present spelling.]

Britain, Europe : *Bri* tun

Brittany, France : *Bri* tun i

Brive-la-Gaillarde, France : Breev la Gah *yahrd*

Brixham, England : *Brik* sum

Brixton, England : *Briks* tun

Brize Norton, England : Briyz *Nawr* tun (UK ... *Naw* tun)

Brno, Czech Republic : *Buhr* noh (UK *Buh* noh) (Czech *Br* naw)
   The German name of the town, *Brünn*, which is easier for the English [speaker] to pronounce, is, of course, no longer used [Ross, p. 52].

Broads, England : Brawdz

Broadstairs, England : *Brawd* sterz (UK *Brawd* stay uz)

Broadus, USA : *Braw* dus

Brocken, Germany : *Brah* kun (UK *Brok* un)

Brockenhurst, England : *Brah* kun huhrst (UK *Brok* un huhst)

Brockton, USA : *Brahk* tun (UK *Brok* tun)

Brockville, Canada : *Brahk* vil (UK *Brok* vil)

Brodick, Scotland : *Brah* dik (UK *Brod* ik)

Broken Hill, Australia; Zambia : Broh kun *Hil*

Bromley, England : *Brahm* li (UK *Brom* li) [The name of the former Kent town and present London borough was earlier pronounced in the US manner as *Brahm* li, as in Edward Lear's 1872 limerick: "There was an old person of Bromley, / Whose ways were not cheerful or comely." But as Pointon comments, p. 36: "The old pronunciation seems to have succumbed completely to the spelling pronunciation." Lloyd James 1936 distinguishes between *Brahm* li for the borough and *Brom* li for the London district alternately known as Bromley-by-Bow.]

Bromsgrove, England : *Brahmz* grohv (UK *Bromz* grohv)

Bromyard, England : *Brahm* yahrd (UK *Brom* yahd)

Bronx, USA : Brahngks (UK Brongks)

Brookfield, USA : *Brook* feeld

Brookhaven, USA : *Brook* hay vun

Brookings, USA : *Brook* ingz

Brookline, USA : *Brook* liyn

Brooklyn, USA : *Brook* lin

Brooks, Canada : Brooks

Brookwood, England : *Brook* wood

Broome, Australia : Broohm

Broons, France : Brawn

Brough, England : Brahf

¹**Broughton**, England : *Braw* tun [There are several villages of the name, with that in Northamptonshire pronounced *Brow* tun.]

²**Broughton**, Wales : *Brahf* tun

Broughty Ferry, Scotland : Braw ti *Fer* i

Brownhills, England : *Brown* hilz

Brownsville, USA : *Brownz* vil

Broxbourne, England : *Brahks* bawrn (UK *Broks* bawn)

Bruchsal, Germany : *Brookh* zahl

Bruck, Austria : Brook

Bruges, Belgium : Broohzh (French Breezh)
    To use a pronunciation with the French vowel would be affected [Ross, p. 53].

Brühl, Germany : Breel

Brunei, Asia : Brooh *niy*

Brunswick, Australia; Germany; USA : *Brahnz* wik

Brussels, Belgium : *Brah* sulz

Bruton, England : *Brooh* tun

Bruz, France : Bree

Bryan, USA : *Briy* un

Bryansk, Russia : Bri *ahnsk*

Bryher, England : *Briy* ur (UK *Briy* a)

Brynmawr, Wales : Brin *mow* ur (UK Brin *mow* a) (Welsh Brin *mowr*)

Bryn Mawr, USA : Brin *Mahr* (UK ... *Maw*)

Brzeg, Poland : Buhr *zheg* (UK Buh *zheg*) (Polish Bu *zhek*)

Bucaramanga, Colombia : Booh kah rah *mahng* gah

Buchan, Scotland : *Bah* kun

Buchanan, Liberia : Byooh *kan* un

Bucharest, Romania : *Booh* ka rest (UK Byooh ka *rest*)

Buchenwald, Germany : *Booh* kun wahld (UK *Booh* kun vald) (German *Booh* khun vahlt)

Buckfastleigh, England : *Bahk* fast lee (UK *Bahk* fahst lee)

Buckie, Scotland : *Bah* ki

¹**Buckingham**, Canada; England : *Bah* king um

²**Buckingham**, USA : *Bah* king ham

Buckley, Wales : *Bahk* li

Budapest, Hungary : *Booh* da pest (UK Byooh da *pest*) (Hungarian *Boo* daw pesht)

Budaun, India : Boo *down*

Bude, England : Byoohd

Budennovsk, Russia : Booh *dyaw* nufsk

Budleigh Salterton, England : Bahd li *Sawl* tur tun (UK ... *Sawl* ta tun)

Buea, Cameroon : Booh *ay* a

Buenaventura, Colombia : Bway nah ven *tooh* rah

Buena Vista, USA : Byooh na *Vis* ta

Buenos Aires, Argentina : Bway nus *Iy* riz (UK Bway nos...) (Spanish Bwe nos *Iy* res)

Buffalo, USA : *Bah* fa loh

Bug, Poland : Boohg (Russian, Polish Book)

Buganda, Uganda : Boo *gan* da

Builth Wells, Wales : Bilth *Welz*

Bujumbura, Burundi : Booh jum *boor* a

Bukavu, Democratic Republic of the Congo : Booh *kah* vooh

Bukhara, Uzbekistan : Baw *khah* ra (Russian Boo kha *rah*)

Bukittingi¸ Indonesia : Booh kit *ting* gi

Bukoba, Tanzania : Booh *koh* bah

Bukovina, Europe : Book o *vee* na

Bulawayo, Zimbabwe : Bool a *way* oh [The town is locally known as Booh lah *wah* yoh.]

Bulgaria, Europe : Bahl *ger* i a (UK Bahl *gay* a ri a)

Bunbury, Australia : *Bahn* ber i (UK *Bahn* bri)

Bundaberg, Australia : *Bahn* da buhrg (UK *Bahn* da buhg)

Bünde, Germany : *Been* da

Bungay, England : *Bahng* gi

Bunkie, USA : *Bahng* ki

Burbank, USA : *Buhr* bank (UK *Buh* bank)

Burford, England : *Buhr* furd (UK *Buh* fud)

Burg, Germany : Boork

Burgas, Bulgaria : Boor *gahs*

Burgenland, Austria : *Buhr* gun land (UK *Buh* gun land) (German *Boor* gun lahnt)

Burgess Hill, Engand : Buhr jis *Hil*

Burgh, England : *Bah* ra [This is the usual pronunciation, but the Suffolk village of this name is US Buhrg, UK Buhg.]

Burgh by Sands, England : Brahf biy *Sandz*

Burghfield, England : *Buhr* feeld (UK *Buh* feeld)

Burgos, Spain : *Boohr* gohs

Burgundy, France : *Buhr* gun di (UK *Buh* gun di)

Burhanpur, India : Bur *hahn* poor

Buriton, England : *Ber* i tun

Burkina Faso, Africa : Bur kee na *Fah* soh (UK Buh kee na *Fas* oh)

Burlingame, USA : *Buhr* ling gaym (UK *Buh* ling gaym)

Burlington, Canada; USA : *Buhr* ling tun (UK *Buh* ling tun)

Burma, Asia : *Buhr* ma (UK *Buh* ma)

Burnaby, Canada : *Buhr* na bi (UK *Buh* na bi)

Burnham-on-Crouch, England : Buhr num ahn *Krowch* (UK Buh num on...)

Burnham-on-Sea, England : Buhr num ahn *See* (UK Buh num on...)

Burnie, Australia : *Buhr* ni (UK *Buh* ni)

Burnley, England : *Buhrn* li (UK *Buhn* li)

Burns, USA : Buhrnz (UK Buhnz)

Burnsville, USA : *Buhrnz* vil (UK *Buhnz* vil)

Burntisland, Scotland : Buhrnt *iy* lund (UK Buhnt *iy* lund) [Some speakers, unaware of the etymological origin of the Fife town's name as "burnt island," mispronounce it US *Buhrnt* is lund, UK *Buhnt* is lund.]

Burpham, England : *Buhr* fum (UK *Buh* fum)

Burrel, Albania : *Boor* el

Bursa, Turkey : *Boor* sah

Burscough Bridge, England : Buhr skoh *Brij* (UK Buh skoh...)

Bursledon, England : *Buhr* zul dun (UK *Buh* zul dun)

Burslem, England : *Buhrz* lum (UK *Buhz* lum)

Burton, USA : *Buhr* tun (UK *Buh* tun)

Burton upon Trent, England : Buhr tun a pahn *Trent* (UK Buh tun a pon...)

Burtonwood, England : Buhr tun *wood* (UK Buh tun *wood*)

Buru, Indonesia : *Booh* rooh

Burundi, Africa : Boo *roon* di

Burwash, England : *Buhr* wahsh (UK *Buh* wosh) [The name of the East Sussex village is locally often pronounced *Bah* rush.]

Bury, England : *Ber* i

Buryatia, Russia : Boor *yah* ti a

Bury St Edmunds, England : Ber i Saynt *Ed* mundz (UK ... Sunt...)

Bushey, England : *Boosh* i

Bushire, Iran : Boo *shir* (UK Boo *shiy* a)

Bussang, France : Bee *sahn*

Busselton, Australia : *Bah* sul tun

Butare, Rwanda : Booh *tah* ray

Bute, Scotland : Byooht

Buton, Indonesia : *Booh* ton

Butte, USA : Byooht

Buttermere, England : *Bah* tur mir (UK *Bah* ta mi a)

Butterworth, Malaysia; South Africa : *Bah* tur wuhrth (UK *Bah* ta wuth)

Butuan, Philippines : Booh *tooh* ahn
Buxar, India : *Bahk* sur
Buxtehude, Germany : Book sta *hee* da
Buxton, England : *Bahk* stun
Buxworth, England : *Bahks* wuhrth
(UK *Bahks* wuhth) [The name of the
Derbyshire village was originally
Bugsworth, pronounced US *Bahgz*
wuhrth, UK *Bahgz* wuhth. It then
adopted its present spelling, although
the earlier pronunciation inevitably
persisted for a while. Placename
changes of this kind are not common
in England, and are not normally
effected as smoothly and simply as
the second quote below implies.]
(1) One cannot command a change
like that without a good deal of con-
sultation and committee-work; public
meetings would seem to be called for,
and the niceties of the arguments put
forward in the suit Bugs *v.* Bux must
have made good hearing [H.G.
Stokes, *English Place-Names*, 1948].
(2) [The village] was Bugsworth
until some vicar decided that Bux-
sounded more refined than Bug-;
villagers still know it colloquially
as Buggy [John Hadfield, ed., *The
Shell Book of English Villages*,
1980].
Buxy, France : Bee *see*
Buzău, Romania : Booh *zow*
Bwlch, Wales : Boolk (Welsh Boolkh)
Bydgoszcz, Poland : *Bid* gawsh (UK *Bid*
gosh) (Polish *Bid* gawshch)
Byfleet, England : *Biy* fleet
Bytom, Poland : *Bit* awm
Bytów, Poland : *Bit* oohf
Byzantium, Turkey : Bi *zan* shum (UK
Bi *zan* ti um)
Caacupé, Paraguay : Kah ah kooh *pay*
Caazapá, Paraguay : Kah ah sah *pah*
Cabaiguán, Cuba : Kah biy *gwahn*
Cabanatuan, Philippines : Kah bah nah
twahn
Cabatuan, Philippines : Kah bah *tooh*
ahn
Cabedelo, Brazil : Kah bi *del* ooh
Cabimas, Venezuela : Kah *bee* mahs

Cabinda, Angola : Ka *bin* da (Portu-
guese Kah *bin* dah)
Caborca, Mexico : Kah *bawr* kah
Cabot (Strait), Canada : *Kab* ut
Cabra, Spain : *Kah* brah
Cáceres, Spain : *Kah* thay rays
Cachoeira do Sul, Brazil : Ka shway ra
dooh *Soohl*
Cachoeiro de Itapemirim, Brazil : Ka
shway rooh dee Ee ta pay mee *reen*
Cader Idris, Wales : Kah dur *Id* ris (UK
Kad ur...)
Cadillac, USA : *Kad* a lak (UK *Kad* i
lak)
¹**Cadiz**, Philippines : *Kah* dees
²**Cadiz**, Spain : Ka *diz* [The former English pronunciation of the seaport
city's name, recommended as recently
as 1937 in Lloyd James, was *Kay* diz,
as in the quotes below.]
(1) But Cadiz, rising on the distant
coast,
Calls forth a sweeter, though ignoble
praise [Lord Byron, *Childe
Harold's Pilgrimage*, 1812].
(2) There was an Old Person of
Cadiz,
Who was always polite to all ladies
[Edward Lear, *A Book of Non-
sense*, 1846].
³**Cadiz**, USA (Kentucky) : *Kay* diz
⁴**Cadiz**, USA (Ohio) : *Kad* iz
Caen, France : Kahn (French Kawn)
Caerleon, Wales : Kahr *lee* un (UK Kah
lee un) [As for **Caerphilly**, the town's
name is an "anglicized" form of the
original, so cannot be given a genuine
Welsh pronunciation.]
Caernarfon, Wales : Kahr *nahr* vun
(UK Ka *nah* vun) (Welsh Kiyr *nahr*
von)
Caerphilly, Wales : Kahr *fil* i (UK Ka *fil*
i) [As for **Caerleon**, the town's name
is an "anglicized" form of the origi-
nal, so cannot be given a genuine
Welsh pronunciation.]
Caersws, Wales : Kiy ur *soohs* (UK Kiy a
soohs) (Welsh Kiyr *soohs*)
Caesarea, Israel : See za *ree* a
Cagayan, Philippines : Kah gah *yahn*

Cagayan de Oro, Philippines : Kah gah
yahn day *Oh* roh

Cagliari, Italy : Ka li *ahr* i (Italian *Kahl*
yah ree)

Cagnes-sur-Mer, France : Kiyn seer
Mer

Cagua, Venezuela : *Kah* gwah

Caguas, Puerto Rico : *Kah* gwahs

Cahors, France : Kah *awr*

Caibarién, Cuba : Kiy bahr *yen*

Caicos (Islands), West Indies : *Kay*
kohs (UK *Kay* kos)

Cairngorm (Mountains), Scotland :
Kern gawrm (UK *Kay* un gawm)

Cairns, Australia : Kernz (UK *Kay* unz)
[In Australia itself, the Queensland
seaport city's name is usually pronounced Kanz.]

¹**Cairo**, Egypt : *Kiy* roh (UK *Kiy* a roh)

²**Cairo**, USA : *Kay* roh
(1) *Cairo*, Ill., is always *Care-o* locally,
never *Ky-ro* [Mencken, p. 541].
(2) Similarities between the Mississippi and Nile rivers prompted the
naming of Cairo after Egypt's capital
city, but Illinois's town has always
been pronounced *kay-ro* [R. Kent
Rasmussen, *Mark Twain A to Z*,
1995].

Caister-on-Sea, England : Kay stur ahn
See (UK ... on...)

Caistor, England : *Kay* stur (UK *Kay*
sta)

Caithness, Scotland : *Kayth* nes [Ac-
cording to Ross, p. 56, the correct
pronunciation of the former county's
name is Kayth *nes*, with the stress on
the second syllable. But this is not the
standard Scots usage.]

Caivano, Italy : Kiy *vah* noh

Cajamarca, Peru : Kah hah *mahr* kah

Calabar, Nigeria : *Kal* a bahr (UK Kal a
bah)

Calabria, Italy : Ka *lay* bri a (UK Ka *lab*
ri a)

¹**Calais**, France : Ka *lay* (UK *Kal* ay)
[The former English pronunciation
of the seaport city's name, spelled
Callis in the 16th century, was as
²**Calais**.]

²**Calais**, USA : *Kal* is

Calama, Chile : Kah *lah* mah

Calamba, Philippines : Kah *lahm* bah

Călăraşi, Romania : Ka la *rahs*

Calatayud, Spain : Kah lah tah *yoohdh*

Calbayog, Philippines : Kahl *bah* yawg

Calcutta, India : Kal *kah* ta

Caldas, Colombia : *Kahl* dahs

Caldas da Rainha, Portugal : Kahl
dahsh dah Rah *ee* nya

Calderdale, England : *Kawl* dur dayl
(UK *Kawl* da dayl)

Caldwell, USA : *Kawld* wel

Caldy (Island), Wales : *Kahl* di (UK
Kawl di)

Caledon, Canada : *Kal* i dun

Caledonia, USA : Ka la *doh* nya

Caledonian (Canal), Scotland : Kal i
doh ni un

Calexico, USA : Ka *lek* si koh

Calgary, Canada : *Kal* ga ri

Cali, Colombia : *Kah* li

Calicut, India : *Kal* i kut

California, USA : Kal a *fawr* nya (UK
Kal a *faw* ni a)

Calistoga, USA : Kal i *stoh* ga

Calke, England : Kawk

Callander, Scotland : *Kal* un dur (UK
Kal un da)

Callao, Peru : Kah *yah* oh

Calne, England : Kahn

Caloocan, Philippines : Kah loh *oh* kahn

Caltagirone, Italy : Kahl tah *jee* roh nee

Caltanissetta, Italy : Kahl tah nees *set*
tah

Calton, Scotland : *Kawl* tun [This is the
pronunciation for Edinburgh's Calton
Hill. The district of Glasgow, however, is usually *Kahl* tun.]

Calumet, USA : *Kal* yoo met

Calvados, France : *Kal* va dohs (UK *Kal*
va dos) (French Kahl vah *dohs*)

Calverley, England : *Kah* vur li (UK
Kah va li)

Calvi, Corsica, France : *Kahl* vee

Calydon, Greece : *Kal* i dun

Camagüey, Cuba : Kah mah *gway*

Camargue, France : Ka *mahrg* (UK Ka
mahg) (French Kah *mahrg*)

Camberley, England : *Kam* bur li (UK *Kam* ba li)

Camberwell, Australia; England : *Kam* bur wul (UK *Kam* ba wul)

Cambodia, Asia : Kam *boh* di a

Camborne, England : *Kam* bawrn (UK *Kam* bawn)

Cambrai, France : Kahm *bray* (UK *Kom* bray) (French Kahn *bray*)

Cambrian (Mountains), Wales : *Kam* bri un

Cambridge, Canada; England; USA : *Kaym* brij

Cambuslang, Scotland : Kam bus *lang*

Camden, Australia; England; USA : *Kam* dun

Camelford, England : *Kam* ul furd (UK *Kam* ul fud)

Camembert, France : Kah mawn *ber*

Cameroon, Africa : Ka ma *roohn*

Cametá, Brazil : Kah may *tah*

Camocim, Brazil : Ka moh *seen*

Campagna, Italy : Kam *pan* ya (Italian Kahm *pah* nyah) [The name of the region surrounding Rome, in full *Campagna di Roma*, is identical in pronunciation with that of **Campania**.]

Campania, Italy : Kam *pan* ya (Italian Kahm *pah* nyah) [The name of the region of southern Italy is identical in pronunciation with that of **Campagna**.]

Campbell, USA : *Kam* bul

Campbellton, Canada : *Kam* bul tun

Campbelltown, Australia : *Kam* bul town

Campbeltown, Scotland : *Kam* bul town [Some Scots also pronounce the port town's name as Kam *bel* town, accenting the second syllable.]

Campeche, Mexico : Kahm *pay* chay

Campina Grande, Brazil : Kam pee na *Gran* dee

Campinas, Brazil : Kam *pee* nus

Campobasso, Italy : Kahm poh *bahs* soh

Campo Grande, Brazil : Kam pooh *Gran* dee

Campo Maior, Brazil : Kam poh Miy *yawr*

Campos, Brazil : *Kam* poohs

Campsie, Scotland : *Kamp* si

Cam Rhan, Vietnam : Kahm *rahn*

Camrose, Canada : *Kam* rohz

Cana, Israel : *Kay* na

Canaan, Israel; USA : *Kay* nun

Canada, North America : *Kan* a da

Çanakkale, Turkey : Chah nah kah *lay*

Cañar, Ecuador : Kah *nyahr*

Canary (Islands), Atlantic Ocean : Ka *ner* i (UK Ka *nay* a ri)

Canaveral, USA : Ka *nav* ral

Canberra, Australia : *Kan* ber a (UK *Kan* bra)

Canchungo, Guinea-Bissau : Kahn *choohng* goh

Cancún, Mexico : Kahn *koohn*

Candaba, Philippines : Kahn dah *bah*

Canea, Greece : Ka *nee* a

Canelones, Uruguay : Kah nay *loh* nays

Cannae, Italy : *Kan* ee

Cannanore, India : Ka na *nawr*

Cannes, France : Kan (French Kahn) [The seaport resort, famed for its international film festival, has a name formerly pronounced Kanz by some English speakers.]

Cannock, England : *Kan* uk

Canoas, Brazil : Ka *noh* us

Canso, Canada : *Kan* soh

Cantabria, Spain : Kan *tab* ri a (Spanish Kahn tah *bree* ah)

Cantal, France : Kahn *tahl*

Canterbury, Australia; England; New Zealand : *Kan* tur ber i (UK *Kan* ta ber i)

Can Tho, Vietnam : Kan *Toh*

¹Canton, China : Kan *tahn* (UK Kan *ton*)

²Canton, USA; Wales : *Kan* tun

Canvey (Island), England : *Kan* vi

Capannori, Italy : Kah *pahn* noh ree

Cap-d'Ail, France : Kahb *diy*

Cap-de-la-Madeleine, Canada : Kap di la Mad *len*

Cape Breton (Island), Canada : Kayp *Bret* un

Cape Cod, USA : Kayp *Kahd* (UK ... *Kod*)

Cape Girardeau, USA : Kayp Ja *rahr* doh (UK ... Ja *rah* doh)

Capel, England : *Kay* pul

Capel Curig, Wales : Kap ul *Kir* ig (Welsh Kap el *Ki* rig)

Capenhurst, England : *Kay* pun huhrst (UK *Kay* pun huhst)

Capernaum, Israel : Ka *puhr* ni um (UK Ka *puh* ni um)

Capestang, France : Kah pay *stahn*

Capesterre, Guadeloupe : Ka pes *ter*

Cape Town, South Africa : *Kayp* Town

Cape Verde, Atlantic Ocean : Kayp *Vuhrd* (UK Kayp *Vuhd*)

Cap Haitien, Haiti : Kap *Hay* shun

Cap-Haïtien, Haiti : Ka piy *syahn*

Cappadocia, Turkey : Ka pa *doh* sha (UK Ka pa *doh* si a)

Capri, Italy : Ka *pree* (Italian *Kah* pree) [The pronunciation of the island's name with the stress on the second syllable, regarded by some as "vulgar," was popularized by Jimmy Kennedy and Will Grosz's 1934 song "The Isle of Capri" ("'Twas on the isle of Capri that I found her").]
Never pronounce Capri as Capree [Guy Egmont, *The Art of Egmontese*, 1961].

Caprivi (Strip), Namibia : Ka *pree* vi

Capua, Italy : *Kap* yoo a (Italian *Kah* poo a)

Caquetá, Colombia : Kah kay *tah*

Caracal, Romania : Kah *rah* kahl

Caracas, Venezuela : Ka *rah* kus (UK Ka *rak* us) (Spanish Kah *rah* kahs)

Caramoan, Philippines : Kah rah *moh* ahn

Caransebeş, Romania : Kah rahn *seb* esh

Caravaggio, Italy : Kah rah *vah* joh

Carbondale, USA : *Kahr* bun dayl (UK *Kah* bun dayl)

Carbonear, Canada : Kahr ba *nir* (UK Kah ba *ni* a)

Carbost, Scotland : *Kahr* bawst (UK *Kah* bost)

Carcassonne, France : Kahr ka *sahn* (UK Kah ka *son*) (French Kahr kah *sawn*)

Carchemish, Syria : *Kahr* ka mish

Carchi, Ecuador : *Kahr* chee

Cárdenas, Cuba : *Kahr* da nas (Spanish *Kahr* dhay nahs)

Cardiff, USA; Wales : *Kahr* duf (UK *Kah* dif)

Cardigan, Wales : *Kahr* dig un (UK *Kah* di gun)

Carhaix-Plouguer, France : Kah ray Plooh *ger*

Caria, Turkey : *Ker* i a (UK *Kay* a ri a)

Cariacica, Brazil : Ka ree a *see* ka

Caribbean (Sea), West Indies : Ka ra *bee* un

Cariboo (Mountains), Canada : *Kar* a booh

Carinthia, Austria : Ka *rin* thi a

Carisbrooke, England : *Kar* iz brook

Carlingford (Lough), Northern Ireland : *Kahr* ling furd (UK *Kah* ling fud)

¹Carlisle, England : Kahr *liyl* (UK Kah *liyl*) [The name of the Cumbria city is locally also stressed as **²Carlisle**.]

²Carlisle, USA : *Kahr* liyl (UK *Kah* liyl)

Carlow, Ireland : *Kahr* loh (UK *Kah* loh)

Carlsbad, USA : *Kahrlz* bad (UK *Kahlz* bad)

Carlton, England : *Kahrl* tun (UK *Kahl* tun)

Carmagnola, Italy : Kahr mah *nyoh* lah

Carmarthen, Wales : Kahr *mahr* dhun (UK Ka *mah* dhun)

¹Carmel, Israel; USA (Indiana) : *Kahr* mul (UK *Kah* mel)

²Carmel, USA (California) : Kahr *mel* (UK Kah *mel*)

Carmen de Patagones, Argentina : Kahr men dhay Pah tah *goh* nays

Carmichael, USA : *Kahr* miy kul

Carmona, Spain : Kahr *moh* nah

Carnac, France : Kahr *nahk*

Carnarvon, South Africa : Kur *nahr* vun (UK Ka *nah* vun)

Carnatic, India : Kahr *nat* ik (UK Kah *nat* ik)

Carnegie, USA : *Kahr* na gi (UK Kah *neg* i) [The name of Carnegie, Pennsylvania, is locally pronounced Kahr *nay* gi.]

Carnforth, England : *Kahrn* fawrth (UK *Kahn* fawth)

Carniola, Europe : Kahr ni *oh* la (UK Kah ni *oh* la)

Carnoustie, Scotland : Kahr *nooh* sti (UK Kah *nooh* sti)

¹Carolina, Puerto Rico : Kah roh *lee* nah

²Carolina, USA : Ka ra *liy* na

Caroline (Islands), Pacific Ocean : *Kar* a liyn

Carpathian (Mountains), Europe : Kahr *pay* thi un (UK Kah *pay* thi un)

Carpentaria, Australia : Kahr pun *ter* i a (UK Kah pun *tay* a ri a)

Carpentras, France : Kahr pahn *trah*

Carpi, Italy : *Kahr* pee

Carrantuohill, Ireland : Kar un *tooh* ul

Carrara, Italy : Ka *rah* ra

Carrickfergus, Northern Ireland : Kar ik *fuhr* gus (UK Kar ik *fuh* gus)

Carrick on Shannon, Ireland : Kar ik ahn *Shan* un (UK ... on...)

Carrick on Suir, Ireland : Kar ik ahn *Shoor* (UK ... on...)

Carrollton, USA : *Kar* ul tun

Carshalton, England : Kahr *shawl* tun (UK Kah *shawl* tun) [At one time the name of the former Surrey village and present district of London was pronounced Kays *haw* tun.]

> (1) CARSHALTON ... (pronounced *Casehorton*) [James Thorne, *Handbook to the Environs of London*, 1876].
> (2) [Pronounced] Casehalton, Casehorton [Johnston, p. 187].

Carson City, USA : Kahr sun *Si* ti (UK Kah sun...)

Carstairs, Scotland : *Kahr* sterz (UK Kah *stay* uz)

Cartagena, Colombia; Spain : Kahr ta *hayn* a (UK Kah ta *jeen* a) (Spanish Kahr tah *hayn* ah)

Cartago, Colombia; Costa Rica : Kahr *tah* goh

¹Carteret, France : Kahr ta *ray*

²Carteret, USA : Kahr ta *ret*

Carthage, Tunisia; USA : *Kahr* thij (UK *Kah* thij)

Cartmel, England : *Kahrt* mul (UK *Kaht* mul)

Caruaru, Brazil : Kah rooh a *rooh*

Cary, USA : *Ker* i (UK *Kay* a ri)

Casablanca, Morocco : Kas a *blang* ka (French Kah zah blawn *kah*) [Although French is still spoken in Morocco as a legacy of the country's colonial period during the first half of the 20th century, the seaport city's name is actually Spanish in origin, meaning "white house." Morocco's official language is Arabic. See Appendix, p. 219.]

Casa Grande, USA : Kah sa *Grahn* day

Casale Monferrato, Italy : Ka sah lay Mawn fer *rah* toh

Casanare, Colombia : Kah sah *nah* ray

Casas Grandes, Mexico : Kah sahs *Grahn* days

Cascade (Range), USA : Kas *kayd*

Cascais, Portugal : Kahsh *kaysh*
> At the beginning of the 19th century, the fishing village of Cascais (pronounced kush-*kaish*) was in a sorry state [*The Times*, August 18, 2006].

Caserta, Italy : Kah *ser* tah

Cashel, Ireland : *Kash* ul

Casilda, Argentina : Kah *seel* dah

Casper, USA : *Kas* pur (UK *Kas* pa)

Caspian (Sea), Eurasia : *Kas* pi un

Cassino, Italy : Kah *see* noh

Cassis, France : Kah *see*

Castel Gandolfo, Italy : Kas tel Gan *dahl* foh (UK ... Gan *dol* foh) [Italian Kahs tel Gahn *dawl* foh]

Castellamare di Stabia, Italy : Kahs tel lah mah ray dee *Stah* byah

Castellón de la Plana, Spain : Kahs tel yohn dhay lah *Plah* nah

Castelnau, England : *Kah* sul naw [According to Willey, p. 82, the name of the London district is "pronounced as in 'neither castle nor city.'"]

Castelnau-le-Lez, France : Kahs tel nohl *Layz*

Castelo Branco, Portugal : Kash tel ooh *Brang* kooh

Castelvetrano, Italy : Kahs tel vay *trah* noh

Castile, Spain : Kas *teel*

Castlebar, Ireland : Kas ul *bahr* (UK Kah sul *bah*)

Castle Combe, England : Kas ul *Koohm* (UK Kah sul...)

Castleford, England : *Kas* ul furd (UK *Kah* sul fud)

Castlemaine, Australia : *Kas* ul mayn (UK *Kah* sul mayn) [The usual Australian pronunciation of the Victoria town's name is as the US one.]

Castlereagh, Northern Ireland : *Kas* ul ray (UK *Kah* sul ray)

Castleton, USA : *Kas* ul tun (UK *Kah* sul tun)

Castres, France : Kahstr

Castries, St. Lucia : Ka *streez*

Castrovillari, Italy : Kahs traw vee *lah* ree

Çatalhüyük, Turkey : Chah tahl hee *yeek*

Catalonia, Spain : Ka tul *oh* ni a (UK Ka ta *loh* ni a)

Cataluña, Spain : Kah tah *looh* nyah

Catamarca, Argentina : Kah tah *mahr* kah

Catanduva, Brazil : Ka tan *dooh* va

Catania, Italy : Ka *tah* nya (Italian Kah *tah* nyah)

Catanzaro, Italy : Kah tahnd *zah* roh

Catawba, USA : Ka *taw* ba

Caterham, England : *Kay* tur ham (UK *Kay* tur um)

Catford, England : *Kat* furd (UK *Kat* fud)

Catonsville, USA : *Kay* tunz vil

Catskill (Mountains), USA : *Kat* skil

Cattenom, France : Kaht *nawm*

Catterick, England : *Kat* ur ik

Cauca, Colombia : *Kow* kah

Caucasus, Eurasia : *Kaw* ka sus

Caughley, England : *Kahf* li

Caulfield, Australia : *Kawl* feeld [Australians often omit the first *l* sound in the Victoria city's name.]

Caulnes, France : Kohn

Caux, France : Koh

Cava de' Tirreni, Italy : Kah vah day Tee *ray* nee

Cavaillon, France : Kah vah *yawn*

Cavan, Ireland : *Kav* un

Caversham, England : *Kav* ur shum (UK *Kav* a shum)

Cavite, Philippines : Kah *vee* tee

Cawdor, Scotland : *Kaw* dur (UK *Kaw* da)

Cawnpore, India : *Kawn* pawr (UK *Kawn paw*)

Caxias, Brazil : Ka *shee* us

Caxias do Sul, Brazil : Ka shee us dooh *Soohl*

Caxito, Angola : Kah *shee* tooh

Cayce, USA : *Kay* si

Cayenne, French Guiana : Kay *en* (French Ka *yen*)

Cayey, Puerto Rico : Kah *yay*

Cayman (Islands), West Indies : *Kay* mun [Ross, p. 60, claims that the stress falls properly on the second syllable, i.e. as Kay *man*. But this would now be regarded as dated, or at best as purely local.]

Cayo, Belize : *Kay* yoh

Cayuga, USA : Ki *ooh* ga

Ceannanus Mór, Ireland : See a nan us *Mawr*

Ceará, Brazil : Syah *rah*

Cebu, Philippines : *Say* booh

Cedar Rapids, USA : See dur *Rap* idz (UK See da...)

Cefalù, Italy : Chay fah *looh*

Celaya, Mexico : Se *liy* a (Spanish Sah *liy* yah)

Celebes (Sea), Indonesia : Sa *lee* biz

Celje, Slovenia : *Tsel* ye

Celle, Germany : *Tse* la

Cemaes Bay, Wales : Kem iys *Bay*

Centerville, USA : *Sen* tur vil (UK *Sen* ta vil)

Cento, Italy : *Chen* toh

Centralia, USA : Sen *tray* li a

Cephalonia, Greece : Kef a *loh* ni a

Ceram, Indonesia : *Say* rahm

Ceredigion, Wales : Ker a *dig* i ahn

(UK Ker a *dig* i on) (Welsh Ke re *dig* yon)

¹Ceres, Scotland : *Si* a riz

²Ceres, USA : *Sir* eez

Cernavodă, Romania : Cher nah *voh* da

Cerne Abbas, England : Suhrn *Ab* us (UK Suhn...)

Cerrigydrudion, Wales : Ker ig a *drid* yahn (UK Ker ig a *drid* yon)

Cerritos, USA : Sa *ree* tus

Cerro de Pasco, Peru : Ser roh dhay *Pahs* koh

César, Colombia : *Say* sahr

Cesena, Italy : Chay *zay* nah

Cēsis, Latvia : *Tsay* sus

Česká Lípa, Czech Republic : Ches kah *Lee* pah

České Budějovice, Czech Republic : Ches ke *Bood* ye yaw veet se

Český Těšín, Czech Republic : Ches kee *Tye* sheen

Cessnock, Australia : *Ses* nahk (UK *Ses* nok)

Cetinje, Montenegro : Tse *tee* nye

Ceuta, Morocco : Say *ooh* ta (UK *Syooh* ta) (Spanish *Thay* oo ta)

Cévennes, France : Say *ven*

Ceylon, Asia : Si *lahn* (UK Si *lon*)

Chablis, France : Shah *bli*

Chacabuco, Argentina : Chah kah *booh* koh

Chaco, Argentina : *Chah* koh

Chad, Africa : Chad

Chadderton, England : *Chad* ur tun (UK *Chad* a tun)

Chadron, USA : *Shad* run

Chaeronea, Greece : Kiy ra *nee* a

Chagford, England : *Chag* furd (UK *Chag* fud)

Chagos (Archipelago), Indian Ocean : *Chah* gus

Chaguanas, Trinidad and Tobago : Chah *gwah* nahs

Chake Chake, Tanzania : Chah kay *Chah* kay

Chalatenango, El Salvador : Chah lah tay *nahng* goh

Chalcedon, Turkey : *Kal* si dahn (UK *Kal* si dun)

Chalcidice, Greece : Kal *sid* i si

Chalcis, Greece : *Kal* sis

Chaldea, Asia : Kal *dee* a

Chalfont St Giles, England : Chal fahnt Saynt *Jiylz* (UK Chal font Sunt...) [A dated alternate local pronunciation of the main name of the Buckingham-shire town, and of its near neighbor, **Chalfont St Peter**, is *Chah* funt.]

Chalfont St Peter, England : Chal fahnt Saynt *Pee* tur (UK Chal font Sunt *Pee* ta)

Chalmette, USA : Shal *met*

Châlons-en-Champagne, France : Shah lawnz ahn Shahn *piyn*

Chalon-sur-Saône, France : Shah lawn seer *Sohn*

Chambéry, France : Shahn bay *ree*

Chambly, Canada : *Sham* bli (French *Shahn* bli)

Chambord, France : Shahn *bawr*

Chamonix, France : Sha ma *nee* (UK *Sha* ma nee) (French Shah moh *nee*)

Champagne, France : Sham *payn* (French Shahn *piyn*)

Champaign, USA : Sham *payn*

Champlain, USA : Sham *playn*

Champotón, Mexico : Chahm poh *tohn*

Chanctonbury (Ring), England : *Changk* tun ber i (UK *Changk* tun bri) [A local pronunciation *Changk* bri also exists for the hilltop Iron Age fort site in West Sussex.]

Chandernagore, India : Chahn dur na *gawr*

Chandigarh, India : *Chahn* dee gur

Changchun, China : Chahng *choon* (UK Chang *choon*)

Changsha, China : Chahng *shah*

Channel-Port aux Basques, Canada : Chan ul Pawr toh *Bask* (UK ... Paw toh...)

Chanthaburi, Thailand : Chahn tah boo *ree*

¹Chantilly, France : Shahn tee *yee*

²Chantilly, USA : Shan *til* i

Chapayevsk, Russia : Cha *pah* yefsk

Chapel-en-le-Frith, England : Chap ul en li *Frith*

Chappaquiddick, USA : Chap a *kwid* ik

Chapra, India : *Chahp* ra

Chapultepec, USA : Chah *poohl* tay pek

Chardzhou, Turkmenistan : *Chahr* joh

Charente, France : Shah *rahnt*

Chari, Chad : *Shah* ree

Charikar, Afghanistan : *Chahr* i kahr

Charing Cross, England : Char ing *Krahs* (UK ... *Kros*)

Chärjew, Turkmenistan : *Chahr* jooh

Charlbury, England : *Chahrl* ber i (UK *Chahl* bri)

[1]**Charleroi**, Belgium : *Shahrl* rwah (UK *Shahl* rwah) (French Sharl *rwah*)

[2]**Charleroi**, USA : *Shahr* la roy

Charlesbourg, Canada : Shahrl *boohr*

Charleston, USA : *Chahrl* stun (UK *Chahl* stun)

Charlestown, St. Kitts and Nevis; USA : *Chahrlz* town (UK *Chahlz* town)

Charleville, Australia : *Chahrl* vil (UK *Chahl* vil)

Charleville-Mézières, France : Shahrl veel May *zyer*

Charlotte, USA : *Shahr* lut (UK *Shah* lut)

Charlotte Amalie, US Virgin Islands : Shahr lut A *mahl* ya (UK ... A *mah* li a)

Charlottenburg, Germany : Shahr *lah* tun buhrg (UK Shah *lot* un buhg) (German Shahr *lawt* un boork)

Charlottesville, USA : *Shahr* luts vil (UK *Shah* luts vil)

Charlottetown, Canada : *Shahr* lut town (UK *Shah* lut town)

Charlton, USA : *Chahrl* tun (UK *Chahl* tun)

Charlton Kings, England : Chahrl tun *Kingz* (UK Chahl tun...)

Charnwood (Forest), England : *Chahrn* wood (UK *Chahn* wood)

Charny, Canada : Shahr *nee*

Charters Towers, Australia : Chahr turz *Tow* urz (UK Chah tuz *Tow* uz)

Chartres, France : Shahrtr

Châteauguay, Canada : Shat a *gay*

Châteauroux, France : Shah toh *rooh*

Château-Thierry, France : Shah toh Tye *ree*

Châtelet, Belgium : Shaht *lay*

Châtellerault, France : Shah tel *roh*

Chatham, Canada; England; USA : *Chat* um

Chatsworth, England : *Chats* wurth (UK *Chats* wuth)

Chattahoochee, USA : Chat a *hooh* chi

Chattanooga, USA : Chat a *nooh* ga

Chatteris, England : *Chat* a ris

Chaudfontaine, Belgium : Shoh fahn *tayn* (UK Shoh fon *tayn*)

Chaumont, France : Shoh *mawn*

Chautauqua, USA : Sha *taw* kwa

Chaves, Portugal : Shah *veesh*

Chawton, England : *Chaw* tun

Cheadle, England : *Chee* dul

Cheam, England : Cheem

Cheb, Czech Republic : Kep

Cheboksary, Russia : Chi bahk *sah* ri

Chechnya, Russia : Chech *nyah*

Cheddar, England : *Ched* ur (UK *Ched* a)

Cheektowaga, USA : Cheek ta *wah* ga

Chegutu, Zimbabwe : Chay *gooh* tooh

Cheju, South Korea : Chay *jooh*

Chełm, Poland : *Khe* oom

Chełmno, Poland : *Khelm* naw

Chelmsford, England; USA : *Chelmz* furd (UK *Chelmz* fud) [The Essex, England, city's name is or was locally also pronounced *Chemz* fud.]

Chelsea, Australia; England; USA : *Chel* si

Cheltenham, England; USA : *Chelt* un ham (UK *Chelt* num)

Chelyabinsk, Russia : Chil *yah* binsk

Chemnitz, Germany : *Kem* nits

Chengde, China : Chahng *dah*

Chengdu, China : Chahng *dooh*

Chennai, India : *Chen* niy

Chenonceaux, France : Shnawn *soh*

Chepstow, Wales : *Chep* stoh

Cher, France : Sher

Cherbourg, France : *Sher* boorg (UK *Shay* a boo ug) (French Sher *boohr*)

Cherepovets, Russia : Cher a *poh* vyets

Cherkassy, Ukraine : Chur *kah* si (UK Chuh *kas* i) (Russian Chir *kah* si)

Cherkessk, Russia : Chir *kyesk*

Chernigov, Ukraine : Chur *nee* gof (UK Chuh *nee* gof) (Russian Chir *nee* guf)

Chernihiv, Ukraine : Chir *nee* hif

Chernivtsi, Ukraine : Chir *nif* tsi

Chernobyl, Russia : Chur *noh* bul (UK Chuh *nob* ul)

Chernovtsy, Ukraine : Chur *nof* tsi (UK Chuh *nof* tsi) (Russian Chir *nawf* tsi)

Chernyakhovsk, Russia : Chir *nyah* khufsk

Cherokee, USA : *Cher* a kee

Cherrapunji, India : Cher a *poon* jee

Chersonese, Turkey; Ukraine : Kuhr sa *nees* (UK Kuh sa *nees*)

Chertsey, England : *Chuhrt* si (UK *Chuht* si)

Cherwell, England : *Chahr* wul (UK *Chah* wul) [The river joins the Thames at Oxford, where it is colloquially known by university members as the *Cher*, US Chahr, UK Chah.]

Chesapeake, USA : *Ches* a peek

Chesham, England : *Chesh* um [The name of the Buckinghamshire town was formerly pronounced *Ches* um.]

Cheshire, England; USA : *Chesh* ur (UK *Chesh* a)

Cheshunt, England : *Ches* unt

Chester, England; USA : *Ches* tur (UK *Ches* ta)

Chesterfield, England; USA : *Ches* tur feeld (UK *Ches* ta feeld)

Chester-le-Street, England : *Ches* tur li Street (UK *Ches* ta...)

Chetumal, Mexico : Chay too *mahl*

Cheviot (Hills), England : *Shev* i ut (UK *Chee* vi ut) [The hills extending along the border between England and Scotland have a common alternate UK pronunciation *Chev* i ut, and the two are considered in the quote below.]

A theory that the first pronunciation [*Chee* vi ut] is used North of the Border, and the other [*Chev* i ut] on the English side, has been discredited by

observation over a long period. The truth appears to be that the former is almost invariably used in the Border country, in both England and Scotland, and that it is speakers from further south who favour the second [Pointon, p. 51].

Chevy Chase, USA : *Chev* i Chays

Cheyenne, USA : Shiy *an* [Lloyd James 1937 recommends a pronunciation *Shiy* en for the name of Wyoming's capital city.]

Chiang Mai, Thailand : Chyahng *Miy*

Chiang Rai, Thailand : Chyahng *Riy*

Chiapas, Mexico : Chi *ah* pus (UK Chi *ap* us) (Spanish *Chyah* pahs)

Chiasso, Switzerland : *Kyah* soh

Chiatura, Georgia : Chee *ah* toor a

Chiavari, Italy : Kee *ah* vah ree

Chiba, Japan : *Chee* bah

Chibougamau, Canada : Sha *booh* ga moh

Chicago, USA : Shi *kah* goh [An alternate local pronunciation of the Illinois city's name is Shi *kaw* goh. The common British pronunciation Chi *kah* goh grates on the American ear.]

Chichén Itzá, Mexico : Chi chen It *sah* (Spanish Chee chen Eet *sah*)

¹**Chichester**, England : *Chi* chi stur (UK *Chi* chi sta)

²**Chichester**, USA : *Chiy* ches tur

Chiclayo, Peru : Chee *kliy* oh

Chico, USA : *Chee* koh

Chicopee, USA : *Chik* a pee

Chicoutimi, Canada : Shi *kooh* ti mi

Chieti, Italy : Kee *ay* tee

Chigasaki, Japan : Chee gah *sah* kee

Chigwell, England : *Chig* wel

Chihuahua, Mexico : Chee *wah* wah

Chile, South America : *Chil* i

Chilkoot (Pass), Canada : *Chil* kooht

Chillán, Chile : Chee *yahn*

Chillicothe, USA : Chil a *kah* thi (UK Chil i *koth* i) [There is a city of this name in each of the three states Illinois, Missouri, and Ohio, and according to Cohen, p. 633, these are respectively pronounced Chi li *kath* i, Chi li *koh* thi, and Chi li *kah* thi.]

Chilliwack, Canada : *Chil* a wak (UK *Chil* i wak)

Chiloé, Chile : Chee loh *ay*

Chilpancingo, Mexico : Cheel pahng *seeng* goh

Chiltern (Hills), England : *Chil* turn (UK *Chil* tun)

Chilung, Taiwan : Jee *loong*

Chimaltenango, Guatemala : Chee mahl tay *nahng* goh

Chimborazo, Ecuador : Chim ba *rah* zoh

Chimbote, Peru : Cheem *boh* tay

Chimkent, Kazakhstan : Chim *kent*

Chimoio, Mozambique : Shi *moy* oh

China, Asia : *Chiy* na

Chinandega, Nicaragua : Chee nahn *day* gah

Chincoteague, USA : Shing ka *teeg*

Chinde, Mozambique : *Cheen* day

Chindwin, Myanmar : *Chin* dwin

Chingford, England : *Ching* furd (UK *Ching* fud)

Chingola, Zambia : Cheeng *goh* lah

Chinhae, South Korea : Chin *hiy*

Chinhoyi, Zimbabwe : Cheen *hoh* yi

Chinju, South Korea : Jin *jooh*

Chinnampo, North Korea : Chin nam *poh*

Chino, USA : *Chee* noh

Chinon, France : Shee *nawn*

Chioggia, Italy : Kee *awj* jah

Chios, Greece : *Kiy* ahs (UK *Kiy* os)

Chipata, Zambia : Chee *pah* ta

Chippenham, England : *Chip* un um

Chippewa, USA : *Chip* i wah

Chipping Sodbury, England : Chip ing *Sahd* ber i (UK ... *Sod* bri)

Chiquimula, Guatemala : Chee kee *mooh* lah

Chiquimulilla, Guatemala : Chee kee mooh *lee* yah

Chirchik, Uzbekistan : Chir *cheek*

Chirk, Wales : Chuhrk (UK Chuhk)

Chisimaio, Somalia : Kee zee *mah* yoh

Chişinău, Moldova : Kee shee *now*

Chislehurst, England : *Chiz* ul huhrst (UK *Chiz* ul huhst)

Chistopol, Russia : Chis *taw* pul

Chiswick, England : *Chiz* ik

Chita, Russia : Chee *tah*

Chitré, Panama : Chee *tray*

Chittagong, Bangladesh : *Chit* a gawng (UK *Chit* a gong)

Chitungwiza, Zimbabwe : Chee toohng *gwee* zah

Chiusi, Italy : *Kyooh* zee

Chivilcoy, Argentina : Chee veel *koy*

Chobham, England : *Chah* bum (UK *Chob* um)

Chocó, Colombia : Choh *koh*

Chofu, Japan : *Choh* fooh

Choiseul, Solomon Islands : Shwah *zuhl*

Chojnice, Poland : Koy *neet* sa

Cholet, France : Shoh *lay*

Choluteca, Honduras : Choh looh *tay* kah

Chomutov, Czech Republic : *Khaw* ma tawf

Chon Buri, Thailand : Chahn Boo *ree*

Ch'ŏngjin, North Korea : Chahng *jin*

Ch'ŏngju, South Korea : Chahng *jooh*

Chongqing, China : Choong *ching*

Chŏnju, South Korea : Chahn *jooh*

Chooz, France : Shoh

Chorley, England : *Chawr* li (UK *Chaw* li)

Chorleywood, England : Chawr li *wood* (UK Chaw li *wood*)

Chorlton cum Hardy, England : Chawrl tun kahm *Hahr* di (UK Chawl tun kahm *Hah* di)

Chorrilos, Peru : Choh *ree* yohs

Chorzów, Poland : *Khaw* zhoohf

Choybalsan, Mongolia : Choy bahl *sahn*

Christchurch, England; New Zealand : *Kriyst* chuhrch (UK *Kriyst* chuhch)

Christiansted, US Virgin Islands : *Kris* chun sted

Christmas (Island), Indian Ocean : *Kris* mus

Chrzanów, Poland : *Khshah* noohf

Chubut, Argentina : Chooh *booht*

Chukchi (Peninsula), Russia : *Chook* chee

Chukotsky (Range), Russia : Choo *kawt* ski

Chula Vista, USA : Chooh la *Vis* ta

Chulmleigh, England : *Chahm* li

Chulucanas, Peru : Chooh looh *kah* nahs

Chungking, China : Choong *king*

Chuquisaca, Bolivia : Chooh kee *sah* kah

Chur, Switzerland : Koor

Churchdown, England : *Chuhrch* down (UK *Chuhch* down) [The name of the Gloucester suburb formerly had a local pronunciation *Choh* zun, preserved in the spelling of nearby Chosen Hill House.]

Churchill, Canada : *Chuhr* chil (UK *Chuh* chil)

Chusovoy, Russia : Chooh sa *voy*

Chuvashia, Russia : Chooh *vash* i a

Chysauster, England : Chiy *saw* sta [The name of the ancient British village near Penzance, Cornwall, is locally pronounced Che *zoy* sta.]

Ciamis, Indonesia : Chi *ah* mis

Cianjur, Indonesia : Chi *ahn* joor

Cibola, USA : *Sib* a la (Spanish *See* boh lah)

Cicero, USA : *Sis* a roh

Ciechanów, Poland : Che *khah* noohf

Ciego de Ávila, Cuba : Si ay goh day *Ah* vi la (Spanish *See* ay goh dhay *Ah* vee lah)

Cienfuegos, Cuba : Syen *fway* gohs

Cieszyn, Poland : *Che* shin

Cilacap, Indonesia : Chi *lah* chahp

Cilicia, Turkey : Sa *lish* a (UK Siy *lis* i a)

Cimahi, Indonesia : Chee *mah* hee

Cimarron, USA : *Sim* a rohn

Cincinnati, USA : Sin sa *nat* i [Ross, p. 63, mentions a UK pronunciation Sin si *nay* ti for the Ohio city, although this is now rarely heard.]

Cinnaminson, USA : Sin a *min* sun

Cintalapa, Mexico : Seen tah *lap* pah

Circassia, Russia : Sur *kash* a (UK Sa *kas* i a)

Cirebon, Indonesia : Chee re *bawn*

Cirencester, England : *Siy* run ses tur (UK *Siy* run ses ta) [The "educated" pronunciation of the Gloucestershire town's name is traditionally held to be US *Si* si tur, UK *Si* si ta, while the local form is the abbreviated *Siy* run. The name regularly surfaces as a subject of discussion in this regard, as instanced in the quotes below.]

(1) In the year 1924 a controversy raged in the *Sunday Times* as to the pronunciation of *Cirencester*. One critic told us that "the correct pronunciation of *Cirencester* should be in full. It is the locals who abbreviate, sometimes beyond recognition." This authoritative gentleman ain't arguing, he's a-telling you [Ernest Weekley, *Adjectives — And Other Words*, 1930].

(2) How long is the name [Cirencester] going to stand out against "Siren," "Sisiter," "Srenster" [*sic*] and all the other spoken versions which befog the stranger? [H.G. Stokes, *English Place-Names*, 1948].

(3) The name of "Cirencester" has always attracted attention, and occasional flutters of letters to *The Times* about its proper pronunciation. Some of its natives pronounce it "sissiter," others pronounce it "syren-sester," and most strangers find some variant between the two [C. Stella Davies and John Levitt, *What's in a Name?*, 1970].

(4) "Sister" to the sophisticated and "Siren" to the locals [Garry Hogg, *The Shell Book of Exploring Britain*, 1971].

Ciskei, South Africa : Sis *kiy*

Città di Castello, Italy : Chee tah dee Kah *stel* loh

Ciudad Bolívar, Venezuela : Syooh dhahdh Boh *lee* vahr

Ciudad del Este, Paraguay : Syooh dhahdh del *Es* tay

Ciudad Guayana, Venezuela : Syooh dhahdh Gah *yay* nah

Ciudad Guzmán, Mexico : Syooh dhahdh Goohs *mahn*

Ciudad Juárez, Mexico : Syooh dhahdh *Hwah* res

Ciudad Madero, Mexico : Syooh dhahdh Mah *dhay* roh

Ciudad Ojeda, Venezuela : Syooh dhahdh Oh *hay* dhah

Ciudad Real, Spain : Syooh dhahdh Ray *ahl*

Ciudad Rodrigo, Spain : Syooh dhahdh Roh *dhree* goh

Ciudad Valles, Mexico : Syooh dhahdh Vah *yays*

Ciudad Victoria, Mexico : Syooh dhahth Veek *toh* ryah

Civitavecchia, Italy : Chi vi ta *vek* i a (Italian Chee vee tah *vek* kyah)

Clackmannan, Scotland : Klak *man* un

Clacton-on-Sea, England : Klak tun ahn *See* (UK ... on...)

Clairvaux, France : Kler *voh*

Clapham, England : *Klap* um [A semi-serious "superior" pronunciation Klahm is sometimes heard for the former Surrey village and present London district, as noted below.]
(1) City [of London] types who reside there refer to Clapham itself as "Clarm" [*The Times*, July 23, 2005].
(2) Pronounced "clappum," despite the jokey, mock-posh "claahm" affected by some residents [Willey, p. 103].

Clare, England; Ireland : Kler (UK *Klay* a)

Claremont, USA : *Kler* mahnt (UK *Klay* a mont)

Claremore, USA : *Kler* mawr (UK *Klay* a maw)

Clarendon (Park), England : *Klar* un dun

Clarksburg, USA : *Klahrks* buhrg (UK *Klahks* buhg)

Clarksdale, USA : *Klahrks* dayl (UK *Klahks* dayl)

Clarksville, USA : *Klahrks* vil (UK *Klahks* vil)

¹Claughton, England : *Klaw* tun (district of Birkenhead, near Liverpool)

²Claughton, England : *Klaf* tun (village near Lancaster, Lancashire)

³Claughton, England : *Klay* tun (village near Preston, Lancashire) [This Claughton and ²**Claughton** are barely 16 miles apart.]

Claverton, England : *Klav* ur tun (UK *Klav* a tun)

Clayton, USA : *Klay* tun

Clayton-le-Moors, England : Klay tun li *Moorz* (UK ... *Moo* uz)

Clearwater, USA : *Klir* waw tur (UK *Kli* a waw ta)

Cleator, England : *Klee* tur (UK *Klee* ta)

Cleburne, USA : *Klee* buhrn (UK *Klee* buhn)

Cleckheaton, England : Klek *hee* tun

Cleethorpes, England : *Klee* thawrps (UK *Klee* thawps)

Clemson, USA : *Klem* sun

Cleobury Mortimer, England : Klib ri *Mawr* ta mur (UK ... *Maw* ti ma)

Clerkenwell, England : *Kluhr* kun wel (UK *Klah* kun wel)

Clermont, England; USA : *Kler* mahnt (UK *Klay* a mont)

Clermont-Ferrand, France : Kler mawn Fay *rahn*

Clevedon, England : *Kleev* dun

Cleveland, England; USA : *Kleev* lund

Cleveleys, England : *Kleev* liz

Cley, England : Kliy [The name of the Norfolk village and former port, also known as *Cley-next-the-Sea*, is pronounced Klay by those unfamiliar with the accepted local form.]
(1) Telephone operators nowadays call it "Clay" [Jonathan Mardle (pseudonym of Eric Fowler), *Broad Norfolk*, 4th ed., 1976].
(2) Cley, pronounced "Cly" [*Reader's Digest Illustrated Guide to Britain's Coast*, 1996].

Clichy, France : Klee *shee*

Clifden, Ireland : *Klif* tun

Clifton, England; USA : *Klif* tun

Clinton, USA : *Klin* tun

Clipsham, England : *Klip* shum

Clitheroe, England : *Klidh* a roh

Clonakilty, Ireland : Klah na *kil* ti (UK Klon a *kil* ti)
Clones, Ireland : *Kloh* nis
Clonmel, Ireland : Klahn *mel* (UK Klon *mel*)
Clontarf, Ireland : Klahn *tahrf* (UK Klon *tahf*)
¹Clough, England : Klahf
²Clough, Northern Ireland : Klokh
Clovelly, England : Kloh *vel* i (UK Kla *vel* i)
Clovis, USA : *Kloh* vis
Cluj-Napoca, Romania : Kloohzh *Nah* poh ka
Cluny, France : *Klooh* ni (French Klee *nee*)
Clwyd, Wales : *Klooh* id
Clydach, Wales : *Klid* ukh
Clyde, Scotland : Kliyd
Clydebank, Scotland : *Kliyd* bangk
Clydesdale, Scotland : *Kliydz* dayl
Coachella, USA : Koh *chel* a
Coahuila, Mexico : Koh ah *wee* lah
Coalinga, USA : Koh *ling* ga
Coalisland, Northern Ireland : Kohl *iy* lund
Coalville, England : *Kohl* vil
Coamo, Puerto Rico : Koh *ah* moh
Coatbridge, Scotland : *Koht* brij
Coatepec, Mexico : Koh ah tay *pek*
Coatepeque, Guatemala : Koh ah tay *pay* kay
Coats (Island), Canada : Kohts
Coatzacoalcos, Mexico : Koh aht sah koh *ahl* kohs
Cobán, Guatemala : Koh *bahn*
Cobar, Australia : *Koh* bahr (UK *Koh* bah)
Cobh, Ireland : Kohv [The name of the Co. Cork seaport is an Irish spelling of English *cove*.]
Cobham, England : *Kah* bum (UK *Kob* um)
Cobija, Bolivia : Koh *bee* hah
Coblenz, Germany : Koh *blents* (German *Koh* blents)
Cobourg, Canada : Koh *buhrg* (UK *Koh* buhg)
Coburg, Australia; Germany : *Koh* buhrg (UK *Koh* buhg) (German *Koh* boork)
Cochabamba, Bolivia : Koh chah *bahm* bah
Cochin, India : *Koh* chin
Cockburn, Australia : *Koh* buhrn (UK *Koh* buhn)
Cockermouth, England : *Kah* kur mowth (UK *Kok* a mowth) [A local pronunciation of the Cumbria town's name is *Kok* a muth.]
Cocos (Islands), Indian Ocean : *Koh* kus
Codó, Brazil : Koh *doh*
Codrington, Antigua and Barbuda : *Kahd* ring tun (UK *Kod* ring tun)
Cody, USA : *Koh* di
Coeur d'Alene, USA : Kawr da *layn* (UK Kaw da *layn*) [The pronunciation of the Idaho city's name has blurred its French origin, meaning "heart of awl."]
    Coeur d'Alene is *Kur-da-lane*, with the accent on the *lane*, and the vowel of *kur* lying between that of *cur* and that of *poor* [Mencken, p. 541].
Coffs Harbour, Australia : Kawfs *Hahr* bur (UK Kofs *Hah* ba)
Coggeshall, England : *Kah* gi shul (UK *Kog* i shul) [An alternate pronunciation of the Essex village's name as *Kok* sul is noted by both Lloyd James 1936 and Forster.]
Cognac, France : Kaw *nyahk*
Cohoes, USA : Ka *hohz*
Coihaique, Chile : Koy *iy* kay
Coimbatore, India : *Koym* ba tawr (UK *Koym* ba taw)
Coimbra, Portugal : *Kweem* bra
Coín, Spain : Koh *een*
Cojutepeque, El Salvador : Koh hooh tay *pay* kay
Colatina, Brazil : Koh la *tee* na
Colchester, England; USA : *Kohl* ches tur (UK *Kohl* ches ta)
Colchis, Georgia : *Kahl* kis (UK *Kol* kis)
Coldstream, Scotland : *Kohld* streem
Coleford, England : *Kohl* furd (UK *Kohl* fud)

Colenso, South Africa : Ka *len* zoh
Coleraine, Northern Ireland : Kohl *rayn*
Colima, Mexico : Koh *lee* mah
Coll, Scotland : Kawl (UK Kol)
College, USA : *Kah* lij (UK *Kol* ij)
Collegno, Italy : Koh *lay* nyoh
Collie, Australia : *Kah* li (UK *Kol* i)
Collingswood, USA : *Kah* lingz wood (UK *Kol* ingz wood)
Collinsville, USA : *Kah* lunz vil (UK *Kol* inz vil)
Colmar, France : *Kohl* mahr
Colne, England : Kohn
Colney, England : *Koh* ni
Cologne, Germany : Ka *lohn*
Colomb-Béchar, Algeria : Kaw lohn Bay *shahr* (UK ... Bay *shah*)
Colombey-les-Deux-Églises, France : Koh lawn bay lay Duh zay *gleez*
Colombia, South America : Ka *lahm* bi a (UK Ka *lom* bi a)
Colombo, Sri Lanka : Ka *lahm* boh
Colomiers, France : Kaw law *myay*
Colón, Cuba; Panama : Ka *lohn* (UK Ka *lon*) (Spanish Koh *lohn*)
Colonia, Uruguay : Koh *loh* nyah
Colonsay, Scotland : *Kah* lun zay (UK *Kol* un zay)
Colorado, USA : Kah la *rad* oh (UK Kol a *rah* doh) [The original Spanish long *a* of the state's name has been preserved in its British pronunciation but not in the American. Mencken, p. 543, mentions a variant pronunciation Kah la *ray* doh.]
Colorado Springs, USA : Kah la rad oh *Springz* (UK Kol a rah doh...)
Colton, USA : *Kohl* tun
Columbia, USA : Ka *lahm* bi a
Columbus, USA : Ka *lahm* bus
Colwich, England : *Kahl* wich (UK *Kol* wich) [The name of the Staffordshire village was formerly pronounced *Kol* ich.]
Colwyn Bay, Wales : Kahl win *Bay* (UK Kol win...)
Comalcalco, Mexico : Koh mahl *kahl* koh

Comayagua, Honduras : Koh mah *yah* gwah
Combs-la-Ville, France : Kawmb la *Veel*
Comitán, Mexico : Koh mee *tahn*
Commack, USA : *Kah* mak (UK *Kom* ak)
Como, Italy : *Koh* moh
Comodoro Rivadavia, Argentina : Koh moh dhoh roh Ree vah *dhah* vee ah
Comoros, Indian Ocean : *Kah* ma rohz (UK *Kom* a rohz)
Compiègne, France : Kawm *pyen*
Compostela, Mexico : Kawm paw *stay* lah
Compton, England; USA : *Kahmp* tun (UK *Komp* tun)
Comrie, Scotland : *Kahm* ri (UK *Kom* ri)
Conakry, Guinea : *Kah* na kree (UK Kon a *kree*)
Concarneau, France : Kawn kahr *noh*
Concepción, Chile; Paraguay : Kawn sep *syawn*
Concepción del Uruguay, Argentina : Kawn sep syawn dhel Ooh rooh *gwiy*
¹Concord, USA (Massachusetts) : *Kahng* kurd (UK *Kong* kud) [The American author of the passage quoted below compares the US pronunciation of the city's name with that of *concord*, "harmony" (US *kahn* kawrd, UK *kong* cawd). *Cp.* ²**Concord**.]
> They are obviously the same word, but they are almost always pronounced differently: *Concord* always sounds exactly like *conquered* (the natural development); *concord* shows the influence of the spelling in being "con cord" or "cong cord" [Eric Partridge and John W. Clark, *British and American English Since 1900*, 1951].

²Concord, USA (North Carolina) : *Kahn* kawrd (UK *Kong* kawd) [The names of Concord, California, and Concord, New Hampshire, are pronounced either thus or as ¹**Concord**.]
Concordia, Argentina : Kun *kawr* dee a (UK Kun *kaw* dee a)

Condamine, Australia : *Kahn* da miyn (UK *Kon* da miyn)

Condom, France : Kawn *dawn*

Condover, England : *Kahn* doh vur (UK *Kahn* doh va)

Conestoga, USA : Kah na *stoh* ga (UK Kon i *stoh* ga)

Coney Island, USA : Koh ni *Iy* lund

Confolens, France : Kawn foh *lahn*

Congleton, England : *Kahn* gul tun (UK *Kong* gul tun)

Congo, Africa : *Kahng* goh (UK *Kong* goh)

Congresbury, England : *Kahngz* ber i (UK *Kongz* bri) [A local pronunciation *Koohms* bri was formerly current for the Somerset village. Ross, p. 68, gives it as the sole correct one.]

Conisbrough, England : *Kah* nus buhr oh (UK *Kon* is bra)

Coniston, England : *Kah* nis tun (UK *Kon* is tun)

Connacht, Ireland : *Kah* nawt (UK *Kon* awt)

Connah's Quay, Wales : Kah nuz *Kee* (UK Kon uz...)

Connaught, Ireland : *Kah* nawt (UK *Kon* awt)

Conneaut, USA : *Kah* nee aht (UK *Kon* ee aht)

Connecticut, USA : Ka *net* i kut

Connemara, Ireland : Kah ni *mah* ra (UK Kon i *mah* ra)

Conselheiro Lafaiete, Brazil : Kon si lyay rooh La fah *yay* tee

Consett, England : *Kahn* sut (UK *Kon* sit)

Constance, Germany : *Kahn* stuns (UK *Kon* stuns)

Constanța, Romania : Kohn *stahn* tsa

Constantine, Algeria; England : *Kahn* stun teen (UK *Kon* stun tiyn) [The village in Cornwall, England, had a distinctive local pronunciation, as the quote below indicates.]

The correct Cornish pronunciation "Costenton" was still known earlier this century [O.J. Padel, *A Popular Dictionary of Cornish Place-Names*, 1988].

Constantinople, Turkey : Kahn stan ta *noh* pul (UK Kon stan ti *noh* pul)

Conway, USA; Wales : *Kahn* way (UK *Kon* way)

Conwy, Wales : *Kahn* wi (UK *Kon* wi) (Welsh *Kon* oo i)

Coober Pedy, Australia : Kooh bur *Pee* di (UK Kooh ba...)

Cooch Behar, India : Koohch Ba *hahr* (UK ... Bi *hah*)

Cook (Islands), Pacific Ocean : Kook

Cookstown, Northern Ireland : *Kooks* town

Cooktown, Australia : *Kook* town

Coolangatta, Australia : Kooh lung *gat* a

Coolgardie, Australia : Koohl *gahr* di (UK Koohl *gah* di)

Coos Bay, USA : Koohs *Bay*

Cootamundra, Australia : Kooh ta *mahn* dra

Copacabana (Beach), Brazil : Koh pa ka *ban* a (Portuguese Kaw pah kah *bah* na)

Copeland, England : *Kohp* lund

Copenhagen, Denmark : *Koh* pun hay gun (UK Koh pun *hay* gun) [Ross, p. 69, gives Koh pun *hah* gun as the usual US pronunciation of the capital's name.]

Copiague, USA : *Koh* payg

Copiapó, Chile : Koh pyah *poh*

Coquet, England : *Koh* kit

Coquimbo, Chile : Koh *keem* boh

Corbeil-Essonnes, France : Kawr bay E *sawn*

Corbridge, England : *Kawr* brij (UK *Kaw* brij)

Corby, England : *Kawr* bi (UK *Kaw* bi)

Corcoran, USA : *Kawr* ka run (UK *Kaw* ka run)

Cordele, USA : Kawr *deel* (UK Kaw *deel*)

Cordillera Central, Colombia; Dominican Republic; Peru; Philippines; Puerto Rico : Kawr dul yer a Sen *trahl* (UK Kaw di lay a ra...) (Spanish Kohr dhee *yay* rah...)

Córdoba, Argentina; Colombia; Mexico; Spain : *Kawr* da ba (UK *Kaw* da ba) (Spanish *Kawr* dhoh bah)

¹**Cordova**, Spain : *Kawr* da va (UK *Kaw* da va)

²**Cordova**, USA : Kawr *doh* va (UK Kaw *doh* va)

Corfe, England : Kawrf (UK Kawf)

Corfu, Greece : *Kawr* fooh (UK Kaw *fooh*)

Corigliano, Italy : Koh ree *lyah* noh

Corinth, Greece; USA : *Kaw* runth (UK *Kor* inth)

Corinto, Nicaragua : Ka *reen* toh

Cork, Ireland : Kawrk (UK Kawk)

Corning, USA : *Kawr* ning (UK *Kaw* ning)

Cornwall, Canada; England : *Kawrn* wawl (UK *Kawn* wawl)

Cornwallis (Island), Canada : Kawrn *wah* lis (UK Kawn *wol* is)

Coro, Venezuela : *Koh* roh

Coroatá, Brazil : Kaw rooh a *tah*

Coromandel (Coast), India : Kawr a *man* dul (UK Kaw roh *man* dul)

Coron, Philippines : Kaw *rawn*

Coronel, Chile : Kaw roh *nel*

Coronel Oviedo, Paraguay : Kaw roh nel Oh *vyay* dhoh

Çorovodë, Albania : Chaw raw *voh* da

Corozal, Belize; Puerto Rico : Koh roh *sahl*

Corpus Christi, USA : Kawr pus *Kris* ti (UK Kaw pus...)

Correggio, Italy : Kaw *red* joh

Corregidor, Philippines : Ka *reg* a dawr (UK Ka *reg* i daw)

Corrèze, France : Kaw *rez*

Corrientes, Argentina : Kawr *yen* tays

Corsica, France : *Kawr* si ka (UK *Kaw* si ka)

Corsicana, USA : Kawr si *kah* na (UK Kaw si *kah* na)

Corsico, Italy : *Kawr* see koh

Corstorphine, Scotland : Kur *stawr* fin (UK Ka *staw* fin)

Cortazar, Mexico : Kawr tah *sahr*

Corte, Corsica, France : Kawr *tay*

Cortina d'Ampezzo, Italy : Kawr tee nah dahm *pet* soh

Cortland, Italy : *Kawrt* lund (UK *Kawt* lund)

Cortona, Italy : Kawr *toh* nah

Çorum, Turkey : *Choh* room

Corumbá, Brazil : Kaw roohm *bah*

Corunna, Spain : Ka *rah* na

Corvallis, USA : Kawr *val* is (UK Kaw *val* is)

Corwen, Wales : *Kawr* wun (UK *Kaw* wun) (Welsh *Kawr* wen)

¹**Coryton**, England (Devon) : *Kaw* ra tun (UK *Kor* i tun)

²**Coryton**, England (Essex) : *Kaw* ri tun [The oil refinery town has a different pronunciation from ¹**Coryton** as it is named for the Cory Brothers who founded it in 1922.]

Cos, Greece : Kahs (UK Kos)

Cosamaloapan, Mexico : Koh sah mah loh *ah* pahn

Cosenza, Italy : Koh *zent* sah

Cosham, England : *Kah* sum (UK *Kos* um) [A popular UK pronunciation *Kosh* um also exists for the district of Portsmouth, Hampshire.]

Cosne-Cours-sur-Loire, France : Kohn Koohr seer *Lwahr*

Costa Mesa, USA : Koh sta *May* sah

Costa Rica, Central America : Koh sta *Ree* ka (UK Kos ta ... (Spanish Kaw stah *Ree* kah)

Costessey, England : *Kah* si (UK *Kos* i) [The name of the Norfolk village was formerly also spelled *Cossey*, preserved in the current unexpected pronunciation.]

Coswig, Germany : *Kaws* vikh

Cotabato, Philippines : Koh tah *bah* toh

Côte d'Azur, France : Koht dah *zeer*

Côte d'Ivoire, Africa : Koht dee *vwahr*

Côte-d'Or, France : Koht *dawr*

Cotentin (Peninsula), France : Koh tahn *tang*

Cotonou, Benin : Koh toh *nooh*

Cotopaxi, Ecuador : Koh ta *pak* si (Spanish Koh toh *pahk* see)

Cotswold (Hills), England : *Kahts* wohld (UK *Kots* wohld)

Cottbus, Germany : *Kaht* bus

Cottesmore, England : *Kahts* mawr (UK *Kots* maw) [The name of the Rutland village is usually pronounced *Kot* is maw by local military personnel and the local media.]

Cottonwood, USA : *Kah* tun wood (UK *Kot* un wood)

Cotuí, Dominican Republic : Koh *twee*

Coucy-Auffrique, France : Kooh see Oh *freek*

Coulsdon, England : *Koohlz* dun [The name of the residential district of the London borough of Croydon has a traditional local pronunciation *Kohlz* dun.]
  Pronounced "coolsdun," although some locals prefer "coalsdun" [Willey, p. 119].

Council Bluffs, USA : Kown sul *Blahfs*

Coupar Angus, Scotland : Kooh pur *Ang* gus

Courcelles, Belgium : Koohr *sel*

Courland, Latvia : *Koor* lund (UK *Koo* a lund)

Courmayeur, Italy : Koor ma *yuhr*

Courtenay, Canada : *Kawrt* ni (UK *Kawt* ni)

Coutances, France : Kooh *tahns*

Coutras, France : Kooh *trah*

Coventry, England : *Kah* vun tri (UK *Kov* un tri) [According to Ross, p.70, *Kah* vun tri is the "better pronunciation" of the former Warwickshire city's name, and it was generally preferred by older "educated" British speakers, but *Kov* un tri is now more widely heard. An analogous duality applies for London's Covent Garden (once *Kah* vunt, now *Kov* unt).]

Coverack, England : *Kah* va rak (UK *Kov* a rak)

Covington, USA : *Kah* ving tun

Cowbridge, Wales : *Kow* brij

Cowdenbeath, Scotland : Kow dun *beeth*

Cowes, England : Kowz

Cowley, England : *Kow* li

Cowra, Australia : *Kow* ra

Coxsackie, USA : Kahk *sak* i (UK Kok *sak* i)

Cracow, Poland : *Krah* kow (UK *Krak* ow) [Lloyd James 1937 recommended a pronunciation *Krak* oh for the city's name in its English spelling. *Cp.* **Kraków**.]

Craigavon, Northern Ireland : Kray *gav* un

Craigie, Scotland : *Kray* gi

Crail, Scotland : Krayl

Crailsheim, Germany : *Kriyls* hiym

Craiova, Romania : Krah *yoh* vah

Cranborne, England : *Kran* bawrn (UK *Kran* bawn)

Cranbrook, Canada; England : *Kran* brook

Cranford, England; USA : *Kran* furd (UK *Kran* fud)

Cranleigh, England : *Kran* li

Crans-sur-Sierre, Switzerland : Krahn seer *Syer*

Cranston, USA : *Kran* stun

Cranwell, England : *Kran* wul

Craon, France : Krawn

Craonne, France : Krahn

Crathes, Scotland : *Kra* thiz

Crato, Brazil : *Kra* tooh

Craven Arms, England : Kray vun Ahrmz (UK ... Ahmz)

Crawley, England : *Kraw* li

Crayford, England : *Kray* furd (UK *Kray* fud)

Crécy, France : Kray *see* (UK *Kres* i) (French Kray *see*)

Crediton, England : *Kred* a tun (UK *Kred* i tun)

Creigiau, Wales : *Kray* ga (Welsh *Kriyg* yiy) [The name is simply the plural form of Welsh *craig*, "rock."]

Creil, France : Kray

Crema, Italy : *Kray* ma

Cremona, Italy : Kri *moh* na (Italian Kre *moh* nah)

Crespin, France : Kray *pang*

Crest, France : Kray

Crete, Greece : Kreet

Créteil, France : Kray *tay*

Creuse, France : Kruhz

Crewe, England : Krooh
Crewkerne, England : *Krooh* kuhrn
(UK *Krooh* kuhn)
Crianlarich, Scotland : Kree un *lar* ikh
Criccieth, Wales : *Krik* i uth (Welsh
Krik yeth)
Crich, England : Kriych [The Der-
byshire village is sometimes referred
to as Krich or even Krikh by those
unfamiliar with the proper pronunci-
ation.]
Crickhowell, Wales : Krik *how* ul
Cricklade, England : *Krik* layd
Crieff, Scotland : Kreef
Crimea, Ukraine : Kriy *mee* a (UK Kriy
mi a)
Crimmitschau, Germany : *Krim* ut
show
Cristóbal, Panama : Kris *toh* bul
Croatia, Europe : Kroh *ay* sha
Croix, France : Krwah
Cromarty, Scotland : *Krah* mur ti (UK
Krom a ti)
Cromer, England : *Kroh* mur (UK *Kroh*
ma)
Crompton, England : *Krahmp* tun (UK
Kromp tun)
Cromwell, New Zealand; USA : *Krahm*
wel (UK *Krom* wel)
Crook, England : Krook
Crosby, England : *Krahz* bi (UK *Kroz*
bi)
Crossmaglen, Northern Ireland : Kraws
ma *glen* (UK Kros ma *glen*)
Crotone, Italy : Kroh *toh* nay
Crowborough, England : *Kroh* buhr oh
(UK *Kroh* bra)
Crowthorne, England : *Kroh* thawrn
(UK *Kroh* thawn)
Croydon, Australia; England : *Kroy* dun
Cruas, France : Kri *ahs*
Cruces, Cuba : *Krooh* ses
Cruz Alta, Brazil : Krooh *zahl* ta
Cruz del Eje, Argentina : Kroohz del *Ay*
hay (Spanish Kroohs dhel *Ay* hay)
Cruzeiro, Brazil : Krooh *zay* rooh
Cuando-Cubango, Angola : Kwahn
doh Kooh *bahng* goh
Cuanza, Angola : *Kwahn* zah

Cuauhtémoc, Mexico : Kwow *tay* mahk
(UK Kwow *tay* mok)
Cuautla, Mexico : *Kwowt* lah
Cuba, West Indies : *Kyooh* ba
Cuckfield, England : *Kook* feeld
Cuckney, England : *Kahk* ni
Cúcuta, Colombia : *Kooh* kooh tah
Cudham, England : *Kood* um
Cudworth, England : *Kahd* wurth (UK
Kahd wuth) [The name of the York-
shire town has an alternate local pro-
nunciation *Kah* duth.]
Cuenca, Ecuador; Spain : *Kweng* kah
Cuernavaca, Mexico : Kwer nah *vah* kah
Cuers, France : Kyer
Cuiabá, Brazil : Kooh ya *bah*
Cuilapa, Guatemala : Kwee *lah* pah
Cuillin (Hills), Scotland : *Kooh* lin
Culcheth, England : *Kahl* chuth
Culiacán, Mexico : Koohl yah *kahn*
Culloden (Moor), Scotland : Ka *lah*
dun (UK Ka *lod* un) [Ross, p. 72,
gives the sole valid pronunciation of
the battlesite's name as Ka *loh* dun,
but this is rarely heard today.]
Cullompton, England : Ka *lahmp* tun
Culoz, France : Ki *lawz*
Culross, Scotland : *Kahl* raws (UK *Kahl*
ros) [The Fife town is locally known
as *Kooh* ros.]
Culver City, USA : Kahl vur *Si* ti (UK
Kahl va...)
Cumae, Italy : *Kyooh* mee
Cumaná, Venezuela : Kooh mah *nah*
Cumberland, England; USA : *Kahm*
bur lund (UK *Kahm* ba lund)
Cumbernauld, Scotland : Kahm bur
nawld (UK Kahm ba *nawld*)
Cumbria, England : *Kahm* bri a
Cumnock, Scotland : *Kahm* nuk
Cundinamarca, Colombia : Koohn di
na *mahr* ka
Cunene, Angola : Kooh *nay* na
Cuneo, Italy : *Kooh* nee oh
Cupar, Scotland : *Kooh* pur (UK *Kooh*
pa)
Ćuprija, Serbia : *Chooh* pree ya
Curaçao, West Indies : *Kyoor* a soh (UK
Kyoo a ra soh)

Curepipe, Mauritius : Koor *peep*
Curicó, Chile : Kooh ree *koh*
Curitiba, Brazil : Koor a *tee* ba
Curragh, Ireland : *Kuhr* a (UK *Kah* ra)
Curuzú Cuatiá, Argentina : Kooh rooh
sooh Kwah *tyah*
Cuttack, India : *Kah* tuk
Cuxhaven, Germany : *Kooks* hah fun
Cuyahoga, USA : Kiy a *hoh* ga
Cuzco, Peru : *Koohs* koh (UK *Koos* koh)
Cwmbran, Wales : Koom *brahn* [The
Welsh vowel *w* of the town's name is
properly pronounced short, although
some say it long.]
First syllable like *cook*, not *doom*
[Kingsley Amis, *The King's English*,
1997].
Cyclades, Greece : *Sik* la deez
Cymru, Europe : *Kahm* ri (Welsh *Kuhm*
ri) [The Welsh name of Wales has
various English mispronunciations,
two others being *Koom* ri and *Kim* ri.]
Cypress, USA : *Siy* prus
Cyprus, Mediterranean Sea : *Siy* prus
Cyrenaica, Libya : Sir a *nay* i ka (UK
Siy ra *nay* i ka)
Cyrene, Libya : Siy *ree* ni
Cysoing, France : See *zwahn*
Cythera, Greece : Si *thir* a
Czechoslovakia, Europe : Chek a sloh
vah ki a (UK Chek a sloh *vak* i a)
Czech (Republic), Europe : Chek
Częstochowa, Poland : Chen sta *koh* va
Dąbrowa Górnicza, Poland : Dawn
braw vah Goor *nee* chah
Dachau, Germany : *Dah* kow (UK *Dak*
ow) (German *Dah* khow)
Dacia, Europe : *Day* sha (UK *Day* si a)
Dagenham, England : *Dag* num
Dagestan, Russia : Dah gi *stahn*
Dagupan, Philippines : Dah *gooh* pahn
Dahlak (Archipelago), Eritrea : Dah
lahk
Dahomey, Africa : Da *hoh* mi
Daimiel, Spain : Diym *yel*
Dajabón, Dominican Republic : Dah
hah *bohn*
Dakar, Senegal : Da *kahr* (UK *Dak* ah)
Dakhla, Western Sahara : *Dah* khla

Dakota, USA : Da *koh* ta
Dakovo, Croatia : *Jah* kaw vaw
Dalaman, Turkey : *Dal* a man
Da Lat, Vietnam : Dah *Laht*
Dalbeattie, Scotland : Dal *bee* ti [Lo-
cally the name of the town is pro-
nounced Dul *bee* ti.]
Dalby, Australia : *Dawl* bi
Dalhart, USA : *Dal* hahrt (UK *Dal*
haht)
Dalhousie, Canada; India : Dal *how* zi
Dalian, China : Dah li *an*
Dalkeith, Scotland : Dal *keeth*
Dallas, USA : *Dal* us
Dalles, USA : Dalz
Dalmatia, Europe : Dal *may* sha
Dalmeny, Scotland : Dal *men* i
Daloa, Côte d'Ivoire : Dah *loh* ah
Dalry, Scotland : Dul *riy*
Dalston, England : *Dawl* stun [Both
the Cumbria village and the London
district have this pronunciation.]
Dalton, USA : *Dawl* tun
Dalton-in-Furness, England : Dawl
tun un *Fuhr* nus (UK ... in *Fuh* nis)
Dalwhinnie, Scotland : Dal *win* i [The
name of the village is locally pro-
nounced Dul *hwin* i.]
Daly City, USA : Day li *Si* ti
Daman, India : Da *mahn*
Damanhur, Egypt : Da man *hoohr* (UK
Da man *hooh* a)
Damar, Indonesia : Dah *mahr*
Damaraland, Namibia : Da *mah* ra
land
Damascus, Syria : Da *mas* kus
Damaturu, Nigeria : Dah mah *tooh* rooh
Damghan, Iran : Dahm *gahn*
Damietta, Egypt : Da mi *et* a
Damoh, India : Da *moh*
Dampier (Archipelago), Australia :
Dam pi ur (UK *Dam* pi a)
Dan, Israel : Dan
Danakil (Desert), Ethiopia : *Dan* a kil
Da Nang, Vietnam : Dah *Nahng* (UK
Dah *Nang*)
Danapur, India : Da na *poor*
Danbury, USA : *Dan* ber i (UK *Dan*
bri)

Dandenong, Australia : Dan da *nahng* (UK Dan da *nong*)
Dandong, China : Dahn *doong*
Dangriga, Belize : Dahn *gree* gah
Dannevirke, New Zealand : *Dan* a vuhrk (UK *Dan* a vuhk)
Danube, Europe : *Dan* yoohb
Danvers, USA : *Dan* vurz (UK *Dan* vuz)
Danville, USA : *Dan* vil
Danzig, Poland : *Dan* tsig (German *Dahn* tsikh)
Dao, Philippines : Dow
Dapitan, Philippines : Da *pee* tahn
Darab, Iran : Da *rahb*
Darby, USA : *Dahr* bi (UK *Dah* bi)
Dardanelles, Turkey : Dahr da *nelz* (UK Dah da *nelz*)
Dar el Beida, Morocco : Dahr el *Biy* dah
Darenth, England : *Dar* unth
Daresbury, England : *Dahrz* ber i (UK *Dahz* bri)
Dar es Salaam, Tanzania : Dahr es Sa *lahm*
Darfur, Sudan : Dahr *foohr* (UK Dah *fooh* a)
Dargaville, New Zealand : *Dahr* ga vil (UK *Dah* ga vil)
Darhan, Mongolia : *Dahr* khahn
¹**Darien**, Panama : *Der* i en (UK *Day* a ri un) (Spanish Dah *ryen*)
²**Darien**, USA : Dar i *en*
Darjeeling, India : Dahr *jee* ling (UK Dah *jee* ling)
Darling, Australia : *Dahr* ling (UK *Dah* ling)
Darlington, England; USA : *Dahr* ling tun (UK *Dah* ling tun)
Darmstadt, Germany : *Dahrm* stat (UK *Dahm* stat) (German *Dahrm* shtaht)
Darnah, Libya : *Dahr* na (UK *Dah* na)
Dartford, England : *Dahrt* furd (UK *Daht* fud)
Dartmoor, England : *Dahrt* moor (UK *Daht* mooh a)
Dartmouth, Canada; England; USA : *Dahrt* muth (UK *Daht* muth)
Darton, England : *Dahr* tun (UK *Dah* tun)

Darwen, England : *Dahr* win (UK *Dah* win) [The Lancashire town's name has an alternate local pronunciation *Dar* un.]
Darwin, Australia : *Dahr* win (UK *Dah* win)
Dashhowuz, Turkmenistan : Dash ha *woohs*
Datchet, England : *Dach* it
Datong, China : Dah *tung*
Daugavpils, Latvia : *Dow* guf pils
Dauphin, Canada : *Daw* fin
Dauphiné, France : Doh fee *nay*
Davao, Philippines : *Dah* vow
Davenport, USA : *Dav* un pawrt (UK *Dav* un pawt)
Daventry, England : *Dav* un tri [The Northamptonshire town's name was formerly pronounced *Dayn* tri. Shakespeare refers to it as *Daintry*, and the modern spelling pronunciation was largely promoted by the BBC, which opened a radio transmitter here in 1925. The quotes below consider the two forms. (*See also* **Sawbridgeworth**.)]
(1) "Education" and the railway are responsible for the replacement of the old local forms by pronunciations based on a traditional spelling. Daintry is giving way to *Daventry*, and Sapsworth has quite yielded to *Sawbridgeworth* [Ernest Weekley, *Adjectives — And Other Words*, 1930].
(2) We are, of course, once again face to face with the perennial question of *Daventry*, and all the storm that its pronunciation raises in the teacups of the curious.... If *Daventry* is really serious in its desire to be known to the world as *Daintry*, then it must dress for the part. It cannot have it both ways [Lloyd James 1936, p. 7].
(3) We have yet to measure the full effect on place-names of such a powerful force as the B.B.C., but in DAVENTRY that body has already provided a rare example of a spelling form overcoming pronunciation ... [Now] Daintry is dead, the broadcast

word is Daventry [H.G. Stokes, *English Place-Names*, 1948].

(4) Fifty years ago ... Daventry was pronounced "Daintry," Sawbridgworth [*sic*] in Hertfordshire is said to have been "Sapsed" [C. Stella Davies and John Levitt, *What's in a Name?*, 1970].

(5) The old pronunciation, to rhyme with *Aintree*, was essentially killed in the nineteen-thirties, because the B.B.C. had a transmitter there, and they pronounced the name as spelt [Ross, p. 74].

David, Panama : Dah *veedh*

Davis, USA : *Day* vis

Davos, Switzerland : Dah *vohs* (UK Da *vohs*)

Dawlish, England : *Daw* lish

Dawson, Canada : *Daw* sun

Dax, France : Dahks

Dayr az Zawr, Syria : Dayr ez *Zawr*

Dayton, USA : *Day* tun

Daytona Beach, USA : Day toh na *Beech*

De Aar, South Africa : Di *Ahr* (UK Di *Ah*)

Deal, England : Deel

Deán Funes, Argentina : Day ahn *Fooh* nes

Dearborn, USA : *Dir* bawrn (UK *Di* a bawn)

Deauville, France : Doh *veel* [Ross, p. 75, recommends *Doh* vil, as "the French pronunciation would be affected."]

Deba Habe, Nigeria : Day bah *Hah* bay

Debenham, England : *Deb* num [The river on which the Suffolk village stands is the Deben, pronounced *Dee* bun.]

Debrecen, Hungary : *Deb* ret sen

Debre Markos, Ethiopia : Deb re *Mahr* kohs (UK ... *Mah* kohs)

Debre Zeyit, Ethiopia : Deb re *Zayt*

Decapolis, Asia : Di *kap* a lis

Decatur, USA : Di *kay* tur (UK Di *kay* ta)

Decazeville, France : D kahz *veel*

Deccan, India : *Dek* un

Děčín, Czech Republic : Dye *cheen*

Decorah, USA : Di *kawr* a

Dedham, England; USA : *Ded* um

Dee, Scotland; Wales : Dee

Deerfield, USA : *Dir* feeld (UK *Di* a feeld)

Deganwy, Wales : Di *gan* wi (Welsh De *gah* noo i)

Dehiwala-Mount Lavinia, Sri Lanka : Day hee wa la Mownt La *vin* i a

Dehra Dun, India : Der a *Doohn* (UK Day a ra...)

Deighton, England : *Dee* tun

Dej, Romania : Dezh

De Kalb, USA : Di *Kalb*

Delagoa (Bay), Mozambique : Del a *goh* a

De Land, USA : Di *Land*

Delano, USA : Da *lay* noh

Delaware, USA : *Del* a wer (UK *Del* a way a)

Delémont, Switzerland : Dlay *mohn*

Delft, Netherlands : Delft

¹Delhi, Canada; USA : *Del* hiy

²Delhi, India : *Del* i

Delitzsch, Germany : *Day* lich

Delmarva (Peninsula), USA : Del *mahr* va (UK Del *mah* va)

Delmenhorst, Germany : *Del* mun hawrst

Delos, Greece : *Dee* lahs (UK *Dee* los)

Delphi, Greece : *Del* fiy

Delray Beach, USA : Del ray *Beech*

Del Rio, USA : Del *Ree* oh

Delyn, Wales : *Del* in

Demerara, Guyana : Dem a *rer* a (UK Dem a *ray* a ra)

Denbigh, Wales : *Den* bi

Denby Dale, England : Den bi *Dayl*

Denderleeuw, Belgium : *Den* dur lay oo

Den Helder, Netherlands : Den *Hel* dur

Denholme, England : *Den* hohlm (UK *Den* holm)

Denison, USA : *Den* a sun (UK *Den* i sun)

Denizli, Turkey : De niz *lee*

Denmark, Europe : *Den* mahrk (UK *Den* mahk)

Denpasar, Indonesia : Den *pah* sahr

Denton, England; USA : *Den* tun

D'Entrecasteaux (Islands), Papua New Guinea : Dawn tra *kas* toh

Denver, USA : *Den* vur (UK *Den* va)

Deoband, India : *Day* a bund

Deoghar, India : *Day* oh gur

Déols, France : Day *awl*

De Pere, USA : Di *Pir* (UK Di *Pi* a)

Depew, USA : Di *pyooh*

Deptford, England : *Det* furd (UK *Det* fud)

Dera Ghazi Khan, Pakistan : Day ra Gah zee *Khahn*

Dera Ismail Khan, Pakistan : Day ra Is miyl *Khahn*

Derbent, Russia : *Duhr* bent (UK *Duh* bent) (Russian Dyir *byent*)

¹**Derby**, Australia; USA : *Duhr* bi (UK *Duh* bi) [The respective US and UK pronunciations of this placename and the identically spelled ²**Derby** show the way an American speaker voices an instinctive *r* even when adopting a British vowel sound. The US author of the passage below illustrates the distinction when he speaks the names of the two horse races.]

> When I speak of the Kentucky Derby, I pronounce it "duhrrby." ... When I speak of the Epsom Downs Derby, I pronounce it "dahrrby." I would never think of saying "dahby," any more than I would think of imitating the Southern British intonation [Eric Partridge and John W. Clark, *British and American English Since 1900*, 1951].

²**Derby**, England : *Dahr* bi (UK *Dah* bi) [A few local people pronounce the city's name as ¹**Derby**, but in general "the town and county are 'Darby' (which is how it was spelled on old maps)." (H.G. Stokes, *English Place-Names*, 1948)].

Derg, Ireland : Duhrg (UK Duhg)

De Ridder, USA : Di *Rid* ur (UK ... *Rid* a)

Derry, Northern Ireland; USA : *Der* i

Derwent, Australia; England : *Duhr* wunt (UK *Duh* wunt)

Derwent Water, England : *Duhr* wunt Waw tur (UK *Dih* wunt Waw ta)

Desamparados, Costa Rica : Day sahm pah *rah* dhohs

Desborough, England : *Dez* buhr oh (UK *Dez* bra)

Descabezado, Chile : Des kah ba *sah* doh

Descartes, France : Day *kahrt*

Dese, Ethiopia : *Day* say

Des Moines, USA : Di *Moyn*

De Soto, USA : Di *Soh* toh

Des Plaines, USA : Des *Playnz*

Dessau, Germany : *Des* ow

Desvres, France : Devr

Detmold, Germany : *Det* mawlt

Detroit, USA : Di *troyt* [The Michigan city's name is also locally pronounced *Dee* troyt.]

Deurne, Belgium; Netherlands : *Duhr* na

Deva, Romania : *Day* vah

Deventer, Netherlands : *Day* vun tur

Devizes, England : Di *viy* ziz

Devon, England; Scotland : *Dev* un [The English county name is pronounced thus, but the Nottinghamshire river is *Dee* vun. The Scottish river is pronounced as the county.]

Devonport, Australia; England; New Zealand : *Dev* un pawrt (UK *Dev* un pawt)

Dewsbury, England : *Doohz* ber i (UK *Dyoohz* bri)

Dezful, Iran : Dez *foohl*

Dezhnev, Russia : *Dezh* nyif

Dhahran, Saudi Arabia : Dah *rahn* (UK Dah *ran*)

Dhaka, Bangladesh : *Dak* a

Dhar, India : Dahr

Dhaulagiri, Nepal : Dow la *gir* ee

Dhekélia, Greece : Di *kay* li a

Diamantina, Brazil : Dee a man *tee* na

Dibër, Albania : *Dee* bur

Dibrugarh, India : *Dib* roo gur

Dickinson, USA : *Dik* un sun (UK *Dik* in sun)

Didcot, England : *Did* kaht (UK *Did* kut)

Diego Garcia, Indian Ocean : Dee ay goh Gahr *see* ah
Diepenbeek, Belgium : *Dee* pun bek
Dieppe, France : Dee *ep* (French Dyep)
Diest, Belgium : Deest
Differdange, Luxembourg : Dee fer *dahnzh*
Digby, Canada : *Dig* bi
Digne, France : Deen
Dijon, France : Dee *zhahn* (UK *Dee* zhon) (French Dee *zhawn*)
Diksmuide, Belgium : Dik *smiy* da
Dikwa, Nigeria : Dik *wah*
Dilbeek, Belgium : *Deel* bek
Dili, Indonesia : Di *lee*
Dillingen, Germany : *Dil* ing un
Dillingham, USA : *Dil* ing ham (UK *Dil* ing um)
Dillon, USA : *Dil* un
Dimitrovgrad, Bulgaria; Russia : Di *mee* truf graht
Dinagat, Philippines : Dee *nah* gaht
Dinan, France : Dee *nahn*
Dinant, Belgium : Dee *nahn*
Dinard, France : Dee *nahr*
Dindigul, India : *Din* di gul
Dinefwr, Wales : Di *nev* oor (UK Di *nev* oo a)
Dingle, Ireland : *Ding* gul
Dingwall, Scotland : *Ding* wawl
Dinkelsbühl, Germany : *Ding* kuls beel
Dinorwic, Wales : Di *nawr* wik (UK Di *naw* wik)
Dinslaken, Germany : *Dins* lah kun
Dinuba, USA : Diy *nooh* ba
Diomede (Islands), Bering Strait : *Diy* a meed
Diourbel, Senegal : Dyoohr *bel*
Dire Dawa, Ethiopia : Dee ray *Dow* ah
Diriamba, Nicaragua : Dee ree *ahm* bah
Dishforth, England : *Dish* furth (UK *Dish* futh)
Disko, Greenland : *Dis* koh
Disley, England : *Diz* li
Dispur, India : Dis *poor*
Diss, England : Dis
Disuq, Egypt : Di *soohk*
Ditchling, England : *Dich* ling
Diu, India : *Dee* ooh

Dixon, USA : *Dik* sun
Diyala, Iraq : Dee *ah* lah
Diyarbakir, Turkey : Di yahr bah *kuhr*
Djakarta, Indonesia : Ja *kahr* ta (UK Ja *kah* ta)
Djelfa, Algeria : *Jel* fa
Djenné, Mali : Je *nay*
Djibouti, Africa : Ji *booh* ti
Djidjelli, Algeria : Jee je *lee*
Dmitri Laptev (Strait), Russia : Dmee tree *Lahp* tif
Dneprodzerzhinsk, Ukraine : Nep roh dzer *zhinsk* (UK Nep roh dzay a *zhinsk*) (Russian Dnyep ra dzir *zheensk*)
Dnepropetrovsk, Ukraine : Nep roh pit *rawfsk* (UK Nep roh pit *rofsk*) (Russian Dnyep ra pit *rawfsk*)
Dnieper, Europe : *Nee* pur (UK *Nee* pa) [Some English speakers sound the initial *D* in this name and that of **Dniester**.]
Dniester, Europe : *Nee* stur (UK *Nee* sta)
Dniprodzerzhynsk, Ukraine : Dnee pra dzir *zheensk*
Dnipropetrovsk, Ukraine : Dnee pra pit *rawfsk*
Döbeln, Germany : *Duh* buln
Dobrich, Bulgaria : *Dob* rich
Dobruja, Europe : *Daw* brooh jah
Dodecanese, Greece : Doh dek a *neez*
Dodge City, USA : Dahj *Si* ti (UK Doj...)
Dodoma, Tanzania : Doh *doh* mah
Dodona, Greece : Da *doh* na (UK Doh *doh* na)
Doetinchem, Netherlands : *Dooh* ti khum
Doha, Qatar : *Doh* hah
Dokkum, Netherlands : *Daw* kum
Dole, France : Dohl
Dolgellau, Wales : Dahl *geth* li (UK Dol *geth* li) (Welsh Dawl *ge* hliy) [*See* **Llanberis** for a note on the pronunciation of Welsh *ll*.]
(1) DOLGELLAU (pronounced Dolgethl-aye) [*The Rough Guide to Wales*, 1998].

(2) Dolgellau (doll-*geth*-lie) is a true Welsh market town [*Lonely Planet Great Britain*, 2005].

Dolgoprudny, Russia : Dawl ga *proohd* ni

Dolisie, Congo : Doh lee *zee*

Dollard des Ormeaux, Canada : Doh lahr day zawr *moh*

Dolomites, Italy : *Doh* la miyts (UK *Dol* a miyts)

¹Dolores, Uruguay : Doh *loh* res

²Dolores, USA : Da *loh* rus

Dolores Hidalgo, Mexico : Doh loh res Ee *dhahl* goh

Dolton, USA : *Dohl* tun

Dombasle-sur-Meurthe, France : Dawn bahl seer *Muhrt*

Domfront, France : Dawn *frawn*

Dominica, West Indies : Dah mi *nee* ka (UK Dom i *nee* ka). [As Ross points out, p. 79, a pronunciation Da *min* i ka for the island republic's name is often used by English speakers, although the local form stresses the third syllable. *Cp*. **Dominican (Republic)**.]

Dominican (Republic), West Indies : Da *min* i kun

Dominion, Canada : Da *min* yun

Domodossola, Italy : Doh moh *daws* soh lah

Dompierre-sur-Besbre, France : Dawn pyer seer *Bebr*

Domrémy-la-Pucelle, France : Dawn ray mee la Pee *sel*

Don, Europe : Dahn (UK Don)

Donaghadee, Northern Ireland : Dah na ha *dee* (UK Don a ha *dee*)

Donauwörth, Germany : *Doh* now vuhrt

Don Benito, Spain : Dohn Bay *nee* toh

Doncaster, England : *Dahng* kus tur (UK *Dong* kas ta)

Dondo, Angola : *Dohn* doh

Donegal, Ireland : Dah ni *gawl* (UK Don i *gawl*) [According to Jones, p. 160, Dah ni *gawl* "appears to be the most usual pronunciation in Ireland" of the town and county's name.]

Donetsk, Ukraine : Doh *nyetsk* (Russian Da *nyetsk*)

Donostia-San Sebastián, Spain : Dhoh noh stee ah Sahn Say bahs *tyahn*

Doorn, Netherlands : Dohrn

Dorchester, England; USA : *Dawr* chus tur (UK *Daw* chis ta)

Dordogne, France : Dawr *dohn* (UK Daw *doyn*) (French Dawr *dawn*)

Dordrecht, Netherlands : *Dawr* drekht

Doris, Greece : *Daw* ris

Dorking, England : *Dawr* king (UK *Daw* king) [The name of the Surrey town was at one time locally pronounced *Dahr* king and generally spelled *Darking*.]

Locally [pronounced] *Darking*, and commonly so written, 1500–1800 [James Thorne, *Handbook to the Environs of London*, 1876].

Dormagen, Germany : *Dohr* mah gun

Dornbirn, Austria : *Dawrn* birn

Dornoch, Scotland : *Dawr* nahk (UK *Daw* nok) [A local pronunciation of the Sutherland town's name is *Dawr* nukh.]

Dorset, England : *Dawr* sit (UK *Daw* sit)

Dorsten, Germany : *Dohr* stun

Dortmund, Germany : *Dawrt* mund (UK *Dawt* mund) (German *Dawrt* moont)

Dothan, USA : *Doh* thun

Douai, France : *Dooh* ay (French Doo *ay*) [The city, with name formerly spelled *Douay*, gave the name of the Douay Bible, the English Roman Catholic version of the Bible, pronounced (especially by Catholics) *Dow* i. This pronunciation is also valid for Douai School, England.]

Douala, Cameroon : Doo *ah* la

Douarnenez, France : Dwahr na *nay*

Doubs, France : Dooh

Douglas, Isle of Man, British Isles; USA : *Dah* glus [According to Johnston, p. 235, the British island's chief town has a name locally pronounced *Dooh* lish.]

Doullens, France : Dooh *lahn*
Dourados, Brazil : Doh *rah* doohs
Douro, Europe : *Doo* roh (UK *Doo* a
   roh) (Portuguese *Doh* rooh)
Dover, England; USA : *Doh* vur (UK
   Doh va)
Down, Northern Ireland : Down
Downey, USA : *Dow* ni
Downpatrick, Northern Ireland :
   Down *pat* rik
Dracut, USA : *Dray* kut
Draguignan, France : Drah gee *nyahn*
Drakensberg, South Africa : *Drah* kuns
   buhrg (UK *Drah* kuns buhg)
Drama, Greece : *Drah* ma
Drammen, Norway : *Drahm* mun
Drenthe, Netherlands : *Dren* ta
Dresden, Germany : *Drez* dun (Ger-
   man *Drays* dun)
Dreux, France : Druh
Driffield, England : *Drif* eeld
Drighlington, England : *Drig* ling tun
Drobeta-Turnu Severin, Romania :
   Droh bay tah Toohr nooh Say va *reen*
Drogheda, Ireland : *Droy* i da
Drogobych, Ukraine : *Drahg* a bich
   (UK *Drog* a bich) (Russian Drug a
   bich)
Droitwich, England : *Droyt* wich
Drôme, France : Drohm
Dromore, Northern Ireland : Dra *mawr*
   (UK Dra *maw*)
Dronfield, England : *Drahn* feeld (UK
   Dron feeld)
Droylsden, England : *Droylz* dun
Drumheller, Canada : *Drahm* hel ur
   (UK *Drahm* hel a)
Drummondville, Canada : *Drah* mund
   vil
Drumnadrochit, Scotland : Drahm na
   drah kit (UK Drahm na *drokh* it)
Druskininkai, Lithuania : *Droohs* kee
   neen kiy
Druzhkovka, Ukraine : Droosh *kawf* ka
Dryburgh (Abbey), Scotland : *Driy*
   buhrg (UK *Driy* bra)
Duarte, USA : *Dwahr* ti
Dubai, United Arab Emirates : Dooh
   biy

Dubbo, Australia : *Dah* boh
Dublin, Ireland; USA : *Dah* blin
Dubna, Russia : *Doohb* na
Dubrovnik, Croatia : Doo *brahv* nik
   (UK Doo *brov* nik) (Croatian Dooh
   brawv nik)
Dubuque, USA : Da *byoohk*
Duchesne, USA : Doo *shayn*
Ducos, France : Di *koh*
Dudelange, Luxembourg : Deed *lahnzh*
Dudinka, Russia : Doo *dying* ka
Dudley, England : *Dahd* li
Dueñas, Philippines : Dooh *ay* nyahs
Duisburg, Germany : *Doohs* buhrg (UK
   Dyoohz buhg) (German *Dees* boork)
Dukinfield, England : *Dah* kin feeld
Duluth, USA : Da *loohth*
Dulverton, England : *Dahl* vur tun
   (UK *Dahl* va tun)
Dulwich, England : *Dah* lij [According
   to Willey, p. 145, the name of the
   London district is pronounced either
   Dah lich or *Dah* lij.]
Dumaguete, Philippines : Dooh mah
   gay tay
Dumaresq, Australia : Da *mer* ik
Dumbarton, Scotland : Dahm *bahr* tun
   (UK Dahm *bah* tun)
Dum Dum, India : *Dahm* Dahm
Dumfries, Scotland : Dahm *frees*
Dumyat, Egypt : Doom *yaht*
Dunaújváros, Hungary : *Dooh* naw ooh
   i vah rohsh [The town's name ana-
   lyzes as Hungarian *Duna*, "Danube,"
   új, "new," *város*, "town."]
Dunbar, Scotland : Dahn *bahr* (UK
   Dahn *bah*)
Dunblane, Scotland : Dahn *blayn*
Duncan, USA : *Dahng* kun
¹**Dundalk**, Ireland : Dahn *dawk*
²**Dundalk**, USA : *Dahn* dawk
Dundas, Canada : Dahn *das*
Dundee, Scotland; South Africa : Dahn
   dee
Dunedin, New Zealand; USA : Dah *nee*
   din [Locally the New Zealand city's
   name is pronounced Dah *nee* dun.]
Dunfermline, Scotland : Dahn *fuhrm*
   lin (UK Dahn *fuhm* lin)

Dungannon, Northern Ireland : Dahn *gan* un

Dungarvan, Ireland : Dahn *gahr* vun (UK Dahn *gah* vun)

Dungeness, England : Dahn ja *nes*

Dunkeld, Scotland : Dahn *keld*

Dunkirk, France : Dahn *kuhrk* (UK Dahn *kuhk*)

Dun Laoghaire, Ireland : Dahn *Ler* i (UK Dahn *Li* a ri) (Irish Doohn *Ler* a) [The name of the Dublin suburb and passenger port was spelled *Dunleary* before it was renamed Kingstown from 1821 through 1920.]

Dunmore, USA : *Dahn* mawr (UK *Dahn* maw)

Dunoon, Scotland : Dah *noohn*

Duns, Scotland : Dahnz

Dunsinane, Scotland : Dahn *sin* un [The hill north of Perth is topped by an ancient fort that Shakespeare identified with the castle of Macbeth, and in his play the name requires the pronunciation Dahn si *nayn*, as can be seen from the lines below.]
I will not be afraid of death and bane Till Birnam forest come to Dunsinane [*Macbeth*, V. iii. 60].

Dunstable, England : *Dahn* sta bul

Dunwich, England : *Dahn* ich

Duque de Caxias, Brazil : Dooh kee dee Ka *shee* us

Duquesne, USA : Doo *kayn* (UK Dyoo *kayn*)

Durango, Mexico; USA : Doo *rang* goh (UK Dyoo *rang* goh)

Durazno, Uruguay : Dooh *rahs* noh

Durban, South Africa : *Duhr* bun (UK *Duh* bun)

Düren, Germany : *Dyooh* run (German *Dee* run)

Durgapur, India : *Door* ga poor

Durham, England; USA : *Duh* rum (UK *Dah* rum)

Durrës, Albania : *Door* us

Dushanbe, Tajikistan : *Dyooh* shahm bay

Düsseldorf, Germany : *Dooh* sul dawrf (UK *Doos* ul dawf) (German *Dee* sul dawrf)

Dutse, Nigeria : *Dooht* say

Duxbury, USA : *Dahks* ber i (UK *Dahks* bri)

Dvina, Europe : *Dvee* na

Dvůr Králové nad Labem, Czech Republic : Dvoohr Krah law vay nahd *Lah* bem

Dyfed, Wales : *Dah* vid (Welsh *Duh* ved) [An erroneous UK pronunciation *Dif* id is sometimes heard for the county name.]

Dyffryn, Wales : *Dahf* rin (Welsh *Duhf* rin)

Dymchurch, England : *Dim* chuhrch (UK *Dim* chuhch)

Dynevor, Wales : *Din* i vur (UK *Din* i va) [A local pronunciation of the castle and community's name is Di *nev* a, reflecting its Welsh spelling, *Dinefwr*.]

Dysart, Scotland : *Diy* zurt (UK *Diy* zut)

Dzerzhinsk, Russia : *Dzuhr* zhinsk (UK *Dzuh* zhinsk) (Russian Dzir *zhinsk*)

Dzhambul, Kazakhstan : Jahm *bool*

Dzhezkazgan, Kazakhstan : Jes kus *gahn*

Dzhizak, Uzbekistan : Jee *zahk*

Dzierżoniów, Poland : Jer *zhaw* nyoohf

Ealing, England : *Ee* ling

Earlston, Scotland : *Uhrl* stun (UK *Uhl* stun)

Easington, England : *Eez* ing tun

Easley, USA : *Eez* li

East : For names prefixed with this word and not given below, as *East Flanders, East London, East Sussex*, see the main name. (*East* is rarely stressed as a separate word.)

Eastbourne, England : *Eest* bawrn (UK *Eest* bawn)

East Dereham, England : Eest *Dir* um (UK ... *Di* a rum)

Easter (Island), Pacific Ocean : *Ees* tur

East Grinstead, England : Eest *Grin* stid

Easthampton, USA : Eest *hamp* tun

East Kilbride, Scotland : Eest Kil *briyd*

Eastlake, USA : *Eest* layk

Eastleigh, England : *Eest* li
Easton, England; USA : *Ees* tun
Eastpointe, USA : *Eest* poynt
East Retford, England : Eest *Ret* furd (UK ... *Ret* fud)
Eastwood, England : *Eest* wood
Eaton Socon, England : Ee tun *Soh* kun
Eau Claire, USA : Oh *Kler* (UK Oh *Klay* a)
Eauze, France : Ay *ohz*
Ebbw Vale, Wales : Eb oo *Vayl*
Eberswalde-Finow, Germany : Ay burs vahl da *Fee* noh
Eboli, Italy : *Ay* baw lee
Ebrington, England : *Eb* ring tun. [The name of the Gloucestershire village long had a local pronunciation US *Yah* bur tun, UK *Yah* ba tun, written *Yubberton*. Stokes precedes quote (1) below by citing a local rhyme beginning: "A Yubberton fool to Campden went," Campden being the nearby town Chipping Campden.]
　(1) "Yubberton" is still the local pronunciation. Will it finally oust Ebrington? [H.G. Stokes, *English Place-Names*, 1948].
　(2) The other [pronunciation], strictly local and used largely by older residents, is a legacy of an earlier form of the name [Pointon, p. 83].
Ebro, Spain : *Ee* broh (Spanish *Ay* broh)
Ecbatana, Iran : Ek *bat* un a
Ecclefechan, Scotland : Ek ul *fek* un
Eccles, England : *Ek* ulz
Eccleston, England : *Ek* ul stun
Ech Cheliff, Algeria : Esh Sha *leef*
Echmiadzin, Armenia : Ech mee a *dzeen*
Echternach, Luxembourg : *Ekh* tur nahkh
Echuca, Australia : Ee *chooh* ka
Ecorse, USA : Ee kawrs (UK *Ee* kaws)
Écouen, France : Ek *wahn*
Ecuador, South America : *Ek* wa dawr (UK *Ek* wa daw) (Spanish Ek wah *dhohr*) [Lloyd James 1937 recommends the pronunciation US Ek wa dawr, UK Ek wa *daw*.]

Edam, Netherlands : *Ee* dam (Dutch *Ay* dahm)
¹Ede, Netherlands : *Ay* da
²Ede, Nigeria : *Ay* day
Edéa, Cameroon : Ay *day* a
Edegem, Belgium : *Ay* da gaym
Eden, Australia; USA : *Ee* dun
Edenbridge, England : *Ee* dun brij
Edessa, Greece : I *des* a
Edgbaston, England : *Ej* bus tun
Edgehill, England : Ej *hil*
Edgewood, USA : *Ej* wood
Edgware, England : *Ej* wer (UK *Ej* way a)
Edina, USA : I *diy* na
Edinburg, USA : *Ed* in buhrg (UK *Ed* in buhg)
¹Edinburgh, Scotland : *Ed* in buhr a (UK *Ed* in bra) [There are various local pronunciations of the Scottish capital's name, rendered by such written forms as *Edinbro* and *Embro*.]
²Edinburgh, USA : *Ed* in buhrg (UK *Ed* in buhg)
¹Edington, England : *Ed* ing tun
²Edington, Scotland : *Ee* ding tun
Edirne, Turkey : Ay *dir* na (UK Ay *dee* a na)
Edison, USA : *Ed* i sun
Edmond, USA : *Ed* mund
Edmonds, USA : *Ed* mundz
Edmonton, Canada : *Ed* mun tun
Edmundston, Canada : *Ed* mun stun
Edom, Asia : *Ee* dum
Eeklo, Belgium : *Ay* kloh
Efate, Vanuatu : Ay *fah* tay
¹Effingham, England : *Ef* ing um
²Effingham, USA : *Ef* ing ham
Egedesminde, Greenland : *Ay* ga dhus min a
Eger, Hungary : *E* ger
Egham, England : *Eg* um
Egremont, England : *Eg* ra mahnt (UK *Eg* ra munt)
Egypt, Africa : *Ee* jipt
Eibar, Spain : *Ay* bahr
Eichstätt, Germany : *Iykh* shtet
Eidsvoll, Norway : *Ayts* vawl
Eifel, Germany : *Iy* ful

Eiger, Switzerland : *Iy* gur (UK *Iy* ga)
Eigg, Scotland : Eg
Eildon (Hills), Scotland : *Eel* dun
Eilean Donan, Scotland : El an *Doh* nun (UK ... *Don* an)
Eilenburg, Germany : *Iy* lun boork
Einbeck, Germany : *Iyn* bek
Eindhoven, Netherlands : *Iynt* hoh vun
Einsiedeln, Switzerland : *Iyn* zee duln
Eisenach, Germany : *Iy* zun ahkh
Eisenberg, Germany : *Iy* zun berk
Eisenhüttenstadt, Germany : *Iy* zun heet un shtaht
Eisenstadt, Austria : *Iy* zun shtaht
Eisleben, Germany : *Iys* lay bun
Ekibastuz, Kazakhstan : Ek ee *bahs* toohs (Russian Ek ee bahs *toohs*)
El Aaiún, Western Sahara : El Ah *yoohn*
El Alamein, Egypt : El *Al* a mayn
El Alto, Bolivia : El *Ahl* toh
Elam, Iran : *Ee* lum
Elat, Israel : *Ee* lat
Elâziğ, Turkey : E lah *zuh*
Elba, Italy : *El* ba (Italian *El* bah)
El Banco, Colombia : El *Bahng* koh
Elbasan, Albania : El bah *sahn*
Elbe, Germany : Elb (German *El* ba)
Elbeuf, France : El *buhf*
Elbląg, Poland : *El* blawngk
Elbrus, Russia : *El* broohs
Elburz (Mountains), Iran : *El* boorz
El Cajon, USA : El Ka *hohn*
El Centro, USA : El *Sen* troh
El Cerrito, USA : El Sa *ree* toh
Elche, Spain : *El* chay
Elda, Spain : *El* dah
¹**El Dorado**, USA (Arkansas, Kansas) : El Da *ray* doh [The pronunciation El Da *rah* doh is normally used for the "golden land" sought by the Spanish conquerors of America.]
²**El Dorado**, USA (California) : El Da *rah* doh
Eldoret, Kenya : El *doh* ret
Elektrostal, Russia : E lyek tra *stahl*
Elephantine, Egypt : E la fan *tiy* ni
El Escorial, Spain : El Es kohr *yahl*
Eleusis, Greece : I *looh* sis (UK I *lyooh* sis)

Eleuthera, Bahamas : I *looh* tha ra
El Faiyûm, Egypt : El Fiy *yoohm*
El Ferrol, Spain : El Fer *rohl*
¹**Elgin**, Scotland; USA (Texas) : *El* gin
²**Elgin**, USA (Illinois) : *El* jin
El Gîza, Egypt : El *Gee* za
Elías Piña, Dominican Republic : Ay lee ahs *Pee* nyah
Elis, Greece : *Ee* lis
Elista, Russia : E *lees* ta
Elizabeth, USA : I *liz* a buth
Elizabethton, USA : I liz a b*eth* tun
Elizabethtown, USA : I *liz* a buth town
El Jadida, Morocco : El Ja *dee* da
Ełk, Poland : Elk
Elkhart, USA : *El* kahrt (UK *Elk* haht)
Elko, USA : *El* koh
Elland, England : *El* und
Ellensburg, USA : *El* unz buhrg (UK *El* inz buhg)
Ellesmere (Island), Canada : *Elz* mir (UK *Elz* mi a)
Ellesmere Port, England : Elz mir *Pawrt* (UK Elz mi a *Pawt*)
Ellingham, England : *El* ing um [This is the usual pronunciation, but the village of this name in Northumberland is *El* in jum.]
Elliot Lake, Canada : El ee ut *Layk*
Ellis (Island), USA : *El* is
Ellsworth (Land), Antarctica : *Elz* wuhrth (UK *Elz* wuhth)
Ellwangen, Germany : *El* vahng un
El Mahalla el Kubra, Egypt : El Ma hal la el *Kooh* bra
El Mansura, Egypt : El Man *sooh* ra
Elmhurst, USA : *Elm* huhrst (UK *Elm* huhst)
Elmina, Ghana : El *mee* na
El Minya, Egypt : El *Min* ya
Elmira, USA : El *miy* ra
El Monte, USA : El *Mahn* ti (UK El *Mon* ti)
Elmshorn, Germany : *Elms* hawrn
El Obeid, Sudan : El Oh *biyd*
El Oro, Ecuador : El *Oh* roh
El Oued, Algeria : El *Wed*
El Paso, USA : El *Pa* soh [The name of the Texas city and port is sometimes

pronounced El *Pah* soh by those aware of its Spanish origin, while an East Coast pronunciation El *Pay* soh may also be heard.]

El Portal, USA : El Pawr *tal* (UK El Paw *tal*)

El Porvenir, Panama : El Pawr vay *neer*

El Progreso, Guatemala; Honduras : El Proh *gray* soh

El Reno, USA : El *Ree* noh

El Salvador, Central America : El *Sal* va dawr (UK El *Sal* va daw) (Spanish El Sahl vah *dhohr*)

El Seibo, Dominican Republic : El *Say* boh

Elsinore, Denmark; USA : El sa *nawr* (UK *El* si naw)

Elstow, England : *El* stoh

Elstree, England : *Els* tree

Elswick, England : *El* sik [The pronunciation is valid for most places of this name, but the district of Newcastle upon Tyne has a local pronunciation *El* zik.]

¹Eltham, Australia; New Zealand : *El* thum

²Eltham, England : *El* tum

El Tigre, Venezuela : El *Tee* gray

Elton, Russia : *El* tun (Russian El *tawn*)

El Tur, Egypt : El *Toohr*

Elven, France : Ayl *vahn*

Ely, England; USA : *Ee* li

Embu, Kenya : *Em* booh

Emden, Germany : *Em* dun

Emi Koussi, Chad : Ay mee *Kooh* see

Emilia-Romagna, Italy : Ay mee lya Roh *mahn* ya

Emmaus, Israel : E *may* us

Emmen, Netherlands : *Em* un

Emmerich, Germany : *Em* a rikh

Empangeni, South Africa : Em pang *gay* ni

Empoli, Italy : *Em* poh lee

Emporia, USA : Em *paw* ri a

Ems, Germany : Emz (German Ems)

Emsworth, England : *Emz* wuhrth (UK *Emz* wuth)

Encarnación, Paraguay : En kahr nah *syohn*

Encinitas, USA : En si *nee* tus

Enderby (Land), Antarctica : *End* ur bi (UK *En* da bi)

Enfield, Australia; England; USA : *En* feeld

Engadine, Switzerland : Eng ga *deen*

En-gedi, Israel : En *gee* diy

Engels, Russia : *Eng* gulz (Russian *Eng* gils)

Enggano, Indonesia : Eng *gah* noh

Enghien, Belgium : Ahn *gyang*

Enghien-les-Bains, France : Ahn gang lay *Bahn*

England, Europe : *Ing* glund [The name is unique in having a stressed "i" sound represented by the letter *e*. (Italian *Inghilterra* represents the sound more faithfully.) In *Spelling Pronunciations* (1901), German linguist Emil Koeppel tells how a discussion with English youngsters convinced him that the pronunciation *Eng* glund was gaining ground. But did he mistake their casual or regional pronunciations for the standard one?] While this word and its derivations are still usable, can we not all agree on their pronunciation, such that the first syllable rhymes with 'sting' and does not take the sound *eng* as spelt, a noise that would be unique in the language? [Kingsley Amis, *The King's English*, 1997].

Englewood, USA : *Eng* gul wood

Enid, USA : *Ee* nid

Enna, Italy : *En* a

Ennerdale, England : *En* ur dayl (UK *En* a dayl)

Ennezat, France : En *zah*

Ennis, Ireland : *En* is

Enniscorthy, Ireland : En is *kawr* thi (UK En is *kaw* thi)

Enniskillen, Northern Ireland : En is *kil* un

Enns, Austria : Ens

Enschede, Netherlands : *En* ska day (Dutch *En* skha day)

Ensenada, Mexico : En say *nah* dhah

Ensisheim, France : En zee *saym*

Entebbe, Uganda : En *teb* i
Entre Ríos, Argentina : En tray *ree* ohs
Entzheim, France : En *tsaym*
Enugu, Nigeria : Ay *nooh* gooh
Epe, Netherlands : *Ay* pa
Épernay, France : Ay per *nay*
Ephesus, Turkey : *Ef* i sus
¹**Ephrata**, USA (Pennsylvania) : *Ef* ra ta
²**Ephrata**, USA (Washington) : Ee *fray* ta
Epidaurus, Greece : Ep i *daw* rus
Épinal, France : Ay pee *nahl*
Epirus, Greece : I *piy* rus
Epping, England : *Ep* ing
Epsom, England : *Ep* sum
Epworth, England : *Ep* wuhrth (UK *Ep* wuth)
Equatorial Guinea, Africa : Eek wa taw ri ul *Gi* ni (UK Ek wa taw ri ul...)
Ercolano, Italy : Er koh *lah* noh
Erebus, Antarctica : *Er* i bus
Erewash, England : *Er* i wosh
Erfurt, Germany : *Er* fuhrt (UK *Ay* a fuht) (German *Er* foort)
Erg Chech, Africa : Erg *Shesh*
Erg Iguidi, Africa : Erg Ee gee *dee*
Eridu, Iraq : *Er* i dooh
Erie, USA : *Ir* i (UK *I* a ri)
Erith, England : *Ir* ith (UK *I* a rith)
Eritrea, Africa : Er i *tree* a (UK Er i *tray* a)
Erlangen, Germany : Er *lahng* un
Erlanger, USA : Ur *lang* gur
Ermelo, Netherlands; South Africa : *Er* ma loh (UK *Ay* a ma loh)
Erne, Northern Ireland : Uhrn (UK Uhn)
Er Rif, Morocco : Er *Rif*
Ersekë, Albania : Er *say* ka
Erstein, France : Er *stayn*
Erythraean (Sea), Asia : Er i *three* un
Erzgebirge, Europe : *Erts* ga bir ga (UK *Ay* uts ga bi a ga)
Erzurum, Turkey : Er za *roohm* (UK Ay a za *roohm*)
Esbjerg, Denmark : *Es* byuhrg (UK *Es* byuhg) (Danish *Es* byer)
Escalante, Philippines : Es kah *lahn* tay
Escanaba, USA : Es ka *nah* ba
Esch, Luxembourg : Esh

Eschwege, Germany : *Esh* vay ga
Eschweiler, Germany : *Esh* viy lur
Escondido, USA : Es kun *dee* doh
Escuintla, Guatemala : Es *kwint* lah
Esfahan, Iran : Es fa *hahn*
Esher, England : *Ee* shur (UK *Ee* sha)
Eskilstuna, Sweden : *Es* kils tee na
Eskişehir, Turkey : Es ki she *hir*
Esmeraldas, Ecuador : Es mah *rahl* dhahs
Espaillat, Dominican Republic : Es piy *yah*
Esperanza, Argentina : Es pay *rahn* sah
Espírito Santo, Brazil : Es pi ri toh *Sahn* toh (Portuguese I shpee ree tooh *Sahn* tooh)
Espíritu Santo, Vanuatu : Es pee ree tooh *Sahn* tyoh
Espoo, Finland : *Es* poh
Esquimalt, Canada : I *skwiy* mawlt
Essaouira, Morocco : Es ah *wee* rah
Essen, Germany : *Es* un
Essendon, Australia : *Es* un dun
Essex, England; USA : *Es* iks
Esslingen, Germany : *Es* ling un
Essonne, France : E *sawn*
Estância, Brazil : Ee *shtahn* sya
Este, Italy : *Es* tay
Estelí, Nicaragua : Es tay *lee*
Esterhazy, Canada : *Es* tur hay zi (UK *Es* ta hay zi)
Estevan, Canada : *Es* ta van
Estonia, Europe : E *stoh* ni a
Estoril, Portugal : Es ta *ril* (Portuguese Eesh too *ril*)
Estremoz, Portugal : Eesh tri *mawsh*
Esztergom, Hungary : *Es* tur gohm
Étampes, France : Ay *tahnp*
Étaples, France : Ay *tahpl*
Etawah, India : Ay *tah* wa
Etchojoa, Mexico : E choh *hoh* ah
Ethiopia, Africa : Ee thi *oh* pi a
Etive, Scotland : *Et* iv
Etna, Italy : *Et* na
Etobicoke, Canada : I *toh* ba kohk
Eton, England : *Ee* tun
Etruria, Italy : I *troor* i a (UK I *troo* a ri a)
Etterbeek, Belgium : *Et* ur bayk

Ettlingen, Germany : *Et* ling un
Ettrick, Scotland : *Et* rik
Eu, France : Uh
Euboea, Greece : Yooh *bee* a (UK Yooh *bi* a)
Eugene, USA : Yooh *jeen*
Euless, USA : *Yooh* lus
Eunice, USA : *Yooh* nis
Eupen, Belgium : *Oy* pun (UK *Uh* pen) (French Uh *pen*)
Euphrates, Asia : Yoo *fray* teez
Eure, France : Uhr
Eureka, USA : Yoo *ree* ka
Europe : *Yoor* up (UK *Yoo* a rup)
Europoort, Netherlands : *Yoo* roh pawrt (UK *Yoo* a roh pawt)
Euskirchen, Germany : *Oys* kir khun
Eustis, USA : *Yooh* stis
Euston, England : *Yooh* stun
Eutin, Germany : Oy *teen*
Euxton, England : *Eks* tun
Evanston, USA : *Ev* un stun
Evansville, USA : *Ev* unz vil
Evenlode, England : *Ee* vun lohd
Evere, Belgium : *Ay* va ra
Everest, Nepal : *Ev* rust (UK *Ev* rist)
Everett, USA : *Ev* rut (UK *Ev* rit)
Evergem, Belgium : *Ay* vur gaym
Everglades, USA : *Ev* ur glaydz (UK *Ev* a glaydz)
Eversholt, England : *Ev* ur shohlt (UK *Ev* a sholt)
Eversley, England : *Ev* urz li (UK *Ev* uz li)
Everton, England : *Ev* ur tun (UK *Ev* a tun)
Evesham, England : *Eev* shum [A local pronunciation *Ee* vi shum also exists for the name of the Worcestershire town.]
Évian-les-Bains, France : Ay vyahn lay *Bahn*
Évora, Portugal : *E* voo ra
Évreux, France : Ay *vruh*
Évry, France : Ay *vree*
Ewell, England : *Yooh* ul
Ewelme, England : *Yooh* elm
Ewhurst, England : *Yooh* huhrst (UK *Yooh* huhst)

Ewing, USA : *Yooh* ing
Exeter, England; USA : *Ek* sa tur (UK *Ek* si ta)
Exmoor, England : *Eks* moor (UK *Eks* moo a)
Exmouth, England : *Eks* muth
Extremadura, Spain : Eks tray ma *dooh* ra (Spanish Es tray mah *dhooh* rah)
Eyam, England : Eem
Eybens, France : Ay *bahns*
Eye, England : Iy
Eymet, France : Ay *may*
Eynsford, England : *Aynz* furd (UK *Aynz* fud)
Eynsham, England : *Ayn* shum [*En* shum also exists as a local pronunciation of the Oxfordshire town's name.]
Eyre, Australia : Er (UK *Ay* a)
[1]**Eyton**, England : *Iy* ton [Places in Shropshire have this pronunciation, but the village of this name in Herefordshire is *Ay* tun.]
[2]**Eyton**, Wales : *Ee* tun
Fabriano, Italy : Fah bree *ah* noh
Faenza, Italy : Fah *en* zah
Faeroe (Islands), Atlantic Ocean : *Fer* oh (UK *Fay* a roh)
Fagatogo, American Samoa : Fahng gah *tohng* goh
Failsworth, England : *Faylz* wurth (UK *Faylz* wuhth)
Fairbanks, USA : *Fer* bangks (UK *Fay* a bangks)
Fairborn, USA : *Fer* bawrn (UK *Fay* a bawn)
Fairfax, USA : *Fer* faks (UK *Fay* a faks)
Fairfield, Australia; USA : *Fer* feeld (UK *Fay* a feeld)
Fairford, England : *Fer* furd (UK *Fay* a fud)
Fairhaven, USA : *Fer* hay vun (UK *Fay* a hay vun)
Fairmont, USA : *Fer* mahnt (UK *Fay* a mont)
Faisalabad, Pakistan : *Fiy* sul a bad
Faizabad, India : *Fiy* za bad
Fajardo, Puerto Rico : Fa *hahr* doh
Fakenham, England : *Fay* kun um
Fakfak, Indonesia : *Fahk* fahk

Falaise, France : Fah *lez*
Falkensee, Germany : *Fahl* kun zay
Falkirk, Scotland : *Fawl* kuhrk (UK *Fawl* kuhk)
Falkland, Scotland : *Fawk* lund (UK *Fawlk* lund)
Falkland (Islands), Atlantic Ocean : *Fawk* lund (UK *Fawlk* lund) [Ross, p. 86, recommends omission of the *l* in the UK pronunciation.]
Falköping, Sweden : *Fahl* shuh ping
Falmouth, England; USA : *Fal* muth
Falster, Denmark : *Fahl* stur
Falun, Sweden : *Fah* loon
Famagusta, Cyprus : Fah ma *goohs* ta (UK Fam a *goos* ta)
Fano, Italy : *Fah* noh
Fao, Iraq : Fow
Fareham, England : *Fer* um (UK *Fay* a rum)
Farghona, Uzbekistan : Fur *gaw* na
Fargo, USA : *Fahr* goh (UK *Fah* goh)
Faridabad, India : Fah *ree* dah bahd
Faringdon, England : *Far* ing dun
Farmington, USA : *Fahr* ming tun (UK *Fah* ming tun)
Farnborough, England : *Fahrn* buhr oh (UK *Fahn* bra)
Farne (Islands), England : Fahrn (UK Fahn)
Farnham, Canada; England : *Fahr* num (UK *Fah* num)
Farnworth, England : *Fahrn* wuhrth (UK *Fahn* wuhth)
Faro, Portugal : *Fah* roh (Portuguese *Fah* rooh)
Faroe (Islands), Atlantic Ocean : *Fer* oh (UK *Fay* a roh)
Fars, Iran : Fahrz
Fashoda, Sudan : Fa *shoh* da
Faslane (Bay), Scotland : *Faz* layn
Fastnet, Ireland : *Fast* net (UK *Fahst* net)
Fategarh, India : Fa *tay* gur
Fatepur, India : *Fah* ta poor
Fátima, Portugal : *Fat* i ma (Portuguese *Fah* tee ma)
Faversham, England : *Fa* vur shum (UK *Fa* va shum)

Fawley, England : *Faw* li
Fayetteville, USA : *Fay* ut vul (UK *Fay* et vil) [Some speakers, especially locally, pronounce the name *Fayt* vul.]
Fazakerley, England : Fa *zak* ur li (UK Fa *zak* a li)
Featherstone, England : *Fedh* ur stun (UK *Fedh* a stun)
Fécamp, France : Fay *kahn*
Fedala, Morocco : Fe *dah* la
Feilding, New Zealand : *Feel* ding
Feira de Santana, Brazil : Fay ra dee Sahn *tahn* na
Felixstowe, England : *Fee* lik stoh
Fellbach, Germany : *Fel* bahkh
Felling, England : *Fel* ing
Felpham, England : *Fel* pum
Felsted, England : *Fel* stid
Feltham, England : *Fel* tum
Feltre, Italy : *Fel* tray
Fenstanton, England : Fen *stan* tun
Fenwick, England : *Fen* ik
Feodosiya, Ukraine : Fee a *doh* si ya
Fergana, Uzbekistan : Fir ga *nah*
Fermanagh, Northern Ireland : Fur *man* a (UK Fa *man* a)
Fermo, Italy : *Fer* moh
Fermoy, Ireland : Fur *moy* (UK Fuh *moy*)
Ferndale, USA : *Fuhrn* dayl (UK *Fuhn* dayl)
Fernie, Canada : *Fuhr* ni (UK *Fuh* ni)
Ferns, Ireland : Fuhrnz (UK Fuhnz)
Ferrara, Italy : Fa *rah* ra (UK Fi *rah* ra) (Italian Fer *rah* rah)
Ferryville, Tunisia : *Fer* ee vil
Fès, Morocco : Fes
Feurs, France : Fuhr
Fez, Morocco : Fez
Fezzan, Libya : Fa *zan*
Ffestiniog, Wales : Fes *tin* i ahg (UK Fes *tin* i og) (Welsh Fes *din* yog) [Welsh double *f* is pronounced as *f*, but a single *f* is pronounced as *v*, as in Dyfed.]
Ffynnongroew, Wales : Fah nun *groy* ooh
Fianarantsoa, Madagascar : Fyah nah rahn *tsoh* a

Fidenza, Italy : Fee *den* tsah
Fier, Albania : *Fee* er
Fiesole, Italy : Fyay *zoh* lay
Fife, Scotland : Fiyf
Figueres, Spain : Fee *gay* res
Fiji, Pacific Ocean : *Fee* jee
Filadelfia, Paraguay : Fee lah dhel *fee* ah
Filchner (Ice Shelf), Antarctica : *Filk* nur
Filey, England : *Fiy* li
Fillmore, USA : *Fil* mawr (UK *Fil* maw)
Finchampstead, England : *Finch* um sted
Finchingfield, England : *Finch* ing feeld
Finchley, England : *Finch* li
Findhorn, Scotland : *Find* hawrn (UK *Find* hawn)
Findlay, USA : *Find* li
Finistère, France : Fee nee *ster*
Finisterre, Spain : Fi ni *ster* (UK Fi ni *stay* a) (Spanish Fee nee *ster* e)
Finland, Europe : *Fin* lund
Finsbury, England : *Finz* ber i (UK *Finz* bri)
Finsteraarhorn, Switzerland : Fin sta *rahr* hawrn
Firminy, France : Feer mee *nee*
Firozabad, India : Fi *roh* za bad
Firozpur, India : Fi *rohz* poor
Firth of Forth, Scotland : Fuhrth uv Fawrth (UK Fuhth uv *Fawth*)
Fishguard, Wales : *Fish* gahrd (UK *Fish* gahd)
Fismes, France : Feem
Fitchburg, USA : *Fich* buhrg (UK *Fich* buhg)
Flagstaff, USA : *Flag* staf (UK *Flag* stahf)
Flamborough (Head), England : *Flam* buhr oh (UK *Flam* bra)
Flanders, Europe : *Flan* durz (UK *Flahn* duz)
Fleetwood, England : *Fleet* wood
Flémalle, Belgium : Flay *mahl*
Flemington, USA : *Flem* ing tun
Flensburg, Germany : *Flents* boork
Flers, France : Fler
Fleurus, Belgium : Fluh *rees*

Flevoland, Netherlands : *Flay* voh lahnt
Flinders, Australia : *Flin* durz (UK *Flin* duz)
Flin Flon, Canada : *Flin* Flahn (UK *Flin* Flon)
Flint, USA; Wales : Flint
Flitwick, England : *Flit* ik
Flodden, England : *Flah* dun (UK *Flod* un)
Florence, Italy; USA : *Flaw* runs (UK *Flor* unts)
Florencia, Colombia : Floh *ren* see ah
Flores, Azores; Brazil; Guatemala; Indonesia : *Flaw* rus (UK *Flaw* riz)
Florianópolis, Brazil : Floh ree a *naw* pooh lis
Florida, Cuba; Uruguay; USA : *Flaw* ri da (UK *Flor* i da) (Spanish Floh *ree* dhah) [The name of the US state is of Spanish origin and would thus have originally been pronounced as shown, with the stress on the second syllable. The present pronunciation, with stress on the first syllable, is of English origin, with the name perhaps copied from a Spanish map and taken as the Latin word *florida*, feminine of *floridus*, "flowery."]
Floridablanca, Philippines : Floh ree dhah *blahng* kah
Florida Keys, USA : Flaw ri da *Keez* (UK Flo ri da...)
Florina, Greece : *Flaw* ree nah
Flotta, Scotland : *Flah* ta (UK *Flot* a)
Flushing, USA : *Flah* shing
Foça, Turkey : Foh *chah*
Fochabers, Scotland : *Fah* ka burz (UK *Fok* a buz)
Focşani, Romania : Fohk *shahn*
Foggia, Italy : *Fahj* ya (UK *Foj* ya) (Italian *Faw* jah)
Fogo, Canada : *Foh* goh
Foix, France : Fwah
Foligno, Italy : Foh *leen* yoh
Folkestone, England : *Fohk* stun
Folschviller, France : Fohlsh vee *ler*
Folsom, USA : *Fohl* sum
Fond du Lac, USA : *Fahnd* Lak (UK *Fawn* ja Lak)

Fongafale, Tuvalu : Fawng gah *fah* lay

Fontaine, France : Fohn *ten*

Fontainebleau, France : *Fahn* tun bloh (UK *Fon* tin bloh) (French Fawn ten *bloh*) [An erroneous or humorous pronunciation of the former royal town's name by some English speakers is *Fown* tin blooh, representing an anglicized spelling "Fountainblue."]

Fontana, USA : Fahn *tan* a (UK Fon *tah* na)

Fontenay-le-Comte, France : Fawnt nayl *Kohnt*

Fontenoy, Belgium : *Fon* tun wah (French Font *nwah*)

Fontevrault, France : Fawnt *vroh*

Footscray, Australia : *Foots* kray

Forbach, France : Fawr *bahk*

Forbes, Australia : Fawrbz (UK Fawbz)

Forcados, Nigeria : Fawr *kah* dohs (UK Faw *kah* dohs)

Forchheim, Germany : *Fawrkh* hiym

Fordingbridge, England : *Fawrd* ing brij (UK *Fawd* ing brij)

Forest, Belgium : Foh *ray*

Forez, France : Faw *ray*

Forfar, Scotland : *Fawr* fur (UK *Faw* fa) [A spelling pronunciation of the town's name also exists as US *Fawr* fahr, UK *Faw* fah.]

Forlì, Italy : Fawr *lee*

Formby, England : *Fawrm* bi (UK *Fawm* bi)

Formia, Italy : *Fawr* mee ah

Formiga, Brazil : Foor *mee* ga

Formosa, Argentina : Fawr *moh* sah (UK Faw *moh* sa)

Forres, Scotland : *Fawr* is (UK *For* is)

Forst, Germany : Fawrst

Fortaleza, Brazil : Fawr ta *lay* za (UK Faw ta *lay* za)

Fort-Archambault, Chad : Fawr Ahr shahm *boh* (UK ... Ah shahm *boh*)

Fort Bragg, USA : Fawrt *Brag* (UK Fawt...)

Fort Collins, USA : Fawrt *Kah* linz (UK Fawt *Kol* inz)

Fort-de-France, Martinique : Fawr da *Frahns* (UK Faw...)

Fort Dodge, USA : Fawrt *Dahj* (UK Fawt *Doj*)

Fort Erie, Canada : Fawrt *Ir* i (UK Fawt *I* a ri)

Fort Frances, Canada : Fawrt *Fran* sus (UK Fawt *Frahn* sis)

Forth, Scotland : Fawrth (UK Fawth)

Fort Jameson, Zambia : Fawrt *Jaym* sun (UK Fawt...)

Fort Johnston, Malawi : Fawrt *Jahn* stun (UK Fawt *Jon* stun)

Fort Knox, USA : Fawrt *Nahks* (UK Fawt *Noks*)

Fort-Lamy, Chad : Fawr La *mee* (UK Faw...)

Fort Lauderdale, USA : Fawrt *Law* dur dayl (UK Fawt *Law* da dayl)

Fort Leavenworth, USA : Fawrt *Lev* un wuhrth (UK Fawt *Lev* un wuhth)

Fort Lee, USA : Fawrt *Lee* (UK Fawt...)

Fort Liard, Canada : Fawrt *Lee* ahrd (UK Fawt *Lee* ahd)

Fort Macleod, Canada : Fawrt Ma *klowd* (UK Fawt...)

Fort McMurray, Canada : Fawrt Muk *mah* ri (UK Fawt...)

Fort McPherson, Canada : Fawrt Muk *fuhr* sun (UK Fawt Muk *fuh* sun)

Fort Madison, USA : Fawrt *Mad* is un (UK Fawt...)

Fort Myers, USA : Fawrt *Miy* urz (UK Fawt *Miy* uz)

Fort Pierce, USA : Fawrt *Pirs* (UK Fawt *Pi* us)

Fort Portal, Uganda : Fawrt *Pawr* tul (UK Fawt *Paw* tul)

Fort Rosebury, Zambia : Fawrt *Rohz* beri (UK Fawt *Rohz* bri)

Fort St. John, Canada : Fawrt Saynt *Jahn* (UK Fawt Sunt *Jon*)

Fort Smith, Canada; USA : Fawrt *Smith* (UK Fawt...)

Fort Sumter, USA : Fawrt *Sahm* tur (UK Fawt *Sahm* ta)

Fort Victoria, Zimbabwe : Fawrt Vik *taw* ri a (UK Fawt...)

Fort Wayne, USA : Fawrt *Wayn* (UK Fawt...)

Fort William, Scotland : Fawrt *Wil* yum (UK Fawt...)

Fort Worth, USA : Fawrt *Wuhrth* (UK Fawt *Wuhth*)

Foshan, China : Foh *shahn*

Fos-sur-Mer, France : Fohs seer *Mer*

Fotheringhay, England : *Fah* dhur ing gay (UK *Fodh* a ring hay) [The name of the Northamptonshire village, famous as the site of the castle where Mary Queen of Scots was executed in 1587, is normally pronounced as shown, although the castle itself, as referred to in historical terms, is usually UK *Fodh* a ring gay. The latter pronunciation is further prompted by the name's alternate spelling of *Fotheringay*.]

Fouesnant, France : Fway *nahn*

Fougères, France : Fooh *zher*

Foula, Scotland : *Fooh* la

Foulness, England : Fowl *nes*

Fouta Djallon, Guinea : Fooh tah Jah *lohn*

Foveaux (Strait), New Zealand : *Foh* voh

Fowey, England : Foy

The form *Foy* in 1576 already shows the modern pronunciation [O.J. Padel, *A Popular Dictionary of Cornish Place-Names*, 1988].

Foxe (Basin), Canada : Fahks (UK Foks)

Foyle, Northern Ireland : Foyl

Framingham, USA : *Fray* ming ham (UK *Fray* ming um)

Framlingham, England : *Fram* ling ham (UK *Fram* ling um)

Franca, Brazil : *Frang* ka

France, Europe : Frants (UK Frahnts) (French Frahns)

Franceville, Gabon : *Frans* vil (UK *Frahns* vil) (French Frahns *veel*)

Franche-Comté, France : Frahnsh Kahn *tay* (UK Fronsh Kon *tay*) (French Frahnsh Kawn *tay*)

Francistown, Botswana : *Fran* sis town (UK *Frahn* sis town)

Franconia, Germany : Frang *koh* ni a

Frankenthal, Germany : *Frahng* kun tahl

Frankfort, USA : *Frangk* furt (UK *Frangk* fut) [This spelling and pronunciation was at one time current in English for **Frankfurt**.]

Frankfurt, Germany : *Frangk* furt (UK *Frangk* fuht) (German *Frahngk* foort) [According to Ross, p. 90, "To use the German pronunciation would be pedantic."]

Frankfurt am Main, Germany : Frahngk foort ahm *Miyn*

Frankfurt an der Oder, Germany : Frahngk foort ahn dur *Oh* dur

Franklin, Canada; USA : *Frangk* lin

Františkovy Lázně, Czech Republic : Frahn teesh kaw vee *Lahz* nye

Franz Josef Land, Russia : Frans *Joh* zuf Land (UK Frans *Joh* zif...)

Frascati, Italy : Frah *skah* tee

Fraser, Canada; USA : *Fray* zur (UK *Fray* za)

Fraserburgh, Scotland : *Fray* zur buhr oh (UK *Fray* za bra)

Frattamaggiore, Italy : Frah tah mah *joh* ray

Frauenfeld, Switzerland : *Frow* un felt

Fray Bentos, Uruguay : Fray *Ben* tohs (UK ... *Ben* tos) (Spanish Friy *Bayn* taws)

Fredericia, Denmark : Fred a *rish* i a (Danish Fray dha *rayd* syah)

Frederick, USA : *Fred* rik

Fredericksburg, USA : *Fred* riks buhrg (UK *Fred* riks buhg)

Fredericton, Canada : *Fred* rik tun

Frederiksberg, Denmark : *Fred* riks buhrg (UK *Fred* riks buhg) (Danish Fredh regz *ber*)

Frederiksborg, Denmark : *Fred* riks bawrg (UK *Fred* riks bawg) (Danish Fredh regz *bawr*)

Frederikshåb, Greenland : Fredh regz *hawp*

Frederikshavn, Denmark : *Fred* riks hah fun (UK *Fred* riks hah vun) (Danish Fredh regz *hown*)

Frederiksted, US Virgin Islands : *Fred* rik sted

Fredonia, USA : Fri *doh* ni a

Fredrikstad, Norway : *Fred* rik stat (UK *Fred* rik staht) (Norwegian *Fred* rik sta)

Freeport, Bahamas; USA : *Free* pawrt (UK *Free* pawt)

Freetown, Sierra Leone : *Free* town

Freiberg, Germany : *Friy* buhrg (UK *Friy* buhg) (German *Friy* berk) [In their English pronunciations, the names of this city and of **Freiburg** are indistinguishable, and even in German they demand differentiation.]

Freiburg, Germany : *Friy* buhrg (UK *Friy* buhg) (German *Friy* boork)

Freising, Germany : *Friy* zing

Freital, Germany : *Friy* tahl

Fréjus, France : *Fray* zhoohs (French Fray *zhees*)

Fremantle, Australia : *Free* man tul [Some Australians favor an alternate pronunciation Fri *man* tul for the Western Australia city.]

Fremont, USA : *Free* mahnt (UK *Free* mont)

Fresnes, France : Fren

Fresnillo, Mexico : Fres *nee* yoh

Fresno, USA : *Frez* noh [Purists claim that the name of the California city, as the Spanish word for "ash," should be pronounced *Fres* noh, but the *z* sound generally prevails.]

Freudenstadt, Germany : *Froy* dun shtaht

Freycinet (Peninsula), Australia : *Fray* sa nay

Fribourg, Switzerland : *Free* buhrg (UK *Free* boo ug) (French Fri *boohr*)

Friedberg, Germany : *Freet* berk

Friedrichshafen, Germany : *Freed* rikhs hah fun

Friern Barnet, England : Friy urn *Bahr* nit (UK Friy un *Bah* nit) [The name of the London district has a variable local pronunciation, as noted below.] Usually pronounced as in "friar" by locals, but some prefer "free-un" [Willey, p. 184].

Friesland, Netherlands : *Freez* lund (Dutch *Fris* lahnt)

Frinton-on-Sea, England : Frin tun ahn *See* (UK ... on...)

Frisian (Islands), Europe : *Free* zhun (UK *Free* zi un)

Friuli, Italy : Free *ooh* lee

Frobisher (Bay), Canada : *Froh* bi shur (UK *Froh* bi sha)

Frodsham, England : *Frahd* shum (UK *Frod* shum)

¹Frome, England : Froohm [Those unfamiliar with the name of the Somerset town sometimes pronounce it as **²Frome**.]

²Frome, Australia : Frohm

Frontenac, USA : *Frahn* ta nak (UK *Fron* ta nak)

Frontera, Mexico : Frawn *tay* rah

Frosinone, Italy : Froh zee *noh* nay

Fuerte Olimpo, Paraguay : Fwer tay Oh *leem* poh

Fuerteventura, Canary Islands : Fwer tay ven *tooh* rah

Fujairah, United Arab Emirates : Foo *jiy* ra

Fuji, Japan : *Fooh* jee

Fujian, China : Fooh *jyen*

Fujisawa, Japan : Fooh jee *sah* wah

Fujiyama, Japan : Fooh jee *yah* mah

Fukuchiyama, Japan : Fooh kooh chee *yah* mah

Fukui, Japan : Fooh *kooh* ee

Fukuoka, Japan : Fooh kooh *oh* kah

Fukushima, Japan : Fooh kooh *shee* mah

Fukuyama, Japan : Fooh kooh *yah* mah

Fulda, Germany : *Fool* da

Fulham, England : *Fool* am

Fullerton, USA : *Fool* ur tun (UK *Fool* a tun)

Fulton, USA : *Fool* tun

Fulwood, England : *Fool* wood

Funabashi, Japan : Fooh nah *bah* shee

Funafuti, Tuvalu : Fooh nah *fooh* tee

Funchal, Madeira : Foon *chahl* (Portuguese Foohn *shahl*)

Fundy, Canada : *Fahn* di

Furneaux (Group), Australia : *Fuhr* noh (UK *Fuh* noh)

Furneux Pelham, England : Fuhr niks *Pel* um (UK Fuh niks...)

Fürstenfeldbruck, Germany : Feer stun *felt* brook
Fürstenwalde, Germany : Feer stun *vahl* da
Fürth, Germany : Feert
Fushun, China : Fooh *shoon*
Füssen, Germany : *Fees* un
Futuna (Islands), Pacific Ocean : Fooh *tooh* nah
Fuxin, China : Fooh *shin*
Fuzhou, China : Fooh *joh*
Fylde, England : Fiyld
Fyn, Denmark : Fuhn
Gabès, Tunisia : Gah *bes*
Gabon, Africa : Ga *bohn* (UK *Gab* on)
Gaborone, Botswana : Gah ba *roh* ni (UK Gab a *roh* ni)
Gabrovo, Bulgaria : *Gah* broh voh
Gadsden, USA : *Gadz* dun
Gaeta, Italy : Gah *ay* tah
Gaetulia, Libya : Ji *tooh* li a (UK Ji *tyooh* li a)
Gafsa, Tunisia : *Gaf* sa
Gagarin, Russia : Ga *gah* rin
Gagnoa, Côte d'Ivoire : Gah *nyoh* ah
Gahanna, USA : Ga *han* a
Gainesville, USA : *Gaynz* vil
Gainsborough, England : *Gaynz* buhr oh (UK *Gaynz* bra)
Gairloch, Scotland : *Ger* lahk (UK *Gay* a lokh)
Gaithersburg, USA : *Gay* thurz buhrg (UK *Gay* thuz buhg)
Galápagos (Islands), Pacific Ocean : Ga *lah* pa gohs (UK Ga *lap* a gus) (Spanish Gah *lah* pah gohs) [A pronunciation Ga la *pay* gohs is sometimes heard for the island group and was actually recommended by Lloyd James 1937.]
Galashiels, Scotland : Ga la *sheelz*
Galaţi, Romania : Ga *lahts*
Galatia, Asia : Ga *lay* sha
Galena, USA : Ga *lee* na
Galesburg, USA : *Gaylz* buhrg (UK *Gaylz* buhg)
Galich, Russia : *Gah* lich
Galicia, Europe : Ga *lish* a (UK Ga *lis* i a)

Galilee, Israel : *Gal* a lee (UK *Gal* i lee)
Gallatin, USA : *Gal* a tun
Galle, Sri Lanka : Gahl
Gallipoli, Italy; Turkey : Ga *lip* a li
Gallipolis, USA : Gal a pa *lees* (UK Gal i pa *lees*)
Galloway, Scotland : *Gal* a way
Gallup, USA : *Gal* up
Galveston, USA : *Gal* va stun
Galway, Ireland : *Gawl* way
Gambia, Africa : *Gam* bi a
Gambier (Islands), Pacific Ocean : *Gam* bir (UK *Gam* bi a)
Gäncä, Azerbaijan : Gahn *jah*
Gander, Canada : *Gan* dur (UK *Gan* da)
Gandhinagar, India : Gahn di *nah* gur
Gandía, Spain : Gahn *dee* ah
Ganges, India : *Gan* jeez
Gangtok, India : Gung *tawk*
Ganshoren, Belgium : *Gahns* haw run
Gansu, China : Gahn *sooh*
Ganzhou, China : Gahn *joh*
Gao, Mali : Gow
Gap, France : Gahp
Garanhuns, Brazil : Ga ra *nyoohns*
Garbsen, Germany : *Gahrp* sun
Gard, France : Gahr
Garda, Italy : *Gahr* da (UK *Gah* da) (Italian *Gahr* dah)
Gardena, USA : Gahr *dee* na (UK Gah *dee* na)
Garfield, USA : *Gahr* feeld (UK *Gah* feeld)
Garforth, England : *Gahr* furth (UK *Gah* futh)
Garioch, Scotland : *Ger* i (UK *Gee* a ri)
Garissa, Kenya : Gah *ree* sah
Garland, USA : *Gahr* lund (UK *Gah* lund)
Garmisch-Partenkirchen, Germany : Gahr mish Pahr tun *kir* khun
Garonne, France : Ga *rohn* (UK Ga *ron*) (French Gah *rawn*)
Garoua, Cameroon : Gah *rooh* ah
Garut, Indonesia : Gah *rooht*
Gary, USA : *Ga* ri
Garza García, Mexico : Gahr sah Gahr *see* ah

Gascony, France : *Gas* ka ni
Gaspé (Peninsula), Canada : Ga *spay* (UK *Gas* pay)
Gastonia, USA : Gas *toh* ni a
Gatchina, Russia : *Ga* chi na
Gateshead, England : *Gayts* hed
Gatlinburg, USA : *Gat* lun buhrg (UK *Gat* lin buhg)
Gatooma, Zimbabwe : Ga *toh* ma
Gatwick, England : *Gat* wik
Gauhati, India : Gow *hah* ti
Gaul, Europe : Gawl
Gauteng, South Africa : *Gow* teng
Gavarnie, France : Gah vahr *nee*
Gävle, Sweden : *Yev* la
Gawler, Australia : *Gaw* lur (UK *Gaw* la)
Gaya, India : Ga *yah*
Gaza, Gaza Strip : *Gah* za [In biblical use the name of the town is also pronounced *Gay* za.]
Gaziantep, Turkey : Gah zee ahn *tep*
Gcuwa, South Africa : *Kooh* wa
Gdańsk, Poland : Ga *dahnsk* (UK Ga *dansk*) (Polish Gdiynsk)
Gdynia, Poland : Ga *din* ia (Polish *Gdin* ya)
Geel, Belgium : Khayl
Geelong, Australia : Ji *lawng* (UK Ji *long*)
Geispolsheim, France : Gays pawl *saym*
Gelderland, Netherlands : *Gel* dur lund (UK *Gel* da lund) (Dutch *Khel* dur lahnt)
Geleen, Netherlands : Kha *layn*
Gelsenkirchen, Germany : Gel zun *kir* khun
Gembloux, Belgium : Zhahn *blooh*
General Pico, Argentina : Khay nay rahl *Pee* koh
General Roca, Argentina : Khay nay rahl *Roh* kah
General San Martín, Argentina : Khay nay rahl Sahn Mahr *teen*
General Santos, Philippines : Khay nay rahl *Sahn* tohs
General Sarmiento, Argentina : Khay nay rahl Sahr *myen* toh
Geneva, Switzerland : Ja *nee* va

Genk, Belgium : Khengk
¹Genoa, Italy : *Jen* oh a
²Genoa, USA : Ja *noh* a
George, South Africa : Jawrj (UK Jawj)
Georgetown, Guyana; USA : *Jawrj* town (UK *Jawj* town) [The name of the Guyanese capital is locally pronounced *Jawj* tahng.]
George Town, Cayman Islands; Malaysia : *Jawrj* Town (UK *Jawj* Town)
Georgia, Asia; USA : *Jawr* ja (UK *Jaw* ja)
Gera, Germany : *Gay* rah
Geraldton, Australia : *Jer* uld tun
Gérardmer, France : Zhay rahr *may*
Germantown, USA : *Juhr* mun town (UK *Juh* mun town)
Germany, Europe : *Juhr* ma ni (UK *Juh* ma ni)
Germiston, South Africa : *Juhr* mi stun (UK *Juh* mi stun)
Gerolstein, Germany : *Ger* ul shtiyn
Gerona, Spain : Ji *roh* na (Spanish Hay *roh* nah)
Gers, France : Zher
Getafe, Spain : Hay *tah* fay
Gets, France : Zhay
Gettysburg, USA : *Get* iz buhrg (UK *Get* iz buhg)
Gex, France : Zheks
Gezira, Sudan : Ja *zeer* a
Ghadames, Libya : Ga *dah* mes
Ghana, Africa : *Gah* na
Ghansi, Botswana : *Gahn* si
Ghardaïa, Algeria : Gahr *dah* ya
Ghat, Libya : Gaht
Ghats, India : Gawts
Ghaziabad, India : *Gah* zi a bahd
Ghazipur, India : *Gah* zi poor
Ghazni, Afghanistan : *Gahz* nee
Ghent, Belgium : Gent
Gia Dinh, Vietnam : Zhah *Din*
Gibara, Cuba : Hee *bah* rah
Gibraltar, Europe : Ji *brawl* tur (UK Ji *brawl* ta)
Gibson (Desert), Australia : *Gib* sun
Gidea Park, England : Gid i a *Pahrk* (UK ... *Pahk*)

Gien, France : Zhyahn
Giessen, Germany : *Gee* sun
Gifu, Japan : *Gee* fooh
Giggleswick, England : *Gig* ulz wik [The name of the North Yorkshire village has or had a local pronunciation *Gil* zik.]
Gigondas, France : Zhee gawn *dahs*
Gijón, Spain : Khee *khohn*
Gila, USA : *Hee* la
Gilbert (Islands), Kiribati : *Gil* burt (UK *Gil* but) [This name gave that of **Kiribati** itself.]
Gilead, Jordan : *Gi* li ud (UK *Gi* li ad)
Gilgit, India : *Gil* gut
Gillette, USA : Ji *let*
¹Gillingham, England (Dorset, Norfolk) : *Gil* ing um
²Gillingham, England (Kent) : *Jil* ing um
Gilroy, USA : *Gil* roy
Gingoog, Philippines : Heeng *goh* awg
Gippsland, Australia : *Gips* land
Girard, USA : Ja *rahrd* (UK Ji *rahd*)
Girardot, Colombia : Khee rahr *dhawt*
Giresun, Turkey : Jee re *soohn*
Gironde, France : Zhee *rawnd*
Girvan, Scotland : *Guhr* vun (UK *Guh* vun)
Gisborne, New Zealand : *Giz* burn (UK *Giz* bun)
Gisors, France : Zhee *zawr*
Gitega, Burundi : Gee *tay* gah
Giurgiu, Romania : *Joohr* jooh
Giza, Egypt : *Gee* za
Gjirokastër, Albania : Gyi roh *kahs* tur
Glace Bay, Canada : Glays *Bay*
Gladsakse, Denmark : *Glahdh* sahk sa
Gladstone, Australia; USA : *Glad* stohn (UK *Glad* stun)
Glamis, Scotland : Glahmz
Glamorgan, Wales : Gla *mawr* gun (UK Gla *maw* gun)
Glarus, Switzerland : *Glah* roos
Glasgow, Scotland; USA : *Glas* goh (UK *Glahz* goh) [The Scottish city's name has various local pronunciations, written in spellings such as *Glesca, Glescay, Glesga, Glesgae, Glesgie*.]

Glaslyn, Wales : *Glas* lin
Glaston, England : *Glay* stun
Glastonbury, England, USA : *Glas* tun ber i (UK *Glas* tun bri) [The Somerset, England, town has a name also pronounced *Glahs* tun bri, although Ross, p. 96, disapproves of the lengthened vowel.]
Glauchau, Germany : *Glow* khow
¹Glencoe, Scotland : Glen *koh*
²Glencoe, USA : *Glen* koh
Glendale, USA : *Glen* dayl
Glendive, USA : *Glen* diyv
Glendora, USA : Glen *daw* ra
Glenelg, Scotland : Glen *elg*
Glen Ellyn, USA : Glen *El* un
Glen Innes, Australia : Glen *In* is
Glen More, Scotland : Glen *Mawr* (UK Glen *Maw*)
Glenorchy, Australia : Glen *awr* ki (UK Glen *aw* ki)
Glenrothes, Scotland : Glen *rah* this (UK Glen *roth* is)
Gliwice, Poland : Gli *veet* se
Głogów, Poland : *Gwaw* goohf
Glossop, England : *Glah* sup (UK *Glos* up)
Gloucester, Canada; England; USA : *Glahs* tur (UK *Glos* ta) [A "county" (aristocratic) pronunciation of the English city's name as *Glaw* sta was formerly current, and is still occasionally heard. Places of the name in the USA are mostly pronounced as for the English city, but Gloucester, Massachusetts, is usually *Glaw* stur.]
Glückstadt, Germany : *Gleek* shtaht
Glyder, Wales : *Glid* ur (UK *Glid* a) (Welsh *Gluh* der) [The name is that of twin peaks, *Glyder Fach*, Vahkh ("Small"), and *Glyder Fawr*, Vowr ("Big").]
Glyndebourne, England : *Gliynd* bawrn (UK *Gliynd* bawn)
Gmunden, Austria : *Gmoon* dun
Gnadenhutten, USA : Ja *nay* dun hut un [The Ohio village was founded by Moravians in 1772 and given a German name (properly *Gnadenhütten*,

pronounced *Gnah* dun hee tun)
meaning literally "mercy huts."]

Gniezno, Poland : *Gnyez* naw

Gnosall, England : *Noh* sul

Goa, India : *Goh* a

Goathland, England : *Gohth* lund

Goba, Ethiopia : *Goh* ba

Gobabis, Namibia : Goh *bah* bis

Gobi, Asia : *Goh* bi

Goch, Germany : Gawkh

Godalming, England : *Gahd* ul ming
(UK *God* ul ming)

Goderich, Canada : *Gahd* rich (UK
God rich)

Godhavn, Greenland : *Gohdh* hown

Godmanchester, England : *Gahd* mun
ches tur (UK *God* mun ches ta)

Gödöllö, Hungary : *Guh* duh luh

Godthåb, Greenland : *Gaht* hahb (UK
Got hahb) (Danish *Gawt* hawp)

Goiânia, Brazil : Goy *yah* nya

Goiás, Brazil : Goy *yahs*

Golan (Heights), Syria : *Goh* lahn (UK
Goh lan)

Golborne, England : *Gohl* bawrn (UK
Gohl bawn)

Golconda, India : Gahl *kahn* da (UK
Gol *kon* da)

Goldsboro, USA : *Gohldz* buhr oh (UK
Gohldz bra)

Goliad, USA : *Goh* li ad

Goma, Democratic Republic of the
Congo : *Goh* mah

Gomel, Belarus : Gah *mel* (UK Go *mel*)
(Russian Ga *myel*)

Gómez Palacio, Mexico : Goh mes Pah
lah syoh

Gomshall, England : *Gahm* shul (UK
Gom shul)

Gonaïves, Haiti : Goh nah *eev*

Gondal, India : *Gohn* dul

Gonder, Ethiopia : *Gawn* dur (UK *Gon*
da)

Goodwin (Sands), England : *Good* win

Goodwood, England : *Good* wood

Goole, England : Goohl

Goosnargh, England : *Goohs* nur (UK
Goohs na)

Göppingen, Germany : *Guh* ping un

Gorakhpur, India : Gor uk *poor* (UK
Gor uk *poo* a)

Gorgan, Iran : Gohr *gawn*

Gorgonzola, Italy : Gawr gun *zoh* la
(UK Gaw gun *zoh* la) (Italian Gawr
gawn *zoh* lah)

Gorizia, Italy : Goh *reet* syah

Gorleston, England : *Gawrl* stun (UK
Gawl stun)

Gorlice, Poland : Gawr *leet* se (UK Gaw
leet se)

Görlitz, Germany : *Guhr* lits

Gorlovka, Ukraine : *Gawr* luf ka

Gorno-Altay, Russia : Gawr noh Al *tiy*
(UK Gaw noh...)

Goroka, Papua New Guinea : Goh roh
kah

Gorontalo, Indonesia : Goh ron *tah* loh

Gorseinon, Wales : Gawr *siy* nun (UK
Gaw *siy* nun)

Gorzów Wielkopolski, Poland : Gaw
zhoohf Vyel kaw *pawl* skee

Gosford, Australia : *Gahs* furd (UK *Gos*
fud)

Gosforth, England : *Gahs* fawrth (UK
Gos futh)

Goshen, Egypt; USA : *Goh* shun

Goslar, Germany : *Gaws* lahr

Gosnells, Australia : *Gahz* nulz (UK
Goz nulz)

Gosport, England : *Gahs* pawrt (UK
Gos pawt)

Göteborg, Sweden : *Guh* ta bawrg (UK
Guh ta bawg) (Swedish *Yuh* tah bawr)
[*Cp.* **Gothenburg**]

Gotha, Germany : *Goh* ta

Gotham, England : *Goh* tum [As a
nickname for New York City made
famous by Washington Irving, the
name of the Nottinghamshire village
is pronounced US *Gahth* um, UK
Goth um.]

Gothenburg, Sweden : *Gahth* un buhrg
(UK *Goth* un buhg) [Ross, p. 97, re-
gards these pronunciations as dated:
"To-day, people usually make some
attempt at the Swedish name [**Göteborg**], which is not pronounced in a
manner at all obvious to the English-

man." The English spelling of the seaport city's name was also pronounced US *Gah* tun buhrg, UK *Got* un buhg, a form recommended by Lloyd James 1937.]

Gotland, Sweden : *Gaht* land (UK *Got* lund) (Swedish *Gawt* lant)

Goto (Islands), Japan : *Goh* toh

Göttingen, Germany : *Guh* ting un

Gouda, Netherlands : *Gow* da (Dutch *Khow* da)

Goudhurst, England : *Gowd* huhrst (UK *Gowd* huhst)

Goulburn, Australia : *Gohl* buhrn (UK *Gohl* buhn)

Gourock, Scotland : *Goor* uk (UK *Goo* a ruk)

Gouyave, Grenada : Gooh *yahv*

Governador Valadares, Brazil : Gooh vur na dohr Va la *dar* is

Gower, Wales : *Gow* ur (UK *Gow* a)

Goya, Argentina : *Goh* yah

Gozo, Malta : *Goh* zoh

Graaff-Reinet, South Africa : Grahf *Riy* nut

Gracias, Honduras : *Grah* syahs

Grafham, England : *Graf* um [This is the regular pronunciation, but the Cambridgeshire village is *Grah* fum.]

Grafton, Australia; England; USA : *Graf* tun (UK *Grahf* tun)

Graham Land, Antarctica : *Gray* um Land

Grahamstown, South Africa : *Gray* umz town

Grampian (Hills), Scotland : *Gram* pi un

Gramsh, Albania : Grahmsh

Granada, Nicaragua; Spain : Gra *nah* da (Spanish Grah *nah* dhah)

Granby, Canada; USA : *Gran* bi

Gran Canaria, Canary Islands : Grahn Ka *nah* ri a (UK Gran Ka *nay* a ri a) (Spanish Grahng Kah *nah* ryah)

Gran Chaco, South America : Gran *Cha* koh (Spanish Grahn *Chah* koh)

Grand Bassam, Côte d'Ivoire : Grahn Bah *sahm*

Grand-Bourg, Guadeloupe : Grahn *Boohr*

Grand Coulee, USA : Gran *Kooh* li

Grande, Rio *see* **Río Grande**

Grande Prairie, Canada : Gran *Prer* i (UK ... *Pray* a ri)

Grand Forks, USA : Gran *Fawrks* (UK Gran *Fawks*)

Grand'Mère, Canada : *Grahn* mer (UK *Gran* may a)

Grand Prairie, USA : Gran *Prer* i (UK ... *Pray* a ri)

Grand Rapids, USA : Gran *Rap* idz

Grangemouth, Scotland : *Graynj* mowth

Grange-over-Sands, England : Graynj oh vur *Sandz* (UK ... oh va...)

Granma, Cuba : Grahn *mah*

Grantchester, England : *Gran* ches tur (UK *Grahn* chis ta)

Grantham, England : *Gran* thum [Ross, p. 98, recommends a pronunciation *Grahn* tum for the Lincolnshire town, but this is rarely if ever heard today.]

Grantown-on-Spey, Scotland : Gran town ahn *Spay* (UK ... on...)

¹Granville, France : Grahn *veel*

²Granville, USA : *Gran* vil

Grapevine, USA : *Grayp* viyn

Grasmere, England : *Gras* mir (UK *Grahs* mi a)

Grasse, France : Grahs

Graubünden, Switzerland : Grow *been* dun

Graulhet, France : Groh *yay*

Gravelines, France : Grahv *leen*

Graves, France : Grahv

Gravesend, England : Grayvz *end*

Graz, Austria : Grahts

Great Ayton, England : Grayt *Ay* tun

Great Bardfield, England : Grayt *Bahrd* feeld (UK *Bahd* feeld)

Great Bookham, England : Grayt *Book* um

Great Casterton, England : Grayt *Kas* tur tun (UK ... *Kah* sta tun)

¹Greatham, England (Co. Durham) : *Gree* tum

²**Greatham**, England (Hampshire) :
Gret um

Great Malvern, England : Grayt *Mawl*
vurn (UK ... *Mawl* vun)

Great Missenden, England : Grayt *Mis*
un dun

Great Salkeld, England : Grayt *Sawl*
kuld [An alternate local pronunciation Gurt *Saf* ul has been recorded for
the Cumbria village.]

Great Shelford, England : Grayt *Shel*
furd (UK ... *Shel* fud)

Great Tew, England : Grayt *Tooh* (UK
... *Tyooh*)

Great Waltham *see* **Waltham Abbey**

Great Witley, England : Grayt *Wit* li

Great Yarmouth, England : Grayt *Yahr*
muth (UK ... *Yah* muth)

Greece, Europe : Grees

Greeley, USA : *Gree* li

Greenbelt, USA : *Green* belt

Greendale, USA : *Green* dayl

Greeneville, USA : *Green* vil

Greenfield, USA : *Green* feeld

Greenland, North America : *Green*
lund

Greenlawn, USA : *Green* lawn

Greenock, Scotland : *Gree* nuk [Ross,
p. 99, recommends a pronunciation
Gren uk for the name of the town and
port.]

Greensboro, USA : *Greenz* buhr oh
(UK *Greenz* bra)

Greenville, Liberia; USA : *Green* vil

Greenwich, England; USA : *Gren* ich
[Ross, p. 99, prefers *Grin* ij for the
name of the London town and borough, and this is equally valid for
Greenwich Village, New York.
Greenwich, Connecticut, is also
known as *Green* wich, with a spelling
pronunciation.]
(1) *Greenwich* as the name of a Connecticut town is pronounced *Gren-
nidge* as in England, but as the name
of a San Francisco street it is *Green-
witch* [Mencken, p. 540].
(2) Greenwich is pronounced
"Grinidge," "Grinitch," or "Grenitch"

[A.D. Mills, *A Dictionary of London
Place Names*, 2001].

Greenwood, USA : *Green* wood

Greifswald, Germany : *Griyfs* vahlt

Greiz, Germany : Griyts

Grenada, West Indies : Gri *nay* da

Grenadines, West Indies : *Gren* a deenz

Grenoble, France : Gri *noh* bul (French
Gri *nawbl*) [According to Ross, p.
98, "To use the French pronunciation
would be affected."]

Gresham, England; USA : *Gresh* um

Gresik, Indonesia : Gre *seek*

Gretna, USA : *Gret* na

Gretna Green, Scotland : Gret na *Green*

Grevenbroich, Germany : *Gray* vun
broykh

Greymouth, New Zealand : *Gray*
mowth

Griffin, USA : *Grif* un (UK *Grif* in)

Grimbergen, Belgium : *Grim* ber gun

Grimsby, Canada; England : *Grimz* bi

Grindelwald, Switzerland : *Grin* dul
vahlt

Griqualand, South Africa : *Gree* kwa
land

Griswold, USA : *Griz* wuld

Grodno, Belarus : *Grawd* na

Gronau, Germany : *Groh* now

Groningen, Netherlands : *Groh* ning un
(Dutch *Khroh* ning un)

Groote Eylandt, Australia : *Grooht* Iy
lund

Grootfontein, Namibia : *Grooht* fon
tayn

¹**Grosmont**, England : *Groh* mahnt (UK
Groh munt) [An alternate local pronunciation of the North Yorkshire
village's name is *Grohs* munt.]

²**Grosmont**, Wales : *Grahs* mahnt (UK
Gros munt)

Grosse Pointe, USA : *Grohs* Poynt

Grosseto, Italy : Groh *say* toh

Grosvenor (Mountains), Antarctica :
Grohv nur (UK *Grohv* na)

¹**Groton**, England : *Graw* tun

²**Groton**, USA : *Grah* tun (UK *Grot* un)

Grozny, Russia : *Grahz* ni (UK *Groz* ni)
(Russian *Grawz* ni) [A common En-

glish mispronunciation of the city's name, prevalent during the civil war of the mid–1990s, is US *Grahzh* ni, UK *Grozh* ni. This may have arisen from the familiar combination *-zhn-* in Russian names, such as *Brezhnev* and *Nizhny Novgorod.*]

Grudziądz, Poland : *Grooh* jawnts

Gruinard (Bay), Scotland : *Grin* yurd (UK *Grin* yud)

Gruyère, Switzerland : Gri *yer*

Gstaad, Switzerland : Ga *shtahd* (German Kshtaht)

Guadalajara, Mexico; Spain : Gwah da la *hah* ra (Spanish Gwah dhah lah *hah* rah)

Guadalcanal, Solomon Islands : Gwah dul ka *nal* (Spanish Gwah dhahl kah *nahl*)

Guadalquivir, Spain : Gwah dul *kwi* vur (UK Gwah dul kwi *vi* a) (Spanish Gwah dhahl kee *vir*)

Guadalupe, Mexico : *Gwah* da loohp (UK Gwah da *loohp*) (Spanish Gwah dhah *looh* pay)

Guadeloupe, West Indies : *Gwah* da loohp (UK Gwah da *loohp*) (French Gwahd *loohp*)

Guáimaro, Cuba : *Gwiy* mah roh

Guainía, Colombia : Gwiy *nee* a

Gualeguay, Argentina : Gwah lay *gwiy*

Gualeguaychú, Argentina : Gwah lay gwiy *chooh*

Guam, Pacific Ocean : Gwahm

Guanacaste, Costa Rica : Gwah nah *kahs* tay

Guanajuato, Mexico : Gwah nah *hwah* toh

Guanare, Venezuela : Gwah *nah* ray

Guangdong, China : Gwahng *doong* (UK Gwang *doong*)

Guangxi, China : Gwahng *shee*

Guangzhou, China : Gwahng *joh* (UK Gwang *joh*)

Guantánamo, Cuba : Gwahn *tah* na moh (UK Gwan *tah* na moh)

Guaranda, Ecuador : Gawh *rahn* dah

Guarda, Portugal : *Gwahr* da

Guarulhos, Brazil : Gwa *roohl* yoohs

Guatemala, Central America : Gwah ta *mah* la

Guaviare, Colombia : Gwahv *yah* ray

Guayama, Puerto Rico : Gwah *yah* mah

Guayaquil, Ecuador : Gwiy ah *keel* (Spanish Gwah yah *kil*)

Guayas, Ecuador : *Gwiy* ahs

Guaymas, Mexico : *Gwiy* mahs

Guaynabo, Puerto Rico : Gwiy *nah* boh

Gubbio, Italy : *Gooh* bi oh

Guben, Germany : *Gooh* bun

Guebwiller, France : Geb vee *ler*

Guéckédou, Guinea : Ge *kay* dooh

Guelma, Algeria : Gel *mah*

Guelmim, Morocco : Goohl *meem*

Guelph, Canada : Gwelf

Guéméné-Penfao, France : Gay may nay Pahn *foh*

Guer, France : Ger

Guéret, France : Gay *ray*

Guernica, Spain : *Gwer* ni ka (UK *Guh* ni ka) (Spanish Ger *nee* kah)

Guernsey, Channel Islands, Europe : *Guhrn* zi (UK *Guhn* zi)

Guiana, South America : Gi *an* a (UK Gi *ahn* a)

Guichen, France : Gee *shahn*

Guienne, France : Gee *en*

Guildford, England : *Gil* furd (UK *Gil* fud)

Guilford, USA : *Gil* furd (UK *Gil* fud)

Guilherand-Granges, France : Gee ya rahn *Grahnzh*

Guilin, China : Gwee *lin*

Guimarães, Portugal : Gee ma *riynsh*

Guinea, Africa : *Gin* i

Guinea-Bissau, Africa : Gin i Bi *sow*

Güines, Cuba : *Gwee* nays

Guingamp, France : Gan *gahn*

Guipavas, France : Gee pah *vahs*

Güira de Melena, Cuba : Gwee rah dhay May *lay* nah

Guisborough, England : *Giz* buhr oh (UK *Giz* bra)

Guise, France : Gweez

Guiseley, England : *Giyz* li

Guiyang, China : Gway *yahng* (UK Gway *yang*)

Guizhou, China : Gway *joh*

Gujan-Mestras, France : Gi zhahn May *strahs*

Gujarat, India : Gooh ja *raht*

Gujranwala, Pakistan : Gooj run *wah* la

Gulfport, USA : *Gahlf* pawrt (UK *Gahlf* pawt)

Gulistan, Uzbekistan : Gooh li *stahn*

Gulu, Uganda : *Gooh* looh

Gumel, Nigeria : Gooh *mel*

Guntur, India : Goon *toor*

Gurupi, Brazil : Gooh rooh *pee*

Guryev, Kazakhstan : *Goohr* yif

Gusau, Nigeria : Gooh *zow*

Gusev, Russia : *Gooh* sif

Gus-Khrustalnyy, Russia : Goos Khroo *stahl* ni

Güstrow, Germany : *Gees* troh

Gütersloh, Germany : *Gooh* tur sloh (UK *Gooh* ta sloh) (German *Gee* turz loh)

Guyana, South America : Giy *an* a [Guyana was formerly British **Guiana**.]

Guymon, USA : *Giy* mun

Gwalior, India : *Gwah* li awr (UK *Gwah* li aw)

Gwent, Wales : Gwent

Gweru, Zimbabwe : *Gway* rooh

Gwynedd, Wales : *Gwi* nedh

Gyandzha, Azerbaijan : Gyahn *jah*

Gympie, Australia : *Gim* pi

Győngyős, Hungary : *Juhn* juhsh

Győr, Hungary : Juhr

Gyumri, Armenia : *Gyoom* ri

Haaltert, Belgium : *Hahl* tert

Haarlem, Netherlands : *Hahr* lum (UK *Hah* lum)

Habsburg, Germany : *Haps* buhrg (UK *Haps* buhg) (German *Hahps* boork)

Habsheim, France : Ahp *saym*

Hachinohe, Japan : Hah chee *noh* hay

Hachioji, Japan : Hah chee *oh* jee

Hackensack, USA : *Hak* un sak

Hackney, England : *Hak* ni

Hadano, Japan : Hah *dah* noh

Haddington, Scotland : *Had* ing tun

Haddonfield, USA : *Had* un feeld

Hadejia, Nigeria : Hah *day* jee ah

Haderslev, Denmark : *Hah* durs lev

(UK *Had* us lev) (Danish *Hah* dhurz le oo)

Ḩaḑramawt, Yemen : Hah drah *mowt*

Haeju, North Korea : *Hiy* jooh

Hafnarfjörthur, Iceland : *Hahp* nahr fyuhr dhoor

Hagen, Germany : *Hah* gun

Hagerstown, USA : *Hay* gurz town (UK *Hay* guz town)

Hagetmau, France : Ah zhet *moh*

Hague, Netherlands : Hayg

Haguenau, France : Ahg *noh*

Haifa, Israel : *Hiy* fa

Haikou, China : Hiy *koh*

Haileybury, Canada : *Hay* li ber i

Hailsham, England : *Hayl* shum

Hainan, China : Hiy *nahn* (UK Hiy *nan*)

Hainault, England : *Hay* nawlt (UK *Hay* nawt)

Hainaut, Belgium : *Hay* noh (French Ay *noh*)

Haiphong, Vietnam : Hiy *fawng*

Haiti, West Indies : *Hay* ti [A spoken form A *ee* ti also exists, from *Haïti*, the French spelling of the island republic's name, itself more precisely pronounced Ah ee *tee*.]

Hajdúböszörmény, Hungary : *Hoy* doo buh suhr mayn

Hajdúszoboszló, Hungary : *Hoy* doo soh boh sloh

Haka, Myanmar : *Hah* ka

Hakodate, Japan : Hah koh *dah* tay

Halab, Syria : *Ha* lab

Halberstadt, Germany : *Hahl* bur shtaht

Halden, Norway : *Hawl* dun

Haldimand, Canada : *Hawl* da mund

Hale, England : Hayl

Haleakala (Crater), USA : Hah li ah ka *lah*

Halesowen, England : Haylz *oh* in

Halesworth, England : *Haylz* wurth (UK *Haylz* wuhth)

Halicarnassus, Turkey : Hal i kahr *nas* us (UK Hal i kah *nas* us)

Halifax, Canada; England; USA : *Hal* a faks (UK *Hal* i faks)

Halle, Germany : *Hah* la
Halle Neustadt, Germany : Hah la *Noy* shtaht
Hallstatt, Austria : *Hawl* stat (UK *Hal* stat) (German *Hahl* shtaht)
Halmahera, Indonesia : Hal ma *huhr* a (UK Hal ma *hi* a ra)
Halmstad, Sweden : *Hahlm* stahd
Halq al-Wadi, Tunisia : Halk al *Wah* di
Hälsingborg, Sweden : *Hel* sing bawrg (UK *Hel* sing bawg)
Halstead, England : *Hal* sted
Haltemprice, England : *Hawl* tum priys
Halton, England : *Hawl* tun
Haltwhistle, England : *Hawlt* wis ul [The name of the Northumberland town, in origin combining Old French *haut*, "high," with Old English *twisla*, "fork (junction of streams)," has or had a local pronunciation *Hoh* ta sul.]
Ham, France : Ahm
Hamadan, Iran : Ha ma *dan*
Hamah, Syria : *Hah* ma
Hamamatsu, Japan : Hah mah *maht* sooh
Hamar, Norway : *Hah* mahr
Hamble, England : *Ham* bul
Hamburg, Germany; USA : *Ham* buhrg (UK *Ham* buhg) (German *Hahm* boork)
Hamden, USA : *Ham* dun
Hämeenlinna, Finland : *Hah* mayn li na
Hamelin, Germany : *Ham* lin
Hameln, Germany : *Hah* muln
Hamersley (Range), Australia : *Ham* urz li (UK *Ham* uz li)
Hamhŭng, North Korea : *Hahm* hung
Hamilton, Bermuda; Canada; New Zealand; Scotland; USA : *Ham* ul tun
Hamina, Finland : *Hah* mee nah
Hamm, Germany : Hahm
Hammamet, Tunisia : Ham a *met*
Hammam Lif, Tunisia : Ha mahm *Leef*
Hamme, Belgium : *Hah* ma
Hammerfest, Norway : *Ham* ur fest

(UK *Ham* a fest) (Norwegian *Hah* mur fest)
Hammersmith, England : *Ham* ur smith (UK *Ham* a smith)
Hammond, USA : *Ham* und
Hampshire, England : *Hamp* shur (UK *Hamp* sha)
Hampstead, Canada; England : *Hamp* stid
Hampton, England; USA : *Hamp* tun
Hamtramck, USA : Ham *tram* ik
Hanau, Germany : *Hah* now
Handan, China : Hahn *dahn*
Hanford, USA : *Han* furd (UK *Han* fud)
Hangzhou, China : Hahng *joh*
Hankou, China : Hahn *koh*
Hanley, England : *Han* li
Hannibal, USA : *Han* a bul (UK *Han* i bul)
Hanoi, Vietnam : Ha *noy*
Hanover, Canada; Germany; USA : *Han* oh vur (UK *Han* oh va)
Hanyang, China : Hahn *yahng*
Happisburgh, England : *Hayz* bra [The name of the Norfolk resort is spelled in a more phonetically faithful form as that of the Hazeborough Sands off the coast here.]
[Happisburgh] will never be found unless its correct pronunciation is used — "Haysborough" [John Hadfield, ed., *The New Shell Guide to England*, 1981].
Harare, Zimbabwe : Ha *rah* ri
Harbel, Liberia : *Hahr* bel (UK *Hah* bel)
Harbin, China : *Hahr* bun (UK *Hah* bin)
Harbour Grace, Canada : Hahr bur *Grays* (UK Hah ba...)
Hardanger (Fjord), Norway : Hahr *dahng* ur
Hardenburg, Netherlands : *Hahr* den berkh
Harderwijk, Netherlands : *Hahr* dur viyk
Hardwick, England : *Hahrd* wik (UK *Hahd* wik)

Harer, Ethiopia : *Hah* rur (UK *Hah* ra)

Harewood, England : *Her* wood (UK *Hay* a wood) [This is the pronunciation for the West Yorkshire estate village. But the name of Harewood House, for which the village is noted, is pronounced US *Hahr* wood, UK *Hah* wood, and according to Jones, p. 244, this pronunciation "may sometimes be heard from old people there."]

Harfleur, France : Hahr *fluhr* (UK Hah *fluh*) (French Ahr *fluhr*)

Hargeysa, Somalia : Hahr *gay* sa (UK Hah *gay* sa)

Haridwar, India : *Hah* ri dwahr (UK *Hah* ri dwah)

Haringey, England : *Har* ing gay

Hari Rud, Asia : Har ee *Roohd*

Harlech, Wales : *Hahr* luk (UK *Hah* luk) (Welsh *Hahr* lekh)

Harlem, USA : *Hahr* lum (UK *Hah* lum)

Harlesden, England : *Hahrlz* dun (UK *Hahlz* dun)

¹Harlingen, Netherlands : *Hahr* ling un (UK *Hah* ling un)

²Harlingen, USA : *Hahr* lun jun (UK *Hah* lin jun)

Harlow, England : *Hahr* loh (UK *Hah* loh)

Harmondsworth, England : *Hahr* mundz wurth (UK *Hah* mundz wuhth)

Härnösand, Sweden : Her nuh *sand*

Harpenden, England : *Hahr* pun dun (UK *Hah* pun dun)

Harper, Liberia : *Hahr* pur (UK *Hah* pa)

Harpers Ferry, USA : Hahr purz *Fer* i (UK Hah puz...)

Harrietsham, England : *Har* i ut shum

Harrisburg, USA : *Har* is buhrg (UK *Har* is buhg)

Harrison, USA : *Har* a sun (UK *Har* i sun)

Harrisonburg, USA : *Har* a sun buhrg (UK *Har* is un buhg)

Harrogate, England : *Har* oh gayt (UK *Har* a gut)

Harrow, England : *Har* oh

Hartford, USA : *Hahrt* furd (UK *Haht* fud)

Hartlepool, England : *Hahrt* li poohl (UK *Haht* li poohl)

Harvard, USA : *Hahr* vurd (UK *Hah* vud)

Harwell, England : *Hahr* wul (UK *Hah* wul)

¹Harwich, England : *Har* ij

²Harwich, USA : *Hahr* wich

Haryana, India : Hah ree *ah* na

Harz, Germany : Hahrts (UK Hahts)

Haslemere, England : *Hayz* ul mir (UK *Hayz* ul mi a)

Haslingden, England : *Haz* ling dun

Hasparren, France : Ahs pah *rahn*

Hassan, India : *Hah* sun

Hasselt, Belgium : *Hah* sult

Hassi R'Mel, Algeria : Hah seer *Mel*

Hastings, Australia; England; New Zealand; USA : *Hay* stingz

Hatay, Turkey : Hah *tiy*

Hatfield, England : *Hat* feeld

Hathersage, England : *Hadh* ur sayj (UK *Hadh* a sayj)

Hatillo, Puerto Rico : Ah *tee* oh

Hato Mayor, Dominican Republic : Ah toh Mah *yawr*

Hatteras, USA : *Hat* ur us

Hattiesburg, USA : *Hat* iz buhrg (UK *Hat* iz buhg)

Hatvan, Hungary : *Hawt* vawn

Haugesund, Norway : *Haw* ga sund

Haute-Loire, France : Oht *Lwahr* [The word *Haute* ("High") occurs in the names of many French departments and is always pronounced as here. But see also the entries below.]

Hautes-Alpes, France : Oht *zalp*

Hautes-Pyrénées, France : Oht Pee ray *nay*

Haut-Rhin, France : Oh *Rahn*

Hauts-de-Seine, France : Ohd *Sen*

Havana, Cuba : Ha *van* a

Havant, England : *Hav* unt

Havelock, USA : *Hav* lahk (UK *Hav* lok)

Haverford, USA : *Hav* ur furd (UK *Hav* a fud)

Haverfordwest, Wales : Hav ur furd *west* (UK Hav a fud *west*) [An elided pronunciation US Hah furd *west*, UK Hah fud *west* also exists for the name of the Pembrokeshire town.]

Haverhill, England; USA : *Hay* vur ul (UK *Hay* vril)

Havering, England : *Hay* vur ing

Havířov, Czech Republic : *Hah* veer zhawf

Havlíčkův Brod, Czech Republic : *Hahv* leech koohv Brawt

Havre, USA : *Hav* ur (UK *Hav* a)

Havre de Grace, USA : Hav ur da *Gras* (UK Hav a...) [The pronunciation of the Maryland city's name is an Americanized form of the original French.]
> *Havre de Grace* is pronounced *Haver de Grass*, with two flat *a*'s [Mencken, p. 541].

Hawaii, USA : Ha *wiy* i [A local pronunciation Ha *viy* i is alternately heard from native residents of the island state.]

¹**Hawarden**, USA : *Hay* wawr dun (UK *Hay* waw dun)

²**Hawarden**, Wales : *Hahr* dun (UK *Hah* dun)

Hawera, New Zealand : *Hah* wa ra

Hawes, England : Hawz

Hawick, England : *Haw* ik

Hawkesbury, Australia : *Hawks* ber i

¹**Haworth**, England : *Haw* wurth (UK *How* uth)

²**Haworth**, USA : *Haw* wurth (UK *Haw* wuth)

Hawthorne, USA : *Haw* thawrn (UK *Haw* thawn)

Hay, Australia : Hay

Haydock, England : *Hay* dahk (UK *Hay* dok)

Hayes, England : Hayz

Hayle, England : Hayl

Hay-on-Wye, Wales : Hay ahn *Wiy* (UK ... on...)

Hays, USA : Hayz

Hayward, USA : *Hay* wurd (UK *Hay* wud)

Haywards Heath, England : Hay wurdz *Heeth* (UK Hay wudz...)

Hazaribag, India : Ha *zah* ri bahg

Hazleton, USA : *Hay* zul tun

Heacham, England : *Hech* um

Headingley, England : *Hed* ing li

Healaugh, England : *Hee* la

Healdsburg, USA : *Heeldz* buhrg (UK *Heeldz* buhg)

Heanor, England : *Hee* nur (UK *Hee* na)

Heard (Island), Indian Ocean : Huhrd (UK Huhd)

Hearst (Island), Antarctica : Huhrst (UK Huhst)

Heather, England : *Hee* dhur (UK *Hee* dha)

Heathfield, England : *Heeth* feeld

Heathrow, England : *Heeth* roh (UK Heeth *roh*)

Heaton, England : *Hee* tun

Hebburn, England : *Heb* urn (UK *Heb* uhn)

Hebden Bridge, England : Heb dun *Brij*

Hebei, China : Hah *bay* (UK Huh *bay*)

Hebrides, Scotland : *Heb* ra deez

Hebron, West Bank : *Heb* run (UK *Heb* ron)

Hechingen, Germany : *Hekh* ing un

Heckmondwike, England : *Hek* mund wiyk

Hednesford, England : *Hens* furd (UK *Hens* fud) [The name of the Staffordshire town has also had a local pronunciation US *Hej* furd, UK *Hej* fud, written *Hedgeford*. Cp. *Wedgefield* for **Wednesfield**.]

Hedon, England : *Hed* un

Heemskerk, Netherlands : *Hayms* kerk

Heerenveen, Netherlands : *Her* un vayn

Heerlen, Netherlands : *Her* la

Hefei, China : Huh *fay*

Heidelberg, Australia; Germany : *Hiy* dul buhrg (UK *Hiy* dul buhg) (German *Hiy* dul berk)

Heidenheim, Germany : *Hiy* dun hiym

Heilbronn, Germany : *Hiyl* brahn (UK *Hiyl* bron) (German *Hiyl* brawn)

Heiligenhaus, Germany : *Hiy* lig un hows

Heilongjiang, China : Hay loong ji *ahng* (UK Hay long *jang*)

Hejaz, Saudi Arabia : He *jaz*

Hekla, Iceland : *Hek* la

Helena, USA : *Hel* un a [The pronunciation is valid for most US places, although Helena, Georgia, is He *lee* na and Helena, South Carolina, is Ha *lay* na.]

Helensburgh, Scotland : *Hel* unz buhrg (UK *Hel* unz bra)

Helicon, Greece : *Hel* a kahn (UK *Hel* i kun)

Heligoland, Germany : *Hel* i goh land

Heliopolis, Egypt : Hee li *ah* pa lis (UK Hee li *op* a lis)

Hellendoorn, Netherlands : *Hel* un dawrn

Hellespont, Turkey : *Hel* is pahnt (UK *Hel* is pont)

Helmand, Afghanistan : *Hel* mund

Helmond, Netherlands : *Hel* mawnt

Helmsley, England : *Helmz* li [A local pronunciation of the North Yorkshire town's name is *Hemz* li.]

Helmstedt, Germany : *Helm* shtet

Helsingør, Denmark : *Hel* sing uhr (UK *Hel* sing uh)

Helsinki, Finland : Hel *sing* ki (Finnish *Hel* sing ki)

Helston, England : *Hel* stun

Helvellyn, England : Hel *vel* un

Helwân, Egypt : Hel *wahn*

Hem, France : Em

Hemel Hempstead, England : Hem ul *Hemp* stid

Hemer, Germany : *Hay* mur

Hemet, USA : *Hem* ut (UK *Hem* et)

Hempstead, USA : *Hemp* sted

Hemsworth, England : *Hemz* wurth (UK *Hemz* wuth)

Henan, China : Ha *nahn* (UK Hay *nan*)

Hendaye, France : Ahn *diy*

Henderson, USA : *Hen* dur sun (UK *Hen* da sun)

Hendersonville, USA : *Hen* dur sun vil (UK *Hen* da sun vil)

Hendon, England : *Hen* dun

Hengelo, Netherlands : *Heng* a loh

Hengyang, China : Heng *yahng* (UK Heng *yang*)

Henley, England : *Hen* li

Henzada, Myanmar : Hen za *dah*

Heraklion, Greece : He *rak* li un

Herat, Afghanistan : He *raht*

Hérault, France : Ay *roh*

Herceg-Novi, Montenegro : Her tseg *Naw* vee

Herculaneum, Italy : Huhr kya *lay* ni um (UK Huh kyoo *lay* ni um)

Heredia, Costa Rica : Ay *ray* dhyah

¹Hereford, England : *Her* i furd (UK *Her* i fud) [A US pronunciation as ²**Hereford** also exists for the name of the town.]

²Hereford, USA : *Huhr* furd (UK *Huh* fud)

Herent, Belgium : *Hay* runt

Herentals, Belgium : *Hay* run tahls

Herford, Germany : *Hayr* fawrt

Herisau, Switzerland : *Her* i zow

Hermon, Lebanon : *Huhr* mun (UK *Huh* mun)

Hermosillo, Mexico : Er moh *see* yoh

Hernandarias, Paraguay : Er nahn *dahr* yahs

Herne, Germany : *Her* na

Herne Bay, England : Huhrn *Bay* (UK Huhn...)

Herrnhut, Germany : *Hern* heet

Hershey, USA : *Huhr* shi (UK *Huh* shi)

Herstal, Belgium : *Ayr* stahl

Herstmonceux, England : Huhrst mun sooh (UK Huhst mun *syooh*) [The name of the East Sussex village, site of the Royal Observatory from 1958 through 1990, has a name of varying pronunciation and spelling (as *Hurstmonceux* or *Hurstmonceaux*). Ross, p. 103, recommends stress of the first syllable, as *Huhst* mun syooh, while the *-ceux* is also pronounced zooh.] *Hurstmonceaux Castle* (pronounced *Herstmonsiou*) [Ruth McKenney & Richard Bransten, *Here's England*, 1955].

¹**Hertford**, England : *Hahrt* furd (UK *Haht* fud) [Ross, p. 103, says the *t* in the name should not be sounded, so that it is *Hah* fud. This was long the traditional pronunciation for the town and county, as well as for the Oxford college. But the spelling pronunciation now prevails, albeit with *e* sounding as *a*, as for **Hartford.**]

²**Hertford**, USA : *Huhrt* furd (UK *Huht* fud)

Herve, Belgium : Ayrv

Hervey Bay, Australia : Hahr vi *Bay* (UK Hah vi...)

Herzegovina, Bosnia-Herzegovina : Herts a *goh* vi na (UK Huhts a *gov* i na)

Herzliyaa, Israel : Herts a *lee* a (UK Huhts a *lee* a)

Hesdin, France : Ay *dahn*

Hesperia, USA : Hes *pir* i a

Hesse, Germany : Hes

Hessle, England : *Hez* ul

Heswall, England : *Hez* wawl (UK *Hez* wul)

Hetton-le-Hole, England : Het un li *Hohl*

Hettstedt, Germany : *Het* shtet

Hever, England : *Hee* vur (UK *Hee* va)

Hexham, England : *Hek* sum

Heysham, England : *Hee* shum [The Lancashire town is often called *Hay* shum by those unfamiliar with the accepted pronunciation.]

Heythrop, England : *Heeth* rup

Heywood, England : *Hay* wood

Hialeah, USA : Hiy a *lee* a

Hibbing, USA : *Hib* ing

Hickory, USA : *Hik* a ri

Hicksville, USA : *Hiks* vil

Hierro, Canary Islands : *Yayr* roh

Higashiosaka, Japan : Hee gah shee *oh* sah kah

Higham, England : *Hiy* um [There are several villages of this name. That of Higham near Barnsley, Yorkshire, is locally also pronounced *Hik* um.]

Higham Ferrers, England : Hiy um *Fer* urz (UK ... *Fer* uz)

Highbury, England : *Hiy* ber i (UK *Hiy* bri)

Highgate, England : *Hiy* gayt

Highland, Scotland; USA : *Hiy* lund

High Point, USA : *Hiy* Poynt

High Wycombe, England : Hiy *Wik* um

Higüey, Dominican Republic : Ee *gway*

Hildburghausen, Germany : *Hilt* boork how zun

Hildesheim, Germany : *Hil* dus hiym

Hillerød, Denmark : *Hee* la ruhdh

Hillhead, Scotland : Hil *hed*

Hillingdon, England : *Hil* ing dun

Hillsboro, USA : *Hilz* buhr oh

Hillsborough, England; USA : *Hilz* buhr oh (UK *Hilz* bra)

Hilo, USA : *Hee* loh

Hilversum, Netherlands : *Hil* vur sum (UK *Hil* va sum)

Himachal Pradesh, India : Hi mah chul Pra *daysh*

Himalaya, Asia : Him a *lay* a

Himeji, Japan : Hee *may* jee

Hinchinbrook, Australia : *Hinch* in brook

Hinchley, England : *Hinch* li

Hinckley, England : *Hink* li

Hindhead, England : *Hiynd* hed

Hindley, England : *Hind* li

Hindmarsh, Australia : *Hiynd* mahrsh (UK *Hiynd* mahsh)

Hindu Kush, Asia : Hin dooh *Koosh*

Hingham, USA : *Hing* um

Hinton, Canada : *Hin* tun

Hirakata, Japan : Hee rah *kah* tah

Hiratsuka, Japan : Hi *raht* soo kah

Hirosaki, Japan : Hee *raw* sah kee

Hiroshima, Japan : Hir oh *shee* ma (UK Hi *rosh* i ma)

Hirwaun, Wales : *Hir* wiyn (UK *Hi* a wiyn) [An alternate local pronunciation of the village's name is *Huh* win.]

Hisar, India : Hi *sahr*

Hispaniola, West Indies : His pun *yohl* a (UK His pan i *oh* la)

Hitachi, Japan : Hee *tah* chee

Hitchin, England : *Hich* in

Hjørring, Denmark : *Yuh* ring
Hluhluwe, South Africa : Shloo *shlooh* way
Ho, Ghana : Hoh
¹**Hobart**, Australia : *Hoh* bahrt (UK *Hoh* baht)
²**Hobart**, USA : *Hoh* burt (UK *Hoh* but)
Hobbs, USA : Hahbz (UK Hobz)
Hoboken, USA : *Hoh* boh kun
Hochfelden, France : *Ohk* fel den
Hochheim, Germany : *Hohkh* hiym
Ho Chi Minh City, Vietnam : Hoh Chee Min *Si* ti
Hoddesdon, England : *Hahdz* dun (UK *Hodz* dun)
Hódmezővásárhely, Hungary : *Hohd* me zuh vah shahr hay [The city's name analyzes as Hungarian *hód*, "beaver," *mező*, "field," *vásár*, "market," and *hely*, "place," meaning "place of the market by the field of beavers." Hence the stress on the first syllable, as if "Beavermarket."]
Hof, Germany : Hohf
Hohenlinden, Germany : *Hoh* un lin dun
Hohenzollern, Germany : *Hoh* un zah lurn (UK Hoh un *zol* un) (German Hoh un *tsaw* lurn)
Hohhot, China : Hoh *hawt* (UK Hoh *hot*)
Hokitika, New Zealand : Hoh ki *tee* ka
Hokkaido, Japan : Hoh *kiy* doh
Holbeach, England : *Hohl* beech
Holborn, England : *Hohl* bawrn (UK *Hoh* bun) [The UK pronunciation of the London district's name normally omits the *l* although it is not incorrect to sound it.]
    The pronunciation of Holborn is "Holeburn" or "Hoeburn" [A.D. Mills, *A Dictionary of London Place Names*, 2001].
Holbrook, USA : *Hohl* brook
Holden, USA : *Hohl* dun
Holderness, England : *Hohl* dur nes (UK *Hohl* da nes)
Holguín, Cuba : Awl *geen*

Holland, Europe; USA : *Hah* lund (UK *Hol* und) (Dutch *Haw* lahnt)
Holliston, USA : *Hah* lis tun (UK *Hol* is tun)
Hollywood, USA : *Hah* li wood (UK *Hol* i wood)
Holmfirth, England : Hohm *fuhrth* (UK Hohm *fuhth*)
Holon, Israel : Ho *lohn*
Holstein, Germany : *Hohl* steen (UK *Hol* stiyn) (German *Hawl* shtiyn)
Holsteinsborg, Greenland : *Hohl* stiynz bawrg
Holyhead, Wales : *Hah* li hed (UK *Hol* i hed) [Ross, p. 104, cautions against pronouncing the first part of the port town's name as *holy*, although this is the etymological sense ("holy headland").]
Holyoke, USA : *Hohl* yohk
Holyport, England : *Hah* li pawrt (UK *Hol* i pawt)
Holywell, Wales : *Hah* li wel (UK *Hol* i wel)
Holzminden, Germany : *Hawlts* min dun
Homberg, Germany : *Hahm* buhrg (UK *Hom* buhg) (German *Hawm* berk)
Homerton, England : *Hah* mur tun (UK *Hom* a tun)
Homestead, USA : *Hohm* sted
Homewood, USA : *Hohm* wood
¹**Homs**, Libya : Homs
²**Homs**, Syria : Hahmz (UK Homz)
Homyel, Belarus : *Khawm* yel
Honduras, Central America : Hahn *door* us (UK Hon *dyoo* a rus)
Honfleur, France : Hahn *fluhr* (UK Hon *fluh*) (French Awn *fluhr*)
Hong Gai, Vietnam : Hawng *Giy*
Hong Kong, China : *Hahng* Kahng (UK Hong *Kong*)
Honiara, Solomon Islands : Hoh ni *ah* ra
Honiton, England : *Hah* ni tun [Ross, p. 104, elects *Hon* i tun for the name of the Devon town, and his preference is still shared by many. Accord-

ing to some sources, including Jones, p. 258, the prime pronunciation is *Hon* i tun, with *Hah* ni tun as the local variant.]

Honokaa, USA : Hah na *kah* ah (UK Hon a *kah* ah)

Honolulu, USA : Hah na *looh* looh (UK Hon a *looh* looh) [As indicated by the quote below, the Hawaiian capital city's name was at one time pronounced Hoh noh *looh* looh.] *Honolulu*, in the original native speech, was *Ho-nolulu*, but now it is *Hon-olulu* [Mencken, p. 541].

Honshu, Japan : *Hahn* shooh (UK *Hon* shooh)

Hoofddorp, Netherlands : *Hohft* dawrp

Hoogeveen, Netherlands : Hoh kha *vayn*

Hooghly, India : *Hooh* gli

Hook of Holland, Netherlands : Hook uv *Hah* lund (UK ... *Hol* und)

Hoorn, Netherlands : Hawrn (UK Hawn) (Dutch Hohrn)

Hoover, USA : *Hooh* vur (UK *Hooh* va)

Hopatcong, USA : Ha *pat* kahn (UK Ha *pat* kong)

Hopetown, South Africa : *Hohp* town

Hopewell, USA : *Hohp* wel

Hopkinsville, USA : *Hahp* kinz vil (UK *Hop* kinz vil)

Hoquiam, USA : *Hoh* kwee um

Horbury, England : *Hawr* ber i (UK *Haw* bri)

Horgen, Switzerland : *Hawr* gun

Horley, England : *Hawr* li (UK *Haw* li)

Horlivka, Ukraine : *Hawr* luf ka

Hormuz, Iran : Hawr *moohz* (UK Haw *moohz*)

Horncastle, England : *Hawrn* kas ul (UK *Hawn* kah sul) [Ross, p. 105, opts for stress on the second syllable of the Lincolnshire town's name, giving UK Hawn *kah* sul.]

Hornchurch, England : *Hawrn* chuhrch (UK *Hawn* chuhch)

Hornsea, England : *Hawrn* see (UK *Hawn* see)

Hornsey, England : *Hawrn* zi (UK *Hawn* zi)

Horsens, Denmark : *Hawr* suns

Horsham, Australia; England : *Hawr* shum (UK *Haw* shum)

Horsmonden, England : Hawrz mun *den* (UK Hawz mun *den*) [Jones, p. 259, gives Haw sun *den* as an "old-fashioned local pronunciation" of the Kent village's name.]

Horsted Keynes, England : Hawr stid *Kaynz* (UK Haw stid...) [The second word of the West Sussex village's name has a distinct pronunciation from that of **Milton Keynes**.]

Horwich, England : *Haw* rich (UK *Hor* ich)

Hospitalet, Spain : *Hahs* pit a let (UK *Hos* pit a let) (Spanish Ohs pee tah *let*)

Hot Springs, USA : *Haht* Springz (UK *Hot*...)

Houghton, England; USA : *Hoh* tun [Most Houghtons in England have names pronounced as here, although many have an alternate form *How* tun which locally may predominate.]

Houghton-le-Spring, England : Hoh tun li *Spring*

Houma, USA : *Hoh* ma

Hounslow, England : *Hownz* loh

Housatonic, USA : Hooh sa *tahn* ik (UK Hooh sa *ton* ik)

¹Houston, USA (Georgia) : *How* stun [This is also the pronunciation for New York City's Houston Street.]

²Houston, USA (Texas) : *Hyooh* stun

Houtman Abrolhos, Australia : Howt man A *brah* lus (UK ... A *brol* us)

Hovd, Mongolia : *Hawv* da

Hove, England : Hohv

Howden, England : *How* dun

Howick, New Zealand; South Africa : *How* ik

Howland (Island), Pacific Ocean : *How* lund

Howrah, India : *How* ra

Howth, Ireland : Hohth [Ross, p. 106, favors Howdh for the name of the Co. Dublin port and resort.]

Hoxne, England : *Hahk* sun (UK *Hok*

sun) [Those unfamiliar with the name of the Suffolk village usually pronounce it US *Hahks* ni, UK *Hoks* ni.]

(1) Hoxne (to be pronounced "Hoxen" if you are not to evoke the hint of a smile from a Suffolk man) [Garry Hogg, *The Shell Book of Exploring Britain*, 1971].

(2) The name of this village is pronounced "hoxen" and may refer to the village site, comparing it to the shape of muscles in the heel of a horse [i.e. its hock] [John Hadfield, ed., *The Shell Book of English Villages*, 1980].

Hoyerswerda, Germany : Hoy urs *ver* da

Hoylake, England : *Hoy* layk

Hradec Králové, Czech Republic : Hrah dets *Krah* law ve

Hrazdan, Armenia : *Hrahz* dun

Hrodna, Belarus : *Khrawd* na

Huainan, China : Hwiy *nahn*

Huambo, Angola : *Wahm* boh

Huancavelica, Peru : Wahng kah vah *lee* kah

Huancayo, Peru : Wahng *kiy* oh

Huánuco, Peru : *Wah* nuh koh

Hubei, China : Hooh *bay*

Hubli-Dharwar, India : Hoo bli Dahr *wahr*

Hucknall, England : *Hahk* nul

Huddersfield, England : *Hah* durz feeld (UK *Hah* duz feeld)

Huddinge, Sweden : *Hoo* ding a

Hudson, Canada; USA : *Hahd* sun

Hue, Vietnam : Hooh *ay*

Huehuetenango, Guatemala : Way way tay *nahng* goh

Huelgoat, France : Wel *gwaht*

Huelva, Spain : *Wel* vah

Huesca, Spain : *Wes* kah

Hugo, USA : *Hyooh* goh

Huila, Colombia : *Wee* lah

Huíla, Angola : *Wee* la

Huizen, Netherlands : *Hoy* zun

Hull, Canada; England; USA : Hahl

Humacao, Puerto Rico : Ooh ma *kow*

Humansdorp, South Africa : *Hooh* muns dawrp (UK *Hooh* muns dawp)

Humber, England : *Hahm* bur (UK *Hahm* ba)

Humboldt, USA : *Hahm* bohlt

Hunan, China : Hooh *nahn* (UK Hooh *nan*)

Hunedoara, Romania : Hooh nay *dwah* rah

Hungary, Europe : *Hahng* ga ri

Hungerford, England : *Hahng* gur furd (UK *Hahng* ga fud)

Hunstanton, England : Hahn *stan* tun [The name of the Norfolk seaside resort is locally also pronounced *Hahn* stun.]

If you asked the way to HUNSTANTON, ... your guide would probably remark "Oh, you mean Hunston" [H.J. Stokes, *English Place-Names*, 1948].

Huntingdon, England; USA : *Hahn* ting dun

Huntington, USA : *Hahn* ting tun

Huntington Beach, USA : Hahn ting tun *Beech*

Huntly, Scotland : *Hahnt* li

Huntsville, USA : *Hahnts* vil

Huron, USA : *Hyoor* un (UK *Hyoo* a run)

Hurstmonceux *see* **Herstmonceux**

Hurstpierpoint, England : Huhrst pir *poynt* (UK Huhst pi a *poynt*)

Hurstville, Australia : *Huhrst* vil (UK *Huhst* vil)

Hürth, Germany : Heert

Husum, Germany : *Hooh* zum

Hutchinson, USA : *Hah* chun sun (UK *Hah* chin sun)

Huy, Belgium : Wee

Huyton, England : *Hiy* tun

Hvar, Croatia : Hvahr (UK Hvah)

Hvidovre, Denmark : *Vee* dhaw ra

Hwange, Zimbabwe : *Hwahng* gay

Hwang Ho, China : Hwang *Hoh*

Hyannis, USA : Hiy *an* is

Hyde, England : Hiyd

Hyderabad, India; Pakistan : *Hiy* dur a bad [Both Lloyd James 1937 and Ross, p.106, prefer a trisyllabic pronunciation Hiy dra *bad* for the city's name, with a final stress.]

Hyères, France : I *yayr*
Hyrcania, Iran : Huhr *kay* ni a (UK Huh *kay* ni a)
Hythe, England : Hiydh
Hyvinkää, Finland : *Hee* ving ka
Iaşi, Romania : Yahsh
Ibadan, Nigeria : Ee *bah* dun (UK I *bad* un)
Ibagué, Colombia : Ee bah *gay*
Ibaraki, Japan : Ee bah *rah* kee
Ibarra, Ecuador : Ee *bahr* rah
Iberia, Europe : Iy *bir* i a (UK Iy *bi* a ri a)
Ibiza, Balearic Islands : I *bee* tha [A spelling pronunciation I *bee* sa is sometimes heard for the island, a popular tourist destination, but this is regarded as incorrect by many.]
    Ibiza is pronounced Ibbeetha [Guy Egmont, *The Art of Egmontese*, 1961].
Ibstock, England : *Ib* stahk (UK *Ib* stok)
Ica, Peru : *Ee* kah
Icaria, Greece : I *ker* i a (UK I *kay* a ri a)
Içel, Turkey : *Ee* chel
Iceland, Europe : *Iys* lund
Ichinomiya, Japan : Ee chee *noh* mee yah
Icod, Canary Islands : Ee *kawdh*
Idaho, USA : *Iy* da hoh
Idar-Oberstein, Germany : Ee dahr *Oh* bur shtiyn
Iddesleigh, England : *Idz* li
Idfu, Egypt : *Id* fooh
Iditarod, USA : Iy *dit* a rahd (UK Iy *dit* a rod)
Idrija, Slovenia : Id *ree* ah
Ieper, Belgium : *Ee* pur
Ife, Nigeria : *Ee* fay
Ifield, England : *Iy* feeld
Ifni, Morocco : *If* nee
Igarka, Russia : I *gahr* ka
Ightham, England : *Iy* tum
Iglesias, Sardinia, Italy : Ee *glez* yahs
Iguaçu, Brazil : Ee gwah *sooh*
Iguala, Mexico : Ee *gwah* lah
Igualada, Spain : Ee gwah *lah* dhah
Iguatu, Brazil : Ee gwa *tooh*
Ijebu-Ode, Nigeria : Ee jay booh *Oh* day

IJsselmeer, Netherlands : *Ay* sul mer (UK *Ay* sul may a) [Dutch *ij* is regarded as a single letter, pronounced *ay* or *iy*, and both parts are capitalized accordingly.]
Ikeda, Japan : Ee *kay* dah
Ikeja, Nigeria : Ee *kay* yah
Ikorodu, Nigeria : Ee koh roh *dooh*
Ila, Nigeria : *Ee* lah
Ilam, Iran : Ee *lahm*
Iława, Poland : Ee *wah* vah
Ilchester, England : *Il* ches tur (UK *Il* chis ta)
Île-de-France, France : Eeld *Frahns*
Ilesha, Nigeria : Ee *lay* shah
Ilford, England : *Il* furd (UK *Il* fud)
Ilfracombe, England : *Il* fra koohm
Ilhéus, Brazil : Il *yay* oos
Iligan, Philippines : Ee *lee* gahn
Ilkeston, England : *Il* ka stun
Ilkley, England : *Ilk* li [A local pronunciation *Ilk* la is also heard for the West Yorkshire town, especially in the popular song "On Ilkley Moor baht 'at" (the last two words are dialect for "without a hat"), as reflected in its variant title, cited in the quote below.]
    This spa town in the moors gave Yorkshire its national anthem, "On Ikla Moor baht 'at," a ballad about the uselessness of it all, set to a hymn tune [John Hadfield, ed., *The Shell Book of England*, 1971].
Illawarra, Australia : Il a *waw* ra (UK Il a *wor* a)
Illampu, Bolivia : Ee *lyahm* pooh
Illimani, Bolivia : Ee yee *mah* nee
Illinois, USA : Il a *noy* [An alternate pronunciation of the state's name, especially formerly or locally, is Il a *noyz*.]
Illyria, Europe : I *lir* i a
Illzach, France : Eel *zahk*
Ilmen, Russia : *Il* mun
Ilmenau, Germany : *Il* ma now
Ilminster, England : *Il* min stur (UK *Il* min sta)
Ilo, Peru : *Ee* loh

Ilocos Norte, Philippines : I loh kohs *Nawr* tay

Ilocos Sur, Philippines : I loh kohs *Soohr*

Iloilo, Philippines : Ee loh *ee* loh

Ilorin, Nigeria : Ee *loh* reen

Imabari, Japan : Ee mah *bah* ree

Imatra, Finland : *I* mah trah

Imbabura, Ecuador : Eem bah *booh* rah

Imeritia, Georgia : I ma *rish* a

Immingham, England : *Im* ing um

Imola, Italy : *Ee* moh la

Imperia, Italy : Im *pir* ee a

Imphal, India : *Imp* hul

Inari, Finland : *Ee* nah ree

Inca, Spain : *Ing* kah

Ince-in-Makerfield, England : Ins in *May* kur feeld (UK ... *May* ka feeld)

Inch'ŏn, South Korea : In *chahn* (UK In *chon*)

Independence, USA : In di *pen* duns

Independencia, Dominican Republic : Een day pen *den* see ah

India, Asia : *In* di a

Indiana, USA : In di *an* a [An alternate pronunciation of the state's name is In di *ah* na, recommended by Lloyd James 1937.]

Indianapolis, USA : In di a *nap* a lis

Indigirka, Russia : In di *gir* ka

Indio, USA : *In* di oh

Indo-China, Asia : In doh *Chiy* na

Indonesia, Asia : In da *nee* zha

Indore, India : In *dawr* (UK In *daw*)

Indramayu, Indonesia : In dra *mah* yooh

Indre, France : Ahndr

Indus, Asia : *In* dus

Ingatestone, England : *Ing* gut stohn

Ingleborough, England : *Ing* gul buhr oh (UK *Ing* gul bra)

Inglewood, USA : *Ing* gul wood

Ingolstadt, Germany : *Ing* gul shtaht

Ingrid Christensen (Coast), Antarctica : In grud *Kris* tun sun

Ingushetia, Russia : Ing gooh *shee* sha (UK Ing goo *shet* i a)

Inhambane, Mozambique : Een yahm *bah* nay

Inkerman, Ukraine : *Ing* kur mun (UK *Ing* ka mun) (Russian In kir *mahn*)

Inkster, USA : *Ingk* stur (UK *Ingk* sta)

Innsbruck, Austria : *Inz* brook (German *Ins* brook)

Inowrocław, Poland : Ee naw *vrawt* swahf

In Salah, Algeria : In Sa *lah*

Interlaken, Switzerland : *In* tur lah kun (UK *In* ta lah kun)

Inuvik, Canada : *I* noo vik

Inveraray, Scotland : In va *rer* i (UK In va *ray* a ri)

Invercargill, New Zealand : In vur *kahr* gul (UK In va *kah* gil)

Inverell, Australia : In va *rel*

Invergordon, Scotland : In vur *gawr* dun (UK In va *gaw* dun)

Inverkeithing, Scotland : In vur *kee* dhing (UK In va *kee* dhing)

Invermoriston, Scotland : In vur *maw* ris tun (UK In va *mor* is tun)

¹**Inverness**, Scotland : In vur *nes* (UK In va *nes*)

²**Inverness**, USA : *In* vur nes (UK *In* va nes)

Inverurie, Scotland : In vur *oor* i (UK In va *roo* a ri)

Inyanga, Zimbabwe : In *yang* ga

Iona, Scotland : Iy *oh* na

Ionia, Asia : Iy *oh* ni a

Iowa, USA : *Iy* a wa (UK *Iy* oh a) [The quote below refers to a local pronunciation of the state's name familiar from the "Iowa Corn Song" ("We're from I-O-way, I-O-way").]

In the early days the pronunciation of *Iowa* was always *Ioway*, but the schoolmarm has brought in *Iowuh*, with the accent on the first syllable [Mencken, p. 541].

Ipameri, Brazil : Ee pa mi *ree*

Ipoh, Malaysia : *Ee* poh

Ipswich, Australia; England; USA : *Ips* wich [A former local pronunciation of the English town's name was *Ip* sij, as was that of the US town named for it.]

Iqaluit, Canada : Ee *kah* loo it

Iquique, Chile : Ee *kee* kay
Iquitos, Peru : Ee *kee* tos
Iráklion, Greece : Ee *rah* klee awn
Iran, Asia : I *rahn*
Irapuato, Mexico : Ee rah *pwah* toh
Iraq, Asia : I *rahk*
Irbid, Jordan : *Ir* bid
Ireland, Europe : *Iy* ur lund (UK *Iy* a lund)
Irian Jaya, Indonesia : Ir i un *Jiy* a
Iringa, Tanzania : Ee *ring* gah
Irkutsk, Russia : Ir *koohtsk* (UK Uh *kootsk*) (Russian Ir *kootsk*)
Irlam, England : *Uhr* lum (UK *Uh* lum)
Ironbridge, England : *Iy* urn brij (UK *Iy* un brij)
Iroquois, USA : *Ir* a kwoy
Irrawaddy, Myanmar : Ir a *wah* di (UK Ir a *wod* i)
Irtysh, Russia : Ir *tish*
Irún, Spain : I *roohn*
¹Irvine, Scotland : *Uhr* vun (UK *Uh* vin)
²Irvine, USA : *Uhr* viyn (UK *Uh* viyn) [But the name of Irvine, Kentucky, is as **¹Irvine**.]
Irving, USA : *Uhr* ving (UK *Uh* ving)
Irvington, USA : *Uhr* ving tun (UK *Uh* ving tun)
Irwell, England : *Uhr* wel (UK *Uh* wel)
Isabela, Philippines; Puerto Rico : Ee sah *bay* lah
Ísafjördhur, Iceland : *Ee* sah fyuhr dhur
Ischia, Italy : *Is* kee a
Ise, Japan : *Ee* say
Isère, France : Ee *zer*
Iserlohn, Germany : Ee zer *lohn*
Isernia, Italy : Ee *zer* nee ah
Iseyin, Nigeria : Ee *say* yin
Isham, England : *Iy* shum
Ishimbay, Russia : Ee shim *biy*
Iskenderun, Turkey : Is ken da *roohn*
Isla Cristina, Spain : Eez lah Kris *tee* nah
Isla de la Juventud, Cuba : Ees lah dhay lah Hooh ven *toohdh*
Islamabad, Pakistan : Iz *lahm* a bad
Islay, Scotland : *Iy* la
Isle of Man, British Isles : Iyl uv *Man*

Isle of Wight, England : Iyl uv *Wiyt*
Isleworth, England : *Iy* zul wurth (UK *Iy* zul wuhth) [At one time the name of the former Middlesex village and present London district acquired the form *Thistleworth*, and this affected the local pronunciation. The *Isle-* represents a personal name and has nothing to do with *isle*.]
   Thistleworth appears to have been the local pronunciation down almost to our own day [James Thorne, *Handbook to the Environs of London*, 1876].
Islington, England : *Iz* ling tun
Islip, England; USA : *Iy* slup (UK *Iy* slip)
Islwyn, Wales : *Is* loo in
Ismailia, Egypt : Iz may a *lee* a (UK Iz miy *lee* a)
Isparta, Turkey : Is *pahr* ta (UK Is *pah* ta)
Israel, Asia : *Iz* ri ul (UK *Iz* rayl)
Issus, Turkey : *Is* us
Issyk-Kul, Kyrgyzstan : Is ik *Kuhl*
Istanbul, Turkey : Is tan *bool* (Turkish Is *tahn* boohl)
Istria, Croatia : *Is* tri a
Itabaiana, Brazil : Ee tah bah *yan* a
Itabuna, Brazil : Ee tah *booh* na
Itajaí, Brazil : Ee tah zhah *ee*
Itajubá, Brazil : Ee tah zhoo *bah*
Italy, Europe : *It* a li
Itanagar, India : Ee ta *nah* gur
Itapetininga, Brazil : Ee tah pay tee *ning* ga
Itapipoca, Brazil : Ee tah pee *poh* ka
Itasca, USA : Iy *tas* ka
Itchen, England : *Ich* in
Ithaca, Greece; USA : *Ith* i ka (UK *Ith* a ka)
Ittoqqortoormiit, Greenland : Ee tawk kawr *tohr* meet
Ituiutaba, Brazil : Ee tooh yooh *tah* ba
Itumbiara, Brazil : Ee toom *byah* ra
Ivano-Frankovsk, Ukraine : I vah noh *Frang* kovsk
Ivanovo, Russia : Ee *vah* na voh (Russian Ee *vah* na va)
Iver, England : *Iy* vur (UK *Iy* va)

Ivory Coast, Africa : Iy vur i *Kohst* (UK Iy vri...)
Ivrea, Italy : Ee *vray* ah
Iwaki, Japan : Ee *wah* kee
Iwakuni, Japan : Ee wah *kooh* nee
Iwerne Courtney, England : Yooh uhrn *Kawrt* ni (UK Yooh uhn *Kawt* ni)
Iwo, Nigeria : *Ee* woh
Iwo Jima, Japan : Ee woh *Jee* mah
Ixelles, Belgium : Eek *sel*
Ixmiquilpan, Mexico : Ees mee *keel* pahn
Izegem, Belgium : *Ee* za khum
Izhevsk, Russia : *Ee* zhefsk
Izmayil, Ukraine : Ees mah *eel*
Izmir, Turkey : Iz *mir* (UK Iz *mee* a)
Izmit, Turkey : Iz *mit*
Iztaccíhuatl, Mexico : Ees tahk *see* wah tul
Iztapalapa, Mexico : Ees tah pah *lah* pah
Izumi, Japan : Ee *zooh* mee
Izumo, Japan : Ee *zooh* moh
Izyum, Ukraine : Iz *yoohm*
Jabalpur, India : *Jab* ul poor
Jablonec nad Nisou, Czech Republic : Yah blaw nets nahd *Nee* sooh
Jaboatão, Brazil : Zha bwa *town*
Jaca, Spain : *Hah* kah
Jacareí, Brazil : Zhah kah ree *ee*
Jáchymov, Czech Republic : Yah khee mawf
Jackson, USA : *Jak* sun
Jacksonville, USA : *Jak* sun vil
Jacmel, Haiti : Zhahk *mel*
Jacobabad, Pakistan : *Jay* kub a bahd (UK *Jay* kub a bad)
Jaén, Spain : Hah *ayn*
Jaffa, Israel : *Jah* fa
Jaffna, Sri Lanka : *Jaf* na
Jagersfontein, South Africa : *Yah* kurs fahn tayn (UK *Yah* kus fon tayn)
Jagüey Grande, Cuba : Hah gway *Grahn* day
Jaipur, India : *Jiy* poor
Jaisalmer, India : *Jiy* sul mer
Jajce, Bosnia-Herzegovina : *Yiyt* se
Jakarta, Indonesia : Ja *kahr* ta (UK Ja *kah* ta)

Jakobshavn, Greenland : *Yah* kups hown
Jalalabad, Afghanistan : Ja *lahl* a bahd
Jalapa, Guatemala; Mexico : Hah *lah* pah
Jalingo, Nigeria : Jah *ling* goh
Jalna, India : *Jahl* na
Jamaica, West Indies : Ja *may* ka
Jamalpur, India : Ja *mahl* poor
Jambi, Indonesia : *Jahm* bi (UK *Jam* bi)
Jamestown, USA : *Jaymz* town
Jammu, India : *Jah* mooh
Jamnagar, India : *Jahm* na gur
Jamshedpur, India : *Jahm* shed poor
Janesville, USA : *Jaynz* vil
Jan Mayen (Island), Arctic Ocean : Yahn *Miy* un
Januária, Brazil : Zhahn *wah* rya
Japan, Asia : Ja *pan*
Jarocin, Poland : Yah *rawt* shin
Jarosław, Poland : Yah *raw* swahf
Jarrow, England : *Jar* oh
Jarvenpaa, Finland : *Yahr* ven pah
Jarvis (Island), Pacific Ocean : *Jahr* vis (UK *Jah* vis)
Jasło, Poland : *Yah* swaw
Jasper, USA : *Jas* pur (UK *Jas* pa)
Jastrzębie-Zdrój, Poland : Yahs *jem* bee Zdroy
Jászberény, Hungary : *Yahz* be rayn
Jaú, Brazil : Zha *ooh*
Jaunpur, India : *Jown* poor
Java, Indonesia : *Jah* va
Jawor, Poland : *Yah* vawr
Jaworzno, Poland : Yah *vawzh* naw
Jayapura, Indonesia : Jah yah *pooh* rah
Jeannette, USA : Ja *net*
Jedburgh, Scotland : *Jed* bur a (UK *Jed* bra)
Jedda, Saudi Arabia : *Jed* a
Jefferson, USA : *Jef* ur sun (UK *Jef* a sun)
Jefferson City, USA : Jef ur sun *Si* ti (UK Jef a sun...)
Jeffersontown, USA : *Jef* ur sun town (UK *Jef* a sun town)
Jeffersonville, USA : *Jef* ur sun vil (UK *Jef* a sun vil)
Jehol, China : Ja *hohl*

Jelenia Góra, Poland : Ye len ya *Goh* ra (Polish Ye len yah *Gooh* rah)
Jelgava, Latvia : *Yel* ga va
Jember, Indonesia : *Jem* bur (UK *Jem* ba)
Jena, Germany : *Yay* na
Jennings, USA : *Jen* ingz
Jepara, Indonesia : Ja *pah* rah
Jequié, Brazil : Zhe *kyay*
Jerécuaro, Mexico : He *ray* kwah roh
Jérémie, Haiti : Zhay ray *mee*
Jerez de García Salinas, Mexico : Hay res dhay Gahr see a Sah *lee* nahs
Jerez de la Frontera, Spain : Hay reth dhay lah Frawn *tay* rah
Jerez de los Caballeros, Spain : Hay reth dhay lohs Kah bah *lyay* rohs
Jericho, USA; West Bank : *Jer* i koh
Jersey, Channel Islands, Europe : *Juhr* zi (UK *Juh* zi)
Jersey City, USA : Juhr zi *Si* ti (UK Juh zi...)
Jerusalem, Israel : Ja *rooh* sa lum
Jervaulx, England : *Juhr* voh (UK *Juh* voh) [The name of the medieval Yorkshire abbey had a former local pronunciation *Jah* vis, like the family name Jarvis. A.H. Smith, in "A Note on Yorkshire Place-Names" (1935), says he never heard this "except at Hawes, a little village at the head of the dale." But Johnston, p. 322, gives it as the sole pronunciation.]
Jessore, India : Je *sawr* (UK Je *saw*)
Jette, Belgium : Zhet
Jezreel, Israel : *Jez* ri ul
Jhang Maghiana, Pakistan : Jahng Mah gee *ah* na
Jhansi, India : *Jahn* si
Jhelum, Pakistan : *Jay* lum [Lloyd James 1937 recommended *Jee* lum for the town and river's name.]
Jiangsu, China : Jang *sooh*
Jiangxi, China : Jang *shee*
Jidda, Saudi Arabia : *Jid* a [Lloyd James 1937 favored Ji *dah* for the seaport city's name.]
Jihlava, Czech Republic : Yee *hlah* va
Jilin, China : Jee *lin*

Jima, Ethiopia : *Jee* ma
Jimaní, Dominican Republic : Hee mah *nee*
Jinan, China : Jee *nahn* (UK Jee *nan*)
Jingdezhen, China : Jing da *jen*
Jinja, Uganda : *Jin* jah
Jinotega, Nicaragua : Hee noh *tay* gah
Jinotepe, Nicaragua : Hee noh *tay* pay
Jinzhou, China : Jin *joh*
Jiujiang, China : Jooh ji *ahng* (UK Jooh *jang*)
Jizzakh, Uzbekistan : Jee *zahk*
João Pessoa, Brazil : Zhwown Pe *soh* a
Jodhpur, India : *Jahd* pur (UK *Jod* pa) [Lloyd James 1937 recommends *Johd* poor for the city and former state's name, and US *johd* purz, UK *jod* puz was a former alternate pronunciation for the riding breeches (jodhpurs), now US *jahd* purz, UK *jod* puz.]
Jodrell Bank, England : Jahd rul *Bangk* (UK Jod rul...)
Joensuu, Finland : *Yaw* en sooh
Johannesburg, South Africa : Joh *han* us buhrg (UK Joh *han* is buhg) [Jones, p. 294, notes that many English-speaking South Africans pronounce the city's name Ja *hon* is buhg, inverting the vowel sounds of the first two syllables.]
John o'Groats, Scotland : Jahn a *Grohts* (UK Jon...)
Johnson, USA : *Jahn* sun (UK *Jon* sun)
Johnson City, USA : Jahn sun *Si* ti (UK Jon sun...)
Johnston, USA : *Jahn* stun (UK *Jon* stun)
Johnstone, Scotland : *Jahn* stun (UK *Jon* stun)
Johnstown, USA : *Jahnz* town (UK *Jonz* town)
Johor, Malaysia : Ja *hawr* (UK Ja *haw*)
Johor Bahru, Malaysia : Ja hawr *Bah* rooh (UK Ja haw...)
Joigny, France : Zhwah *nyee*
Joinvile, Brazil : Zhwayn *vee* lee
Joliet, USA : Joh li *et* [Those unfamiliar with the Illinois city's name may pronounce it US Jah li *et*, UK Jol i *et*.]

Joliette, Canada : Zhoh *lyet*
Jolo, Philippines : *Hoh* loh
Jonesboro, USA : *Johnz* bur oh (UK *Johnz* bra)
Jönköping, Sweden : *Yuhn* shuh ping
Jonquière, Canada : Zhawn *kyer* (UK Zhon ki *ay* a)
Joplin, USA : *Jahp* lin (UK *Jop* lin)
Joppa, Israel : *Jah* pa (UK *Jop* a)
¹Jordan, Asia : *Jawr* dun (UK *Jaw* dun)
²Jordan, Philippines : Hawr *dahn*
Jos, Nigeria : Jaws (UK Jos)
Jotunheim (Mountains), Norway : *Yoh* tun haym
Jovellanos, Cuba : Hoh vay *yah* nohs
Juana Díaz, Puerto Rico : Hwah nah *Dhee* ahs
Juan de Fuca (Strait), Canada : Hwahn da *Fyooh* ka
Juan Fernández, Pacific Ocean : Hwahn Fer *nahn* days
Juan-les-Pins, France : Zhwahn lay *Pang*
Juàzeiro, Brazil : Zhwah *zay* rooh
Juàzeiro do Norte, Brazil : Zhwah zay rooh dooh *Nawr* tee
Jubaland, Somalia : *Jooh* bah land (UK *Jooh* ba land)
Judaea, Israel : Joo *dee* a (UK Joo *di* a)
Judah, Israel : *Jooh* da
Juigalpa, Nicaragua : Hwee *gahl* pah
Juiz de Fora, Brazil : Zhweez dee *Faw* ra
Jujuy, Argentina : Hooh *hwee*
Julianehåb, Greenland : Yooh lee *ah* nah hawp
Jülich, Germany : *Yee* likh
Jullundur, India : *Jahl* un dur
Jumilla, Spain : Hooh *mee* lyah
Junagadh, India : Joo *nah* gud
Jundiaí, Brazil : Zhoohn dya *ee*
Juneau, USA : *Jooh* noh
Jungfrau, Switzerland : *Yoong* frow
Junín, Argentina; Peru : Hooh *neen*
Jupiter, USA : *Jooh* pi tur (UK *Jooh* pi ta)
¹Jura, France; Switzerland : *Joor* a (UK *Joo* a ra) (French Zhee *rah*) [Ross, p. 112, prefers a pronunciation *Jaw* ra for

the mountain range rather than an attempt at the French form.]
²Jura, Scotland : *Joor* a (UK *Joo* a ra)
Jūrmala, Latvia : *Yoohr* ma la
Jutiapa, Guatemala : Hooh *tyah* pah
Juticalpa, Honduras : Hooh tee *kahl* pah
Jutland, Denmark : *Jaht* lund
Jyväskylä, Finland : *Yee* vas kee la
Kabaena, Indonesia : Kah bah *ay* nah
Kabalega (Falls), Uganda : Ka ba *lay* ga
Kabardino-Balkaria, Russia : Ka bar dee noh Bawl *ker* i a (UK Ka ba *dee* no Bawl *kay* a ri a)
Kabul, Afghanistan : *Kah* bul [Ross, p. 112, recommends *Kaw* bul as a pronunciation of the capital city's name, but this would now be uncommon. Ka *bool* was in fact long current.]
Properly pronounced to rhyme with *bauble*, although when I have to refer to the place, which is seldom, I find I prefer to call it the capital (of Afghanistan) [Kingsley Amis, *The King's English*, 1997].
Kabwe, Zambia : *Kahb* way
Kadesh, Syria : *Kay* desh
Kadiköy, Turkey : Kah *duh* kuh i
Kadoma, Zimbabwe : Kah *doh* ma
Kaduna, Nigeria : Kah *dooh* nah
Kaédi, Mauritania : Kah *ay* di
Kaesŏng, North Korea : Kay *sawng*
Kaffraria, South Africa : Kaf *rer* i a (UK Kaf *ray* a ri a)
Kafr ash Shaykh, Egypt : Kaf rash *Shaykh*
Kafue, Zambia : Kah *fooh* ay
Kagoshima, Japan : Kah goh *shee* mah
Kaiapoi, New Zealand : Kiy a *poy*
Kaifeng, China : Kiy *feng*
Kaikoura (Range), New Zealand : Kiy *koor* a
Kailua, USA : Kiy *looh* ah
Kairouan, Tunisia : Ker *wahn* (UK Kay a *wahn*)
Kaiserslautern, Germany : Kiy zurs *low* turn
Kaiserswerth, Germany : *Kiy* zurs vert

Kakadu (National Park), Australia : *Kak* a dooh
Kakamega, Kenya : Kah kah *may* gah
Kakamigahara, Japan : Kah kah mee gah *hah* rah
Kakhovka, Ukraine : Ka *khawf* ka
Kakinada, India : Kah ka *nah* da (UK Kah ki *nah* da)
Kalaallit Nunaat, North America : Kah laht leet Noo *naht*
Kalahari (Desert), Africa : Ka la *hah* ri
Kalamata, Greece : Kah lah *mah* tah
Kalamazoo, USA : Ka la ma *zooh*
Kalat, India : Ka *laht*
Kalemie, Democratic Republic of the Congo : Kah *lay* mee
Kalgoorlie, Australia : Kal *goor* li (UK Kal *goo* a li)
Kalimantan, Indonesia : Ka li *man* tun
Kaliningrad, Russia : Ka *lee* nin grad (Russian Ka lee nin *graht*)
Kalispell, USA : *Kal* a spel
Kalisz, Poland : *Kah* leesh
Kalmar, Sweden : *Kahl* mahr
Kalmthout, Belgium : *Kahlm* toht
Kalmykia, Russia : Kal *mik* i a
Kalocsa, Hungary : *Kaw* law chaw
Kaluga, Russia : Ka *looh* ga
Kalyan, India : Kul *yahn*
Kama, Russia : *Kah* ma
Kamagaya, Japan : Kah mah *gah* yah
Kamakura, Japan : Kah mah *kooh* rah
Kamchatka, Russia : Kam *chat* ka (Russian Kum *chaht* ka)
Kamenets Podolskiy, Ukraine : Kah mi nets Pa *dawl* ski (UK ... Pa *dohl* ski) (Russian Kuh mi nits Pa *dawl* ski)
Kamensk Uralskiy, Russia : Kah minsk Oo *rahl* ski
Kamenz, Germany : *Kah* ments
Kamienna Góra, Poland : Kah myen nah *Gooh* rah
Kamloops, Canada : *Kam* loohps
Kampala, Uganda : Kahm *pah* la (UK Kam *pah* la)
Kampen, Netherlands : *Kahm* pun
Kampuchea, Asia : Kam poo *chee* a
Kamsack, Canada : *Kam* sak

Kamyanets-Podilskyy, Ukraine : Kahm ya nets Pa *dil* ski
Kamyshin, Russia : Ka *mwee* shin
Kanagawa, Japan : Kah *nah* gah wah
Kananga, Democratic Republic of the Congo : Kah *nahng* gah
Kanazawa, Japan : Kah *nah* zah wah
Kanchanaburi, Thailand : Kahn chah nah boo *ree* [Some sources give a pronunciation Kahn boo *ree* for the town's name, omitting the two middle syllables.]
Kanchenjunga, Nepal : Kahn chun *joong* ga (UK Kan chun *joong* ga)
Kanchipuram, India : Kahn *chee* pa rum
Kandahar, Afghanistan : Kan da *hahr* (UK Kan da *hah*)
Kandalaksha, Russia : Kun da *lak* sha
Kandy, Sri Lanka : *Kan* di
Kangar, Malaysia : *Kahng* gahr
Kangavar, Iran : Kahng gah *vahr*
Kangean, Indonesia : *Kahng* ay ahn
Kangnŭng, South Korea : Kahng *nuhng*
Kankakee, USA : Kang ka *kee*
Kankan, Guinea : Kahn *kahn*
Kannapolis, USA : Ka *nap* a lis
Kano, Nigeria : *Kah* noh
Kanpur, India : *Kahn* poor
Kansas, USA : *Kan* zus [In the state itself Kansas River is often called the *Kaw*, pronounced Kaw.]
Kansas City, USA : Kan zus *Si* ti
Kansk, Russia : Kahnsk
Kanye, Botswana : *Kahn* yay
Kaohsiung, Taiwan : Kow *shoong*
Kaolack, Senegal : *Koh* lak
Kapaa, USA : Ka *pah* ah
Kapfenberg, Austria : *Kahp* fun berk
Kaposvár, Hungary : *Kaw* pohsh vahr
Kapsukas, Lithuania : *Kahp* sa kus
Kapuskasing, Canada : Ka pus *kay* sing
Kara-Bogaz Gol, Turkmenistan : Ka ra Ba gaz *Gawl*
Karabük, Turkey : Kah rah *beek*
Karachay-Cherkessia, Russia : Ka ra chiy Chur *kes* i a (UK ... Chuh *kes* i a)
Karachayevsk, Russia : Ka ra *chiy* efsk (Russian Ku ra *cha* yifsk)

Karachi, Pakistan : Ka *rah* chi
Karaganda, Kazakhstan : Kahr a *gahn* da (UK Ka ra *gan* da) (Russian Ka ra gan *dah*)
Karaj, Iran : Kah *rahj*
Karakalpak (Republic), Uzbekistan : Ka ra kal *pahk* (UK Ka ra kal *pak*)
Karakol, Kyrgyzstan : Kah ra *kuhl*
Karakoram (Range), Pakistan : Kah rah *koh* rahm
Karakorum, Mongolia : Kah rah *koh* room
Kara Kum (Desert), Turkmenistan : Kah ra *Koohm*
Karaman, Turkey : Kah ra *mahn*
Karamea (Bight), New Zealand : Kah ra *may* a
Kara (Sea), Russia : *Kah* ra
Karbala, Iraq : *Kahr* bah lah
Karelia, Russia : Ka *ree* li a
Karen, Myanmar : Ka *ren*
Kariba, Zimbabwe : Kah *ree* ba
Karibib, Namibia : Kah ra *bib*
Karimata, Indonesia : Kah ri *mah* ta
Karimunjawa, Indonesia : Kah ri moohn *jah* va
Karlovac, Croatia : *Kahr* la vahts
Karlovo, Bulgaria : *Kahr* loh voh
Karlovy Vary, Czech Republic : Kahr law vee *Vah* ree
Karlshamn, Sweden : Kahrls *hahmn*
Karlskoga, Sweden : Kahrls *kooh* ga
Karlskrona, Sweden : Kahrls *krooh* na
Karlsruhe, Germany : *Kahrlz* rooh a (UK *Kahlz* rooh a) (German *Kahrls* rooh a)
Karlstad, Sweden : *Kahrl* stahd
Karnak, Egypt : *Kahr* nak (UK *Kah* nak)
Karnal, India : Kur *nahl*
Karnataka, India : Kahr *nah* ta ka
Karonga, Malawi : Kah *rawng* ga
Karoo, South Africa : Ka *rooh*
Kars, Turkey : Kahrs
Karshi, Uzbekistan : *Kahr* shee (UK *Kah* shi)
Karviná, Czech Republic : *Kahr* vee nah
Kasama, Zambia : Kah *sah* mah

Kashan, Iran : Kah *shahn*
Kashi, China : *Kah* shi
Kashira, Russia : Ka *shir* a
Kashiwa, Japan : Kah *shee* wah
Kashmir, India : Kash *mir* (UK Kash *mi* a)
Kassala, Sudan : Kah *sah* la
Kassel, Germany : *Kah* sul
Kasserine, Tunisia : Ka sa *reen*
Kastellórizon, Greece : Kahs te *law* ree zawn
Kasterlee, Belgium : *Kahs* tur lay
Kasugai, Japan : Kah *sooh* giy
Kasungu, Malawi : Kah *soong* gooh
Katanga, Democratic Republic of the Congo : Ka *tahng* ga (UK Ka *tang* ga)
Katherine, Australia : *Kath* a rin [This is the "textbook" pronunciation of the Northern Territory town's name, but a colloquial form *Kath* a riyn is also heard.]
Kathmandu, Nepal : Kat man *dooh*
Katmai, USA : *Kat* miy
Katowice, Poland : Kah taw *veet* se
Katrine, Scotland : *Kat* rin
Katrineholm, Sweden : Kah tree na *hawlm*
Katsina, Nigeria : *Kaht* see nah
Kattegat, Denmark : *Kat* i gat (Danish *Kah* ta gaht)
Katwijk, Netherlands : *Kaht* viyk
Kauai, USA : Kah *wiy*
Kaufbeuren, Germany : Kowf *boy* run
Kaunas, Lithuania : *Kow* nus
Kaura Namoda, Nigeria : Kow rah Nah *moh* dah
Kavála, Greece : Kah *vah* lah
Kavaratti, India : Ka va *rah* tee
Kavieng, Papua New Guinea : Ka vee *eng*
Kawaguchi, Japan : Kah wah *gooh* chee
Kawasaki, Japan : Kah wah *sah* kee
Kayes, Mali : Kayz
Kayseri, Turkey : *Kiy* sa ree
Kazakhstan, Asia : Kaz ak *stahn*
Kazan, Russia : Ka *zahn*
Kazanluk, Bulgaria : Kah zahn *luhk*
Kazbek, Russia : Kuz *byek*
Kazerun, Iran : Kah ze *roohn*

Kealakekua, USA : Kay ah lah kay *kooh* ah

Kearney, USA : *Kahr* ni (UK *Kah* ni)

Kearns, USA : Kuhrnz (UK Kuhnz)

Kearny, USA : *Kahr* ni (UK *Kah* ni)

Kecskemét, Hungary : *Kech* ke mayt

Kedah, Malaysia : *Ked* a

Kediri, Indonesia : Kay *dir* ee

Kedleston, England : *Ked* ul stun [The Derbyshire locality, famous for the Georgian house Kedleston Hall, is locally also known as *Ked* lus tun.]

Kedron, Jordan : *Kee* drun (UK *Ked* ron)

Keetmanshoop, Namibia : *Kayt* mahns hohp

Keewatin, Canada : Kee *way* tin

Keflavík, Iceland : *Kef*la vik (Icelandic *Kyep* la veek)

Keighley, England : *Keeth* li [The West Yorkshire town has an Old English name meaning "Cyhha's wood," and the *th* of the present pronunciation evolved in an attempt to preserve the original *h* sound of the Anglo-Saxon personal name. Until relatively recently, the pronunciation was thus *Keekh* li, as indicated in the quote below.]

It is not called Keeley, as might be supposed, but as if written Keihley, wherein there seems to be a relic of a guttural sound [Alfred Easther, *A Glossary of the Dialect of Almondbury and Huddersfield*, 1883].

Keilor, Australia : *Kee* lur (UK *Kee* la)

Keith, Scotland : Keeth

Kelang, Malaysia : Ka *lahng*

Kelantan, Malaysia : Ka *lahn* tahn

Kelheim, Germany : *Kayl* hiym

Kells, Ireland : Kelz

Kelowna, Canada : Ki *loh* na

Kelso, Scotland; USA : *Kel* soh

Kemerovo, Russia : *Kay* ma roh voh (UK *Kem* i ra voh) (Russian *Kyem* i ru va)

Kemi, Finland : *Ke* mee

Kempen, Germany : *Kem* pun

Kempsey, Australia : *Kemp* si

Kempston, England : *Kemp* stun

Kempten, Germany : *Kemp* tun

Kenadsa, Algeria : Kah nahd *zah*

Kenai, USA : *Kee* niy

Kendal, England : *Ken* dul

Kendari, Indonesia : Ken *dah* ri

Kenema, Sierra Leone : Ke *nem* a

Kenilworth, England; USA : *Ken* ul wuhrth (UK *Ken* ul wuhth)

Kenitra, Morocco : Ka *neet* ra

Kenmare, Ireland : Ken *mer* (UK Ken *may* a)

Kennebunkport, USA : Ken a *bahnk* pawrt (UK Ken i *bahnk* pawt)

Kennewick, USA : *Ken* a wik

Kennington, England : *Ken* ing tun

Kenora, Canada : Ka *naw* ra

Kenosha, USA : Ka *noh* sha (UK Ki *noh* sha)

Kensington, England : *Ken* zing tun

Kent, England; USA : Kent

Kentucky, USA : Kun *tah* ki (UK Ken *tah* ki)

Kentwood, USA : *Kent* wood

Kenya, Africa : *Ken* ya [The country was regularly spoken of as *Keen* ya before gaining its independence in 1963, and this was the form recommended by Lloyd James 1937.]

Keokuk, USA : *Kee* a kuk

Kerala, India : *Ker* a la

Kerch, Ukraine : Kerch (UK Kuhch) (Russian Kyerch)

Keren, Eritrea : *Ker* en

Kerguelen (Islands), Indian Ocean : *Kuhr* ga lun (UK *Kuh* ga lin)

Kermadec (Islands), Pacific Ocean : Kuhr *mad* uk (UK Kuh *mad* ik)

Kerman, Iran : Kuhr *mahn* (UK Kuh *mahn*)

Kerouan, Tunisia : Ker *wahn* (UK Kay a *wahn*)

Kerry, Ireland : *Ker* i

Kesteven, England : Kes *tee* vun

Keswick, England : *Kez* ik

Ketchikan, USA : *Kech* i kan

Kętrzyn, Poland : *Kent* chin

Kettering, England; USA : *Ket* a ring

Ketton, England : *Ket* un

Kew, Australia; England : Kyooh
Key Largo, USA : Kee *Lahr* goh (UK ...
Lah goh)
Keynsham, England : *Kayn* shum
Keyser, USA : *Kiy* zur (UK *Kiy* za)
Key West, USA : Kee *West*
Khabarovsk, Russia : Ka *bah* rofsk
(Russian Kha *bah* rufsk)
Khakassia, Russia : Ka *kahs* i a (UK Ka
kas ia) (Russian Kha *kahs* ya)
Khanty-Mansiysk, Russia : Khun tee
Mun *seesk*
Kharagpur, India : *Kah* rag *poor*
Kharkiv, Ukraine : *Khahr* kuf
Kharkov, Ukraine : *Kahr* kuf (UK *Kah*
kof) (Russian *Khahr* kuf)
Khartoum, Sudan : Kahr *toohm* (UK
Kah *toohm*) [The Arabic pronuncia-
tion of the capital city's name is
Khahr *toohm*.]
Khaskovo, Bulgaria : *Khahs* koh voh
Kherson, Ukraine : Ker *sawn* (UK Kay
a *son*) (Russian Khir *sawn*)
Khimki, Russia : *Kheem* ki
Khiva, Uzbekistan : *Khee* va (Russian
Khee *vah*)
Khmelnitsky, Ukraine : Kmel *nit* skee
(Russian Khmyel *nit* ski)
Khmelnytskyy, Ukraine : Khmyel *nit*
ski
Khodzhent, Tajikistan : Khaw *jent*
Khoms, Libya : Hawms
Khorasan, Iran : Khaw ra *sahn* (UK
Khaw ra *san*)
Khorezm, Uzbekistan : Kha *rez* um
Khorog, Tajikistan : Kha *rohg*
Khorramabad, Iran : Khaw rum a *bahd*
Khorramshahr, Iran : Khaw rum *shah*
hur
Khujand, Tajikistan : Khoo *jahnt*
Khulna, Bangladesh : *Khool* na
Khuzestan, Iran : Khooh zi *stahn*
Khvoy, Iran : Khvoy
Khyber (Pass), Afghanistan : *Kiy* bur
(UK *Kiy* ba)
Kiama, Australia : Kiy *am* a
Kidderminster, England : *Kid* ur min
stur (UK *Kid* a min sta)
Kidlington, England : *Kid* ling tun

Kidsgrove, England : *Kidz* grohv
Kidwelly, Wales : Kid *wel* i
Kiel, Germany : Keel
Kielce, Poland : *Kyel* tse
Kielder, England : *Keel* dur (UK *Keel* da)
Kieta, Solomon Islands : Kee *ay* tah
Kiev, Ukraine : *Kee* ef (Russian *Kee* yif)
Kigali, Rwanda : Kee *gah* lee
Kigoma, Tanzania : Kee *goh* mah
Kilauea, USA : Ki la *way* a
Kilburn, England : *Kil* burn (UK *Kil*
bun)
Kildare, Ireland : Kil *der* (UK Kil *day* a)
Kilgore, USA : *Kil* gawr (UK *Kil* gaw)
Kilimanjaro, Tanzania : Ki li mun *jah*
roh
Kilis, Turkey : *Kee* lees
Kilkenny, Ireland : Kil *ken* i
Killarney, Ireland : Ki *lahr* ni (UK Ki
lah ni)
Killeen, USA : Ki *leen*
Killiekrankie, Scotland : Ki li *krang* ki
Killin, Scotland : Ki *lin*
Killingly, USA : *Kil* ing li
Kilmarnock, Scotland : Kil *mahr* nuk
(UK Kil *mah* nuk)
Kilrush, Ireland : Kil *rahsh*
Kilsyth, Scotland : Kil *siyth*
Kilwinning, Scotland : Kil *win* ing
Kimberley, Australia; Canada; South
Africa : *Kim* bur lee (UK *Kim* ba li)
Kimbolton, England : Kim *bohl* tun
Kim-ch'aek, North Korea : Keem *chak*
Kinabalu, Malaysia : Ki na *bah* looh
Kincardine, Scotland : Kin *kahr* dun
(UK Kin *kah* din)
Kindersley, Canada : *Kin* durz li (UK
Kin duz li)
Kindia, Guinea : *Kin* dee ah
Kindu, Democratic Republic of the
Congo : *Kin* dooh
Kineshma, Russia : *Kee* nish ma
Kingborough, Australia : *King* buhr oh
(UK *King* ba ra)
Kingisepp, Russia : *Keeng* gee sep
Kingman, USA : *King* mun
Kingsbridge, England : *Kingz* brij
Kingskerswell, England : Kingz *kuhrz*
wul (UK Kingz *kuhz* wul)

King's Lynn, England : Kingz *Lin*
Kingsteignton, England : Kingz *tayn* tun
Kingston, Canada; England; Jamaica; USA : *King* stun
Kingston upon Thames, England : King stun a pahn *Temz* (UK ... a pon...)
Kingstown, St. Vincent and the Grenadines : *Kingz* town
Kingsville, USA : *Kingz* vil
Kingswear, England : *Kingz* wir (UK *Kingz* wi a)
Kingswinford, England : King *swin* furd (UK King *swin* fud)
Kingswood, England : *Kingz* wood
Kington, England : *King* tun
Kingussie, Scotland : King *yooh* si
King William's Town, South Africa : King *Wil* yumz Town
Kinross, Scotland : Kin *raws* (UK Kin *ros*)
Kinsale, Ireland : Kin *sayl*
Kinshasa, Democratic Republic of the Congo : Kin *shah* sa
Kinston, USA : *Kin* stun
Kintyre, Scotland : Kin *tiyr* (UK Kin *tiy* a)
Kiowa, USA : *Kee* a wah
Kippax, England : *Kip* aks
Kirchheim unter Teck, Germany : Kirkh hiym oon tur *Tek* [In practice the city's main name is usually pronounced *Kir* khiym, as ch followed by h demands precision.]
Kirghizia, Asia : Kir *gee* zha (UK Kuh *giz* i a)
Kiribati, Pacific Ocean : Ki ri *bah* ti [According to some sources, the name is "correctly" pronounced Ki ri *bas*. It represents a local pronunciation for the **Gilbert** Islands that are the nation's main constituent part and that contain its capital, Tarawa.]
Kirikkale, Turkey : Kuh *ruh* kah lay
Kirin, China : Kee *rin*
Kiritimati, Kiribati : Ki *ree* ti mah ti [According to some sources, the name should be pronounced Ka *ris* mus. It

represents a local pronunciation of *Christmas*, the island's original name, given by Captain James Cook, who discovered it on Christmas Eve 1777.]
Kirkburton, England : Kuhrk *buhr* tin (UK Kuhk *buh* tun)
Kirkby, England : *Kuhr* bi (UK *Kuh* bi) [The middle k is not sounded in the names of Kirkby near Liverpool and many other northern towns, as **Kirkby Lonsdale, Kirkbymoorside,** and **Kirkby Stephen,** but places in central England are usually as **Kirkby in Ashfield.**]
Kirkby in Ashfield, England : Kuhrk bi in *Ash* feeld (UK Kuhk bi...)
Kirkby Lonsdale, England : Kuhr bi *Lahnz* dayl (UK Kuh bi *Lonz* dayl)
Kirkbymoorside, England : Kuhr bi *moor* siyd (UK Kuh bi *moo* a siyd)
Kirkby Stephen, England : Kuhr bi *Stee* vun (UK Kuh bi...)
Kirkcaldy, Scotland : Kur *kah* di (UK Ka *kawd* i) [The identical family name is usually pronounced Ka *kawl* di, sounding the l.]
Kirkcudbright, Scotland : Kur *kooh* bri (UK Ka *kooh* bri) [The town's name represents Scots *kirk*, "church," followed by a Gaelic form of the saint's name *Cuthbert*.]
Kirkenes, Norway : *Khir* ka nays
Kirkham, England : *Kuhr* kum (UK *Kuh* kum)
Kirkintilloch, Scotland : Kur kun *til* ukh (UK Kuh kun *ti* lukh)
Kirkland, England; USA : *Kuhrk* lund (UK *Kuhk* lund)
Kirklees, England : Kuhrk *leez* (UK Kuhk *leez*)
Kirkstall, England : Kuhrk *stawl* (UK *Kuhk* stawl) [A local pronunciation *Kuhk* stul also exists for the name of the district of Leeds.]
Kirksville, USA : *Kuhrks* vil (UK *Kuhks* vil)
Kirkuk, Iraq : Kir *koohk*
Kirkwall, Scotland : *Kuhrk* wawl (UK *Kuhk* wawl)

Kirovograd, Ukraine : Ki *roh* va grad (Russian Kee ra va *graht*)

Kirovohrad, Ukraine : Kee ra va *hraht*

Kirovsk, Russia : *Kee* rawfsk (UK *Kee* a rofsk) (Russian *Kir* ufsk)

Kirriemuir, Scotland : Ki ri *myoor* (UK Ki ri *myoo* a)

Kirşehir, Turkey : Kuhr she *hir*

Kirton in Lindsey, England : Kuhr tun un *Lin* zi (UK Kuh tun in...)

Kiruna, Sweden : *Kee* rooh nah

Kiryu, Japan : *Keer* yooh

Kisangani, Democratic Republic of the Congo : Kee sahn *gah* nee

Kiselevsk, Russia : Ki sil *yawfsk*

Kishinev, Moldova : *Kish* i nef (Russian Ki shi *nyof*)

Kishiwada, Japan : Kee shee *wah* dah

Kiskunfélegyháza, Hungary : *Keesh* koohn fay lej hah zaw [The lengthy Hungarian name analyzes as *kis*, "little," *Kun*, a tribal name, *fél*, "district," and *egyház*, "church."]

Kiskunhalas, Hungary : *Keesh* koohn haw lawsh

Kislovodsk, Russia : Kees la *vodsk* (Russian Kees la *vawtsk*)

Kismaayo, Somalia : Kees *mah* yoh

Kissidougou, Guinea : Kee see *dooh* gooh

Kissimmee, USA : Ki *sim* i

Kisumu, Kenya : Kee *sooh* mooh

Kitakyushu, Japan : Kee *tah* kyoo shooh

Kitale, Kenya : Kee *tah* lay

Kitchener, Canada : *Kich* a nur (UK *Kich* i na)

Kíthira, Greece : *Kee* thee rah

Kitikmeot, Canada : Ki *tik* mee ut

Kitimat, Canada : *Ki* ta mat

Kittatinny (Mountains), USA : Ki ta *tin* i

Kitty Hawk, USA : *Ki* ti Hawk

Kitwe, Zambia : *Keet* way

Kitzbühel, Austria : *Kits* byoo ul (German *Kits* bee ul)

Kitzingen, Germany : *Kit* sing un

Kivu, Africa : *Kee* vooh

Kladno, Czech Republic : *Klahd* naw

Klagenfurt, Austria : *Klah* gun foort

Klaipeda, Lithuania : *Kliy* ped a

Klamath, USA : *Klam* uth

Klaten, Indonesia : *Klah* tun

Klerksdorp, South Africa : *Kluhrks* dawrp (UK *Kluhks* dawp)

Kleve, Germany : *Klay* va [The city's name was long known to English speakers as *Cleves*, pronounced Kleevz, as for Anne of Cleves, fourth wife of Henry VIII.]

Klin, Russia : Kleen

Kłodzko, Poland : *Klawt* skaw

Klondike, Canada : *Klahn* diyk (UK *Klon* diyk)

Klosters, Switzerland : *Kloh* sturz (UK *Kloh* stuz) (German *Klaw* stas)

Kluczbork, Poland : *Kloohj* bawrk

Knaresborough, England : *Nerz* buhr oh (UK *Nay* uz bra)

Knebworth, England : *Neb* wurth (UK *Neb* wuth)

Knighton, Wales : *Niy* tun

Knock, Ireland : Nahk (UK Nok)

Knockholt, England : *Nahk* hohlt (UK *Nok* hohlt)

Knockmealdown, Ireland : Nahk *meel* down (UK Nok *meel* down)

Knokke-Heist, Belgium : Knaw ka *Hiyst*

Knossos, Greece : *Nahs* us (UK *Knos* os)

Knottingley, England : *Nah* ting li (UK *Not* ing li)

Knowle, England : Nohl

Knowsley, England : *Nohz* li

Knox, Australia : Nahks (UK Noks)

Knoxville, USA : *Nahks* vil (UK *Noks* vil)

Knoydart, Scotland : *Noy* dahrt (UK *Noy* daht)

Knutsford, England : *Nahts* furd (UK *Nahts* fud)

Kobe, Japan : *Koh* bay

Koblenz, Germany : Koh *blents* (German *Koh* blents)

Kocaeli, Turkey : Ko *jah* a li

Kochi, Japan : *Koh* chee

Kodiak, USA : *Koh* di ak

Koekelberg, Belgium : *Kooh* kul berkh

Koforidua, Ghana : Koh foh ree *dooh* ah
Kofu, Japan : *Koh* fooh
Kohat, Pakistan : Koh *haht*
Kohima, India : *Koh* hee ma
Kohtla-Järve, Estonia : Kohkht la *Yar* vay
Kokand, Uzbekistan : Koh *kand* (Russian Ka *kahnt*)
Kokchetav, Kazakhstan : *Kahk* chi tav (UK *Kok* chi tav) (Russian Kuk chi *tahf*)
Kokkola, Finland : *Kaw* kaw lah
Kokomo, USA : *Koh* ka moh
Kola (Peninsula), Russia : *Koh* la
Kolding, Denmark : *Kawl* ding (UK *Kohl* ding) (Danish *Kaw* leng)
Kolhapur, India : *Koh* la poor
Kolkata, India : Kawl *kah* tah
Kołobrzeg, Poland : Kaw *wawb* zhek
Kolomna, Russia : Ka *lawm* na
Kolomyya, Ukraine : Kul a *mee* ya
Kolonjë, Albania : Ka *lawn* ya
Kolwezi, Democratic Republic of the Congo : Kohl *way* zee
Komagatake, Japan : Koh mah gah *tah* kay
Komandorskiye (Islands), Russia : Ka mahn *dawr* ski ya (UK Kom un *daw* ski ye)
Komárno, Slovakia : Kaw *mahr* naw
Komárom, Hungary : Koh *mah* rohm
Komi, Russia : *Koh* mi
Komodo, Indonesia : Ka *moh* doh
Kompong Cham, Cambodia : Kahm pawng *Chahm* (UK Kom pong *Cham*)
Kompong Som, Cambodia : Kahm pawng *Sawm* (UK Kom pong *Som*)
Komsomolsk, Russia : Kahm sa *mahlsk* (UK Kom sa *mawlsk*) (Russian Kum sa *moylsk*)
Kong, Côte d'Ivoire : Kawng (UK Kong)
Kongo, Africa : *Kahng* goh (UK *Kong* goh)
Kongsberg, Norway : *Kawngs* ber
Königsberg, Russia : *Kay* nigz buhrg (UK *Kuh* nigz buhg) (German *Kuh* nikhs berk)

Königswinter, Germany : *Kuh* nikhs vin tur
Konin, Poland : *Kaw* neen
Köniz, Switzerland : *Kuh* nits
Konotop, Ukraine : Kun ah *tawp*
Konstantinovka, Ukraine : Kun stahn *tee* nuf ka
Konstanz, Germany : *Kawn* stahnts
Kontagora, Nigeria : Kon tah *goh* rah
Konya, Turkey : *Kawn* yah
Kootenay, North America : *Kooh* tun ay (UK *Kooh* ta nay)
Kópavogur, Iceland : *Kow* pah vaw geer
Koper, Slovenia : *Koh* pur
Kopet Dagh, Asia : Koh pet *Dahg*
Kopeysk, Russia : Koh *paysk* (Russian Ka *pyaysk*)
Köping, Sweden : *Chuh* ping
Korçë, Albania : *Kawr* cha
Kordofan, Sudan : Kawr doh *fahn* (UK Kaw da *fan*)
Korea, Asia : Ka *ree* a (UK Ka *ri* a)
Korhogo, Côte d'Ivoire : Kor *hoh* goh
Koriyama, Japan : Koh ree *yah* mah
Koror, Palau : *Kawr* awr
Korosten, Ukraine : Koh ra *sten*
Korsakov, Russia : *Kawr* sa kuf
Korsør, Denmark : Kawr *suhr*
Korsun-Shevchenkovskiy, Ukraine : Kawr soohn Shef *chen* kuf ski
Kortenberg, Belgium : *Kawr* tun bayrk
Kortrijk, Belgium : *Kawrt* riyk (UK *Kawt* riyk)
Kos, Greece : Kahs (UK Kos)
¹**Kosciusko**, Australia : Kah zee *ahs* koh (UK Koz i *ahs* koh)
²**Kosciusko**, USA : Kah see *ahs* koh (UK Kos i *ahs* koh)
Kosice, Slovakia : *Kaw* shee tse
Kosovo, Serbia : *Koh* sa voh (UK *Kos* a voh) (Serbo-Croat *Kaw* saw vaw)
Kosovska Mitrovica, Serbia : Kaw sawv skah *Meet* raw veet sah
Kostroma, Russia : Kahs *troh* ma (UK Kos *troh* ma) (Russian Kus tra *mah*)
Kostrzyn, Poland : *Kaws* chin
Koszalin, Poland : Kaw *shah* leen
Kőszeg, Hungary : *Kuh* seg
Kota, India : *Koh* ta

Kota Baharu, Malaysia : Koh ta *Bah* hah rooh

Kota Kinabalu, Malaysia : Koh ta Ki na *bah* looh

Kota Kota, Malawi : Koh ta *Koh* ta

Köthen, Germany : *Kuh* tun

Kotka, Finland : *Kawt* ka

Kotlas, Russia : *Kawt* lus

Kotor, Montenegro : *Koh* tawr

Kotri, Pakistan : *Koh* tree

Koudougou, Burkina Faso : Kooh *dooh* gooh

Koulikoro, Mali : Kooh lee *koh* roh

Kouroussa, Guinea : Koo *rooh* sah

Kouvola, Finland : *Kaw* ooh voh lah

Kovel, Ukraine : *Koh* vil

Kovrov, Russia : Kahv *rawf*

Kowloon, China : Kow *loohn*

Kozhikode, India : *Koh* zhi kohd

Kpalimé, Togo : Pah lee *may*

Kragujevac, Serbia : *Krah* gooh ye vahts

Krakatau, Indonesia : Kra ka *tow* [The name of the island volcano is popularly spelled *Krakatoa*, pronounced Kra ka *toh* a.]

Kraków, Poland : *Krah* kow (UK *Krak* ow) (Polish *Krah* koohf)

Kraljevo, Serbia : *Krahl* ye voh

Kramatorsk, Ukraine : Krah ma *tawrsk*

Kranj, Slovenia : *Krahn* ya

Krasnodar, Russia : Krahs na *dahr*

Krasnodon, Ukraine : Krahs na *dawn*

Krasnogorsk, Russia : Krahs na *gawrsk*

Krasnograd, Ukraine : Krahs na *graht*

Krasnohrad, Ukraine : Krahs na *hraht*

Krasnovodsk, Turkmenistan : Krahs na *vawtsk*

Krasnoyarsk, Russia : Krahs na *yarsk*

Krefeld, Germany : *Kray* felt

Kremenchug, Ukraine : Kri min *choohk*

Kreuzlingen, Switzerland : *Kroyts* ling un

Kribi, Cameroon : *Kree* bee

Krishnanagar, India : *Krish* na na gur

Kristiansand, Norway : *Kris* tee un sahn

Kristianstad, Sweden : *Kris* tee un stahd

Kristiansund, Norway : *Kris* tee un soon

Kristinehamn, Sweden : Kris *tee* na hahmn

Krivoy Rog, Ukraine : Kri voy *Rahg* (UK Kri voy *Rog*) (Russian Kri voy *Rawk*)

Krk, Croatia : Kurk (UK Kuhk)

Krkonoše, Czech Republic : Kur kaw *noh* she

Kroměříž, Czech Republic : *Kraw* myer zheesh

Kronshtadt, Russia : *Krohn* shtaht

Kroonstad, South Africa : *Krohn* stat

Kropotkin, Russia : Kra *pawt* kin

Krosno, Poland : *Kraws* noh

Krugersdorp, South Africa : *Krooh* gurz dawrp (UK *Krooh* guz dawp)

Krujë, Albania : *Krooh* ya

Kruševac, Serbia : *Krooh* she vahts

Kryvyy Rih, Ukraine : Kri vi *Rikh*

Ksar el Kebir, Morocco : Ksahr el Ke *bir*

Kuala Lipis, Malaysia : Kwah la *Lee* pus

Kuala Lumpur, Malaysia : Kwah la Loom *poor* (UK ... *Loom* poo a) [Ross, p. 115, cites *Lahm* pa as the correct UK pronunciation of the second word of the capital city's name, but it would be highly unusual to hear this today.]

Kuala Pilah, Malaysia : Kwah la *Pee* lah

Kuala Selangor, Malaysia : Kwah la Sa *lahng* awr

Kuala Terengganu, Malaysia : Kwah la Ta reng *gah* nooh

Kuantan, Malaysia : *Kwahn* tahn

Kuban, Russia : Kooh *bahn*

Kuching, Malaysia : *Kooh* ching

Kudus, Indonesia : *Kooh* doohs

Kudymkar, Russia : Kooh *dim* kur

Kuito, Angola : *Kwee* toh

Kukës, Albania : *Kooh* kus

Kulmbach, Germany : *Koolm* bahkh

Kulyab, Tajikistan : Kooh *lyap*

Kumamoto, Japan : Kooh mah *moh* toh

Kumanovo, Macedonia : Koo *mah* na voh

Kumasi, Ghana : Kooh *mah* si

Kumba, Cameroon : *Koohm* bah

Kumo, Nigeria : *Kooh* moh

Kungur, Russia : Koon *goor* (UK Koon *goo* a)
Kunming, China : Koon *ming*
Kunsan, South Korea : Koon *sahn*
Kuopio, Finland : *Kwaw* pee oh
Kupang, Indonesia : *Kooh* pahng
Kurashiki, Japan : Koo *rah* shee kee
Kurdistan, Turkey : *Kuhrd* a stan (UK Kuhd i *stahn*)
Kure, Japan : *Kooh* ray
Kuressaare, Estonia : Koor a *sah* ray
Kurgan, Russia : Koor *gan* (UK Koo a *gahn*)
Kurgan-Tyube, Tajikistan : Koor gahn Tyooh *bay*
Kuril (Islands), Russia : *Koor* il (UK Koo *reel*)
Kursk, Russia : Kuhrsk (UK Kuhsk) (Russian Koorsk)
Kuruman, South Africa : *Koor* a mahn
Kurume, Japan : *Kooh* rooh may
Kushiro, Japan : *Kooh* shee roh
Kushka, Turkmenistan : *Koohsh* ka
Küsnacht, Switzerland : *Kees* nahkht
Küssnacht, Switzerland : *Kees* nahkht
Kustanay, Kazakhstan : Koos ta *niy*
Kuta, Indonesia : *Koh* ta
Kütahya, Turkey : Kee *tah* yah
Kutaisi, Georgia : Kooh tah *ee* si
Kutch, India : Kahch
Kutná Hora, Poland : Kooht na *Haw* ra
Kutno, Poland : *Kooht* naw
Kuwait, Asia : Koo *wayt* (UK Kyoo *wayt*)
Kuybyshev, Russia : *Kooh* i bi shef
Kuznetsk, Russia : Kooz *nyetsk*
Kwajalein, Marshall Islands : *Kwah* ja layn
KwaNdebele, South Africa : Kwahn di *bel* i (UK Kwon di *bel* i)
Kwangju, South Korea : Kwahng *jooh* (UK Kwong *jooh*)
KwaZulu-Natal, South Africa : Kwah zooh looh Na *tal*
Kwekwe, Zimbabwe : *Kway* kway
Kwidzyn, Poland : *Kfeed* zin
Kwinana, Australia : Kwi *nah* na
Kyakhta, Russia : *Kyahkh* tah
Kyŏngju, South Korea : Kyawng *jooh*
Kyoto, Japan : *Kyoh* toh

Kyrgyzstan, Asia : Kir gi *stahn* (UK Kuh gi *stahn*)
Kyushu, Japan : *Kyooh* shooh
Kyustendil, Bulgaria : Kyooh stun *dil*
Kyyiv, Ukraine : *Kee* if
Kyzyl, Russia : Ki *zil*
Kyzyl Kum, Uzbekistan : Ki zil *Koohm*
Kzyl-Orda, Kazakhstan : Ksil Ur *dah*
La Albuera, Spain : Lahl *bway* rah
La Altagracia, Dominican Republic : Lah Ahl tah *grah* syah
La Araucanía, Chile : Lah Ah row kah *nee* ah
La Asunción, Venezuela : Lah soohn *syohn*
La Baie, Canada : La *Biy*
La Banda, Argentina : Lah *Bahn* dah
La Baule-Escoublac, France : La Bohl Es kooh *blahk*
Labé, Guinea : La *bay*
Labinsk, Russia : La *byinsk*
Labrador, Canada : *Lab* ra dawr (UK *Lab* ra daw) [Lloyd James 1937 favored the pronunciation US Lab ra *dawr*, UK Lab ra *daw* for the peninsula's name.]
Lábrea, Brazil : *Lah* bree a
Labuan, Malaysia : Lah boo *ahn* (UK La *booh* un)
La Carolina, Spain : Lah Kah roh *lee* nah
La Castellana, Philippines : La Kahs te *yah* nah
Laccadive (Islands), India : *Lak* a div
La Ceiba, Honduras : Lah *Say* bah
La Chaux-de-Fonds, Switzerland : La Shohd *Fawn*
Lachine, Canada : La *sheen*
Lachlan, Australia : *Lah* klun (UK *Lok* lun)
La Chorrera, Panama : Lah Chohr *ray* rah
La Ciotat, France : La Syoh *tah*
Lackawanna, USA : Lak a *wah* na (UK Lak a *won* a)
La Clayette, France : La *Klet*
La Clusaz, France : La Klee *zah*
Lacock, England : *Lay* kahk (UK *Lay* kok)

La Condamine, Monaco : Lah Kawn dah *mee* nay

Laconia, Greece; USA : La *koh* ni a

La Coruña, Spain : Lah Koh *rooh* nyah

La Crosse, USA : La *Kraws* (UK La *Kros*)

Ladakh, India : La *dahk*

Ladhar Bheinn, Scotland : Lahr *Ven* (UK Lah...)

Ladoga, Russia : *Lah* da ga

Ladysmith, South Africa : *Lay* di smith

Lae, Papua New Guinea : *Lah* ay

La Esperanza, Honduras : La Es pay *rahn* sah

Lafayette, USA : Lah fay *et* (UK Lah fiy *et*) [The pronunciation holds good for most places of the name, with Lah fee *et* as an alternate form, although Lafayette, Alaska, is Lah *fay* it, and Jones, p. 305, has the Louisiana city as Lah *fayt*.]

La Fayette, USA : La *fay* it [In practice the name of the Georgia town is closer to La *fet*.]

Lafia, Nigeria : Lah *fee* ah

Lafiagi, Nigeria : Lah fee *ah* gi

La Follette, USA : La *Fah* lut

Lagarto, Brazil : Lah *gahr* tooh

Lagash, Iraq : *Lay* gash

Laghouat, Algeria : Lah *gwaht*

¹**Lagos**, Nigeria : *Lay* gahs (UK *Lay* gos) [The name of the former capital city is also sometimes pronounced *Lah* gohs by US speakers unfamiliar with Nigeria.]

²**Lagos**, Portugal : *Lah* goohsh

Lagos de Moreno, Mexico : Lah gohs dhay Moh *ray* noh

La Goulette, Tunisia : Lah Gooh *let*

La Grange, USA : La *Graynj*

La Guaira, Venezuela : Lah *Gwiy* rah

La Guajira, Colombia : Lah Gwah *hee* rah

Laguna, Brazil; Philippines : Lah *gooh* nah

La Habra, USA : La *Hah* bra

Lahore, Pakistan : La *hawr* (UK La *haw*)

Lahti, Finland : *Lah* tee

Lairg, Scotland : Lerg (UK *Lay* ug)

Lajeado, Brazil : La *zhyah* dooh

Lajes, Brazil : *Lah* zhis

La Jolla, USA : La *Hoy* a

La Junta, USA : La *Hahn* ta

Lake : if not below, see under main name, e.g., **Superior**

Lake Charles, USA : Layk *Chahrlz*

Lake Havasu City, USA : Layk Hav a sooh *Si* ti

Lakeland, USA : *Layk* lund

Lakenheath, England : *Lay* kun heeth

Lake Oswego, USA : Layk Ah *swee* goh

Lake Placid, USA : Layk *Pla* sud (UK ... *Pla* sid)

Lakeville, USA : *Layk* vil

Lakewood, USA : *Layk* wood

Lake Worth, USA : Layk *Wuhrth* (UK ... *Wuhth*)

Lakshadweep, India : Luk *shahd* weep

La Laguna, Canary Islands : Lah Lah *gooh* nah

La Libertad, El Salvador; Philippines : Lah Lee ber *tahdh*

La Línea, Spain : Lah *Lee* nay ah

Lalitpur, Nepal : La *lit* poor

La Louvière, Belgium : Lah Looh *vyer*

La Mancha, Spain : Lah *Mahn* chah

Lambaréné, Gabon : Lahm ba *ree* ni (UK Lam ba *ree* ni) (French Lahm bah ray *nay*)

Lambayeque, Peru : Lahm bah *yay* kay

Lambeth, England : *Lam* buth [The London borough, bordering the Thames River, has a name meaning "landing place for lambs."]
    The name Lambeth is pronounced as it is spelt, an interesting reminder that in Old English the *b* in the word *lamb* was not a silent letter [A.D. Mills, *A Dictionary of London Place Names*, 2001].

Lambourn, England : *Lam* bawrn (UK *Lam* bawn)

Lamesa, USA : La *mee* sa [This is the Texas town. *Cp.* **La Mesa**.]

La Mesa, USA : La *May* sa [This is the California city. *Cp.* **Lamesa**.]

Lamía, Greece : Lah *mee* ah

La Mirada, USA : Lah Ma *rah* da (UK
  Lah Mi *rah* da)
Lammermuir, Scotland : *Lam* a myoor
  (UK *Lam* a myoo a)
Lamoni, USA : La *moh* niy
Lampang, Thailand : *Lahm* pahng
Lampedusa, Italy : Lam pa *dooh* za (UK
  Lam pi *dyooh* za) (Italian Lahm pe
  dooh zah)
Lampeter, Wales : *Lam* pa tur (UK *Lam*
  pi ta)
Lamu, Kenya : *Lah* mooh
Lanai, USA : La *niy*
Lanark, Scotland : *Lan* urk (UK *Lan*
  uk)
Lancashire, England : *Lang* ka shir (UK
  Lang ka sha)
Lancaster, England; USA : *Lang* ka stur
  (UK *Lang* kas ta) [There are several
  places of the name in the USA and
  the pronunciation can vary slightly
  from one state to another. Cohen, pp.
  1678–9, specifies *Lan* ka stur in Cali-
  fornia and Ohio, *Lang* ki stur in Mis-
  souri and Pennsylvania, and *Lang* ka
  stur in Texas.]
Lanchester, England : *Lan* ches tur
  (UK *Lan* chis ta)
Lanciano, Italy : Lahn *chah* noh
Lancing, England : *Lan* sing (UK *Lahn*
  sing)
Lancy, Switzerland : Lahn *see*
Landau, Germany : *Lahn* dow
Landes, France : Lahnd
Land's End, England : Landz *End*
Landshut, Germany : *Lahnts* hooht
Landskrona, Sweden : Lahnts *krooh* na
Langbaurgh, England : *Lang* bahrf (UK
  Lang bahf)
Langdale, England : *Lang* dayl
Langen, Germany : *Lahng* un
Langenfeld, Germany : *Lahng* un felt
Langenhagen, Germany : Lahng un
  hah gun
Langensalza, Germany : Lahng un
  zahlt sa
Langholm, Scotland : *Lang* um [The
  town's name is also often pronounced
  US *Lang* hohm, UK *Lang* hohlm by

those unfamiliar with the accepted
  pronunciation.]
Langres, France : Lahngr
Languedoc, France : Lahng ga *dahk*
  (UK Long ga *dok*) (French Lahng
  dawk)
Länkäran, Azerbaijan : Lin ka *ran*
Lansing, USA : *Lan* sing (UK *Lahn*
  sing)
Lanús, Argentina : Lah *noohs*
Lanzarote, Canary Islands : Lahn sa *roh*
  ti (UK Lan za *rot* i) (Spanish Lahn
  thah *raw* tay)
Lanzhou, China : Lahn *joh*
Laoag, Philippines : Lah *wahg*
Laodicea, Syria; Turkey : Lay a da *see* a
  (UK Lay oh di *see* a)
Laoighis, Ireland : Leesh
Laon, France : Lahn
La Oroya, Peru : Lah Oh *roh* yah
Laos, Asia : *Lah* oos (UK Lows)
La Palma, Canary Islands; Panama : La
  Pahl mah
La Pampa, Argentina : Lah *Pahm* pah
La Paz, Argentina; Bolivia; Honduras;
  Mexico : Lah *Pahs*
Laphroaig, Scotland : La *froyg*
La Piedad, Mexico : Lah Pyay *dhahdh*
Lapland, Scandinavia : *Lap* land (Nor-
  wegian *Lahp* lahn)
La Plata, Argentina : Lah *Plah* tah
Lappeenranta, Finland : *Lah* pen rahn
  ta
Laprairie, Canada : La *Prer* ee
Laptev (Sea), Russia : *Lap* tif
La Puente, USA : Lah Poo *en* tee
Lapu-Lapu, Philippines : Lah pooh *Lah*
  pooh
L'Aquila, Italy : *Lah* kwee lah
Lar, Iran : Lahr
Larache, Morocco : La *rash*
Laramie, USA : *La* ra mi
  Laramie, Wyo., is often reduced to
  two syllables locally, and pronounced
  Lormie or *Lahrmie* [Mencken,
  p. 541].
Larbert, Scotland : *Lahr* burt (UK *Lah*
  but)
Laredo, USA : La *ray* doh

Lares, Puerto Rico : *Lah* rays

Largo, Scotland; USA : *Lahr* goh (UK *Lah* goh)

Largs, Scotland : Lahrgz (UK Lahgz)

La Rioja, Argentina; Spain : Lah Ree *oh* hah

Larissa, Greece : La *ris* a

Laristan, Iran : La ra *stan*

Larkhall, Scotland : *Lahrk* hawl (UK *Lahk* hawl)

Larnaca, Cyprus : *Lahr* nah kah (UK *Lah* na ka)

Larne, Northern Ireland : Lahrn (UK Lahn)

La Oroya, Peru : Lah Oh *roh* yah

La Rochelle, France : La Roh *shel* (UK La Ro *shel*) (French La Raw *shel*)

La Roche-sur-Yon, France : La Rawsh seer *Yohn*

La Romana, Dominican Republic : Lah Roh *mah* nah

Larsa, Iraq : *Lar* sa

Lars Christensen (Coast), Antarctica : Lahrz *Kris* tun sun

Larsen (Ice Shelf), Antarctica : *Lahr* sun

Larvik, Norway : *Lahr* vik

Las Cruces, USA : Lahs *Krooh* sus (UK Las...)

La Serena, Chile : Lah Say *ray* nah

La Seyne-sur-Mer, France : La Sayn seer *Mer*

Lasham, England : *Lash* um [An alternate local pronunciation of the Hampshire village's name is *Las* um.]

Las Palmas, Canary Islands : Lahs *Pahl* mus (UK Las *Pal* mus) (Spanish Lahs *Pahl* mahs)

La Spezia, Italy : Lah *Spet* syah

Las Piedras, Puerto Rico; Uruguay : Lahs *Pyay* dhrahs

Lassen (Peak), USA : *Las* un

Lasswade, Scotland : Las *wayd*

Las Tablas, Panama : Lahs *Tah* blahs

Las Tunas, Cuba : Lahs *Tooh* nahs

Las Vegas, USA : Lahs *Vay* gus (UK Las...)

Latacunga, Ecuador : Lah tah *koohng* gah

Latakia, Syria : La ta *kee* a

Latina, Italy : Lah *tee* nah

Latium, Italy : *Lay* shi um

La Trinité, Martinique : La Tree nee *tay*

Latrobe, USA : La *trohb*

Lattes, France : Laht

La Tuque, Canada : La *Teek*

Latvia, Europe : *Lat* vi a

Lauchhammer, Germany : *Lowkh* hah mur

Lauderdale, Scotland; USA : *Law* dur dayl (UK *Law* da dayl)

Laugharne, Wales : Lahrn (UK Lahn) (1) The name of this ancient borough ... is pronounced "Larn" [Wynford Vaughan-Thomas and Alun Llewellyn, *The Shell Guide to Wales*, 1969]. (2) Laugharne (the *ugha* is silent) is a small town [Ruth Thomas, *South Wales*, 1977].

¹Launceston, Australia : *Lahn* sa stun (UK *Lawn* sa stun) [A local pronunciation of the Tasmanian city's name is *Lon* sa stun.]

²Launceston, England : *Lawn* sa stun (UK *Lawn* stun) [A local pronunciation of the Cornish town's name is *Lahn* stun. The four pronunciations in order of "correctness" given by Pointon, p. 140, differ from the above: *Lahn* sun, *Lahn* stun, *Lawn* sun, *Lawn* stun.] Pronounced "Lanson," as shown already [in the spelling *Lanson* recorded] in 1478 [O.J. Padel, *A Popular Dictionary of Cornish Place-Names*, 1988].

La Unión, El Salvador : Lah Ooh *nyawn*

Laurel, USA : *Law* rul (UK *Lor* ul)

Lausanne, Switzerland : Loh *zahn*

Laut, Indonesia : Lowt

Laval, Canada; France : La *vahl*

La Vega, Dominican Republic : Lah *Vay* gah

Lavenham, England : *Lav* num

La Verne, USA : La *Vuhrn* (UK La *Vuhn*)

Lavras, Brazil : *Lahv* rahs

Lawrence, USA : *Law* runs (UK *Lor* uns)

Lawton, USA : *Law* tun
Laxey, Isle of Man, British Isles : *Lak* si
Laxou, France : Lahk *sooh*
Layton, USA : *Lay* tun
Lazio, Italy : *Laht* si oh (UK *Lat* si oh) (Italian *Laht* see oh)
Lead, USA : Leed [The South Dakota town is not named for the metal but for the *lead* or deposit of gold by which it was laid out in 1876. The famous Homestake Mine here is still in operation.]
¹Leamington, Canada : *Lee* ming tun
²Leamington, England : *Lem* ing tun [The Warwickshire town is officially known as *Royal Leamington Spa*.]
Leatherhead, England : *Ledh* ur hed (UK *Ledh* a hed)
Leavenworth, USA : *Lev* un wuhrth (UK *Lev* un wuhth)
Lebanon, Asia; USA : *Leb* un un
Lebbeke, Belgium : Lay *bek*
Le Bec-Hellouin, France : Luh Bek El *wahn*
Le Blanc-Mesnil, France : Luh Blahn May *neel*
Lębork, Poland : *Lem* bawrk
Lebowa, South Africa : Le *boh* a
Lebrija, Spain : Lay *bree* hah
Le Cannet, France : Luh Kah *nay*
Lecce, Italy : *Lay* chee
Le Chesnay, France : Luh Shay *nay*
Lechlade, England : *Lech* layd
Leconfield, England : *Lek* un feeld
Le Creusot, France : Luh Kruh *zoh*
Ledbury, England : *Led* ber i (UK *Led* bri)
Lede, Belgium : Layd
Leeds, England : Leedz
Leek, England : Leek
Leeming, England : *Lee* ming
Leesburg, USA : *Leez* buhrg (UK *Leez* buhg)
Leeuwarden, Netherlands : *Lay* vahr da
Leeuwin, Australia : *Looh* un
Leeward (Islands), Pacific Ocean : *Lee* wurd (UK *Lee* wud)
Lefkosia, Cyprus : Lef koh *see* a
Leforest, France : Luh faw *ray*

Legazpi, Philippines : Li *gas* pee
Leghorn, Italy : *Leg* hawrn (UK *Leg* hawn) [The now dated English name of the seaport city of **Livorno** was formerly pronounced Li *gawn*, as in Edward Lear's 1846 limerick: "There was an Old Man of Leghorn, / The smallest as ever was born."]
Legnago, Italy : Le *nyah* goh
Legnano, Italy : Le *nyah* noh
Legnica, Poland : Leg *neet* sah
Le Havre, France : Luh *Ahvr*
Lehigh, USA : *Lee* hiy
Lehrte, Germany : *Ler* ta
Leicester, England; USA : *Les* tur (UK *Les* ta) [The pronunciation *Lay* ses tur is sometimes heard among US or other non-UK speakers unfamiliar with the name of the English city.]
Leichhardt, Australia : *Liy* kahrt (UK *Liy* kaht)
Leiden, Netherlands : *Liy* dun (Dutch *Lay* da]
Leigh, England : Lee [There are several places so named, with some in the south, such as the village near Reigate, Surrey, being pronounced Liy. The name of the Lancashire town at one time had the local pronunciation Leeth or Leekh.]
There are 14 villages called Leigh in Britain. The word, pronounced *lye*, means a forest clearing [John Hadfield, ed., *The Shell Book of English Villages*, 1980].
Leighton Buzzard, England : Lay tun *Bah* zurd (UK ... *Bah* zud)
Leikanger, Norway : *Lay* kahng ur
Leinster, Ireland : *Len* stur (UK *Len* sta)
Leintwardine, England : *Lent* wur diyn (UK *Lent* wa diyn)
Leipzig, Germany : *Liyp* sig (German *Liyp* tsikh)
Leiria, Portugal : Lay *ree* a
Leith, Scotland : Leeth
Leitrim, Ireland : *Lee* trum
Leix, Ireland : Leesh
Leixões, Portugal : Lay *shoynsh*

Lelystad, Netherlands : *Lay* lee staht

Le Mans, France : Luh *Mahn* [An anglicized pronunciation of the city's name as Li *Manz* was formerly current.]

Lemgo, Germany : *Lem* goh

Lemnos, Greece : *Lem* nahs (UK *Lem* nos)

Le Moule, Guadeloupe : Luh *Moohl*

Lena, Russia : *Lay* na (Russian *Lye* na)

Lenexa, USA : La *nek* sa

Leningrad, Russia : *Len* in grad (Russian Lin in *graht*)

Leninogorsk, Kazakhstan : Len in a *gawrsk* (Russian Li neen a *gawrsk*)

Leninsk-Kuznetskiy, Russia : Lyay neensk Koos *nyet* ski

Lenkoran, Azerbaijan : Lin ka *rahn*

Lennox (Hills), Scotland : *Len* uks

Lens, France : Lahns

Lentini, Italy : Len *tee* nee

Leoben, Austria : Lay *oh* bun

¹Leominster, England : *Lem* stur (UK *Lem* sta) [The form of the Herefordshire town's name, with its unsounded *o*, probably influenced that of the nearby village of **Weobley**.]

²Leominster, USA : *Lem* in stur (UK *Lem* in sta)

León, Mexico; Nicaragua; Spain : Lay *ohn* (UK Lay *on*)

Leonberg, Germany : *Lay* awn berk

Leonding, Austria : *Lay* awn ding

Lepanto, Greece : Li *pan* toh

Le Petit Quevilly, France : Luh Ptee Kvee *yee*

Lepontine (Alps), Italy : Li *pahn* tiyn (UK Li *pon* tiyn)

Le Port, Réunion : Luh *Pawr*

Le Puy, France : Luh *Pwee*

Le Quesnoy, France : Luh Ken *wah*

Lerdo, Mexico : *Ler* doh

Leribe, Lesotho : Lay *ree* bay

Lérida, Spain : *Lay* ree dhah

Lerwick, Scotland : *Luhr* wik (UK *Luh* wik)

Les Andelys, France : Layz Ahnd *lee*

Les Baux-de-Provence, France : Lay Bohd Praw *vahns*

Lesbos, Greece : *Lez* bahs (UK *Lez* bos)

Leskovac, Serbia : *Les* kaw vahts

Lesmahagow, Scotland : Les ma *hay* goh

Lesneven, France : Les ne *vahn*

Lesotho, Africa : Li *sooh* tooh

Les Sables-d'Olonne, France : Lay Sahbl do *lohn*

Leszno, Poland : *Lesh* naw

Letchworth, England : *Lech* wuhrth (UK *Lech* wuth)

Lethbridge, Canada : *Leth* brij

Leticia, Colombia : Le *tee* syah

Leuchars, Scotland : *Looh* kurz (UK *Looh* kuz)

Leuctra, Greece : *Loohk* tra

Leuk, Switzerland : Loyk

Leuze, Belgium : Luhz

Levallois-Perret, France : Luh vahl wah Pe *ray*

Le Vauclin, Martinique : La Voh *klahn*

Levelland, USA : *Lev* a land

Leven, Scotland : *Lee* vun

Levens, France : Luh *vahns*

Leverkusen, Germany : Lay vur *kooh* zun

Levin, New Zealand : La *veen*

Lévis, Canada : *Lev* i

Levittown, USA : *Lev* ut town

Levkás, Greece : Lef *kahs*

Lewes, England; USA : *Looh* us (UK *Looh* is)

Lewis, Scotland : *Looh* is

Lewisham, England : *Looh* ish um [The name of the former Kent village, now a London borough, at one time had the local pronunciation *Looh* is um.]

Lewisporte, Canada : *Looh* us pawrt (UK *Looh* is pawt)

Lewiston, USA : *Looh* a stun (UK *Looh* is tun)

Lexington, USA : *Lek* sing tun

Leyburn, England : *Lay* buhrn (UK *Lay* buhn)

Leyden, Netherlands : *Liy* dun

Leyland, England : *Lay* lund

Leyte, Philippines : *Lay* tee

Leyton, England : *Lay* tun

Leytonstone, England : *Lay* tun stohn

Lezhë, Albania : *Lay* zha
Lhasa, China : *Lah* sa
L'Haÿ-les-Roses, France : Lay lay *Rohz*
Liaoning, China : Lyow *ning*
Liaoyang, China : Lyow *yahng*
Liberec, Czech Republic : *Lee* be rets
[1]Liberia, Africa : Liy *bir* i a (UK Liy *bi* a ri a)
[2]Liberia, Costa Rica : Lee *bay* ree ah
Liberty, USA : *Lib* ur ti (UK *Lib* a ti)
Libertyville, USA : *Lib* ur ti vil (UK *Lib* a ti vil)
Libourne, France : Lee *boohrn*
Librazhd, Albania : Li *brahsht*
Libreville, Gabon : *Lee* bra vil
Libya, Africa : *Lib* i a
Licata, Italy : Lee *kah* tah
Lichfield, England : *Lich* feeld
Lichinga, Mozambique : Lee *shing* gah
Lida, Belarus : *Lee* da
Lidice, Czech Republic : *Lee* dyee tse
Lidingö, Sweden : *Lee* ding uh
Lidköping, Sweden : *Leed* chuh ping
Lido, Italy : *Lee* doh
Liechtenstein, Europe : *Lik* tun stiyn (German *Likh* tun shtiyn)
Liège, Belgium : Li *ayzh* (French Lyezh)
Liepaja, Latvia : *Lyep* ah yah
Lier, Belgium : Lir
Liestal, Switzerland : *Lees* tahl
Liévin, France : Lyay *vahn*
Liffey, Ireland : *Lif* i
Lifford, Ireland : *Lif* urd (UK *Lif* ud)
Ligonier, USA : Lig a *nir*
Liguria, Italy : La *gyoor* i a (UK Li *gyoo* a ri a) (Italian Lee *gooh* ryah)
Lihue, USA : Lee *hooh* ay
Likasi, Democratic Republic of the Congo : Lee *kah* see
Lille, France : Leel
Lillebonne, France : Leel *bawn*
Lillehammer, Norway : *Lil* a hah mur (UK *Lil* i ham a)
Lillers, France : Lee *ler*
Lilongwe, Malawi : Li *lawng* way (UK Li *long* way)
[1]Lima, Peru : *Lee* ma (Spanish *Lee* mah)
[2]Lima, USA : *Liy* mah
Limassol, Cyprus : Lee mah *sawl*

Limavady, Northern Ireland : Li ma *vad* i
Limbe, Cameroon : *Lim* bay
[1]Limburg, Belgium; Netherlands : *Lim* buhrg (UK *Lim* buhg) (Dutch, Flemish *Lim* berkh)
[2]Limburg, Germany : *Lim* boork
Limeira, Brazil : Lee *may* ra
Limerick, Ireland : *Lim* a rik
Limoeiro, Brazil : Lee *mway* rooh
Limoges, France : Li *mohzh* (French Lee *mohzh*)
Limón, Costa Rica : Lee *mohn*
Limonest, France : Lee maw *nay*
Limousin, France : Lee moo *zahn*
Limpopo, Africa : Lim *poh* poh
Linares, Chile; Spain : Lee *nah* rays
Linas, France : Lee *nahs*
Lincoln, Canada; England; USA : *Ling* kun
Lindau, Germany : *Lin* dow
Linden, Guyana; USA : *Lin* dun
Lindi, Tanzania : *Lin* di
Lindisfarne, England : *Lin* dis fahrn (UK *Lin* dis fahn)
Lingen, Germany : *Ling* un
Lingfield, England : *Ling* feeld
Lingga (Archipelago), Indonesia : *Ling* ga
Linhares, Brazil : Leen *yahr* ish
Linköping, Sweden : *Lin* chuh ping
Linlithgow, Scotland : Lin *lith* goh
Linnhe, Scotland : *Lin* i
Lins, Brazil : Leens
Linz, Austria : Lints
Lipa, Philippines : Lee *pah*
Lipari (Islands), Italy : *Lip* ur i (Italian *Lee* pah ri)
Lipetsk, Russia : *Li* pitsk
Lippstadt, Germany : *Lip* shtaht
Lira, Uganda : *Lee* rah
Lisbon, Portugal; USA : *Liz* bun
Lisburn, Northern Ireland : *Liz* burn (UK *Liz* buhn)
Lisichansk, Ukraine : Li si *chahnsk*
Lisieux, France : Lee *zyuh*
Liskeard, England : Lis *kahrd* (UK Lis *kahd*) [A pronunciation of the Cornish town's name with first-syllable

stress, US *Lis* kahrd, UK *Lis* kahd, also exists.]

Liski, Russia : *Lis* ki

Lisle-sur-Tarn, France : Leel seer *Tahrn*

¹**Lismore**, Australia : *Liz* mawr (UK *Liz* maw)

²**Lismore**, Ireland; Scotland : Liz *mawr* (UK Liz *maw*)

Listowel, Ireland : Lis *toh* ul

Litchfield, USA : *Lich* feeld

Litherland, England : *Lidh* ur land (UK *Lidh* a land)

Lithgow, Australia : *Lith* goh

Lithuania, Europe : Lith oo *ay* ni a (UK Lith yoo *ay* ni a)

Litoměřice, Czech Republic : *Lee* taw myer zhit se

Littleborough, England : *Lit* ul buhr oh (UK *Lit* ul bra)

Littlehampton, England : *Lit* ul hamp tun

Little Rock, USA : *Lit* ul Rahk (UK *Lit* ul Rok)

Littleton, USA : *Lit* ul tun

Litvínov, Czech Republic : Lit *vee* nawf

Livadia, Ukraine : Li *vad* i a

Livermore, USA : *Liv* ur mawr (UK *Liv* a maw)

Liverpool, Australia; Canada; England : *Liv* ur poohl (UK *Liv* a poohl)

Liversedge, England : *Liv* ur sej (UK *Liv* a sej)

Livingston, Scotland; USA : *Liv* ing stun

Livingstone, Zambia : *Liv* ing stun

¹**Livonia**, Europe : Li *voh* ni a

²**Livonia**, USA : La *voh* nya

Livorno, Italy : Lee *vawr* noh

Lizard, England : *Liz* urd (UK *Liz* ud) [The most southerly point of the English mainland, in Cornwall, has a Celtic name meaning "court on a height," and accordingly one would have expected a pronunciation US Li *zahrd*, UK Li *zahd*, as explained in the quote below. But it is now identical with that of English *lizard*.]

Such a name should have been stressed on the second syllable, so it must be assumed that the modern pronunciation, "*Liz*ard," is the result of a stress-shift, presumably under English influence [O.J. Padel, *A Popular Dictionary of Cornish Place-Names*, 1988].

Ljubljana, Slovenia : Lee ooh blee *ahn* a (UK Loo bli *ahn* a) (Slovene Lyoo *blyah* na)

Llanberis, Wales : Lan *ber* is (Welsh Hlan *ber* is) [According to the BBC radio course *Welsh for Beginners* (1966), the notorious Welsh *ll* that begins this and other names is produced "by putting the tongue in the *l* position and at the same time emitting a sharp breath." For those who cannot manage this, Leaver (see Bibliography, p. 219) suggests a compromise pronunciation *thl*, so that *Llanberis* would be Thlan *ber* is. The rendering of *Llan-* as *Lan-* in the Welsh names below is thus a UK approximation. The *Llan-* itself, meaning "holy place," "church," and related to Spanish *llano* and English *plain*, is usually followed by a saint's name, so that *Llanberis* means "church of (St.) Peris" (but *Llantrisant* means "church of the three saints").]

Llandaff, Wales : *Lan* duf [The name of the former cathedral village, now a district of Cardiff, has an alternate "Welsh" pronunciation Hlan daf. The actual Welsh spelling of the name is *Llandaf*, pronounced Hlan *dahv*.] Although the first [pronunciation] is widespread local usage, the second is preferred by the clergy of Llandaff Cathedral and by the BBC in Cardiff [Pointon, p. 146].

Llandeilo, Wales : Lan *diy* loh

Llandovery, Wales : Lan *dahv* ri

Llandrindod Wells, Wales : Lan drin dod *Welz*

Llandudno, Wales : Lan *did* noh

Llanelli, Wales : La *neth* li (Welsh Hlan e hli) [The pronunciation of the town's name is a challenge for many

English speakers, not least because of the doubly-present *ll*.]
(1) The two *lls* in Llanelli are a little hard to pronounce, but practice makes it easier, as long as the abomination of "Lan-elthy" is avoided [Wynford Vaughan-Thomas and Alun Llewellyn, *The Shell Guide to Wales*, 1969].
(2) If you must, unlike most of the Welsh, attempt a Welsh pronunciation, at least pronounce the first LL as English L. LuhNETHlih will do very well [Kingsley Amis, *The King's English*, 1997].

Llanfairfechan, Wales : Lan fer *fek* un (UK Lan fay a *fek* un) (Welsh Hlan viyr *vekh* an)

Llanfair P.G., Wales : Lan fer Pee *Jee* (UK Lan fay a ...] [The initials are those of *pwllgwyn*, the next two syllables in the artificially created, 58-letters-long name.]

Llangefni, Wales : Lan *gev* ni

Llangollen, Wales : Lan *goth* lun [Like **Llanelli**, the name has a double occurrence of the distinctive Welsh *ll*, so is properly pronounced more like Hlan *gaw* hlen.]

Llano, USA : *Lan* oh

Llano Estacado, USA : Lahn oh Es ta *kah* doh (Spanish Yah noh...)

Llanos, South America : *Yah* nohs

Llanrwst, Wales : Lan *roohst*

Llantrisant, Wales : Lan *tris* unt

Llanwrtyd Wells, Wales : Lan oo a tid *Welz*

Lleyn (Peninsula), Wales : Leen [The Welsh spelling is *Llŷn*, pronounced Hleen.]

Lloret de Mar, Spain : La ret da *Mahr* (UK ... *Mah*)

Lloydminster, Canada : *Loyd* min stur (UK *Loyd* min sta)

Llullaillaco, Chile : Yooh yiy *yah* koh

Lobatse, Botswana : Loh *baht* say

Löbau, Germany : *Luh* bow

Lobito, Angola : Loh *bee* toh

Locarno, Switzerland : Loh *kahr* noh (UK Loh *kah* noh)

Lochearnhead, Scotland : Lahk uhrn *hed* (UK Lokh uhn *hed*)

Loches, France : Lohsh

Lochgelly, Scotland : Lahk *gel* i (UK Lokh *gel* i)

Lochgilphead, Scotland : Lahk *gilp* hed (UK Lokh *gilp* hed)

Lochinver, Scotland : Lah *kin* vur (UK Lokh *in* va)

Lochmaben, Scotland : Lahk *may* bun (UK Lokh *may* bun)

Lockerbie, Scotland : *Lah* kur bi (UK *Lok* a bi)

Locmariaquer, France : Lawk mah ree ah *ker*

Locris, Greece : *Loh* kris

Lod, Israel : Lohd

¹**Lodi**, Italy : *Law* dee

²**Lodi**, USA : *Loh* diy

Łódź, Poland : Lohdz (UK Wooj) (Polish Woohch)

Lofoten, Norway : *Loh* foh tun (UK Loh *foh* tun)

Lofthouse, England : *Lawft* hows (UK *Loft* hows)

Logan, Australia; USA : *Loh* gun

Logansport, USA : *Loh* gunz pawrt (UK *Loh* gunz pawt)

Logroño, Spain : La *groh* nyoh

Löhne, Germany : *Luh* na

Loikaw, Myanmar : Loy *kaw*

Loing, France : Lwahn

Loire, France : Lwahr

Loiret, France : Lwah *ray*

Loíza, Puerto Rico : Loh *ee* sah

Loja, Ecuador : *Law* hah

Lokeren, Belgium : *Loh* kur a

Lokoja, Nigeria : Loh *koh* jah

Lomas de Zamora, Argentina : Loh mahs dhay Sah *moh* rah

Lombard, USA : *Lahm* bahrd (UK *Lom* bahd)

Lombardy, Italy : *Lahm* bur di (UK *Lom* ba di)

Lomblen, Indonesia : Lahm *blen* (UK Lom *blen*)

Lombok, Indonesia : *Lahm* bahk (UK *Lom* bok)

Lomé, Togo : Loh *may* (UK *Loh* may)

Lomond, Scotland : *Loh* mund
Lomonosov, Russia : Lum a *naw* suf
Lompoc, USA : *Lahm* pahk (UK *Lom* pok)
Łomża, Poland : *Wawm* zhah
Londerzeel, Belgium : *Lawn* dur zayl
London, Canada; England : *Lahn* dun [The British capital's name was formerly pronounced *Lah* nun, represented in writing as *Lunnon*: "In Samuel Rogers' youth everyone said Lunnon; we have now returned to Lundun" (Isaac Taylor, *Words and Places*, c.1908). English poet Samuel Rogers (1763–1855) was a leading figure in London society.]
Londonderry, Northern Ireland; USA : *Lahn* dun der i
Londrina, Brazil : Lohn *dree* na
Long Beach, USA : *Lawng* Beech (UK *Long*...)
Longbenton, England : Lawng *ben* tun (UK Long *ben* tun)
Long Eaton, England : Lawng *Ee* tun (UK Long...)
Longford, Ireland : *Lawng* furd (UK *Long* fud)
Long Island, USA : Lawng *Iy* lund (UK Long...) [The New York island's name is noted for its pronunciation with an "intrusive"*g* by some local residents, especially the progeny of immigrant families, as explained by the American author of the passage quoted below.]
   The classic example [of this trait] (and it *is* classic) is "Long Guyland" for *Long Island*.... I am inclined to accept the opinion of a number of my Jewish friends that the feature originated in Yiddish (or rather in one style of Yiddish pronunciation), though it is now heard from the lips of many Gentile New Yorkers [Eric Partridge and John W. Clark, *British and American English Since 1900*, 1951].
Longjumeau, France : Lohng zhee *moh*
Long Melford, England : Lawng *Mel* furd (UK Long *Mel* fud)

Longmont, USA : *Lawng* mahnt (UK *Long* mont)
Long Mynd, England : *Lawng* Mind (UK *Long*...)
Longridge, England : *Lawng* rij (UK *Long* rij)
Long Sutton, England : Lawng *Sah* tun (UK Long...)
Longtown, England : *Lawng* town (UK *Long* town)
Longueuil, Canada : Lawng *gayl* (UK Long *gayl*)
Longuyon, France : Lawn gwee *yawn*
Longvic, France : Lawn *vee*
Longview, USA : *Lawng* vyooh (UK *Long* vyooh)
Longwy, France : Lohn *wee*
Longyearbyen, Norway : *Lawng* yir byooh un (UK *Long* yi a byooh en) [The town's name translates as "Longyear town," after the US miner J.M. Longyear.]
Lons-le-Saunier, France : Lohn luh Soh *nyay*
Looe, England : Looh
Loon, Philippines : Loh *awn*
Loon op Zahnt, Netherlands : Lohn awp *Zahnt*
Loos, France : Lohs
Loose, England : Loohz [The name of the Kent village has regularly had this pronunciation, with no cause for specific championing of the kind described in quote (1) below.]
   (1) The women of the village prefer its name to be pronounced as in "lose" [John Hadfield, ed., *The Shell Guide to England*, 1970].
   (2) Loose is pronounced "lose" [John Hadfield, ed., *The New Shell Guide to England*, 1981].
Lop Nur, China : Lawp *Noor* (UK Lop *Noo* a)
Lora del Río, Spain : Loh rah dhel *Ree* oh
Lorain, USA : La *rayn*
Lorca, Spain : *Lawr* kah
Lorena, Brazil : Looh *ray* na
Lorenskog, Norway : *Loh* runs kawg

Loreto, Peru : Loh *ray* toh
Lorient, France : Lawr *yahn*
Lörrach, Germany : *Luhr* ahkh
Lorraine, France : La *rayn* (French Law *ren*)
Lorris, France : Law *rees*
Los Alamos, USA : Laws *Al* a mohs (UK Los *Al* a mos)
Los Altos, USA : Laws *Al* tus
Los Andes, Chile : Laws *Ahn* days
Los Angeles, USA : Laws *An* ja lus (UK Los *An* ja leez) [There has long been a dispute as to whether the main word of the California city's name should be pronounced *An* ja lus or *Ang* ga lus, with a hard *g*. The pronunciation given here is now generally regarded as the norm, although there are still many variants, as illustrated by the quotes below. **Los Ángeles** is the Spanish equivalent.]
    (1) "O" long, "g" hard and rhyme with "es" — That's how to say Los Angeles [Local rhyme, quoted in Alfred Holt, *American Place Names*, 1938].
    (2) For years the Los Angeles *Times* has printed a standing notice that the name of the city should be pronounced *Loce Ahng-hayl-ais*, but the resident boosters and Bible-searchers continue to say *Loss Angle-iss, Loss Anjell-iss, Loce Angle-iss, Loce Angle-ez*, and even *Sang-lis* [Mencken, p. 541].
    (3) There are still some enthusiasts who insist on a "Spanish" pronunciation, not realizing, however, that the Spanish *g*, correctly pronounced, is an entirely foreign sound to Americans [Erwin G. Gudde, *California Place Names*, revised and enlarged by William Bright, 1998].
Los Ángeles, Chile : Laws *Ahng* hay lays
Los Banos, USA : Laws *Ban* us (UK Los *Ban* os)
Los Baños, Philippines : Laws *Bah* nyohs (UK Los...)
Los Dos Caminos, Venezuela : Laws Dhaws Kah *mee* naws
Los Gatos, USA : Laws *Gah* tohs

Los Lagos, Chile : Laws *Lah* gaws
Los Ríos, Ecuador : Laws *Ree* aws
Lossiemouth, Scotland : Law si *mowth* (UK Los i *mowth*) [The name of the fishing port and resort is alternately stressed US *Law* si mowth, UK *Los* i mowth.]
Los Teques, Venezuela : Laws *Tay* kes
Lostwithiel, England : Laws *twidh* i ul (UK Los *with* i ul)
Lot, France : Lawt
Lota, Chile : *Loh* tah
Lothian, Scotland : *Loh* dhi un
Louangphrabang, Laos : Lwahng prah *bahng*
Loubomo, Congo : Looh *boh* moh
Loudonville, USA : *Low* dun vil
Loudun, France : Looh *duhn*
Loughborough, England : *Lahf* buhr oh (UK *Lahf* bra)
Loughor, Wales : *Lah* kur (UK *Lah* kha)
Loughrea, Ireland : Lahk *ray*
Loughton, England : *Low* tun
Louhans, France : Looh *ahn*
Louisburg, USA : *Looh* is buhrg (UK *Looh* is buhg)
Louisiade (Archipelago), Papua New Guinea : Loo ee zee *ahd*
Louisiana, USA : Loo eez i *an* a [Locally the state's name is pronounced Looh zee *an* a.]
Louis Trichardt, South Africa : Looh is *Tri* churt
Louisville, USA : *Looh* i vil [The Kentucky city's name is usually pronounced thus, but is subject to local variation, as indicated in the quotes below. Places of the name in other states are normally *Looh* is vil.]
    (1) *Louisville*, to its denizens, is *Louie-ville*, with the first syllable French and the second American [Mencken, p. 541].
    (2) Call it Looeyville, Lewisville or Louahvul; the locals don't mind [*Lonely Planet USA*, 2004].
Louny, Czech Republic : *Loh* nee
Lourdes, France : Loohrd [Some En-

glish speakers refer to the town, famous as a center of Catholic pilgrimage, as US Loordz, UK *Loo* udz.]

Lourenço Marques, Mozambique : Loh ren soh Mahr *kes* (UK ... Mah *kes*)

¹**Louth**, England : Lowth

²**Louth**, Ireland : Lowdh

Louvain, Belgium : Loo *van*

Lovech, Bulgaria : Loh *vech*

Loveland, USA : *Lahv* lund

Lowell, USA : *Loh* ul

Lowestoft, England : *Loh* stawft (UK *Loh* stoft) [A local pronunciation of the Suffolk town's name as *Loh* stuf also exists.]

Łowicz, Poland : *Waw* vich

Lowther, Scotland : *Low* dhur (UK *Low* dha)

Lozère, France : Loh *zer*

Lualaba, Democratic Republic of the Congo : Looh ah *lah* bah

Luanda, Angola : Loo *ahn* da

Luang Prabang, Laos : Lwahng Prah *bahng*

Luanshya, Zambia : Looh *ahn* shah

Lubango, Angola : Loo *bahng* gooh

Lubbock, USA : *Lah* buk

Lübeck, Germany : *Looh* bek (German *Lee* bek)

Lubin, Poland : *Looh* bin

Lublin, Poland : *Looh* blin

Lubny, Ukraine : *Loohb* ni

Lubumbashi, Democratic Republic of the Congo : Looh boohm *bah* shee

Lucapa, Angola : Looh *kah* pa

Lucca, Italy : *Looh* kah

Lucena, Philippines : Looh *say* nah

Lucera, Italy : Looh *chay* rah

Lucerne, Switzerland : Looh *suhrn* (UK Looh *suhn*) (French Looh *sern*)

Luckenwalde, Germany : Look un *vahl* da

Lucknow, India : *Lahk* now

Luçon, France : Lee *sohn*

Lüdenscheid, Germany : *Lee* dun shiyt

Lüderitz, Namibia : *Lee* da rits

Ludhiana, India : Looh di *ah* na

Ludlow, England; USA : *Lahd* loh

Ludvika, Sweden : *Loohd* vi ka

Ludwigsburg, Germany : *Leed* viks boork

Ludwigshafen, Germany : *Leed* viks hah fun

Luena, Angola : *Lway* na

Luga, Russia : *Looh* ga

Lugano, Switzerland : Looh *gah* noh

Lugansk, Ukraine : Looh *gahnsk*

Luganville, Vanuatu : Looh gun *veel*

Lugo, Spain : *Looh* goh

Lugoj, Romania : *Looh* gawzh

Luhansk, Ukraine : Looh *hahnsk*

Luján, Argentina : Looh *hahn*

Luleå, Sweden : *Looh* la oh

Lumajang, Indonesia : Looh ma *jahng*

Lund, Sweden : Loond

Lunda, Angola : *Loohn* da

Lundy, England : *Lahn* di

Lüneburg, Germany : *Looh* na buhrg (UK *Looh* na buhg) (German *Lee* na boork)

Lünen, Germany : *Lee* nun

Lunéville, France : Lee nay *veel*

Luoyang, China : Lwaw *yahng*

Luque, Paraguay : *Looh* kay

Lurgan, Northern Ireland : *Luhr* gun (UK *Luh* gun)

Lusaka, Zambia : Loo *sah* ka

Lusatia, Germany : Loo *say* sha

Lushenjë, Albania : *Loohsh* nya

Lüshun, China : Lee *shoon*

Lusignan, France : Lee zee *nyahn*

Lusitania, Portugal : Looh si *tay* ni a

Luton, England : *Looh* tun

Lutsk, Ukraine : Loohtsk

Lutter, Germany : *Loot* ur

Lutterworth, England : *Lah* tur wuhrth (UK *Lah* ta wuth)

Luxembourg, Europe : *Lahk* sum buhrg (UK *Lahk* sum buhg) (French Leek sahm *boohr*) [This spelling and pronunciation is also valid for the Belgian province.]

Luxemburg, Europe : *Lahk* sum buhrg (UK *Lahk* sum buhg) (German Look sum *boork*) [This spelling of the grand duchy's name is sometimes used to avoid French influence.]

Luxor, Egypt : *Lahk* sawr (UK *Lahk* saw)

Luxulyan, England : Lahk *sil* yun [The name of the Cornish village means "chapel of *Sulyen*."]
Pronounced "Luk*sill*yan," with regular change of Cornish *u* to *i* [O.J. Padel, *A Popular Dictionary of Cornish Place-Names*, 1988].

Luzern, Switzerland : Looh *tsern*

Luzhou, China : Looh *joh*

Luzon, Philippines : Looh *zahn* (UK Looh *zon*)

Lviv, Ukraine : Lveef

Lvov, Ukraine : La *vahf* (UK La *vof*) (Russian Lvawf)

Lycia, Turkey : *Lish* a (UK *Lis* i a)

Lydd, England : Lid

Lydgate, England : *Lid* gayt [The pronunciation is valid for the Manchester district of this name, but the identically named West Yorkshire village is *Lid* git, while Lydgate Lane, Sheffield, running east off Manchester Road, is *Lij* it.]

Lydia, Turkey : *Lid* i a

Lyell, Australia : *Liy* ul

Lyme Regis, England : Liym *Ree* jis

Lymington, England : *Lim* ing tun

Lymm, England : Lim

Lympne, England : Lim [The name of the Kent village was formerly pronounced Liym, as in the anonymous limerick: "There was an old fellow of Lympne / Who married three wives at one time." However, according to Arnold Silcock's *Verse and Worse* (1952), which quotes these lines, "purists ... asseverate that Lympne should be pronounced 'Limb.'"]

Lynchburg, USA : *Linch* buhrg (UK *Linch* buhg)

Lyndhurst, England; USA : *Lind* huhrst (UK *Lind* huhst)

Lynmouth, England : *Lin* muth

Lynn, USA : Lin

Lynton, England : *Lin* tun

Lynwood, USA : *Lin* wood

Lyon, France : Lee *ahn* (UK Lee on)

(French Lyawn) [In its alternate spelling of *Lyons*, the city's name formerly had the regular English pronunciation *Liy* unz, or, according to Ross, p. 122, Lahnz. But an essayal at the French pronunciation is now generally *de rigueur*.]

Lyonnais, France : Lyaw *nay*

Lyons-la-Forêt, France : Lee awns la Faw *ray*

Lysychansk, Ukraine : Li si *chahnsk*

Lytham St Anne's, England : Lidh um Saynt *Anz* (UK ... Sunt...)

Lyttelton, New Zealand : *Lit* ul tun

Lyubertsy, Russia : Lyooh *byert* si

Ma'an, Jordan : Ma *ahn*

Maas, Netherlands : Mahs

Maaseik, Belgium : *Mah* zayk

Maassluis, Netherlands : Mahs *sluh* is

Maastricht, Netherlands : *Mahs* trikt (Dutch Mahs *trikht*)

Mabalacat, Philippines : Mah bah *lah* kaht

Mablethorpe, England : *May* bul thawrp (UK *May* bul thawp)

Macabebe, Philippines : Mah kah *bay* bay

Macaé, Brazil : Mah kah *e*

McAlester, USA : Ma *kal* us tur (UK Ma *kal* us ta)

McAllen, USA : Ma *kal* un

Macao, China : Ma *kow*

Macapá, Brazil : Mah kah *pah*

Macas, Ecuador : *Mah* kahs

Macclesfield, England : *Mak* ulz feeld

M'Clintock (Channel), Canada : Ma *klin* tuk (UK Ma *klin* tok)

M'Clure (Strait), Canada : Ma *kloor* (UK Ma *kloo* a)

McCook, USA : Ma *kook*

Macdonnell (Ranges), Australia : Muk *dah* nul (UK Muk *don* ul)

Macedonia, Europe : Mas i *doh* ni a [The pronunciation is valid for the ancient kingdom, the modern Greek region, and the republic formed in 1991 from the former Yugoslavia.]

Maceió, Brazil : Ma say *oh*

Macenta, Guinea : Mah *sen* tah

Macerata, Italy : Mah chay *rah* tah
Macgillycuddy's Reeks, Ireland : Ma gil i kah diz *Reeks*
Machala, Ecuador : Mah *chah* lah
Machen, Wales : *Makh* un
Machida, Japan : Mah *chee* dah
Machilipatnam, India : Ma sha lee *paht* num
Machrihanish, Scotland : Mak ri *han* ish
Machu Picchu, Peru : Mah chooh *Peek* choo (UK Ma chooh *Pik* chooh)
Machynlleth, Wales : Ma *khahn* hleth
Mackay, Australia : Ma *kiy*
McKeesport, USA : Ma *keez* pawrt (UK Ma *keez* pawt)
Mackenzie, Canada : Ma *ken* zee
Mackinaw, USA : *Mak* i naw
McKinley, USA : Ma *kin* li
McMurdo (Sound), Antarctica : Muk *muhr* doh (UK Muk *muh* doh)
Macomb, USA : Ma *kohm*
Macon, USA : *May* kun
Mâcon, France : Mah *kawn*
Macquarie, Australia : Ma *kwah* ri (UK Ma *kwor* i)
MacRobertson (Land), Antarctica : Muk *rah* burt sun (UK Muk *rob* ut sun)
Mactan, Philippines : Mahk *tahn*
Macuspana, Mexico : Mah kooh *spah* nah
Ma'daba, Jordan : Mah da *bah*
Madagascar, Africa : Mad a *gas* kur (UK Mad a *gas* ka)
Madang, Papua New Guinea : Mah *dahng* (UK Ma *dang*)
Madeira, Atlantic Ocean : Ma *dir* a (UK Ma *di* a ra) (Portuguese Mah *day* ra)
Madhya Pradesh, India : Mah dya Pra *daysh*
Madison, USA : *Mad* a sun (UK *Mad* i sun)
Madiun, Indonesia : Mah dee *oohn*
¹**Madras**, India : Ma *dras* (UK Ma *drahs*)
²**Madras**, USA : *Mad* rus
Madrid, Spain : Ma *drid* (Spanish Mah *dhreedh*)

Madura, Indonesia : Mah *door* a
Madurai, India : Mah da *riy*
Maebashi, Japan : May yay *bah* shee
Maentwrog, Wales : Miyn *toor* ahg (UK Miyn *too* a rog) (Welsh Miyn *too* rog)
Maerdy, Wales : *Mahr* di (UK *Mah* di) (Welsh *Miyr* di)
Maesteg, Wales : Miys *tayg*
Mafeteng, Lesotho : *Maf* a teng
Mafikeng, South Africa : *Maf* e king
Mafra, Brazil; Portugal : *Maf* ra
Magadan, Russia : Mug a *dahn*
Magallanes, Chile : Mah gah *lyah* nays
Magangué, Colombia : Mah gahng *gay*
Magdala, Israel : *Mag* da la
Magdalena, Colombia : Mag da *lay* na (Spanish Mahg dah *lay* nah)
Magdalen (Islands), Canada : *Mag* da lun
Magdeburg, Germany : *Mag* da buhrg (UK *Mag* da buhg) (German *Mahg* da boork)
Magelang, Indonesia : Mah gay *lahng*
Magellan (Strait), Chile : Ma *jel* un (UK Ma *gel* un)
Magenta, Italy : Mah *jen* tah
Maggiore, Italy : Mah *joh* ray
Magherafelt, Northern Ireland : Mak ra *felt*
Maghreb, Africa : *Mah* greb
Maghull, England : Ma *gahl*
Magnesia, Greece : Mag *nee* sha
Magnitogorsk, Russia : Mug nee ta *gawrsk*
Magwe, Myanmar : Ma *gway*
Mahajanga, Madagascar : Mah hah *jahng* gah
Maharashtra, India : Mah ha *rahsh* tra
Mahdia, Tunisia : Ma *dee* a
Mahe, India : *Mah* ay
Mahé, Seychelles : Mah *ay*
Mahebourg, Mauritius : Mah ay *boor*
Mahilyow, Belarus : Ma khi *lyawf*
Mahón, Menorca, Spain : Mah *awn*
Maidan, Iraq : Miy *dan*
Maidenhead, England : *May* dun hed
Maidstone, England : *Mayd* stohn (UK *Mayd* stun)
Maiduguri, Nigeria : Miy *dooh* ga ree

Maillane, France : Mah *yahn*
Main, Germany : Miyn
Mai-Ndombe, Democratic Republic of
   the Congo : Miy un *dawm* bay
¹Maine, France : Men
²Maine, USA : Mayn
Mainland, Scotland : *Mayn* land
Mainz, Germany : Miynts
Maiquetía, Venezuela : Miy kay *tee* ah
Maitland, Australia : *Mayt* lund
Maizuru, Japan : *Miy* zooh rooh
Majorca, Spain : Ma *jawr* ka (UK Ma
   jaw ka) [The name of the largest is-
   land in the Balearic group, as Ross
   says, p. 125, is pronounced as spelled.
   "But the many English tourists have
   tended, rather affectedly, to introduce
   the pronunciation belonging to its
   Spanish name, *Mallorca*." *See* **Mal-
   lorca** in Appendix, p. 219.]
Majuro, Marshall Islands : Mah *jooh*
   roh
Makassar (Strait), Indonesia : Ma *kas*
   ur (UK Ma *kas* a)
Makati, Philippines : Mah kah *tee*
Makeyevka, Ukraine : Ma *kay* uf ka
Makhachkala, Russia : Ma khahch ka
   lah
Makiyivka, Ukraine : Ma *kee* uf ka
Makó, Hungary : *Maw* koh
Makthar, Tunisia : *Mak* tur (UK *Mak*
   ta)
Makurdi, Nigeria : Mah *koor* dee
Malabar (Coast), India : *Mal* a bahr
   (UK *Mal* a bah)
Malabo, Equatorial Guinea : Mah *lah*
   boh
Malabon, Philippines : Mah lah *bawn*
Malacca (Strait), Indonesia : Ma *lak* a
Maladzyechna, Belarus : Ma la *dyech* na
Málaga, Spain : *Mal* a ga (Spanish *Mah*
   lah ga)
Malahide, Ireland : *Mal* a hiyd
Malang, Indonesia : Mah *lahng*
Malanje, Angola : Ma *lahn* zhee
Mälaren, Sweden : *May* lah run
Malatya, Turkey : Mah *lah* tyah
Malawi, Africa : Ma *lah* wi
Malaya, Malaysia : Ma *lay* a

Malaysia, Asia : Ma *lay* zha (UK Ma *lay*
   zi a)
Malbork, Poland : *Mahl* bawrk
Malden, Kiribati; USA : *Mawl* dun
Maldives, Indian Ocean : *Mawl* deevz
Maldon, England : *Mawl* dun
Maldonado, Uruguay : Mahl doh *nah*
   doh
Male, Maldives : *Mah* lay
Malegaon, India : Mah la *gown*
Malesherbes, France : Mahl *zerb*
Malestroit, France : Mah lay *trwah*
Mali, Africa : *Mah* li
Malibu, USA : *Mal* a booh (UK *Mal* i
   booh)
Malindi, Kenya : Mah *lin* dee
Malin (Head), Ireland : *Mal* un
Malita, Philippines : Mah *lee* tah
Mallaig, Scotland : *Mal* ayg
Mallawi, Egypt : Ma *lah* wee
Mallee, Australia : *Mal* ee
Mallow, Ireland : *Mal* oh
Malmédy, Belgium : Mahl may *dee*
Malmesbury, England : *Mahmz* ber i
   (UK *Mahmz* bri)
Malmö, Sweden : *Mal* moh (Swedish
   Mahl muh)
Malolos, Philippines : Mah *loh* lohs
Maloyaroslavets, Russia : Mul a yir a
   slah vits
¹Malpas, England (Cheshire) : *Mawl*
   pus
²Malpas, England (Cornwall) : *Moh* pus
³Malpas, Wales : *Mal* pus
Malta, Europe : *Mawl* ta
Maltby, England : *Mawlt* bi
Malton, England : *Mawl* tun
¹Malvern, Australia : *Mawl* vurn (UK
   Mawl vun)
²Malvern, USA : *Mal* vurn (UK *Mal*
   vun)
Malvern (Hills), England : *Mawl* vurn
   (UK *Mawl* vun)
Malvinas, Atlantic Ocean : Mal *vee* nuz
Mamaroneck, USA : Ma *mar* a nek
Mamers, France : Mah *mers*
Mamou, Guinea : Mah *mooh*
Man, Côte d'Ivoire : Mahn
Man *see* **Isle of Man**

Manabí, Ecuador : Mah nah *bee*
Manacor, Mallorca, Spain : Mah nah
    kawr
Manado, Indonesia : Ma *nah* doh
Managua, Nicaragua : Ma *nahg* wa (UK
    Ma *nag* wa)
Manama, Bahrain : Mah *nah* ma
Manassas, USA : Ma *nas* us
Manaus, Brazil : Ma *nows*
Manche, France : Mahnsh
Manchester, England; USA : *Man* ches
    tur (UK *Man* chis ta)
Manchukuo, Asia : Man chooh *kwoh*
Manchuria, China : Man *choor* i a (UK
    Man *choo* a ri a)
Mandalay, Myanmar : Man da *lay*
Mandan, USA : *Man* dun
Mandeville, Jamaica : *Man* da vil
Mandurah, Australia : Man *joo* ra
Manea, England : *May* ni
Manfredonia, Italy : Mahn fray *daw*
    nyah
Mangalore, India : *Mahng* ga lawr (UK
    Mahng ga law)
Mangoche, Malawi : Mahng *goh* chee
Mangotsfield, England : *Mang* guts
    feeld
Mangyshlak, Kazakhstan : Mahng gish
    lahk
Manhattan, USA : Man *hat* un
Manila, Philippines : Ma *nil* a
Manipur, India : *Mah* ni poor
Manisa, Turkey : *Mah* nee sa
Manitoba, Canada : Man a *toh* ba (UK
    Man i *toh* ba)
Manitoulin (Island), Canada : Man a
    tooh lin (UK Man i *tooh* lin)
Manitowoc, USA : *Man* a ta wahk (UK
    Man i ta wok)
Manizales, Colombia : Mah nee *sah*
    lays
Mankato, USA : Man *kay* toh
Manly, Australia : *Man* li
Mannheim, Germany : *Man* hiym
    (German *Mahn* hiym)
Manokwari, Indonesia : Mah noh *kwah*
    ri
Manorbier, Wales : Man ur *bir* (UK
    Man a *bi* a)

Manresa, Spain : Mahn *ray* sah
Mansa, Zambia : *Mahn* sah
Mansfield, Australia; England; USA :
    Manz feeld
Manta, Ecuador : *Mahn* tah
Manteca, USA : Man *tee* ka
Mantinea, Greece : Man ti *nee* a
Mantua, Italy : *Man* choo a (UK *Man*
    tyoo a)
Manua (Islands), American Samoa :
    Mah *nooh* ah
Manukau, New Zealand : *Mah* na kow
    (UK *Man* a kow)
Manzanares, Spain : Mahn thah *nah*
    rays
Manzanillo, Cuba : Mahn sah *nee* yoh
Manzini, Swaziland : Mahn *zee* nee
Mao, Chad; Dominican Republic :
    Mow
Maputo, Mozambique : Mah *pooh* toh
Maracaibo, Venezuela : Ma ra *kiy* boh
    (Spanish Mah rah *kiy* boh)
Maracay, Venezuela : Mah rah *kiy*
Maradi, Niger : Mah *rah* di
Maranhão, Brazil : Ma ra *nyown*
Marans, France : Mah *rahn*
Marathon, Greece : *Mar* a thahn (UK
    Mar a thun)
Marazion, England : Ma ra *ziy* un
Marbella, Spain : Mahr *bay* a (UK Mah
    bay a) (Spanish Mahr *bay* lyah) [The
    Mediterranean resort is sometimes re-
    ferred to by English speakers with the
    spelling pronunciation US Mahr *bel*
    a, UK Mah *bel* a.]
Marblehead, USA : *Mahr* bul hed (UK
    Mah bul hed)
Marburg, Germany : *Mahr* buhrg (UK
    Mah buhg) (German *Mahr* boork)
March, England : Mahrch (UK Mahch)
¹**Marche**, France : Mahrsh
²**Marche**, Italy : *Mahr* kay
Mardan, Pakistan : *Mahr* dan
Mar del Plata, Argentina : Mahr del
    Plah tah
Marden, England : *Mahr* dun (UK *Mah*
    dun) [The Kent village so named has
    an occasional pronunciation *Mah*
    den.]

Marengo, Italy : Ma *reng* goh
Margaretting, England : Mahr ga *ret* ing (UK Mah ga *ret* ing)
Margarita, Venezuela : Mahr gah *ree* tah
Margate, England; USA : *Mahr* gayt (UK *Mah* gate)
Marghilon, Uzbekistan : Mahr ga *lawn*
Margilan, Uzbekistan : Mahr ga *lahn*
Marham, England : *Mar* um [The name of the Norfolk village is commonly pronounced *Mah* rum by Royal Air Force personnel stationed locally.]
Maria (Island), Australia : Ma *riy* a
Mariana (Islands), Pacific Ocean : Mar i *an* a (UK Mar i *ahn* a)
Marianao, Cuba : Mah ree ah *now*
Mariánské Lázně, Czech Republic : *Mahr* yahn ske Lahz nye
María Trinidad Sanchez, Dominican Republic : Mah ree ah Tree nee dhahdh *Sahn* chays
Maribor, Slovenia : *Mah* ree bawr
Marie Byrd (Land), Antarctica : Ma *ree* Buhrd (UK ... Buhd)
Mariehamn, Finland : Ma *ree* a hahmn
Mari El, Russia : Mah ree *El*
Marienbad, Czech Republic : *Mar* i un bad
Mariestad, Sweden : Ma *ree* stahd
Marietta, USA : Ma ri *et* a
Marignane, France : Mah ree *nyahn*
Marília, Brazil : Ma *ree* lya
Marin, USA : Ma *rin*
Marín, Spain : Mah *reen*
Marinette, USA : Ma ra *net* (UK Ma ri *net*)
Maringá, Brazil : Ma rin *gah*
Marion, Australia; USA : *Mar* i un
Mariupol, Ukraine : Ma ri *ooh* pul
Market Bosworth, England : Mahr kut *Bahz* wurth (UK Mah kit *Boz* wuth)
Market Drayton, England : Mahr kut *Dray* tun (UK Mah kit...)
Market Harborough, England : Mahr kut *Hahr* buhr oh (UK Mah kit *Hah* bra)
Market Rasen, England : Mahr kut *Ray* zun (UK Mah kit...)

Market Weighton, England : Mahr kut *Wee* tun (UK Mah kit...)
Markham, Canada; USA : *Mahr* kum (UK *Mah* kum)
Marks, Russia : Mahrks (UK Mahks)
Marl, Germany : Mahrl
Marlboro, USA : *Mawl* ba ra [This is the usual pronunciation for Marlboro, New Jersey, and Marlboro, New York, but Marlboro, Vermont, is normally *Mahrl* buhr oh.]
[1]Marlborough, England : *Mawl* bra
[2]Marlborough, USA : *Mahrl* buhr oh [The name of the Massachusetts city is alternately spelled as for **Marlboro.**]
Marlow, England : *Mahr* loh (UK *Mah* loh)
Marmara, Turkey : *Mahr* ma ra (UK *Mah* ma ra)
Marne, France : Mahrn
Maroua, Cameroon : Mah *rooh* ah
Marple, England; USA : *Mahr* pul (UK *Mah* pul)
Marquesas (Islands), Pacific Ocean : Mahr *kay* zus (UK Mah *kay* zus)
Marquette, USA : Mahr *ket* (UK Mah *ket*)
Marrakech, Morocco : Mar a *kesh*
Marrickville, Australia : *Mar* ik vil
Marsala, Italy : Mahr *sah* la (UK Mah *sah* la) (Italian Mahr *sah* lah)
Marsden, England : *Mahrz* dun (UK *Mahz* dun)
Marseille, France : Mahr *say* (UK Mah *say*) [A former English pronunciation of the seaport city's name, in its alternate spelling *Marseilles*, was US Mahr *saylz*, UK Mah *saylz*, as in Edward Lear's 1846 limerick: "There was an Old Man of Marseilles, / Whose daughters wore bottle-green veils." This form was actually recommended by Lloyd James 1937.]
Marshall (Islands), Pacific Ocean : *Mahr* shul (UK *Mah* shul)
Marshalltown, USA : *Mahr* shul town (UK *Mah* shul town)
Marske-by-the-Sea, England : Mahrsk biy dha *See* (UK Mahsk...)

Marston Moor, England : Mahr stun *Moor* (UK Mah stun *Moo* a)

Martha's Vineyard, USA : Mahr thuz *Vin* yurd (UK Mah thuz *Vin* yud)

Martigues, France : Mahr *teeg*

Martínez de la Torre, Mexico : Mahr tee nays dhay lah *Tohr* ray

Martinique, West Indies : Mahr tun *eek* (UK Mah ti *neek*)

Martinsburg, USA : *Mahr* tunz buhrg (UK *Mah* tinz buhg)

Martinsville, USA : *Mahr* tunz vil (UK *Mah* tinz vil)

Martock, England : *Mahr* tuk (UK *Mah* tuk)

Martos, Spain : *Mahr* tohs

Marvejols, France : Mahrv *zhol*

Mary, Turkmenistan : Mah *ree*

Maryborough, Australia : *Mer* i buhr oh (UK *May* a ri ba ra)

Maryland, USA : *Mer* lund (UK *May* a ri lund) [British speakers may even refer to the state as *May* a ri land, a pronunciation which to Americans sounds stilted or simply incorrect. It is, however, the pronunciation given in the *Oxford English Dictionary* in connection with expressions such as "Maryland chicken."]

Maryland, at home, is always *Mare-l'nd* [Mencken, p. 540].

Marylebone, England : *Mer* a la bohn (UK *Mar* a la bun) [A traditional local pronunciation of the London district's name is *Mar* a bun, omitting the *-le-* which is anyway inorganic. Pointon, p. 167, gives four UK pronunciations, the first being "preferred by the local educated population": *Mar* i la bun, *Mar* a la bun, *Mar* i bun, and *Mah* li bun. The very form and sound of the name seems to demand a shortening or slurring of its four syllables to three or even less, as instanced in quote (2) below.]

(1) Ask any Londoner the way to "Mary-le-bone." "Oh," he will say, "you mean *Marybone*!" [H.G. Stokes, *English Place-Names*, 1948].

(2) The process [of slurring a name] is well illustrated by the street in London called Marylebone Road. Visitors from abroad often misread it as "Marleybone." Provincial Britons tend to give it its full phonetic value: "Mary-luh-bone." Londoners are inclined to slur it to "Mairbun" or something similar, while those who live or work along it slur it even further to something not far off "Mbn" [Bill Bryson, *Mother Tongue*, 1990]. (3) [The added] *-le-* is usually sounded now in current pronunciations of the name, "Marrylebon" or "Marlibon" [A.D. Mills, *A Dictionary of London Place Names*, 2001].

Maryport, England : *Mer* i pawrt (UK *May* a ri pawt)

Marysville, USA : *Mer* iz vil (UK *May* a riz vil)

Masan, South Korea : *Mah* sahn

Masaya, Nicaragua : Mah *sah* yah

Masbate, Philippines : Mahs *bah* tay

Mascara, Algeria : *Mas* ka ra

Mascarene (Islands), Indian Ocean : Mas ka *reen*

Maseru, Lesotho : *Maz* a rooh (UK Ma *si* a rooh)

Masham, England : *Mas* um

Mashhad, Iran : Ma *shahd*

Mashonaland, Zimbabwe : Ma *shah* na land (UK Ma *shon* a land)

Masjed Soleyman, Iran : Mahs jid Sooh lay *mahn*

Mason City, USA : May sun *Si* ti

Masqat, Oman : Mus *kaht*

Massa, Italy : *Mahs* sah

Massachusetts, USA : Mas a *chooh* suts

Massapequa, USA : Mas a *peek* wa

Massawa, Eritrea : Mah *sah* wah

Massenya, Chad : Mah *say* nyah

Massif Central, France : Ma seef Sahn *trahl*

Massillon, USA : *Mas* a lun (UK *Mas* i lon)

Masterton, New Zealand : *Mas* tur tun (UK *Mahs* ta tun)

Masuria, Poland : Ma *zoor* i a

Masvingo, Zimbabwe : Mahs *ving* goh

Mat, Albania : Maht
Matabeleland, Zimbabwe : Ma ta *bee* li
land
Matadi, Democratic Republic of the
Congo : Mah *tah* dee
Matagalpa, Nicaragua : Mah tah *gahl*
pah
Matamoros, Mexico : Mah tah *moh*
rohs
Matane, Canada : Ma *tan*
Matanzas, Cuba : Ma *tan* zus (Spanish
Mah *tahn* sahs)
Matapan, Greece : *Mat* a pan
Mataram, Indonesia : Ma *tah* rum
Mataura, New Zealand : Ma *tow* ra
Matehuala, Mexico : Mah tay *wah* lah
Matera, Italy : Mah *tay* rah
Mathura, India : *Mah* ta ra
Matlock, England : *Mat* lahk (UK *Mat*
lok)
Matochkin Shar, Russia : Mah tuch kin
Shahr
Mato Grosso, Brazil : Ma toh *Groh* soh
(UK ... *Gros* oh) (Portuguese Mah
tooh *Groh* sooh)
Matruh, Egypt : Ma *trooh*
Matsu, China : *Maht* sooh (UK *Mat*
sooh)
Matsudo, Japan : Maht *sooh* doh
Matsue, Japan : Maht *sooh* ay
Matsumoto, Japan : Maht sooh *moh*
toh
Matsuyama, Japan : Maht sooh *yah*
mah
Matterhorn, Switzerland : *Mat* ur
hawrn (UK *Mat* a hawn)
Mattoon, USA : Ma *toohn*
Maturín, Venezuela : Mah tooh *reen*
(UK Mat yoo a *rin*)
Maubeuge, France : Moh *buhzh*
Mauchline, Scotland : *Mawkh* lin
Maui, USA : *Mow* i
Maule, Chile : *Mow* lay
Maumee, USA : Maw *mee*
Maun, Botswana : Mah *oon*
Mauna Kea, USA : Mow na *Kay* a
Mauna Loa, USA : Mow na *Loh* a
Mauretania, Africa : Mor i *tay* ni a
Mauritania, Africa : Mor i *tay* ni a

Mauritius, Indian Ocean : Maw *rish* us
(UK Ma *rish* us)
Maurs, France : Mawrs
Mauthausen, Austria : *Mowt* how zun
Mayagüez, Puerto Rico : Miy ah *gways*
Mayarí, Cuba : Miy ah *ree*
Maybole, Scotland : May *bohl*
Mayenne, France : Mah *yen*
Maykop, Russia : Miy *kawp*
Maynooth, Ireland : Ma *noohth*
Mayo, Ireland : *May* oh
Mayotte, Indian Ocean : Miy *yaht* (UK
Miy *ot*) (French Miy *yawt*)
May Pen, Jamaica : *May* Pen
Mazagan, Morocco : Ma za *gahn*
Mazar-e Sharif, Afghanistan : Ma zahr
ee Sha *reef*
Mazatenango, Guatemala : Mah zah
tay *nahng* goh
Mazatlán, Mexico : Mah sah *tlahn*
Mbabane, Swaziland : M bah *bah* nay
Mbala, Zambia : M *bah* lah
Mbale, Uganda : M *bah* lay
Mbandaka, Democratic Republic of the
Congo : M bahn *dah* kah
M'banza Congo, Angola : M bahn zah
Kahng goh (UK ... *Kong* goh)
Mbeya, Tanzania : M *bay* ah
Mbini, Equatorial Guinea : M *bee* nee
Mbuji-Mayi, Democratic Republic of
the Congo : M booh jee *Miy* ee
Mc- : All names beginning *Mc-* are al-
phabetized as if beginning *Mac-*.
Mdina, Malta : Ma *dee* nah
Meagher, USA : Mahr (UK Mah)
Mearns, Scotland : Mernz (UK *May*
unz) [The Scots pronunciation of the
region's name is closer to the US than
the UK.]
Meath, Ireland : Meedh [The county
name is commonly pronounced
Meeth by non–Irish. The same is true
of **Westmeath**.]
Meaux, France : Moh
Mecca, Saudi Arabia : *Mek* a
Mechanicsville, USA : Mi *kan* iks vil
Mechelen, Belgium : *May* kha lun
Mechlin, Belgium : *Mek* lin
Mecklenburg, Germany : *Mek* len

buhrg (UK *Mek* len buhg) (German
May klun boork)

Medan, Indonesia : May *dahn* (UK *May*
dan)

Médéa, Algeria : May day *ah*

Medellín, Colombia : Med ul *en* (Spanish May dhay *yeen*)

Medford, USA : *Med* furd (UK *Med*
fud)

Medgidia, Romania : May jee *dee* ah

Media, Iran : *Mee* di a

Mediaş, Romania : May dee *ahsh*

Medicine Hat, Canada : *Med* sun Hat

¹**Medina**, Saudi Arabia : Ma *dee* na

²**Medina**, USA : Ma *diy* na

Mediterranean (Sea), Europe : Med i ta
ray ni an

Medmenham, England : *Med* num

Médoc, France : May *dawk*

Medway, England : *Med* way

Meeker, USA : *Mee* kur (UK *Mee* ka)

Meerane, Germany : May *rah* na

Meerssen, Netherlands : *Mer* sun

Meerut, India : *Mi* rut

Mégara, Greece : *Meg* a ra

Megève, France : Mi *zhev*

Meghalaya, India : May ga *lay* a

Megiddo, Israel : Mi *gid* oh

Meije, France : Mayzh

Meiktila, Myanmar : *Mek* ta la

Meiningen, Germany : *Miy* ning un

Meirionnydd, Wales : Mer i *ahn* idh
(UK Mer i *on* idh) (Welsh Mayr *yon*
idh)

Meissen, Germany : *Miy* sun

Mejicanos, El Salvador : May hee *kah*
nohs

Mekele, Ethiopia : *May* ka lay

Meknès, Morocco : Mek *nes*

Mekong, Asia : May *kawng* (UK Mee
kong)

Melaka, Malaysia : Ma *lah* kah

Melanesia, Pacific Ocean : Mel a *nee*
zha (UK Mel a *nee* zi a)

¹**Melbourne**, Australia; USA : *Mel*
burn (UK *Mel* bun) [The Australian
state capital's name is often pronounced by non–Australians as ²**Melbourne**.]

²**Melbourne**, England : *Mel* bawrn (UK
Mel bawn)

Melilla, Morocco : Ma *lee* lyah

Melitopol, Ukraine : Mel a *taw* pul

Melksham, England : *Melk* shum

Melo, Uruguay : *May* loh

Melos, Greece : *Mee* lahs (UK *Mee* los)

Melrose, Scotland; USA : *Mel* rohz

Meltham, England : *Mel* thum

Melton, Australia : *Mel* tun

Melton Mowbray, England : Mel tun
Moh bri

Melun, France : Mi *luhn*

Melville (Island), Australia; Canada :
Mel vil

Memmingen, Germany : *Mem* ing un

Memphis, Egypt; USA : *Mem* fus (UK
Mem fis)

Menai (Strait), Wales : *Men* iy

Mende, France : Mahnd

Menden, Germany : *Men* dun

Menderes, Turkey : Men de *res*

Mendip (Hills), England : *Men* dip

Mendocino, USA : Men da *see* noh

Mendoza, Argentina : Men *doh* za

Menen, Belgium : *May* nun

Menlo (Park), USA : *Men* loh

Menomonie, USA : Ma *nah* ma ni (UK
Ma *nom* a ni)

Menongue, Angola : May *nawng*

Mentawai, Indonesia : Men *tah* wiy

Menton, France : Mahn *tawn*

Menzel Bourguiba, Tunisia : Men zel
Boor *gee* ba

Meols, England : Melz

Meopham, England : *Mep* um

Merano, Italy : May *rah* noh

Merapi, Indonesia : Ma *rah* pi

Merauke, Indonesia : Ma *row* ka

Merced, USA : Mur *sed* (UK Muh *sed*)

Mercedes, Argentina; Uruguay; USA :
Mur *say* deez (Spanish Mer say
dhays)

Mercia, England : *Muhr* sha (UK *Muh*
si a)

Merelbeke, Belgium : *May* rul bayk

Mergui, Myanmar : Mur *gwee*

Mérida, Mexico; Spain; Venezuela :
Mer i da (Spanish *May* ree dhah)

Meriden, England; USA : *Mer* a dun
(UK *Mer* i dun)
Meridian, USA : Ma *rid* i un
Merioneth, Wales : Mer i *ahn* uth (UK
Mer i *on* uth)
Merlo, Argentina : *Mer* loh
Meroë, Sudan : *Mer* oh wee
Merrick, USA : *Mer* ik
Merrillville, USA : *Mer* ul vil
Merrimack, USA : *Mer* a mak (UK *Mer*
i mak)
Merseburg, Germany : *Mer* za boork
Mersey, England : *Muhr* zi (UK *Muh*
zi)
Mersin, Turkey : Mer *seen*
Mers-les-Bains, France : Mers lay *Bahn*
Merstham, England : *Muhrs* tum (UK
Muhs tum) [The name of the Surrey
village was formerly pronounced US
Mir stum, UK *Mi* a stum, as evi-
denced by the quotes below.]
   (1) At *Mearstam* there is a field of cab-
bages [William Cobbett, *Rural Rides*,
July 26, 1823 (1830)].
   (2) *Mearstam*, the country people call
it, and so Cobbett writes it in his
"Rural Rides" [James Thorne, *Hand-
book to the Environs of London*, 1876].
Merthyr Tydfil, Wales : Muhr thur *Tid*
vil (UK Muh tha...)
Merton, England : *Muhr* tun (UK *Muh*
tun)
Meru, Kenya : *May* rooh
Merzifon, Turkey : Mer zee *fawn*
Mesa, USA : *May* sa
Mesagne, Italy : May *sah* nyay
Mesopotamia, Iraq : Mes a pa *tay* mi a
Mesquite, USA : Me *skeet*
Messenia, Greece : Ma *see* ni a
Messina, Italy; South Africa : Me *see*
nah
Meta, Colombia : *May* ta
Métabief, France : May tah *byay*
Methuen, USA : Ma *thooh* un (UK Ma
thyooh un)
Methven, Scotland : *Meth* vun
Metu, Ethiopia : *Met* ooh
Metuchen, USA : Mi *tah* chun
Metz, France : Mets (French Mes)

Meudon, France : Muh *dawn*
Meung-sur-Loir, France : Muhng seer
Lwahr
Meuse, Europe : Myoohz (UK Muhz)
Mevagissey, England : Mev a *gis* i
Mexborough, England : *Meks* buhr oh
(UK *Meks* bra)
Mexia, USA : Ma *hay* a
Mexicali, Mexico : Mek see *kah* lee
Mexico, Central America : *Mek* si koh
Mexico City, Mexico : Mek si koh *Si* ti
Mézenc, France : May *zahnk*
Mezhdurechensk, Russia : Mezh doo
rye chinsk
Mhow, India : Mow
Miami, USA : Miy *am* i
Miass, Russia : Mee *ahs*
Michalovce, Slovakia : *Mee* khah low
tse
Micheldever, England : *Mich* ul dev ur
(UK *Mich* ul dev a)
Michigan, USA : *Mish* i gun [A UK
pronunciation *Mich* i gun, recognized
by Ross, p. 120, was formerly current
for the state, and is still sometimes
heard.]
Michurinsk, Russia : Mi *chooh* rinsk
Mickleover, England : *Mik* ul oh vur
(UK *Mik* ul oh va)
Micronesia, Pacific Ocean : Miy kra *nee*
zha (UK Miy kroh *nee* zi a)
Middelburg, Netherlands; South Af-
rica : *Mid* ul buhrg (UK *Mid* ul
buhg)
Middelkerke, Belgium : *Mid* ul kerk
Middlebury, USA : *Mid* ul ber i (UK
Mid ul bri)
Middlesborough, USA : *Mid* ulz buhr
oh (UK *Mid* ulz bra)
Middlesbrough, England : *Mid* ulz bra
Middlesex, England; USA : *Mid* ul seks
Middleton, England; USA : *Mid* ul tun
Middletown, USA : *Mid* ul town
Middlewich, England : *Mid* ul wich
Midhurst, England : *Mid* huhrst (UK
Mid huhst)
Midland, Canada; USA : *Mid* lund
[1]**Midlothian**, Scotland : Mid *loh* dhi un
[2]**Midlothian**, USA : Mid *loh* thi un

Midnapore, India : *Mid* na pohr
Midsayap, Philippines : Mid sah *yahp*
Midvale, USA : *Mid* vayl
Midway (Islands), Pacific Ocean : *Mid* way
Mielec, Poland : *Mye* lets
Miercurea-Ciuc, Romania : Myer koohr yah *Choohk*
Mieres, Spain : *Myay* rays
Mihara, Japan : Mee *hah* rah
Mikhaylovgrad, Bulgaria : Mi *khiy* luv graht
Mikkeli, Finland : *Mee* ke lee
Mikołów, Poland : Mee *kaw* woohf
Milagro, Ecuador : Mee *lah* groh
¹**Milan**, Italy : Mi *lan* [The former English pronunciation of the city's name was *Mil* un. Hence its occurrence with this stress in Shakespeare, especially in *The Tempest* (1611), in which the chief character, Prospero, is "the right Duke of Milan."]
　Was Milan thrust from Milan, that his issue
　Should become kings of Naples? [V. i. 205].
²**Milan**, USA : *Miy* lun
Milazzo, Italy : Mee *laht* soh
Mildenhall, England : *Mil* dun hawl
Mildura, Australia : Mil *dyoo* ra
Miletus, Turkey : Miy *lee* tus
Milford, England; USA : *Mil* furd (UK *Mil* fud)
Milford Haven, Wales : Mil furd *Hay* vun (UK Mil fud...)
Miliana, Algeria : Mil *yah* nah
Millas, France : Mee *yahs*
Millau, France : Mee *yoh*
Milledgeville, USA : *Mil* ij vil
Millom, England : *Mil* um
Millville, USA : *Mil* vil
Milngavie, Scotland : Mil *giy*
Milnrow, England : *Miln* roh [A local pronunciation *Mil* droh was at one time current for the former Lancashire town.]
Milpitas, USA : Mil *pee* tus
Milton, Canada; England; USA : *Mil* tun

Milton Keynes, England : Mil tun *Keenz* [The second word of the former Buckinghamshire town's name has a different pronunciation from that of **Horsted Keynes**.]
Milverton, England : *Mil* vur tun (UK *Mil* va tun)
Milwaukee, USA : Mil *waw* ki
Minas, Uruguay : *Mee* nahs
Minas de Ríotinto, Spain : Mee nahs dhay Ree oh *teen* toh
Minas Gerais, Brazil : Mee nus Zhee *riys*
Minatitlán, Mexico : Mee nah teet *lahn*
Mindanao, Philippines : Min da *now*
Mindelo, Cape Verde : Min *del* ooh
Minden, Germany; USA : *Min* dun
Mindoro, Philippines : Min *doh* roh
Minehead, England : *Miyn* hed
Mineola, USA : Mi nee *oh* la
Mineralnyye Vody, Russia : Mi ni rahl nee a *Vaw* di
Mingechaur, Azerbaijan : Meen gi *chyoohr*
Mingrelia, Georgia : Min *gree* li a
Mingulay, Scotland : *Ming* goo lay
Minna, Nigeria : *Min* a
Minneapolis, USA : Mi nee *ap* a lis
Minnesota, USA : Mi na *soh* ta (UK Mi ni *soh* ta)
Minnetonka, USA : Mi na *tahng* ka (UK Mi ni *tong* ka)
Minoo, Japan : *Mee* noh oh
Minorca, Spain : Mi *nawr* ka (UK Mi *naw* ka)
Minot, USA : *Miy* naht (UK *Miy* not) [As the quote below esoterically implies, the name of the North Dakota city (unrelated to Asian currency) requires a proper pronunciation.]
　Minot (rhymes with "Thai Baht") [*Lonely Planet USA*, 2004].
Minsk, Belarus : Minsk
Minto, Scotland : *Min* toh
Minusinsk, Russia : Mee nooh *seensk*
Miquelon, St. Pierre and Miquelon : *Mee* ka lahn (UK *Mee* ka lon) (French Mee *klawn*)
Mirabel, Canada : *Mir* a bel (French Mee rah *bel*)

Miraflores, Peru : Mee rah *floh* rays

¹**Miramar**, Argentina : Mee rah *mahr*

²**Miramar**, USA : *Mir* a mahr

Mirandola, Italy : Mee *rahn* doh lah

Mirano, Italy : Mee *rah* noh

Mirditë, Albania : Meer *dee* ta

Mirfield, England : *Muhr* feeld (UK *Muh* feeld)

Miri, Malaysia : *Mee* ree

Mirim, South America : Mee *reem*

Mirzapur, India : *Mir* za poor

Misantla, Mexico : Mee *sahnt* lah

Mishawaka, USA : Mi sha *waw* ka

Mishima, Japan : Mee *shee* mah

Misiones, Argentina; Paraguay : Mee *syoh* nays

Miskolc, Hungary : *Mish* kohlts

Misool, Indonesia : *Mee* sol

Misratah, Libya : Mees *rah* ta

Mississauga, Canada : Mi si *saw* ga

Mississippi, USA : Mi sa *sip* i (UK Mi si *sip* i)

Missolonghi, Greece : Mis a *lawng* gi (UK Mis a *long* gi)

Missoula, USA : Mi *zooh* la

Missouri, USA : Ma *zoor* i (UK Mi *zoo* a ri) [An alternate local pronunciation of the state's name is Ma *zoor* a.] *Missouri*, at home, is *Mizzoora*, although efforts have been made for many years by the local schoolmarms and other purists to unvoice the *z*'s and to convert the final *a* into a *y* [Mencken, p. 541].

Misurata, Libya : Mee sooh *rah* ta

Mitaka, Japan : Mee *tah* kah

Mitcham, England : *Mich* um

Mitchell, USA : *Mich* ul

Mito, Japan : *Mee* toh

Mits'iwa, Eritrea : Mit *see* wah

Mittagong, Australia : *Mit* a gahng (UK *Mit* a gong)

Mittenwald, Germany : *Mit* un vahlt

Mitú, Colombia : Mee *tooh*

Mixco, Guatemala : *Meesh* koh

Miyazaki, Japan : Mee *yah* zah kee

Mizda, Libya : *Miz* da

Mizoram, India : Mi *zaw* rum

Mkoani, Tanzania : M koh *ah* ni

Mladá Boleslav, Czech Republic : Mlah dah *Baw* les lahf

Mława, Poland : *Mwah* vah

Mmabatho, South Africa : Mah *bah* toh

Moab, Syria; USA : *Moh* ab

Mobile, USA : Moh *beel*

Mobridge, USA : *Moh* brij

Moca, Dominican Republic; Puerto Rico : *Moh* kah

Moçambique, Mozambique : Mooh sum *bee* ka

Môçamedes, Angola : Mooh *sah* ma dish

Mocha, Yemen : *Moh* ka (UK *Mok* a)

Mochudi, Botswana : Moh *chooh* dee

Mocoa, Colombia : Moh *koh* ah

Mocorito, Mexico : Moh koh *ree* toh

Modena, Italy : *Moh* da na (UK *Mod* in a) (Italian *Maw* day nah)

Modesto, USA : Ma *des* toh

Modica, Italy : *Maw* dee kah

Mödling, Austria : *Muhd* ling

Moengo, Suriname : *Moohng* oh

Moers, Germany : Muhrs

Moesia, Europe : *Mee* sha (UK *Mee* si a)

Mogadishu, Somalia : Mah ga *dish* ooh (UK Mog a *dish* ooh)

Mogador, Morocco : Mah ga *dawr* (UK Mog a *daw*)

Mogi das Cruzes, Brazil : Moh zhee dahs *Krooh* zees

Mogilev, Belarus : Ma gi *lyawf*

Mogilev-Podolski, Ukraine : Ma gi lyawf Pa *dawl* ski

Mogollon (Mountains), USA : Moh ga *yohn*

Mohács, Hungary : *Moh* hahch

Mohales Hoek, Lesotho : Moh hah les *Hook*

Mohammedia, Morocco : Moh ah may *dyah*

Mojave (Desert), USA : Mo *hah* vi

Mojokerto, Indonesia : Moh joh *ker* toh (UK Moh joh *kay* a toh)

Moknine, Tunisia : *Mok* ni ni

Mokp'o, South Korea : *Mahk* poh (UK *Mok* poh)

Mol, Belgium : Mawl

Mold, Wales : Mohld

Moldavia, Europe : Mahl *day* vi a (UK Mol *day* vi a)

Molde, Norway : *Mawl* da

Moldova, Europe : Mahl *doh* va (UK Mol *doh* va)

Molepolole, Botswana : Moh lay poh *loh* lay

Moline, USA : Moh *leen*

Molitg-les-Bains, France : Maw lich lay *Bahn*

Mollendo, Peru : Moh *yen* doh

Mölndal, Sweden : *Muhln* dahl

Molokai, USA : Moh loh *kiy*

Moluccas, Indonesia : Ma *lah* kuz

Mombasa, Kenya : Mahm *bah* sa (UK Mom *bas* a) (Swahili Mohm *bah* sah)

Momostenango, Guatemala : Moh moh stay *nahng* goh

Monaco, Europe : *Mah* na koh (UK Mon a koh) (French Maw nah *koh*, Italian Maw nah koh)

Monadhliath (Mountains), Scotland : Moh na *lee* a

Monadnock, USA : Ma *nad* nahk (UK Ma *nad* nok)

Monaghan, Ireland : *Mah* na hun (UK Mon a hun)

Monastir, Tunisia : Mah na *stir* (UK Mon a *sti* a)

Monchegorsk, Russia : Mun cha *gawrsk*

Mönchengladbach, Germany : Mahn shun *glad* bak (German Muhn khun *glaht* bahkh)

Monclova, Mexico : Mawng *kloh* vah

Moncton, Canada : *Mahng* tun

Mondragone, Italy : Mawn drah *goh* nay

Monemvasía, Greece : Maw nem vah *see* ah

Monfalcone, Italy : Mawn fahl *koh* nay

Mongolia, Asia : Mahng *goh* li a (UK Mong *goh* li a)

Mongu, Zambia : *Mawng* gooh

Monheim, Germany : *Mawn* hiym

Monifieth, Scotland : Mah ni *feeth*

Monkwearmouth, England : Mahnk *wir* mowth (UK Mahnk *wi* a mowth)

Monmouth, Wales; USA : *Mahn* muth (UK *Mon* muth)

Mono, USA : *Moh* noh

Monocacy, USA : Ma *nah* ka si (UK Ma *nok* a si)

Monongahela, USA : Ma nahng ga *hee* la (UK Ma nong ga *hee* la)

Monopoli, Italy : Moh *naw* poh lee

Monreale, Italy : Mohn ree *ah* lay

Monroe, USA : Mun *roh*

Monrovia, Liberia : Mun *roh* vi a

Mons, Belgium : Mahnz (UK Monz) (French Mawns)

Monseñor Nouel, Dominican Republic : Mawn say nyawr Noh *wel*

Montana, USA : Mahn *tan* a (UK Mon *tan* a) [A fairly frequent UK pronunciation of the state's name is Mon *tah* na, as recommended by Lloyd James 1937.]

Montauban, France : Mawn toh *bahn*

Montbéliard, France : Mawn bay *lyahr*

Mont Blanc, France : Mahnt *Blahng* (UK Mont *Blong*) (French Mawn *Blahn*)

Mont Cenis, France : Mawn *Snee*

Montclair, USA : Mahnt *kler* (UK Mont *klay* a)

Mont-de-Marsan, France : Mawnd Mahr *sahn*

Montdidier, France : Mawn dee *dyay*

Montebello, USA : Mahn ta *bel* oh (UK Mon ti *bel* oh)

Monte Carlo, Monaco : Mahn ti *Kahr* loh (UK Mon ti *Kah* loh) (French Mawn tay Kahr *loh*)

Montecatini-Terme, Italy : Mawn tay kah tee nee *Ter* may

Monte Cristi, Dominican Republic : Mawn tay *Krees* tee

Montego Bay, Jamaica : Mahn tee goh *Bay* (UK Mon tee goh…)

Montélimar, France : Mawn tay lee *mahr*

Montenegro, Europe : Mahn ta *nee* groh (UK Mon ti *nee* groh)

Monte Plata, Dominican Republic : Mawn tay *Plah* tah

Monterey, USA : Mahn ta *ray* (UK Mon ta *ray*)

Montería, Colombia : Mawn tay *ree* ah

Monterrey, Mexico : Mahn ta *ray* (UK Mon ta *ray*) (Spanish Mawn ter *ray*)

Montes Claros, Brazil : Mohn teesh *Kla* roohs

¹**Montevideo**, Uruguay : Mahn ta va *day* oh (UK Mon ti vi *day* oh) (Spanish Mawn tay vee *dhay* oh) [An alternate pronunciation US Mahn ta *vid* i oh, UK Mon ti *vid* i oh also exists for the capital city's name, no doubt for Americans influenced by that of ²**Montevideo**.]

²**Montevideo**, USA : Mahn ta *vid* i oh (UK Mon ti *vid* i oh) [The name of the Minnesota town has the alternate pronunciation of ¹**Montevideo**.]

Montgomery, USA; Wales : Munt *gahm* ri (UK Mont *gom* ri)

Monticello, USA : Mahn ta *sel* oh (UK Mon ti *chel* oh) [Monticello, Minnesota, is generally Mawn ti *sel* oh, while Thomas Jefferson's home near Charlottesville, Virginia, is also Mahn ti *chel* oh, closer to the name's Italian origin, meaning "little mountain."]

Montier-en-Der, France : Mawn tyay ahn *Der*

Montigny, France : Mawn tee *nyee*

Montijo, Portugal; Spain : Mawn *tee* hoh

Montilla, Spain : Mawn *tee* lyah

Mont-Laurier, Canada : Mon *Law* ri ay

Montluçon, France : Mawn li *sawn*

Montmagny, Canada : Mon mah *nyee*

Montmorency, Canada; France : Mahnt ma *ren* si (UK Mont ma *ren* si) (French Mawn moh rahn *see*)

Montpelier, USA : Mahnt *peel* yer (UK Mont *pee* li a)

Montpellier, France : Mohn pel *yay* (UK Mont *pel* i a) (French Mawn puh *lyay*)

Montreal, Canada : Mahn tri *awl* (UK Mon tri *awl*)

Montréal, Canada : Mawn ray *al*

Montréjeau, France : Mawn ray *zhoh*

Montreuil, France : Mawn *truh* i

Montreux, Switzerland : Mohn *troo* (UK Mon *truh*) (French Mawn *truh*)

Montrichard, France : Mawn tree *shahr*

Montrose, Scotland; USA : Mahn *trohz* (UK Mon *trohz*)

Montrouge, France : Mawn *roohzh*

Mont-St.-Michel, France : Mohn San Mi *shel* (UK Mont...) (French Mawn Sahn Mee *shel*)

Montségur, France : Mawn say *geer*

¹**Montserrat**, Spain : Mawnt ser *raht*

²**Montserrat**, West Indies : Mahnt sa *rat* (UK Mont sa *rat*) [The usual local pronunciation of the island's name is *Mont* sa rat.]

Montsûrs, France : Mawn *seer*

Montville, USA : *Mahnt* vil (UK *Mont* vil)

Monymusk, Scotland : Mah ni *mahsk* (UK Mon i *mahsk*)

Monza, Italy : *Mahn* za (UK *Mon* za) (Italian *Mohn* tsah)

Moorabbin, Australia : Moo *rab* in

Moorhead, USA : *Moor* hed (UK *Moo* a hed)

Moorpark, USA : *Moor* pahrk (UK *Moo* a pahk)

Moose Jaw, Canada : *Moohs* Jaw

Mopti, Mali : *Mawp* ti

Moquegua, Peru : Moh *kay* gwah

Moradabad, India : Ma *rah* da bahd

Moratuwa, Sri Lanka : *Moh* ra too wa

Morava, Slovakia : Maw *rah* vah

Moravia, Czech Republic : Ma *ray* vi a

Moray, Scotland : *Muh* ri (UK *Mah* ri) [The region and sea inlet (Moray Firth) is sometimes called *Mor* i by those unfamiliar with the pronunciation, which is identical with that of Australia's **Murray** River.]

Morbihan, France : Mawr bee *ahn*

Morcenx, France : Mawr *sahns*

Morden, England : *Mawr* dun (UK *Maw* dun)

Mordialloc, Australia : Mawr di *al* uk (UK Maw di *al* uk)

Mordvinia, Russia : Mawrd *vin* i a (UK Mawd *vin* i a)

Morea, Greece : Maw *ree* a (UK Maw *ri* a)

Morecambe, England : *Mawr* kum (UK *Maw* kum)

Moree, Australia : *Maw* ree

Morehead, USA : *Mawr* hed (UK *Maw* hed)

Morelia, Mexico : Moh *ray* lyah

Morena, India : Maw *ray* na

Moreno Valley, USA : Ma ree noh *Val* i

Moresby, England : *Mor* is bi [The name is generally pronounced US *Mawrz* bi, UK *Mawz* bi, as for **Port Moresby**, but the Cumbria village is distinctively as here.]

Moreton (Bay), Australia : *Mawr* tun (UK *Maw* tun)

Moretonhampstead, England : Mawr tun *hamp* stid (UK Maw tun *hamp* stid)

Morez, France : Maw *ray*

Morfa Harlech, Wales : Mawr va *Hahr* luk (UK Maw va *Hah* luk) (Welsh Mawr vah *Hahr* lekh) [The name is that of an area of marshland (Welsh *morfa*, "marsh") near **Harlech**.]

Morgan, USA : *Mawr* gun (UK *Maw* gun)

Morgantown, USA : *Mawr* gun town (UK *Maw* gun town)

Morges, Switzerland : Mawrzh

Morioka, Japan : Moh ree *oh* kah

Morlaàs, France : Mawr *lahs*

Morlaix, France : Mawr *lay*

Morlanwelz, Belgium : *Mawr* lahn way

Morley, England : *Mawr* li (UK *Maw* li)

Morocco, Africa : Ma *rah* koh (UK Ma *rok* oh)

Morogoro, Tanzania : Moh roh *goh* roh

Moroleón, Mexico : Moh roh lay *awn*

Morón, Argentina; Cuba; Spain; Venezuela : Moh *rawn*

Morona-Santiago, Ecuador : Moh roh nah Sahn tee *ah* goh

Moroni, Comoros : Maw *roh* nee

Morotai, Indonesia : Moh roh *tiy*

Morovis, Puerto Rico : Moh roh *vees*

Morpeth, England : *Mawr* puth (UK *Maw* puth)

Morristown, USA : *Mawr* is town (UK *Mor* is town)

Morshansk, Russia : Mar *shahnsk*

Mortehoe, England : *Mawrt* hoh (UK *Mawt* hoh)

Mortlake, England : *Mawrt* layk (UK *Mawt* layk)

Mortsel, Belgium : *Mawrt* sel

Morwell, Australia : *Mawr* wel (UK *Maw* wel)

¹Moscow, Russia : *Mahs* kow (UK *Mos* koh)

²Moscow, USA : *Mahs* koh (UK *Mos* koh)

Moselle, Europe : Moh *zel* [The German name of the river is *Mosel*, pronounced *Moh* zul.]

Moshi, Tanzania : *Moh* shi

Mosman, Australia : *Mahs* mun (UK *Mos* mun)

Mosonmagyaróvár, Hungary : *Maw* shawn maw dyaw roh vahr

Moss, Norway : Maws

Mosselbaai, South Africa : Maw sul *biy*

Mossley, England : *Maws* li (UK *Mos* li)

Mossoró, Brazil : Moh soh *raw*

Most, Czech Republic : Mawst

Mostaganem, Algeria : Mos tah gah *nem*

Mostar, Bosnia-Herzegovina : *Mohs* tahr (UK *Mos* tah) (Croatian *Maws* tahr)

Mosul, Iraq : *Moh* sul

Motala, Sweden : *Mooh* tah lah

Motherwell, Scotland : *Mah* dhur wul (UK *Mah* dha wul)

Motril, Spain : Moh *treel*

Mouaskar, Algeria : *Mooh* us kahr (UK *Mooh* us kah)

Mouilleron-en-Pareds, France : Mwee rawn ahn Pah *ray*

Moulins, France : Mooh *lahn*

Moulmein, Myanmar : Moohl *mayn*

Moundou, Chad : *Moohn* dooh

Mount : if not below, see under main name, e.g., **Tacoma**

Mountain Ash, Wales : Mown tun *Ash*

Mount Gambier, Australia : Mownt *Gam* bir (UK ... *Gam* bi a)

Mount Isa, Australia : Mownt *Iy* za

Mount Pearl, Canada : Mownt *Puhrl* (UK ... *Puhl*)

Mount Pleasant, Australia; England; USA : Mownt *Plez* unt

Mount Prospect, Canada : Mownt *Prahs* pekt (UK ... *Pros* pekt)

Mount Vernon, USA : Mownt *Vuhr* nun (UK ... *Vuh* nun)

Mourenx, France : Mooh *rahns*

Mourne (Mountains), Northern Ireland : Mawrn (UK Mawn)

Mousa, Scotland : *Mooh* za

Mousehole, England : *Mow* zul [The Cornish village gets its name from a nearby cave.]
(1) Pronounced "Mowzle" (rhyming with "tousle"), by natural development, as seen already [in the spelling *Mowssal*] in 1580 [O.J. Padel, *A Popular Dictionary of Cornish Place-Names*, 1988].
(2) The little port, whose name is pronounced "Mowzull" [*Reader's Digest Illustrated Guide to Britain's Coast*, 1996].

Moxico, Angola : *Maw* shee kooh

Moyle, Northern Ireland : Moyl

Moyobamba, Peru : Moy oh *bahm* bah

Mozambique, Africa : Moh zahm *beek* (UK Moh zum *beek*)

Mozhaysk, Russia : Ma *zhiysk*

Mpumalanga, South Africa : M pooh mah *lahng* gah

M'Sila, Algeria : M See *lah*

Mtwara, Tanzania : M *twah* rah

Mubi, Nigeria : *Mooh* bi

Much Wenlock, England : Mahch *Wen* lahk (UK ... *Wen* lok)

Muck, Scotland : Mahk

Muckle Flugga, Scotland : Mah kul *Flah* ga

Mudeford, England : *Mah* di furd (UK *Mah* di fud)

Mufulira, Zambia : Mooh fooh *lee* rah

Muggia, Italy : *Mooh* jah

Muharraq, Bahrain : Maw *hah* ruk

Mühlhausen, Germany : *Meel* how zun

Mukacheve, Ukraine : Mooh ka *choh* va

Mukden, China : *Mook* dun

Mulanje, Malawi : Ma *lahn* jay

Mulhacén, Spain : Mooh lah *thayn*

Mülheim, Germany : *Meel* hiym

Mulhouse, France : Mee *loohz*

Mull, Scotland : Mahl

Mullingar, Ireland : Mah lun *gahr*

Multan, Pakistan : Mool *tahn*

Mumbai, India : Moom *biy*

Muna, Indonesia : *Mooh* na

Muncie, USA : *Mahn* si

Münden, Germany : *Meen* dun

Mundesley, England : *Mahnz* li

Munich, Germany : *Myooh* nik [Some English speakers attempt a "German" pronunciation of the name as *Myooh* nikh, although the city's actual German name is *München*. See **München** in Appendix, p. 219.]

¹Munster, France : Muhn *ster*

²Munster, Ireland; USA : *Mahn* stur (UK *Mahn* sta)

Münster, Germany : *Meen* stur

Murang'a, Kenya : Mooh *rahng* gah

Murchison (Falls), Uganda : *Muhr* chi sun (UK *Muh* chi sun)

Murcia, Spain : *Muhr* sha (UK *Muh* si a) (Spanish *Moohr* thyah)

Murfreesboro, USA : *Muhr* friz buhr oh (UK *Muh* friz bah ra)

Murmansk, Russia : Moor *mahnsk* (UK Muh *mansk*) (Russian *Moor* munsk)

Murom, Russia : *Mooh* rum

Muroran, Japan : Mooh *roh* rahn

Muros, Spain : *Mooh* rohs

Murray, Australia : *Muh* ri (UK *Mah* ri)

Murrumbidgee, Australia : Muh rum *bij* i (UK Mah rum *bij* i)

Murshidabad, India : *Moor* shid a bahd

Mururoa, Pacific Ocean : Mooh rooh *roh* a (UK Moo ra *roh* a)

Murzuq, Libya : Moor *zoohk*

Musala, Bulgaria : Mooh sah *lah*

Musan, North Korea : Mooh *sahn*

Muscat, Oman : *Mahs* kat

Mushin, Nigeria : *Mooh* shin

Muskegon, USA : Mus *kee* gun

Muskogee, USA : Mus *koh* gi

Musoma, Tanzania : Mooh *soh* mah

Musselburgh, Scotland : *Mah* sul buhr oh (UK *Mah* sul bra)

Mustique, St. Vincent and the Grenadines : Moos *teek*

Mutare, Zimbabwe : Mooh *tah* ray

Muttenz, Switzerland : *Moo* tents

Muzaffarabad, Pakistan : Moo zah fur a *bahd*

Muzaffarnagar, India : Moo *zah* fur nuh gur

Muzaffarpur, India : Moo *zah* fur poor

Mwanza, Tanzania : *Mwahn* zah

Mweru, Africa : *Mway* rooh

Myanmar, Asia : *Myahn* mahr (UK *Myahn* mah)

Mycenae, Greece : Miy *see* ni

Myingyan, Myanmar : Myin *jahn*

Myitkyina, Myanmar : Myit chee *nah*

Mykolayiv, Ukraine : Mee ka *lah* yif

Mykonos, Greece : *Mee* ka nahs (UK *Mee* ka nos)

Mysłowice, Poland : Mees waw *veet* se

Mysore, India : Miy *sawr* (UK Miy *saw*)

Myszkow, Poland : *Meesh* koohf

My Tho, Vietnam : Mee *Toh*

Mytholmroyd, England : Miy dhum *royd*

Mytilene, Greece : Mi ta *lee* ni (UK Mi ti *lee* ni)

Mytishchi, Russia : Mwi *tish* chi

Mzuzu, Malawi : M *zooh* zooh

Naaldwijk, Netherlands : *Nahlt* viyk

Naarden, Netherlands : *Nahr* da

Naas, Ireland : Nays

Naberezhnyye Chelny, Russia : Na bi rezh ni ya Chil *nee*

Nabeul, Tunisia : Na *buhl*

Nablus, West Bank : *Nab* lus

Nacaome, Honduras : Nah kah *oh* may

Náchod, Czech Republic : *Nah* kawt

Nacogdoches, USA : Nak a *doh* chuz (UK Nak a *doh* chiz)

Nador, Morocco : Na *dawr* (UK Na *daw*)

Næstved, Denmark : *Nest* vedh

Nagaland, India : *Nah* ga land

Nagano, Japan : *Nah* gah noh

Nagaoka, Japan : Nah gah *oh* kah

Nagapattinam, India : Na ga *paht* a num

Nagareyama, Japan : Nah gah *ray* yah mah

Nagasaki, Japan : Nah gah *sah* kee

Nagercoil, India : *Nah* gur koyl

Nagorno-Karabakh, Azerbaijan : Na gawr na Ka ra *bahkh*

Nagoya, Japan : Nah *goy* ah

Nagpur, India : *Nahg* poor

Nagua, Dominican Republic : *Nah* gwah

Naguabo, Puerto Rico : Nah *gwah* boh

Nagykanizsa, Hungary : *Nawj* kaw nee zhaw

Nagykörös, Hungary : *Nawj* kuh ruhsh

Naha, Japan : *Nah* hah

Nahavand, Iran : Nah ha *vand*

Nailsea, England : *Nayl* see

Nailsworth, England : *Naylz* wurth (UK *Naylz* wuth)

Nairn, Scotland : Nern (UK *Nay* un)

Nairobi, Kenya : Niy *roh* bee

Naivasha, Kenya : Niy *vah* shah

Najibabad, India : Na *jee* ba bahd

Najin, North Korea : Nah *jeen*

Nakatsu, Japan : Nah *kaht* sooh

Nakhichevan, Azerbaijan : Na khee chi *vahn*

Nakhodka, Russia : Na *khawt* ka

Nakhon Nayok, Thailand : Nah kawn *Nah* yuk

Nakhon Pathom, Thailand : Nah kawn Pah *tahm*

Nakhon Phanom, Thailand : Nah kawn Pah *nahm*

Nakhon Ratchasima, Thailand : Nah kawn Rah cha *see* mah

Nakhon Sawan, Thailand : Nah kawn Sah *wahn*

Nakhon Si Thammarat, Thailand : Nah kawn See Tah ma *raht*

Nakło nad Notecią, Poland : Nah kwaw nahd Naw *te* chaw

Nakuru, Kenya : Nah *kooh* rooh

Nalchik, Russia : *Nahl* chik

Namaland, Namibia : *Nah* ma land

Namangan, Uzbekistan : Nah mahng *gahn*

Namaqualand, Africa : Na *mah* kwa land

Nam Dinh, Vietnam : Nahm *Deen*
Namib (Desert), Namibia : *Nah* mib
Namibe, Angola : Nah *mee* bay
Namibia, Africa : Na *mib* i a
Nampa, USA : *Nam* pa
Namp'o, North Korea : Nahm *poh*
Nampula, Mozambique : Nahm *pooh* lah
Namsos, Norway : *Nahm* sohs
Namur, Belgium : Na *myoor* (UK Na *myoo* a) (French Na *meer*)
Nanaimo, Canada : Na *niy* moh
Nanchang, China : Nahn *chahng* (UK Nan *chang*)
Nancy, France : Nahn *see*
Nanga Parbat, Pakistan : Nahn ga *Puhr* but (UK ... *Puh* but)
Nanjing, China : Nan *jing*
Nanking, China : Nan *king*
Nanning, China : Nahn *ning*
Nanterre, France : Nahn *ter*
Nantes, France : Nawnt
Nantgarw, Wales : Nant *gar* ooh
Nanticoke, USA : *Nan* ti kohk
Nantong, China : Nahn *tong*
Nantucket, USA : Nan *tah* kut (UK Nan *tah* kit)
Nantwich, England : *Nant* wich
Napa, USA : *Nap* a
Naperville, USA : *Nay* pur vil (UK *Nay* pa vil)
Napier, New Zealand : *Nay* pee ur (UK *Nay* pi a)
Naples, Italy; USA : *Nay* pulz
Napo, Ecuador : *Nah* poh
Nara, Japan : *Nah* rah
Narathiwat, Thailand : Nah ra tee *waht*
Narayanganj, Bangladesh : Na *rah* yun gunj
Narberth, Wales : *Nahr* burth (UK *Nah* buth)
Narbonne, France : Nahr *bawn*
Nardò, Italy : Nahr *doh*
Nariño, Colombia : Nah *ree* nyoh
Narita, Japan : Nah *ree* tah
Narodnaya, Russia : *Nah* rud na ya [The highest peak in the Urals was discovered in 1927 on the 10th anniversary of the Russian Revolution by a team from the Soviet Academy of Sciences and named by them as now but with the pronunciation Na *rod* na ya, "of the people," in honor of the Soviet people (Russian *narod*). The name was later influenced by that of the nearby Narod (*Nah* rud) River, and came to adopt its present altered stress.]
Naro-Fominsk, Russia : Nah ra Fa *minsk*
Narón, Spain : Nah *rawn*
Narrabri, Australia : *Nar* a bri
Narragansett, USA : Na ra *gan* sut (UK Na ra *gan* sit)
Narrandera, Australia : Na *ran* da ra
Narrogin, Australia : *Nar* a jun
Narva, Estonia : *Nahr* vah
Narvik, Norway : *Nahr* vik
Naryan-Mar, Russia : Nur *yahn* Mahr
Naryn, Kyrgyzstan : Na *rin*
Naseby, England : *Nayz* bi
Nashua, USA : *Nash* oo wa
Nashville, USA : *Nash* vil [As elsewhere in the USA, the *-ville* of the Tennessee capital city's name is liable to be minimized, giving a local pronunciation *Nash* vul.]
Nasik, India : *Nah* sik
¹**Nassau**, Bahamas; USA : *Nas* aw
²**Nassau**, Germany : *Nah* sow
Nässjö, Sweden : *Ne* shuh
Natal, Brazil; South Africa : Na *tahl*
Natchez, USA : *Nach* uz (UK *Nach* iz)
Natchitoches, USA : *Nak* a tahsh (UK *Nak* a tosh) [A Native American tribe lies behind the tricky spelling and unexpected pronunciation of the Louisiana town's name.]
　Natchitoches (mysteriously pronounced *nak*-id-esh) [*Lonely Planet USA*, 2004].
Natick, USA : *Nay* tik
Natron (Lakes), Egypt : *Nay* trun
Natuna (Islands), Indonesia : Na *tooh* na
Naucratis, Egypt : *Naw* kra tis
Naugatuck, USA : *Naw* ga tuk
Naumburg, Germany : *Nowm* boork

Nauplia, Greece : *Naw* pli a
Nauru, Pacific Ocean : Nah *ooh* rooh
Nauvoo, USA : Naw *vooh*
Navajo, USA : *Nah* va hoh
Navan, Ireland : *Nav* un
Navanagar, India : Na va *nah* gur [According to Lloyd James 1937, the name of the former state should be pronounced Now *nah* gur.]
Navarino, Greece : Nav a *ree* noh
Navarre, France; Spain : Na *vahr* (UK Na *vah*) (French Nah *vahr*)
Navojoa, Mexico : Nah voh *hoh* ah
Návpaktos, Greece : *Nahf* pahk taws
Nawabganj, Bangladesh; India : Na *wahb* gunj
Nawabshah, Pakistan : Na *wahb* shah
Naxçivan, Azerbaijan : Nakh chi *vahn*
Naxos, Greece : *Nak* sahs (UK *Nak* sos)
Nayland, England : *Nay* lund
Nazareth, Israel : *Naz* a ruth
Nazca, Peru : *Nahs* ka (UK *Naz* ka)
Nazeing, England : *Nay* zing
Nazilli, Turkey : Nah zee *lee*
Nazret, Ethiopia : *Nahz* ret
Ndalatando, Angola : N dah lah *tahn* doh
N'Djamena, Chad : N jah *may* nah
Ndola, Zambia : N *doh* lah
Neagh, Northern Ireland : Nay
Neapolis, Greece : Nee *ap* a lis
Neasden, England : *Neez* dun
Neath, Wales : Neeth
Nebitdag, Turkmenistan : Nyi beet *dahk*
¹Nebo, Jordan; USA : *Nee* boh
²Nebo, Wales : *Neb* oh [The various villages of this name are named for the biblical Mt. ¹**Nebo**, better known as Mt. Pisgah.]
Nebraska, USA : Na *bras* ka
Necochea, Argentina : Nay koh *chay* ah
Nederland, USA : *Nee* dur land
Needham, England; USA : *Nee* dum
Neenah, USA : *Nee* na
Nefta, Tunisia : *Nef* ta
Neftechala, Azerbaijan : Nyef ti cha *lah*
Neftegorsk, Russia : Nyef ti *gawrsk*
Neftekamsk, Russia : Nyef ti *kahmsk*

Nefteyugansk, Russia : Nyef ti yoo *gahnsk*
Nefyn, Wales : *Nev* in
Negev, Israel : *Neg* ev
Negombo, Sri Lanka : Nay *gawm* boh
Negro, South America : *Nay* groh
Negros, Philippines : *Nay* grohs
Neiba, Dominican Republic : *Nay* bah
Neisse, Europe : *Niy* sa
Neiva, Colombia : *Nay* vah
Nejd, Saudi Arabia : Nezhd
Nekemte, Ethiopia : Ne *kem* ti
Nellore, India : Ne *lohr*
Nelson, Canada; England; New Zealand; USA : *Nel* sun
Nelspruit, South Africa : *Nel* sproyt
Neman, Europe : *Nem* un
Nemby, Paraguay : *Naym* bi
Nemea, Greece : Ni *mee* a
Nemi, Italy : *Nay* mee
Nemours, France : Na *moohr*
Nenagh, Ireland : *Nee* nah
Nene, England : Neen [The river of central and eastern England has a name pronounced Nen in its upper reaches, as at Northampton, but as Neen in its lower reaches, as at Peterborough and in Cambridgeshire.]
Nepal, Asia : Na *pawl* (UK Ni *pawl*) [Locally the kingdom's name is pronounced *Nay* pahl.]
Nepalganj, Nepal : *Nay* pahl gunj
Nepean, Canada : Ni *pee* un
Nephi, USA : *Nee* fiy
Neptune, USA : *Nep* toohn (UK *Nep* tyoohn)
Nerchinsk, Russia : *Ner* chinsk
Nesebŭr, Bulgaria : Ne *se* bur
Nesle, France : Nel
Ness, Scotland : Nes
Neston, England : *Nes* tun
Netanya, Israel : Na *tah* nyah
Netheravon, England : *Nedh* ur ay vun
Netherlands, Europe : *Nedh* ur lundz (UK *Nedh* a lundz)
Nether Stowey, England : Nedh ur *Stoh* i
Netley, England : *Net* li

Netzahualcóyotl, Mexico : Nay tsah wahl *koh* yoh tul

Neubrandenburg, Germany : Noy *brahn* dun boork

Neuchâtel, Switzerland : Nuh sha *tel*

Neuf-Brizach, France : Nuh Bree *zahk*

Neufchâteau, Belgium; France : Nuh shah *toh*

Neufchâtel-en-Bray, France : Nuh shah tel ahn *Bray*

Neuilly, France : Nuh *yee*

Neumünster, Germany : Noy *meen* stur

Neunkirchen, Austria; Germany : *Noyn* kir khun

Neuquén, Argentina : Ne oo *kayn*

Neuruppin, Germany : Noy roo *peen*

Neuss, Germany : Noys

Neustadt, Germany : *Noy* shtaht

Neustrelitz, Germany : Noy *shtray* lits

Neu-Ulm, Germany : Noy *Oolm*

Neuwied, Germany : Noy *veet*

Neva, Russia : *Nay* va (Russian Nyi *vah*)

Nevada, USA : Ni *vad* a (UK Ni *vah* da) [Thus the state, but Nevada, Iowa, and Nevada, Missouri, have names pronounced Ni *vay* da.]

Nevers, France : Nuh *ver*

Neves, Brazil : *Nev* is

Nevinnomyssk, Russia : Ni vin na *mwisk*

Nevis, St. Kitts and Nevis : *Nee* vis

Nevşehir, Turkey : *Nev* sha hir

New : For names prefixed with this word and not given below, as *New Brunswick, New Delhi, New England*, see the main name. (*New* is rarely stressed as a separate word.)

New Alresford, England : Nooh *Awls* furd (UK Nyooh *Awls* fud) [An alternate pronunciation of the Hampshire town's name is *Ahlz* fud. *Cp.* **Alresford**.]

> Some say "Awlsfd" and some say "Arlsfd" [John Hadfield, ed., *The Shell Book of English Villages*, 1980].

¹Newark, England : *Nooh* urk (UK *Nyooh* uk)

²Newark, USA : *Nooh* ahrk [A pronunciation as **¹Newark** is also valid for some US places, but Newark, Delaware, and Newark, Ohio, are usually as here.]

Newberg, USA : *Nooh* buhrg (UK *Nyooh* buhg)

Newbiggin, England : *Nooh* big un (UK *Nyooh* big in)

New Braunfels, USA : Nooh *Brown* fulz (UK Nyooh...)

Newbridge, Ireland; Wales : *Nooh* brij (UK *Nyooh* brij)

Newbrough, England : *Nooh* brahf (UK *Nyooh* brahf)

Newburgh, Scotland; USA : *Nooh* buhrg (UK *Nyooh* bra)

Newbury, England; USA : *Nooh* ber i (UK *Nyooh* bri)

Newburyport, USA : *Nooh* ber i pawrt (UK *Nyooh* bri pawt)

Newcastle, Australia; Canada; England; South Africa; USA : *Nooh* kas ul (UK *Nyooh* kah sul) [The English port city of **Newcastle upon Tyne** is locally referred to as Nyooh *kas* ul and increasingly generally as *Nyooh* kas ul. Pointon, p. 180, refers to the respective regular and local pronunciations (*Nyooh* kah sul and Nyooh *kas* ul) as below.]

> The second, being the local pronunciation, should normally take precedence over the other. Here, however, is a case where the first is firmly established national usage.

Newcastle-under-Lyme, England : Nooh kas ul ahn dur *Liym* (UK Nyooh kah sul ahn da...)

Newcastle upon Tyne, England : Nooh kas ul a pahn *Tiyn* (UK Nyooh kah sul a pon...) [See comment at **Newcastle**.]

Newfoundland, Canada : *Nooh* fun lund (UK *Nyooh* fun lund) [The island and province is locally known as Nyooh fun *land*, and as Jones points out, p. 365, this is also the UK nautical pronunciation. An alternate UK pronunciation Nyooh *fownd* lund is preferred by some, as in the quote below.]

The old pronunciation with stressed first syllable is becoming archaic and incomprehensible, so if in doubt stress the second [Kingsley Amis, *The King's English*, 1997].

New Glasgow, Canada : Nooh *Glas* goh (UK Nyooh *Glahz* goh)

Newham, England : *Nooh* um (UK *Nyooh* um) [The London borough was originally referred to as *Nyooh* ham when created in 1965 from the boroughs of East Ham and West Ham.] This [name] was the final choice out of ninety suggestions. (The Town Clerk hoped that people would take care to pronounce the middle "h." It is unlikely they will.) [C. Stella Davies and John Levitt, *What's in a Name?*, 1970].

Newhaven, England : *Nooh* hay vun (UK *Nyooh* hay vun)

New Haven, USA : Nooh *Hay* vun (UK Nyooh *Hay* vun)

Newington, England; USA : *Nooh* ing tun (UK *Nyooh* ing tun)

New Liskeard, Canada : Nooh Lis *kahrd* (UK Nyooh *Lis* kahd)

Newlyn, England : *Nooh* lin (UK *Nyooh* lin)

Newmarket, Canada; England : *Nooh* mahr kit (UK *Nyooh* mah kit)

Newnham, England : *Nooh* num (UK *Nyooh* num)

New Norfolk, Australia : Nooh *Nawr* fuk (UK Nyooh *Naw* fuk)

New Orleans, USA : Nooh *Awr* lunz (UK Nyooh *Awl* i unz) [Locally the Louisiana city is often referred to as *Nyaw* linz, rendered in written form as N'Yawlins or N'Awlins.]

New Orleans is *New Oar-lins*, with a heavy accent on the first syllable, but when *New* is omitted and *Orleans* is used as an adjective modifying a following noun it becomes *Or-leens*, with the accent on the second syllable. In Baltimore *Orleans* street is always *Or-leens* [Mencken, p. 541].

New Plymouth, New Zealand : Nooh *Plim* uth (UK Nyooh...)

Newport, England; USA; Wales : *Nooh* pawrt (UK *Nyooh* pawt)

Newport News, USA : Nooh pawrt *Noohz* (UK Nyooh pawt *Nyoohz*)

Newport Pagnell, England : Nooh pawrt *Pag* nul (UK Nyooh pawt...)

Newquay, England : *Nooh* kee (UK *Nyooh* kee)

New Quay, Wales : Nooh *Kee* (UK Nyooh...)

Newry, Northern Ireland : *Nooh* ri (UK *Nyoo* a ri)

New South Wales, Australia : Nooh Sowth *Waylz* (UK Nyooh...)

Newstead, England; Scotland : *Nooh* stid (UK *Nyooh* stid)

Newton, England; USA : *Nooh* tun (UK *Nyooh* tun)

Newton Abbot, England : Nooh tun *A* but (UK Nyooh tun...)

Newton Aycliffe, England : Nooh tun *Ay* clif (UK Nyooh tun...)

Newton Ferrers, England : Nooh tun *Fer* urz (UK Nyooh tun *Fer* uz)

Newton-le-Willows, England : Nooh tun li *Wil* ohz (UK Nyooh tun...)

Newtonmore, Scotland : Nooh tun *mawr* (UK Nyooh tun *maw*)

Newton Stewart, Scotland : Nooh tun *Stooh* urt (UK Nyooh tun *Styooh* ut)

Newtownabbey, Northern Ireland : Nooh tun *ab* i (UK Nyooh tun *ab* i)

Newtownards, Northern Ireland : Nooh tun *ahrdz* (UK Nyooh tun *ahdz*)

New York, USA : Nooh *Yawrk* (UK Nyooh *Yawk*) [There are various pronunciations of the city's name, rendered in such spellings as Noo Yawk and Noo Yoik. Broadly speaking, the former of these, without the *r* sound, is common on the East Coast, while this letter is clearly sounded in Western states. In the center of the city itself, Nyawk (written N'Yawk) may be heard, while in the region of 33rd Street Nyoyk (N'Yoik) is a speech form.]

New Zealand, Oceania : Noo *Zee* lund (UK Nyoo...) [The main word of the island country's name is locally sometimes pronounced *Zil* und.]

Neyshabur, Iran : Nay shah *boohr*

Nezhin, Ukraine : *Nye* zhin

Nganjuk, Indonesia : Ng *gahn* joohk

Ngaoundéré, Cameroon : Ng gown day *ray*

Ngawi, Indonesia : Ng *gah* wi

Ngozi, Burundi : Ng *goh* zee

Nguru, Nigeria : Ng *gooh* rooh

Nha Trang, Vietnam : Nyah *Trahng*

Nhulunbuy, Australia : *Nooh* lun boy

Niagara, Canada; USA : Niy *ag* ra

Niamey, Niger : *Nyah* may

Nias, Indonesia : *Nee* us

Nicaea, Turkey : Niy *see* a

Nicaragua, South America : Ni ka *rahg* wa (UK Ni ka *rag* yoo a) (Spanish Nee kah *rah* gwah)

Nice, France : Nees

Nichelino, Italy : Nee ke *lee* noh

Nickel Centre, Canada : *Nik* ul Sen tur (UK ... Sen ta)

Nicobar (Islands), Indian Ocean : *Nik* a bahr (UK *Nik* a bah)

Nicosia, Cyprus : Ni ka *see* a

Nidwalden, Switzerland : *Need* vahl dun

Niedersachsen, Germany : Nee dur *sahk* sun (UK Nee da *sak* sun) (German *Nee* da zahk sun)

Nieuw Nickerie, Suriname : Nyooh *Nik* a ree

Nieuwpoort, Belgium : *Nyooh* pohrt

Nièvre, France : Nyevr

Niğde, Turkey : Nee *day*

¹Niger, Africa (country) : *Niy* jur (UK Nee *zhay* a) [The UK pronunciation is based on that of the French, the country's official language.]

²Niger, Africa (river) : *Niy* jur (UK *Niy* ja)

Nigeria, Africa : Niy *jir* i a (UK Niy *ji* a ri a)

Niigata, Japan : Nee *gah* tah

Nijmegen, Netherlands : *Niy* may gun (Dutch *Nay* may kha)

Nikolayev, Ukraine : Ni ka *lah* yif

¹Nikopol, Bulgaria : Ni *kaw* pohl

²Nikopol, Ukraine : *Nee* ka pul

Nikšić, Montenegro : *Nik* shich

Nile, Africa : Niyl

Niles, USA : Niylz

Nilgiri, India : *Nil* ga ree

Nilópolis, Brazil : Nee *law* poo lees

Nîmes, France : Neem

Nineveh, Iraq : *Nin* a va (UK *Nin* i va)

Ningbo, China : Ning *boh*

Ningxia, China : Ning shi *ah*

Ninove, Belgium : Nee *nawv*

Nioro du Sahel, Mali : Nyoh roh di Sah *el*

Niort, France : Nyawr

Nipawin, Canada : *Nip* a win

Nipissing, Canada : *Nip* a sing

Nippur, Iraq : Ni *poor*

Niquero, Cuba : Nee *kay* roh

Niš, Serbia : Neesh

Nishinomiya, Japan : Nee shee *noh* mee yah

Niterói, Brazil : Nee tay *roy*

Nitra, Slovakia : *Nyee* trah

Niue, Pacific Ocean : Nee *ooh* ay

Nivelles, Belgium : Nee *vel*

Nivernais, France : Nee ver *nay*

Nizamabad, India : Ni *zah* ma bahd

Nizhnekamsk, Russia : Nizh ni *kahmsk*

Nizhnevartovsk, Russia : Nizh ni *vahr* tufsk

Nizhny Novgorod, Russia : Nizh ni *Nahv* ga rahd (UK ... *Nov* ga rod) (Russian ... *Nawv* ga rut)

Nizhny Tagil, Russia : Nizh ni Ta *gil*

Nkayi, Congo : Ng *kah* yee

Nkongsamba, Cameroon : Ng kawng *sahm* bah

Noailles, France : Noh *iy*

Nobeoka, Japan : Noh bee *oh* kah

Noda, Japan : *Noh* dah

Nogales, Mexico; USA : Noh *gah* lays

Noginsk, Russia : Naw *ginsk*

Nogoyá, Argentina : Noh goh *yah*

Noirmoutier, France : Nwahr mooh *tyay*

Nokia, Finland : *Noh* kee ah

Nola, Italy : *Noh* lah

Nome, USA : Nohm

Nonthaburi, Thailand : Nun ta boo *ree* [According to some sources the town's name is pronounced Nun boo *ree*, omitting the second syllable.]

Noordwijk, Netherlands : *Nohrt* viyk

Nootka, Canada : *Noot* ka

Nord, France : Nawr

Norden, Germany : *Nawr* dun

Nordhausen, Germany : *Nawrt* how zun

Nordhorn, Germany : *Nawrt* hawrn

Nordjylland, Denmark : *Nawrd* yee lan

Nördlingen, Germany : *Nuhrt* ling un

Nordrhein-Westfalen, Germany : Nawrt riyn Vest *fah* lun

Norfolk, England; USA : *Nawr* fuk (UK *Naw* fuk) [An alternate pronunciation for many US places is *Nawr* fawk.]

Norfolk (Island), Pacific Ocean : *Nawr* fuk (UK *Naw* fuk) [The local pronunciation of the island's name is *Naw* fohk.]

Norilsk, Russia : Na *reelsk*

Normal, USA : *Nawr* mul (UK *Naw* mul)

Norman, USA : *Nawr* mun (UK *Naw* mun)

Normanby, England : *Nawr* mun bi (UK *Naw* mun bi)

¹**Normandy**, England : *Nawr* mun di (UK *Naw* mun di) [A local pronunciation of the Surrey village's name is Naw *man* di.]

²**Normandy**, France : *Nawr* mun di (UK *Naw* mun di)

Normanton, England : *Nawr* mun tun (UK *Naw* mun tun)

Norristown, USA : *Naw* rus town (UK *Nor* is town)

Norrköping, Sweden : *Nawr* shuh ping

Norrland, Sweden : *Nawr* lahnd

North : For names prefixed with this word and not given below, as *North Carolina*, *North York*, see the main name. (*North* is rarely stressed as a separate word.)

Northallerton, England : Nawr *thal* ur tun (UK Naw *thal* a tun)

¹**Northam**, Australia : *Nawr* thum (UK *Naw* thum)

²**Northam**, England : *Nawr* dhum (UK *Naw* dhum)

Northampton, England; USA : Nawr *thamp* tun (UK Naw *thamp* tun) [Although the English city's name is etymologically "North Hampton," the second *h* is not normally pronounced, as against **Southampton**, where it is usually heard. The *p* sound is often omitted in both, as it is in the local pronunciation Na *tham* tun.]

North Berwick, Scotland : Nawrth *Ber* ik (UK Nawth...) [The Scottish town's name relates to that of **Berwick-upon-Tweed**, just south of the border.]

Northbrook, USA : *Nawrth* brook (UK *Nawth* brook)

Northcote, Australia : *Nawrth* koht (UK *Nawth* kut)

Northenden, England : *Nawr* dhun dun (UK *Naw* dhun dun)

Northern Ireland, Europe : Nawr dhurn *Iy* ur lund (UK Naw dhun *Iy* a lund)

Northern Territory, Australia : Nawr dhurn *Ter* a taw ri (UK Naw dhun *Ter* a tri)

Northfield, USA : *Nawrth* feeld (UK *Nawth* feeld)

Northfleet, England : *Nawrth* fleet (UK *Nawth* fleet)

Northiam, England : *Nawr* dhi um (UK *Naw* dhi um)

North Island, New Zealand : *Nawrth* Iy lund (UK *Nawth*...)

Northolt, England : *Nawr* thohlt (UK *Naw* thohlt) [Ross, p. 134, recommends a UK pronunciation *Nawth* hohlt for the former location of London's main airport, but this is now rarely heard.]

North Shields, England : Nawrth *Sheeldz* (UK Nawth...)

North Uist, Scotland : Nawrth *Yooh* ist (UK Nawth...)

Northumberland, England : Nawr

thahm bur lund (UK Naw *thahm* ba lund)

Northumbria, England : Nawr *thahm* bri a (UK Naw *thahm* bri a)

North Walsham, England : Nawrth *Wawl* shum (UK Nawth...) [The main name of the Norfolk town is also locally pronounced *Wol* sum.]

Northwich, England : *Nawrth* wich (UK *Nawth* wich)

Northwood, England : *Nawrth* wood (UK *Nawth* wood)

Norton, England; USA : *Nawr* tun (UK *Naw* tun)

Norumbega, North America : Naw rum *bee* ga

Norwalk, USA : *Nawr* wawk (UK *Naw* wawk)

Norway, Europe : *Nawr* way (UK *Naw* way)

¹Norwich, England : *Naw* rij (UK *Nor* ij)

²Norwich, USA : *Nawr* wich (UK *Naw* wich)

Norwood, England; USA : *Nawr* wood (UK *Naw* wood)

Noto, Italy : *Noh* toh

Notre Dame, USA : Noh tur *Daym* (UK Noh tra...)

Nottingham, England : *Nah* ting um (UK *Not* ing um)

Notting Hill, England : Nah ting *Hil* (UK Not ing...)

Nouadhibou, Mauritania : Nwah dee *booh*

Nouakchott, Mauritania : Nooh ahk *shaht* (UK Nooh ak *shot*) (French Nwahk *shawt*)

Nouméa, New Caledonia : Nooh *may* a

Nova Friburgo, Brazil : Naw va Free *boohr* gooh

Nova Gorica, Slovenia : Naw va *Gaw* reet sah

Nova Iguaçu, Brazil : Naw va Ee gwah *sooh*

Nova Lima, Brazil : Naw va *Lee* ma

Nova Lisboa, Angola : Naw va Leezh *voh* ah

Novara, Italy : Noh *vah* rah

Nova Scotia, Canada : Noh va *Skoh* sha

Nova Sofala, Mozambique : Noh va Sooh *fah* la

Novato, USA : Noh *vah* toh

Novaya Zemlya, Russia : Noh va ya *Zem* li a (Russian Naw va ya Zim *lyah*)

Nové Zámky, Slovakia : Naw ve *Zahm* kee

Novgorod, Russia : *Nahv* ga rahd (UK *Nov* ga rod) (Russian *Nawv* ga rut)

Novi, USA : *Noh* viy

Novi Ligure, Italy : Naw vee Lee *goor* ay

Novi Pazar, Serbia : Naw vee Pa *zahr*

Novi Sad, Serbia : Naw vee *Sahd*

Novocherkassk, Russia : Naw va chur *kahsk*

Novo Hamburgo, Brazil : Noh vooh Ahm *boohr* gooh

Novokuybyshevsk, Russia : Naw va *kwee* bi shefsk

Novokuznetsk, Russia : Naw va koohz *nyetsk*

Novomoskovsk, Russia : Naw va mas *kawfsk*

Novo Redondo, Angola : Naw voh Re *dahn* doh

Novorossiysk, Russia : Naw va ra *seesk*

Novoshakhtinsk, Russia : Naw va *shahkh* teensk

Novosibirsk, Russia : Naw va si *birsk*

Novotroitsk, Russia : Naw va *traw* itsk

Nový Jičín, Czech Republic : Naw vee *Yee* cheen

Nowa Ruda, Poland : Naw vah *Rooh* dah

Nowa Sól, Poland : Naw va *Soohl*

Nowy Dwór Mazowiecki, Poland : Naw vi Dvoohr Mah zaw *vyet* skee

Nowy Sącz, Poland : Naw vi *Sawnch*

Nowy Targ, Poland : Naw vi *Tahrg*

Noyers, France : Nwah *yer*

Noyon, France : Nwah *yohn*

Nsawam, Ghana : N sah *wahm*

Nsukka, Nigeria : N *sook* kah

Nubia, Africa : *Nooh* bi a (UK *Nyooh* bi a)

Nueva Gerona, Cuba : Nway vah He *roh* nah

Nueva Loja, Ecuador : Nway vah *Loh* hah
Nueva Ocotepeque, Honduras : Nway vah Oh koh tay *pay* kay
Nueva Paz, Cuba : Nway vah *Pahs*
Nueva Rosita, Mexico : Nway vah Roh *see* tah
Nueva San Salvador, El Salvador : Nway vah Sahn *Sahl* vah dhawr
Nuevitas, Cuba : Nway *vee* tahs
Nuevo Laredo, Mexico : Nway voh Lah *ray* dhoh
Nuku'alofa, Tonga : Nooh kooh ah *loh* fa
Nukus, Uzbekistan : Nooh *koohs*
Nullarbor (Plain), Australia : *Nahl* a bawr (UK *Nahl* a baw)
Numantia, Spain : Noo *man* cha (UK Nyoo *man* shi a)
Numazu, Japan : Nooh *mah* zooh
Numidia, Africa : Noo *mid* i a (UK Nyoo *mid* i a)
Nunavut, Canada : *Nooh* na vooht
Nunawading, Australia : Nah na *wah* ding (UK Nah na *wod* ing)
Nuneaton, England : Nah *nee* tun
Nunivak, USA : *Nooh* na vak (UK *Nooh* ni vak)
Nuoro, Sardinia, Italy : *Nooh* oh roh
Nuremberg, Germany : *Noor* um buhrg (UK *Nyoor* um buhg)
Nuristan, Afghanistan : Noor i *stan* (UK Noo a ri *stahn*)
Nürnberg, Germany : *Neern* berk
Nutley, England; USA : *Naht* li
Nuuk, Greenland : Noohk
Nuwara Eliya, Sri Lanka : Nooh va ra *Ay* lee a
Nyack, USA : *Niy* ak
Nyala, Sudan : *Nyah* lah
Nyanda, Zimbabwe : *Nyahn* dah
Nyanza, Kenya : *Nyahn* zah
Nyborg, Denmark : *Nee* bawr
Nybro, Sweden : *Nee* brooh
Nyeri, Kenya : *Nye* ree
Nyíregyháza, Hungary : *Nee* rej hah zaw
Nykøbing, Denmark : *Nee* kuh bing
Nyköping, Sweden : *Nee* chuh ping

Nymburk, Czech Republic : *Nim* boork
Nyon, Switzerland : Nyohn
Nyons, France : Nyawns
Nysa, Poland : *Ni* sa
Nzérékoré, Guinea : N zay ray kaw *ray*
Oadby, England : *Ohd* bi
Oahu, USA : Oh *wah* hooh
Oakdale, USA : *Ohk* dayl
Oakengates, England : *Oh* kun gayts
Oakham, England : *Oh* kum
Oakland, USA : *Ohk* lund
Oakleigh, Australia : *Ohk* li
Oakmont, USA : *Ohk* mahnt (UK *Ohk* mont)
Oak Ridge, USA : Ohk *Rij*
Oakville, Canada : *Ohk* vil
Oakwood, USA : *Ohk* wood
Oamaru, New Zealand : *Ahm* a rooh (UK *Om* a rooh)
Oates (Coast), Antarctica : Ohts
Oaxaca, Mexico : Wah *hah* kah
Ob, Russia : Ohb (UK Ob) (Russian Awp)
Oban, Scotland : *Oh* bun
Obbia, Somalia : *Ob* yah
Oberammergau, Germany : Oh ba *rah* mur gow (UK Oh ba *ram* a gow) (German Oh ber *ahm* er gow)
Oberhausen, Germany : *Oh* ber how zun
Oberlin, USA : *Oh* bur lun (UK *Oh* ba lin)
Óbidos, Brazil : *Aw* bi doohs
Obihiro, Japan : Oh bee *hee* roh
Obi (Islands), Indonesia : *Oh* bi
Obninsk, Russia : *Awb* ninsk
Obuasi, Ghana : Oh *bwah* si
Obwalden, Switzerland : *Awp* vahl dun
Ocala, USA : Oh *kal* a
Ocaña, Colombia : Oh *kay* nyah
Oceania, Pacific Ocean : Oh shi *an* i a (UK Oh si *ah* ni a)
Oceanside, USA : *Oh* shun siyd
Ochakov, Ukraine : A *chah* kuf
Ochil (Hills), Scotland : *Oh* kul
Ochiltree, Scotland : *Ah* kul tree (UK *Ok* ul tree)
Ocoee, USA : Oh *koh* ee

Oconomowoc, USA : A *kah* na ma wawk (UK A *kon* a ma wawk)
Ocosingo, Mexico : Oh koh *seeng* goh
Ocotal, Nicaragua : Oh koh *tahl*
Ocotlán, Mexico : Oh koh *tlahn*
Ocracoke (Island), USA : *Ohk* ra kohk
Odawara, Japan : Oh dah *wah* rah
Odendaalsrus, South Africa : Oh dun dahls *rahs*
Odense, Denmark : *Oh* dun sa (Danish *Oh* dhun sa) [A local pronunciation of the city's name is *Oo* un za.]
Odenwald, Germany : *Oh* dun vahlt
Oder, Europe : *Oh* dur (UK *Oh* da)
Odessa, Ukraine; USA : Oh *des* a (Russian A *dyes* a)
Odienné, Côte d'Ivoire : Oh *dyen* ay
Odiham, England : *Oh* di um
Odintsovo, Russia : A dyin *tsaw* va
O'Fallon, USA : Oh *Fal* un
Offa, Nigeria : *Aw* fah
Offaly, Ireland : *Aw* fa li (UK *Of* a li)
Offenbach, Germany : *Aw* fun bahkh
Offenburg, Germany : *Aw* fun boork
Ogaden, Ethiopia : Ah ga *den* (UK *Og* a *den*)
Ogaki, Japan : Oh *gah* kee
Ogalalla, USA : Oh ga *lah* la
Ogbomosho, Nigeria : Ohg boh *moh* shoh
Ogden, USA : *Awg* dun (UK *Og* dun)
Ogdensburg, USA : *Awg* dunz buhrg (UK *Og* dunz buhg)
Oglethorpe, USA : *Oh* gul thawrp (UK *Oh* gul thawp)
Ogmore, Wales : *Awg* mawr (UK *Og* maw)
Ogwr, Wales : *Aw* goor (UK *Og* oo a) (Welsh *O* goor)
Ohio, USA : Oh *hiy* oh
Ohrid, Macedonia : *Ohk* reed
Oimyakon, Russia : Oy mya *kawn*
Oise, France : Wahz
Oita, Japan : *Oh* ee tah
Oka, Russia : Oh *kah*
Okara, Pakistan : Oh *kah* ra
Okavango (Swamps), Botswana : Oh ka *vang* goh
Okayama, Japan : Oh kah *yah* mah

Okazaki, Japan : Oh kah *zah* kee
Okeechobee, USA : Oh ka *choh* bi (UK Oh ki *choh* bi)
Okefenokee (Swamp), USA : Oh ka fa *noh* ki (UK Oh ki fi *noh* ki)
Okeford Fitzpaine, England : Ohk furd Fits *payn* (UK Ohk fud...) [The form of the Dorset village's name below, representing an inversion of the two words, hardly applies now.]
   Perhaps the strangest [pronunciation] of all is Okeford Fitzpaine, Dorset, which many locals pronounce — for reasons no one can begin to guess at — "fippenny ockford" [Bill Bryson, *Mother Tongue*, 1990].
Okehampton, England : *Ohk* hamp tun (UK Ohk *hamp* tun)
Okhotsk, Russia : A *khawtsk*
Okinawa, Japan : Oh kee *nah* wah
Oklahoma, USA : Ohk la *hoh* ma
Oktyabrskiy, Russia : Ak *tyah* bur ski
Öland, Sweden : *Uh* lahnd
Olathe, USA : Oh *lay* tha
Olavarría, Argentina : Oh lah vah *ree* yah
Olbia, Italy : *Awl* byah
Oldbury, England : *Ohld* ber i (UK *Ohld* bri)
Oldenburg, Germany : *Ohl* dun buhrg (UK *Ohl* dun buhg) (German *Awl* dun boork)
Oldenzaal, Netherlands : *Awl* dun zahl
Oldham, England : *Ohl* dum
Olduvai (Gorge), Tanzania : *Awl* da viy (UK *Ol* da viy)
Oleśnica, Poland : Aw lesh *neet* sa
Olifants, Africa : *Ah* la funts (UK *Ol* i funts)
Olinda, Brazil : Oh *lin* da
Olkusz, Poland : *Awl* koohsh
Ollerton, England : *Ahl* ur tun (UK *Ol* a tun)
Olney, England : *Ohl* ni
Olomouc, Czech Republic : *Oh* loh mowts (UK *Ol* a mowts) (Czech *Aw* law mohts)
Olonets, Russia : A *law* nyets

Olongapo, Philippines : Oh lawng gah *poh*

Olot, Spain : Oh *lawt*

Olsztyn, Poland : *Awlsh* tun

Olteniţa, Romania : Ohl *tay* neet sah

Olympia, Greece; USA : Oh *lim* pi a (UK A *lim* pi a)

Olympus, Greece : Oh *lim* pus (UK A *lim* pus)

Olynthus, Greece : Oh *lin* thus

Omagh, Northern Ireland : *Oh* ma

Omaha, USA : *Oh* ma hah [The name of the Nebraska city has an alternate local pronunciation *Oh* ma haw.]

Oman, Asia : Oh *mahn*

Omaruru, Namibia : Oh mah *rooh* rooh

Omdurman, Sudan : Ahm dur *mahn* (UK Om duh *mahn*)

Omiya, Japan : Oh *mee* ah

Omsk, Russia : Awmsk

Ondjiva, Angola : On *jee* va

Ondo, Nigeria : *Awn* doh

Onega, Russia : Oh *neg* a (UK O *nay* ga) (Russian A *nyeg* a)

Oneida, USA : Oh *niy* da

O'Neill, USA : Oh *Neel*

Oneonta, USA : Oh ni *ahn* ta (UK Oh ni *on* ta)

Oneşti, Romania : Aw *nesht*

Onex, Switzerland : Aw *nay*

Onitsha, Nigeria : Oh *nee* chah

Onondaga, USA : Ahn un *dah* ga (UK On un *dah* ga)

Ontario, Canada; USA : Ahn *ter* i oh (UK On *tay* a ri oh)

Ontinyent, Spain : Awn tee *nyent*

Oosterhout, Netherlands : *Oh* stur howt

Oostkamp, Belgium : *Ohst* kamp

Opatija, Croatia : Aw *pah* tee ya

Opava, Czech Republic : *Aw* pah vah

Opole, Poland : Aw *paw* le

Oporto, Portugal : Oh *pawr* toh (UK Oh *paw* toh) (Portuguese Oo *pawr* too)

Opsterland, Netherlands : *Awp* stur lahnt

Oradea, Romania : Aw *rah* dyah

Öræfajökull, Iceland : *Uh* riy vah yuh kootl

Oral, Kazakhstan : Aw *rahl*

Oran, Algeria : Aw *rahn*

¹Orange, Australia; South Africa; USA : Aw rinj (UK *Or* inj)

²Orange, France : Aw *rahnzh*

Orangeburg, USA : Aw rinj buhrg (UK *Or* inj buhg)

Oranienburg, Germany : Oh *rah* nee un boork

Oranjestad, Netherlands Antilles : Oh *rahn* ya staht

Ordu, Turkey : Awr dooh

Örebro, Sweden : Uhr a *brooh*

Oregon, USA : Aw ri gun (UK *Or* i gun) [Outsiders sometimes refer to the state as Aw ri gahn.]

Orekhovo-Zuyevo, Russia : A ryekh a va *Zooh* ya va

Orel, Russia : Ar *yawl*

Orem, USA : *Oh* rum

Orenburg, Russia : Aw run buhrg (UK Aw run buhg) (Russian A ryen *boork*)

Orense, Spain : Aw *ren* say

Øresund, Scandinavia : *Uhr* a sun

Orford, England : *Awr* furd (UK Aw fud)

Orihuela, Spain : Oh ree *way* lah

Orillia, Canada : Oh *ril* ya

Orinoco, Venezuela : Awr a *noh* koh (UK Or i *noh* koh) (Spanish Oh ree *noh* koh)

Orion, Philippines : Ohr *yohn*

Oriskany, USA : Aw *ris* ka ni

Orissa, India : Aw *ris* a

Oristano, Italy : Oh ree *stah* noh

Orizaba, Mexico : Oh ree *sah* bah

Orkney (Islands), Scotland : *Awrk* ni (UK *Awk* ni)

Orlando, USA : Awr *lan* doh (UK Aw *lan* doh)

Orleans, USA : Awr *leenz* [This is the pronunciation for the Massachusetts town. Places of the name in other states vary the spoken form, as Louisiana's Awr lee unz or Awr lunz, New York's Awr leenz, and Vermont's Awr *leenz*. *See also* **New Orleans**.]

Orléans, France : *Awr* li unz (UK Aw *lee* unz) (French Awr lay *ahn*)
Orlová, Czech Republic : *Awr* law vah
Orly, France : *Awr* li (UK *Aw* li) (French Awr *lee*)
Ormskirk, England : *Awrmz* kuhrk (UK *Awmz* kuhk)
Ornans, France : Awr *nahn*
Orne, France : Awrn
Oronsay, Scotland : *Awr* un say (UK *Or* un say)
Orosháza, Hungary : *Oh* rohsh hah zaw
Orpington, England : *Awr* ping tun (UK *Aw* ping tun)
Orrell, England : *Aw* rul (UK *Or* ul)
Orsha, Belarus : *Awr* sha
Orsk, Russia : Awrsk
Orthez, France : Awr *tes*
Orton, England : *Awr* tun (UK *Aw* tun) [The name is that of the district of the former Cambridgeshire city of Peterborough comprising Orton Longueville and Orton Waterville. The railroad station at the latter, now closed, was originally *Overton*, pronounced as now.]
Ortona, Italy : Awr *toh* nah
Orumiyeh, Iran : Oo rooh *mee* ya
Oruro, Bolivia : Aw *rooh* roh
Orvieto, Italy : Awr *vyay* toh
Orwell, England : *Awr* wel (UK *Aw* wel)
Osage, USA : Oh *sayj*
Osaka, Japan : Oh *sah* kah
Osawatomie, USA : Oh sa *wah* ta mi
Osasco, Brazil : Oh *sahs* kooh
Osceola, USA : Oh see *oh* la
Oschatz, Germany : *Aw* shahts
Osh, Kyrgyzstan : Awsh
Oshakati, Namibia : Oh shah *kah* ti
Oshawa, Canada : *Ah* sha wa (UK *Osh* a wa)
Oshkosh, USA : *Ahsh* kahsh (UK *Osh* kosh)
Oshogbo, Nigeria : Oh *shohg* boh
Osidge, England : *Ah* sij (UK *Os* ij) [According to Willey, p. 369, the name of the London district is "pronounced to rhyme with 'sausage.'"]

Osijek, Croatia : *Oh* see yek
Osimo, Italy : *Aw* zee moh
Oskarshamn, Sweden : Aws kurs *hah* mun
Öskemen, Kazakhstan : *Uhs* ki min
Oslo, Norway : *Ahz* loh (UK *Oz* loh) (Norwegian *Oohs* looh)
Osmanabad, India : Ahs *mah* na bahd
Osmotherly, England : Ahz *mah* dhur li (UK *Oz mah* dha li)
Osnabrück, Germany : *Ahz* na brook (UK *Oz* na brook) (German *Aws* na breek)
Osney, England : *Ohz* ni
Osorno, Chile : Oh *sawr* noh
Oss, Netherlands : Aws
Ossetia, Europe : Ah *set* i a (UK O *set* i a)
Ossett, England : *Ah* sut (UK *Os* it)
Ossining, USA : *Ah* sun ing (UK *Os* un ing)
Ossun, France : Aw *suhn*
Ostend, Belgium : Ahs *tend* (UK Os *tend*)
Osterley, England : *Ahs* tur li (UK *Os* ta li)
Osterode, Germany : Aws ta *roh* da
Östersund, Sweden : *Uhs* tur sund
Ostia, Italy : *Ahs* ti a (UK *Os* ti a)
Ostrava, Czech Republic : *Aws* tra va (UK *Os* tra va)
Ostróła, Poland : Aw *strooh* da
Ostrołęka, Poland : Aw stroh *wen* kah
Ostrowiec Świętokrzyski, Poland : Aw straw vyets Shfyen taw *kshis* ki [The second word of the town's name represents the combining form of Polish *święty*, "holy," and the adjectival form of *krzyż*, "cross," referring to a nearby Benedictine abbey.]
Ostrów Wielkopolski, Poland : Aw stroohf Vyel kaw *pawl* ski
Osuna, Spain : Oh *sooh* nah
Oswaldtwistle, England : *Ahz* wul twis ul (UK *Oz* wul twis ul)
Oswego, USA : Ahs *wee* goh (UK Os *wee* goh)
Oswestry, England : *Ahz* wus tri (UK *Oz* wus tri)

Oświęcim, Poland : Awsh *fyen* cheem [The town's name is more familiar under its German form of **Auschwitz.**]

Otago, New Zealand : Oh *tah* goh

Otaru, Japan : Oh *tah* rooh

Otford, England : *Aht* furd (UK *Ot* fud)

Otley, England : *Aht* li (UK *Ot* li)

Otranto, Italy : Oh *trahn* toh (UK O *tran* toh) (Italian *Aw* trahn taw)

Otsu, Japan : *Oht* sooh

Ottawa, Canada; USA : *Ah* ta wa (UK *Ot* a wa)

Otterburn, England : *Ah* tur buhrn (UK *Ot* a buhn)

Ottery St Mary, England : Ah tur i Saynt *Mer* i (UK Ot a ri Sunt *May* a ri)

Ottumwa, USA : A *tahm* wa

Otwock, Poland : *Awt* vawtsk

Ouachita, USA : *Wah* sha taw (UK *Wosh* a taw)

Ouadane, Mauritania : Wah *dahn*

Ouagadougou, Burkina Faso : Wah gah *dooh* gooh

Ouahigouya, Burkina Faso : Wiy *gooh* yah

Ouargla, Algeria : *Wahr* glah

Oudenaarde, Belgium : *Ooh* da nahrd (UK *Ooh* da nahd) (Flemish *Ow* dun ahr da)

Oudh, India : Owd

Oudtshoorn, South Africa : *Ohts* hawrn

Oued Zem, Morocco : Wed *Zem*

Ouessant, France : Wes *ahn*

Ouezzane, Morocco : We *zahn*

Oughtershaw, England : *Ow* tur shaw (UK *Ow* ta shaw)

Oughtibridge, England : *Ooh* ti brij [The pronunciation of the Yorkshire village's name is subject to variation, as illustrated by the quote below.] Oughtibridge, South Yorkshire, has four [pronunciations]: "owtibrij," "awtibrij," "ootibrij," and "ōtibrij" [Bill Bryson, *Mother Tongue*, 1990].

Ouistreham, France : Wees tra *hahm*

Oujda, Morocco : Oohj *dah*

Oulton, England : *Ohl* tun

Oulu, Finland : *Ow* looh [Lloyd James 1937 gives *Oh* looh as the appropriate pronunciation of the seaport city's name.]

Oundle, England : *Own* dul

Ouro Prêto, Brazil : Oh rooh *Pray* tooh

Ouse, England : Oohz

Outremont, Canada : *Ooh* tra mahnt (UK *Ooh* tra mont) (French Ooh tra *mawn*)

Ovamboland, Namibia : Oh *vahm* boh land (UK Oh *vam* bo land)

Overijse, Belgium : Aw va *rays*

Overijssel, Netherlands : Oh vur *ay* sul

Overton, England : *Oh* vur tun (UK *Oh* va tun)

Ovid, USA : *Oh* vid

Oviedo, Spain : Oh vi *ay* doh (UK Ov i *ay* doh) (Spanish Oh *vyay* dhoh)

Oving, England : *Oh* ving

Ovingdean, England : *Oh* ving deen

Owensboro, USA : *Oh* unz ber oh

Owen Sound, Canada : Oh un *Sownd* (UK Oh in...)

Ower, England : *Ow* ur (UK *Ow* a)

Owerri, Nigeria : Oh *wer* ee

Owo, Nigeria : *Oh* woh

Owyhee, USA : Oh *wiy* hee

Oxford, England; USA : *Ahks* furd (UK *Oks* fud)

Oxnard, USA : *Ahks* nahrd (UK *Oks* nahd)

Oxshott, England : *Ahk* shaht (UK *Ok* shot)

Oxted, England : *Ahks* tud (UK *Oks* tid)

Oxus, Uzbekistan : *Ahk* sus (UK *Ok* sus)

Oyo, Nigeria : *Oh* yoh

Oyonnax, France : Aw yoh *nah*

Oystermouth, Wales : *Oy* stur mowth (UK *Oy* sta mowth)

Ozark, USA : *Oh* zahrk (UK *Oh* zahk)

Ózd, Hungary : Ohzd

Pa-an, Myanmar : *Bah* ahn

Paarl, South Africa : Pahrl (UK Pahl)

Pabianice, Poland : Pah byah *neet* se

Pabna, Bangladesh : *Pahb* nah

Pachuca, Mexico : Pah *chooh* kah
Pacific (Ocean) : Pa *sif* ik
Padang, Indonesia : *Pah* dahng
Padangpanjang, Indonesia : Pah dang *pahn* jahng
Paddington, Australia; England : *Pad* ing tun
Paderborn, Germany : *Pah* dur bawrn
Padiham, England : *Pad* i um
Padstow, England : *Pad* stoh
Padua, Italy : *Paj* oo a (UK *Pad* yoo a)
Paducah, USA : Pa *dooh* ka
Pagadian, Philippines : Pah gah *dee* ahn
Pagan, Myanmar : Pa *gahn*
Pagham, England : *Pag* um
Pago Pago, American Samoa : Pahng goh *Pahng* goh (UK Pah goh *Pah* goh)
Pahala, USA : Pa *hah* la
Pahang, Malaysia : Pa *hahng* (UK Pa *hang*)
Paignton, England : *Payn* tun
Paimpol, France : Pahn *pawl*
Painswick, England : *Paynz* wik
Paisley, Scotland : *Payz* li
Pakanbaru, Indonesia : Pa *kahn* bah rooh
Pakenham, England : *Payk* num
Pakistan, Asia : *Pak* i stan (UK Pah ki *stahn*)
Pakokku, Myanmar : Pah *kaw* kooh
Pakxé, Laos : Pahk *say*
Palana, Russia : Pah *lah* na
Palangkaraya, Indonesia : Pah *lahng* kah rah yah
Palapye, Botswana : Pah *lah* pyay
Palau, Pacific Ocean : Pa *low*
Palawan, Philippines : Pa *lah* wun
Palembang, Indonesia : Pah lem *bahng*
Palencia, Spain : Pah *len* thyah
Palermo, Italy : Pa *ler* moh (UK Pa *lay* a moh) (Italian Pah *ler* moh)
Palestine, Asia : *Pal* a stiyn
Palestrina, Italy : Pah lay *stree* nah
Palghat, India : *Pahl* gaht
Palk (Strait), Asia : Pawk
Palma, Mallorca, Spain : *Pahl* ma (UK *Pal* ma) (Spanish *Pahl* mah)
Palma Soriano, Cuba : Pahl mah Sohr *yah* noh

Palm Beach, USA : Pahm *Beech*
Palmdale, USA : *Pahm* dayl
Palmeira das Missões, Brazil : Pal may ra dahs Mee *sahwns*
Palmer (Archipelago), Antarctica : *Pah* mur (UK *Pah* ma)
Palmerston, Australia; Pacific Ocean : *Pah* mur stun (UK *Pah* ma stun)
Palmerston North, New Zealand : Pah mur stun *Nawrth* (UK Pah ma stun *Nawth*)
Palmira, Colombia : Pahl *mee* rah
Palm Springs, USA : Pahm *Springz*
Palmyra, Syria; USA : Pal *miy* ra
Palo Alto, USA : Pal oh *Al* toh
Palomar (Mountain), USA : *Pal* a mahr (UK *Pal* oh mah)
Palouse, USA : Pa *loohs*
Palu, Indonesia : *Pah* looh
Pamekasan, Indonesia : Pah may kah *sahn*
Pamir, Tajikistan : Pa *mir* (UK Pa *mi* a)
Pamlico (Sound), USA : *Pam* li koh
Pampanga, Philippines : Pahm *pahng* gah
Pampas, South America : *Pam* puz (UK *Pam* pus)
Pamphylia, Turkey : Pam *fil* i a
Pamplona, Colombia; Spain : Pam *ploh* na (Spanish Pahm *ploh* nah)
Panaitan, Indonesia : Pa *niy* tun
Panaji, India : Pah *nah* jee
Panama, Central America : *Pan* a mah
Panay, Philippines : Pa *niy*
Pančevo, Serbia : *Pahn* che voh
Panchiaou, Taiwan : Pahn *chyow*
Pandharpur, India : *Pahn* dur poor
Pando, Bolivia : *Pahn* doh
Panevėžys, Lithuania : Pah nye ve *zhees*
Pangani, Tanzania : Pahng *gah* ni
Pangbourne, England : *Pang* bawrn (UK *Pang* bawn)
Pangkalanbrandan, Indonesia : Pahng kah lahn *brahn* dahn
Pangkalpinang, Indonesia : Pahng kahl pi *nahng*
Panipat, India : *Pah* nee put
P'anmunjŏm, North Korea : Pahn moon *jahm* (UK Pan moon *jom*)

Pannonia, Hungary : Pa *noh* ni a
Pantar, Indonesia : Pahn *tahr*
Pantelleria, Italy : Pan tel a *ree* a
Pápa, Hungary : *Pah* paw
Papakura, New Zealand : Pa pa *koor* a
Papatoitoi, New Zealand : Pa pa toy *toy*
Papeete, Tahiti : Pah pay *ay* tay [A popular pronunciation Pa *pee* ti is also current for the capital of French Polynesia.]
Paphlagonia, Turkey : Paf la *goh* ni a
Paphos, Cyprus : *Pay* fahs (UK *Paf* os)
Papua, Papua New Guinea : *Pap* yoo a
Par, England : Pahr (UK Pah)
Pará, Brazil : Pa *rah*
Paraburdoo, Australia : Par a bur *dooh* (UK Par a ba *dooh*)
Paracel (Islands), South China Sea : Par a *sel*
Paradise, USA : *Par* a diys
Paragould, USA : *Par* a goohld
Paraguarí, Paraguay : Pah rah gwah *ree*
Paraguay, South America : *Par* a gwiy (Spanish Pah rah *gwiy*)
Paraíba, Brazil : Pah ra *ee* ba
Paraíso, Mexico : Pah rah *ee* soh
Parakou, Benin : Pah rah *kooh*
Paramaribo, Suriname : Par a *mar* a boh (UK Par a *mar* i boh) (Dutch Pah rah *mah* ree boh)
Paramount, USA : *Par* a mownt
Paramus, USA : Pa *ram* us
Paraná, Argentina; Brazil : Pah rah *nah*
Paranaguá, Brazil : Pah ra nah *gwah*
Parchim, Germany : *Pahr* khim
Pardubice, Czech Republic : *Pahr* dooh beet se
Parepare, Indonesia : Pah ray pah *ray*
Parham, England : *Par* um
Paris, France; USA : *Par* us (UK *Par* is) (French Pah *ree*)
Parkersburg, USA : *Pahr* kurz buhrg (UK *Pah* kuz buhg)
Parkes, Australia : Pahrks (UK Pahks)
Parkeston, England : *Pahrk* stun (UK *Pahk* stun)
Parkstone, England : *Pahrk* stohn (UK *Pahk* stun)

Parma, Italy; USA : *Pahr* ma (UK *Pah* ma) (Italian *Pahr* mah)
Parnaíba, Brazil : Pahr na *ee* ba
Parnassus, Greece : Pahr *nas* us (UK Pah *nas* us)
Pärnu, Estonia : *Per* nooh
Paropamisus, Afghanistan : Par a pa *miy* sus
Paros, Greece : *Par* ahs (UK *Par* os)
Parracombe, England : *Par* a koohm
Parral, Mexico : Pahr *rahl*
Parramatta, Australia : Par a *mat* a
Parry (Islands), Canada : *Par* i
Parsippany-Troy (Hills), USA : Pur *sip* an i Troy (UK Pa *sip* a ni...)
Parsons, USA : *Pahr* sunz (UK *Pah* sunz)
Parthenay, France : Pahrt *nay*
Parthia, Iran : *Pahr* thi a (UK *Pah* thi a)
Partington, England : *Pahr* ting tun (UK *Pah* ting tun)
Parys, South Africa : Pa *riys*
Pasadena, USA : Pas a *dee* na
Pasargadae, Iran : Pa *sahr* ga dee (UK Pa *sah* ga dee)
Pasay, Philippines : *Pah* siy
Pascagoula, USA : Pas ka *gooh* la
Pasco, USA : *Pas* koh
Pas-de-Calais, France : Pahd Ka *lay*
Pasig, Philippines : *Pah* sig
Passaic, USA : Pa *say* ik
Passamaquoddy (Bay), USA : Pas a ma *kwah* di (UK Pas a ma *kwod* i)
Passau, Germany : *Pah* sow
Passchendaele, Belgium : *Pash* un dayl (Flemish *Pah* sun dah la)
Passo Fundo, Brazil : Pah sooh *Foohn* dooh
Passos, Brazil : *Pah* soohs
Pastaza, Ecuador : Pah *stah* sah
Pasto, Colombia : *Pahs* toh
Pasuruan, Indonesia : Pah soo rooh *ahn*
Patagonia, Argentina : Pat a *goh* ni a
Patan, India : *Pah* tun
Patchogue, USA : Pa *chawg*
Pateley Bridge, England : Payt li *Brij*
Paterson, USA : *Pat* ur sun (UK *Pat* a sun)
Pati, Indonesia : *Pah* ti

Patiala, India : Pat i *ah* la
Patmos, Greece : *Pat* mus (UK *Pat* mos)
Patna, India : *Pat* na
Patos, Brazil : *Pah* toohs
Patras, Greece : *Pat* rus (UK *Pat* ras)
Patterdale, England : *Pat* a dayl
Pátzcuaro, Mexico : *Pahts* kwah roh
Pau, France : Poh
Paulista, Brazil : Pow *lees* ta
Paulo Afonso, Brazil : Pow looh A *fohn* sooh
Pavia, Italy : Pah *vee* ah [A pronunciation *Pay* vi a was formerly current among English speakers for the city's name.]
Pavlodar, Kazakhstan : *Pav* la dahr (UK *Pav* la dah) (Russian Puv la *dahr*)
Pavlograd, Ukraine : *Pav* la grad (Russian Puv la *graht*)
Pavlohrad, Ukraine : Puv la *khraht*
Pavlovo, Russia : *Pahv* la va
Pavlovsk, Russia : *Pahv* lufsk
Pawtucket, USA : Pa *tah* kut (UK Paw *tah* kit)
Paxos, Greece : *Pak* sus (UK *Pak* sos)
Paysandú, Uruguay : Piy sahn *dooh*
Pazardzhik, Bulgaria : *Pah* zahr jeek
Peabody, USA : *Pee* ba dee (UK *Pee* bod i)
Peacehaven, England : *Pees* hay vun
Pearl Harbor, USA : Puhrl *Hahr* bur (UK Puhl *Hah* ba)
Peary (Land), Greenland : *Pir* i (UK *Pi* a ri)
Peć, Serbia : Pech
Pechenga, Russia : Pe *cheng* gah
Pechora, Russia : Pi *chaw* ra
Peckham, England : *Pek* um
Peconic (Bay), USA : Pi *kah* nik (UK Pi *kon* ik)
Pecos, USA : *Pay* kus
Pécs, Hungary : Paych
Pedernales, Dominican Republic : Pay der *nah* lays
Pedro Juan Caballero, Paraguay : Pay dhroh Hwahn Kah bah *yay* roh
Peebles, Scotland : *Pee* bulz
Pee Dee, USA : Pee *Dee*
Peenemünde, Germany : Pay na *meen* da

Pegu, Myanmar : Pe *gooh*
Peine, Germany : *Piy* na
Peiping, China : Pay *ping*
Peipus, Europe : *Piy* pus
Pekalongan, Indonesia : Pi kah *lawng* ahn
Pekanbaru, Indonesia : Pi *kahn* bah rooh
Pekin, USA : *Pee* kun
Peking, China : Pee *king* [The capital city is now usually known as **Beijing**. The two Chinese names are actually identical. *Peking* represents the Wade-Giles romanization *Pei-ching*, while *Beijing* is the Pinyin form.]
Pelée, Martinique : Pa *lay* (UK *Pel* ay)
Peleng, Indonesia : *Pay* leng
Pelham, Canada; USA : *Pel* um
Pelion, Greece : *Pee* li un
Peloponnese, Greece : Pel a pa *neez* (UK Pel a pa *nees*)
Pelotas, Brazil : Pay *law* tas
Pemalang, Indonesia : Pay ma *lahng*
Pematangsiantar, Indonesia : Pi ma tahng syahn *tahr*
Pemba, Mozambique; Tanzania : *Pem* ba
Pemberton, Australia : *Pem* bur tun (UK *Pem* ba tun)
Pembrey, Wales : Pem *bray*
Pembridge, England : *Pem* brij
Pembroke, Canada; USA; Wales : *Pem* brohk (UK *Pem* brook)
Pembury, England : *Pem* bri
Penang, Malaysia : Pi *nang*
Penarth, Wales : Pen *ahrth* (UK Pen *ahth*)
Pencoed, Wales : Pen *koyd*
Pendine, Wales : Pen *diyn*
Pendle, England : *Pen* dul
Pendlebury, England : *Pen* dul ber i (UK *Pen* dul bri)
Pendleton, USA : *Pen* dul tun
Pend Oreille, USA : Pahn da *ray*
Penedo, Brazil : Piy *nay* dooh
Penfield, USA : *Pen* feeld
Penge, England : Penj
Penicuik, Scotland : *Pen* i kook
Penistone, England : *Pen* is tun

Penjamo, Mexico : *Pen* hah moh
Penkridge, England : *Penk* rij
Penmaenmawr, Wales : Pen mun *mow* ur (UK Pen mun *mow* a) (Welsh Pen miyn *mowr*)
Penmarch, France : Pahn *mahr*
Pennines, England : *Pen* iynz
Pennsauken, USA : Pen *saw* kun
Pennsylvania, USA : Pen sul *vay* nya (UK Pen sul *vay* ni a) [The state name also has a rapid pronunciation Pen sa *vay* nya.]
Penobscot, USA : Pa *nahb* skut (UK Pa *nob* skot)
Penonomé, Panama : Pay noh noh *may*
Penrhyndeudraeth, Wales : Pen rin *diy* druth (Welsh Pen rin *day* driyth) [The village's lengthy name comprises Welsh *penrhyn*, "promontory," *dau*, "two," and *traeth*, "beach."]
Penrith, Australia; England : Pen *rith* [Many sources give a pronunciation *Pen* rith for the English town, but Pen *rith* is more generally current. A local pronunciation is *Pi* a rith. The Australian city's name is locally pronounced *Pen* ruth.]
Penryn, England : Pen *rin*
Pensacola, USA : Pen sa *koh* la
Penshurst, England : *Penz* huhrst (UK *Penz* huhst)
Penticton, Canada : Pen *tik* tun
Pentire, England : Pen *tiyr* (UK Pen *tiy* a)
Pentland (Firth), Scotland : *Pent* lund
Pentland (Hills), Scotland : *Pent* lund [This name and that above have become identical in spelling and pronunciation but differ in their origins. The firth, a sea channel in the north of Scotland, has a name meaning "land of Picts"; the hills, in southeastern Scotland, have a name meaning "land of heights."]
Pentre, Wales : *Pen* tra
Penwith, England : Pen *with*
Pen-y-Bont, Wales : Pen a *Bont*
Pen-y-ghent, England : Pen i *gent*
Penza, Russia : *Pen* za

Penzance, England : Pen *zans*
Peoria, USA : Pi *ohr* i a
Peover, England : *Pee* vur (UK *Pee* va)
Perak, Malaysia : *Per* a (UK *Pay* a ra) [Some English speakers pronounce the state and river's name as US Pi *rahk*, UK Pa *rak*.]
Peravia, Dominican Republic : Pay rah *vee* yah
Percé, Canada : Per *say* (UK Pay a *say*)
Perche, France : Persh
Pereira, Colombia : Pe *ray* rah
Perekop, Ukraine : Per a *kahp* (UK Per i *kop*) (Russian Pi ri *kawp*)
Pereslavl-Zalesskiy, Russia : Pi ri slah vul Za *lyes* ki
Pereyaslav, Ukraine : Pi ri *yah* sluv
Pereyaslav-Khmelnytskyy, Ukraine : Pi ri yah sluv Khmel *neet* ski
Pergamino, Argentina : Per gah *mee* noh
Pergamum, Turkey : *Puhr* ga mum (UK *Puh* ga mum)
Perico, Cuba : *Pay* ree koh
Périgord, France : Pay ree *gawr*
Périgueux, France : Pay ree *guh*
Peristérion, Greece : Per ee *ster* ee awn
Perlis, Malaysia : *Per* lis (UK *Puh* lis)
Perm, Russia : Puhrm (UK Puhm) (Russian Pyerm)
Përmet, Albania : Pur *met*
Pernambuco, Brazil : Puhr num *booh* koh (UK Puh num *booh* koh) (Portuguese Per num *booh* kooh)
Pernik, Bulgaria : *Per* nik
Péronne, France : Pay *rawn*
Perpignan, France : Puhr pee *nyahn* (UK *Puh* pee nyon) (French Per pee *nyahn*)
Perranporth, England : *Per* un pawrth (UK *Per* un pawth)
Perris, USA : *Per* us (UK *Per* is)
Perry, USA : *Per* i
Perryville, USA : *Per* i vil
Persepolis, Iran : Pur *sep* a lis (UK Puh *sep* a lis)
Pershore, England : *Puhr* shawr (UK *Puh* shaw)
Persia, Asia : *Puhr* zha (UK *Puh* sha)

Perth, Australia; Scotland : Puhrth (UK Puhth)

Perth Amboy, USA : Puhrth *Am* boy (UK Puhth...)

Peru, South America : Pa *rooh*

Perugia, Italy : Pay *rooh* jah

Peruwelz, Belgium : Pay ri *way*

Pervomaysk, Ukraine : Pir va *miysk*

Pervouralsk, Russia : Pir va ooh *rahlsk*

Pesaro, Italy : *Pay* zah roh

Pescadores, Taiwan : Pes ka *daw* reez

Pescara, Italy : Pes *kah* rah

Peshawar, Pakistan : Pa *shah* wur (UK Pa *shah* wa)

Peshkopi, Albania : Pesh *kaw* pee

Pessac, France : Pe *sahk*

Pest, Hungary : Pest (Hungarian Pesht)

Petach Tikva, Israel : Pe tukh *Tik* va

Petaling Jaya, Malaysia : Pa tah ling *Jiy* a

Petaluma, USA : Pet a *looh* ma

Peterborough, Canada; England : *Pee* tur buhr oh (UK *Pee* ta bra)

Peterhead, Scotland : Pee tur *hed* (UK Pee ta *hed*)

Peterlee, England : Pee tur *lee* (UK Pee ta *lee*)

Petersburg, USA : *Pee* turz buhrg (UK *Pee* tuz buhg)

Petersfield, England : *Pee* turz feeld (UK *Pee* tuz feeld)

¹Petersham, England : *Pee* tur shum (UK *Pee* ta shum)

²Petersham, USA : *Pee* turz ham

Pétionville, Haiti : Pay tyawn *veel*

Petit-Bourg, Guadeloupe : Pa tee *Boohr*

Petoskey, USA : Pa *tahs* ki (UK Pa *tos* ki)

Petra, Jordan : *Pet* ra

Petrodvorets, Russia : Pit ra dvah *ryets*

Petrograd, Russia : *Pet* ra grad (Russian Pit ra *graht*)

Petrokrepost, Russia : Pit ra *kryep* ust

Petrolina, Brazil : Pet rooh *lee* na

Petropavlovsk, Russia : Pet ra *pav* lawfsk (UK Pet roh *pav* lofsk) (Russian Pit ra *pahv* lufsk)

Petropavlovsk-Kamchatskiy, Russia : Pit ra pahv lufsk Kum *chaht* ski

Petrópolis, Brazil : Pet *raw* pooh lees

Petroşani, Romania : Pet roh *shahn*

Petrovaradin, Serbia : Pet ra va *rah* deen

Petrozavodsk, Russia : Pit ra za *vawtsk*

Petworth, England : *Pet* wurth (UK *Pet* wuhth)

Pevensey, England : *Pev* un zi [A local pronunciation of the East Sussex village's name is *Pem* zi.]

Pewsey, England : *Pyooh* zi

Peyruis, France : Pay *rwee*

Pézenas, France : Payz *nahs*

Pforzheim, Germany : *Pfawrts* hiym

Pharos, Egypt : *Fer* ahs (UK *Fay* a ros)

Pharr, USA : Fahr (UK Fah)

Pharsalus, Greece : Fahr *say* lus (UK Fah *say* lus)

Phetchabun, Thailand : Pet chah *boohn*

Phetchaburi, Thailand : Pet chah *boo* ri [According to some sources, the accepted pronunciation of the seaport town's name is *Pet* boo ree, omitting the second syllable.]

Philadelphia, USA : Fil a *delf* i a

Philae, Egypt : *Fiy* li

¹Philippi, Greece : Fi *lip* iy [The name of the historic (now ruined) town has an alternate pronunciation US *Fil* a piy, UK *Fil* i piy.]

²Philippi, USA : *Fil* a pi

Philippines, Asia : *Fil* a peenz [Ross, p. 141, gives primary preference to *Fil* i piynz for the island republic, but this is rarely if ever heard now.]

Philistia, Israel : Fi *lis* ti a

Philleigh, England : *Fil* i

Phitsanulok, Thailand : *Pit* sah noo lohk

Phnom Penh, Cambodia : Nahm *Pen* (UK Nom...) [Some speakers sound the initial *P* of the capital city's name, giving US Pa nahm *Pen*, UK Pa nom *Pen*.]

Phocaea, Turkey : Foh *see* a

Phocis, Greece : *Foh* sis

Phoenicia, Syria : Fa *nish* a

Phoenix, USA : *Fee* niks

Phra Nakhon Si Ayutthaya, Thailand :

Prah Nah kawn See Ah yooh *tiy* a
[The city's full formal name, meaning
"lord town of the good and invincible
one," is often shortened to *Ayut-
thaya.*]
Phrygia, Turkey : *Frij* i a
Phuket, Thailand : Pooh *ket*
Phuntsholing, Bhutan : *Pin* soh ling
Phuthaditjhaba, South Africa : Pooh
tah dee *chah* bah
Piacenza, Italy : Pyah *chen* tsah
Piaseczno, Poland : Pyah *sech* noh
Piastow, Poland : *Pyah* stoohf
Piatra-Neamţ, Romania : Pyah trah
Nyahms
Piauí, Brazil : Pyow *ee*
Picardy, France : *Pik* ur di (UK *Pik* a
di)
Picayune, USA : Pik ee *yoohn*
Pichincha, Ecuador : Pee *cheen* chah
Pickering, Canada; England : *Pik* a
ring
Pico Rivera, USA : Pee koh Ri *vir* a
Picton, Canada; New Zealand : *Pik* tun
Pictou, Canada : *Pik* tooh
Pidurutalagala. Sri Lanka : Pi da rooh
ta *lah* ga la
Piedmont, Italy; USA : *Peed* mahnt
(UK *Peed* mont)
Piedras Negras, Mexico : Pyay dhrahs
Nay grahs
Piekary Śląskie, Poland : Pye kah ree
Shlawn skee
Pierre, USA : Pir (UK *Pi* a) [The pro-
nunciation of the South Dakota state
capital's name is unexpected for the
first name of the French fur trader
Pierre Chouteau who gave it.]
　　Pierre (pronounced peer — no one is
　　sure why) [*Lonely Planet USA*, 2004].
Pierrefonds, Canada : Pyer *fawn*
Pieštany, Slovakia : *Pyesh* tyah ni
Pietermaritzburg, South Africa : Pee
tur *mar* uts buhrg (UK Pee ta *mar* its
buhg)
Pietersburg, South Africa : *Pee* turz
buhrg (UK *Pee* tuz buhg)
Piet Retief, South Africa : Peet Ra *teef*
Pikesville, USA : *Piyks* vil

Piła, Poland : *Pee* wah
Pilar, Argentina; Paraguay : Pee *lahr*
Pilsen, Czech Republic : *Pil* zun
Pima, USA : *Pee* ma
Pinar del Río, Cuba : Pi nahr del *Ree*
oh
Pinatubo, Philippines : Pee na *tooh* boh
Pindus (Mountains), Greece : *Pin* dus
Pine Bluff, USA : *Piyn* Blahf
Pinerolo, Italy : Pee nay *raw* loh
Pinetown, South Africa : *Piyn* town
P'ingtung, Taiwan : Ping *tahng*
Pinheiro, Brazil : Pee *nyer* ooh
Pinner, England : *Pin* ur (UK *Pin* a)
Pinos, Mexico : *Pee* nohs
Pinsk, Belarus : Pinsk
Pinxton, England : *Ping* stun
Piombino, Italy : Pyohm *bee* noh
Piotrków Trybunalski, Poland : Pyaw
tur koohf Tri booh *nahl* skee
Piqua, USA : *Pik* way
Piracicaba, Brazil : Pee rah see *kah* ba
Piraeus, Greece : Piy *ree* us
Pirapora, Brazil : Pee ra *poh* ra
Pirbright, England : *Puhr* briyt (UK
Puh briyt)
Pirmasens, Germany : *Pir* ma zens
Pirna, Germany : *Pir* na
Pisa, Italy : *Pee* za (Italian *Pee* sah)
Písek, Czech Republic : *Pee* sek
Pisgah, Jordan; USA : *Piz* gah
Pisidia, Turkey : Piy *sid* i a
Pistoia, Italy : Pees *toy* ah
Pitcairn (Island), Pacific Ocean : *Pit*
kern (UK *Pit* kay un) [According to
Ross, p. 142, the local pronunciation
of the British colony's name is *Pit*
kuhn.]
Piteå, Sweden : *Pee* ta oh
Piteşti, Romania : Pee *tesht*
Pitlochry, Scotland : Pit *lahk* ri (UK Pit
lokh ri)
Pitsea, England : *Pit* see
Pittenweem, Scotland : *Pit* un weem
Pittsburg, USA : *Pits* buhrg (UK *Pits*
buhg)
Pittsburgh, USA : *Pits* buhrg (UK *Pits*
buhg)
Pittsfield, USA : *Pits* feeld

Placentia, Canada; USA : Pla *sen* cha
Placetas, Cuba : Plah *say* tahs
Plainfield, USA : *Playn* feeld
Plainview, USA : *Playn* vyooh
Plainville, USA : *Playn* vil
Plaistow, England : *Plah* stoh [There are two districts of the name in London, that in Newham having an alternate pronunciation *Plas* toh, and that in Bromley also known as *Play* stoh. The first of these is also valid for the West Sussex village of the same name.]
   (1) The current local pronunciation [for the Newham neighborhood] is "Plasstow" [A.D. Mills, *A Dictionary of London Place Names*, 2001].
   (2) Although it [i.e. the Newham district] has now acquired the cockney pronunciation "plarstow," the name probably derives from "play-stow," a place of recreation [Willey, p. 389].
Plano, USA : *Play* noh
Plantation, USA : Plan *tay* shun (UK Plahn *tay* shun)
Plaridel, USA : Plah ree *del*
Plasencia, Spain : Plah *sen* syah
Plata, South America : *Plah* ta
Plataea, Greece : Pla *tee* a
Platte, USA : Plat
Plattsburgh, USA : *Plats* buhrg (UK *Plats* buhg)
Plauen, Germany : *Plow* un
Plaxtol, England : *Plaks* tul
Pleasanton, USA : *Plez* un tun
Pleasantville, USA : *Plez* unt vil
Pleven, Bulgaria : *Ple* ven
Płock, Poland : Pwawtsk
Ploemeur, France : Ploh ay *muhr*
Ploërmel, France : Ploh er *mel*
Plœuc-sur-Lié, France : Pluhk seer *Lyay*
Ploieşti, Romania : Plaw *yesht*
Ploumanac'h, France : Plooh mah *nahk*
Plovdiv, Bulgaria : *Plahv* div (UK *Plov* div) (Bulgarian *Plawv* dif)
Plumstead, England : *Plahm* stid
Plymouth, England; USA : *Plim* uth [Despite the American tendency to favor a spelling pronunciation, this historically significant name, found not only for the Massachusetts city but elsewhere in the USA, is pronounced as that of the English city, i.e. not with -mowth. The same holds for **Portsmouth**.]
Plynlimon, Wales : Plin *lim* un
Plzeň, Czech Republic : *Pul* zen
Po, Italy : Poh
Pobeda (Peak), Kyrgyzstan : Pa *byed* a
Pocatello, USA : Poh ka *tel* oh
Pocklington, England : *Pahk* ling tun (UK *Pok* ling tun)
Poços de Caldas, Brazil : Paw soohs dee *Kahl* des
Podgorica, Montenegro : *Pawd* gaw reet sah
Podolia, Ukraine : Pa *doh* li a
Podolsk, Russia : Pa *dawlsk*
Podor, Senegal : *Poh* dawr (UK *Poh* daw)
Pogradec, Albania : Paw grah *dets*
P'ohang, South Korea : Poh *hahng*
Pohnpei, Micronesia : *Pohn* pay
Pointe-à-Pitre, Guadeloupe : Pwahnt a *Peetr*
Pointe-Noire, Republic of the Congo : Pwahnt *Nwahr*
Point Fortin, Trinidad and Tobago : Poynt *Fawr* tin (UK ... *Faw* tin)
Poissy, France : Pwah *see*
Poitiers, France : Pwah *tyay* [Ross, p. 143, favors the anglicized pronunciation Poy *tee* uz. This is now obsolete, but existed formerly, when the city's name was spelled *Poictiers*.]
   Maine, Blois, Poictiers, and Tours are won away,
   'Long all of Somerset and his delay [William Shakespeare, *Henry VI, Part 1*, IV. iii. 45, *c.* 1592].
Poitou, France : Pwah *tooh*
Pokhara, Nepal : *Poh* ka ra
Poland, Europe : *Poh* lund
Polesworth, England : *Pohlz* wurth (UK *Pohlz* wuth)
Polesye, Europe : Paw *lyes* ye
Polk, USA : Pohk
Pollokshields, Scotland : Pah luk *sheeldz* (UK Pol uk *sheeldz*)

Polmont, Scotland : *Pohl* mahnt (UK *Pohl* mont) [The local pronunciation of the town's name is *Pohl* munt.]

Polotsk, Belarus : *Paw* lutsk

Polperro, England : Pahl *per* oh (UK Pol *per* oh)

Poltava, Ukraine : Pul *tah* va

Polwarth, Scotland : *Pohl* wurth (UK *Pohl* wuth)

Polynesia, Pacific Ocean : Pahl a *neezh* a (UK Pol i *neez* i a)

Polzeath, England : Pohl *zeth* (UK Pol *zeth*)

Pomerania, Europe : Pahm a *ray* ni a (UK Pom a *ray* ni a)

Pomona, Scotland; USA : Pa *moh* na

Pompano Beach, USA : Pahm pa noh *Beech* (UK Pom pa noh...)

Pompeii, Italy : Pahm *pay* i (UK Pom *pay* i)

Ponape, Micronesia : *Poh* nah pay

Ponce, Puerto Rico : *Pawn* say (UK *Pon* say)

Pondicherry, India : Pahn da *cher* ee (UK Pon di *cher* i)

Pondoland, South Africa : *Pahn* doh land (UK *Pon* doh land)

Ponferrada, Spain : Pawn fer *rah* dhah

Ponorogo, Indonesia : Poh noh *roh* goh

Pons, France : Pawn

Ponta Delgada, Azores : Pawn ta Del *gah* da

Ponta Grossa, Brazil : Pohn ta *Graw* sa

Pontardawe, Wales : Pahn tur *dow* i (UK Pont a *dow* i) (Welsh Pawn tahr *dow* e)

Pontarddulais, Wales : Pahn tur *dil* us (UK Pon ta *dil* us) (Welsh Pawn tahr *dhi* liys)

Pont-Aven, France : Pawn ta *ven*

Pontchartrain, USA : *Pahn* shur trayn (UK *Pon* sha trayn) [The name of the Louisiana lake, of French origin, may be pronounced with a final stress, as in the lines below.]

> Where summer's falling roses stain
> The tepid waves of Pontchartrain
> [Oliver Wendell Holmes,
> *Songs in Many Keys*, 1826].

Pontefract, England : *Pahn* ti frakt (UK *Pon* ti frakt) [This is really a modern spelling pronunciation of the Yorkshire town's name, based on the medieval Latin form *Pontefracto*, "(at the) broken bridge." An earlier pronunciation was *Pahm* fri (as if *Pomfrey*), with local forms *Pahm* frut or *Pom* frit, written *Pomfret*, from the Old French equivalent of the Latin.]

> Lord Rivers and Lord Gray are sent to Pomfret [William Shakespeare, *Richard III*, II. iv. 42, *c.* 1592].

Ponteland, England : Pahn *tee* lund (UK Pon *tee* lund)

Pontevedra, Philippines; Spain : Pawn tay *vay* drah

Pontiac, USA : *Pahn* ti ak (UK *Pon* ti ak)

Pontianak, Indonesia : Pahn ti *ah* nuk (UK Pon ti *ah* nuk)

Pontine (Marshes), Italy : *Pahn* tiyn (UK *Pon* tiyn)

Pontoise, France : Pawn *twahz*

Pontus, Asia Minor : *Pahn* tus (UK *Pon* tus)

Pontyclun, Wales : Pahn ti *kleen* (UK Pon ti *kleen*)

Pontypool, Wales : Pahn ti *poohl* (UK Pon ti *poohl*)

Pontypridd, Wales : Pahn ti *preedh* (UK Pon ti *preedh*)

Ponza (Islands), Italy : *Pawnt* sah

Poole, England : Poohl

Poolewe, Scotland : Pool *yooh*

Poona, India : *Pooh* na

Popayán, Colombia : Poh pah *yahn*

Poplar, England : *Pahp* lur (UK *Pop* la)

Popocatépetl, Mexico : Poh pa kat a *pet* ul (UK Pop a kat a *pet* ul) (Spanish Paw paw kah *tay* petl)

Poprad, Slovakia : Paw *praht*

Porbandar, India : Pawr *bahn* dur

Pordenone, Italy : Pawr day *noh* nay

Pori, Finland : *Paw* ree

Porirua, New Zealand : Por a *rooh* a

Porlock, England : *Pawr* lahk (UK *Paw* lok)

Port Adelaide, Australia : Pawrt *A* da layd (UK Pawt...)

Portadown, Northern Ireland : Pawrt a *down* (UK Pawt a *down*)

Portage, USA : *Pawr* tij (UK *Paw* tij)

Portage la Prairie, Canada : Pawr tij la *Prer* i (UK Paw tij la *Pray* a ri)

Port Alberni, Canada : Pawrt Al *buhr* ni (UK Pawt Al *buh* ni)

Portalegre, Portugal : Poohr ta *le* gree

Portales, USA : Pawr *tal* us (UK Paw *tal* us)

Port Angeles, USA : Pawrt *An* ja lus (UK Pawt *An* ja leez)

Port Antonio, Jamaica : Pawrt An *toh* ni oh (UK Pawt...)

Port Arthur, China; USA : Pawrt *Ahr* thur (UK Pawt *Ah* tha)

Port Askaig, Scotland : Pawrt *As* kayg (UK Pawt...)

Port Augusta, Australia : Pawrt A *gahs* ta (UK Pawt...)

Port-au-Prince, Haiti : Pawrt oh *Prins* (UK Pawt...) (French Pawrt oh *Prahns*)

Port Blair, India : Pawrt *Bler* (UK Pawt *Blay* a)

Port-Cartier, Canada : Pawr Kahr *tyay* (UK Paw Kah *tyay*)

Port Chalmers, New Zealand : Pawrt *Chal* murz (UK Pawt *Chahl* muz)

Port Chester, USA : *Pawrt* Ches tur (UK *Pawt* Ches ta)

Port Colborne, Canada : Pawrt *Kohl* buhrn (UK Pawt *Kohl* buhn)

Port Coquitlam, Canada : Pawrt Koh *kwit* lum (UK Pawt...)

Port-de-Paix, Haiti : Pawr da *Pay* (UK Paw...)

Port Dickson, Malaysia : Pawrt *Dik* sun (UK Pawt...)

Port Elizabeth, South Africa : Pawrt I *liz* a buth (UK Pawt...)

Porterville, USA : *Pawr* tur vil (UK *Paw* ta vil)

Port Eynon, Wales : Pawrt *Ayn* un (UK Pawt...)

Port-Gentil, Gabon : Pawr Zhahn *tee*

Port Glasgow, Scotland : Pawrt *Glas* goh (UK Pawt *Glahz* goh)

Port Harcourt, Nigeria : Pawrt *Hahr* kurt (UK Pawt *Hah* kawt)

Porthcawl, Wales : Pawrth *kawl* (UK Pawth *kawl*)

Port Hedland, Australia : Pawrt *Hed* lund (UK Pawt...)

Porthleven, England : Pawrth *lev* un

Porthmadog, Wales : Pawrth *mad* awg (UK Pawth *mad* og)

Port Hueneme, USA : Pawrt Wiy *nee* mi (UK Pawt...)

Port Huron, USA : Pawrt *Hyoo* run (UK Pawt *Hyoo* a run)

Portici, Italy : *Pawr* tee chee

Portishead, England : *Pawr* tis hed (UK *Paw* tis hed)

Port Jackson, Australia : Pawrt *Jak* sun (UK Pawt...)

Port Kelang, Malaysia : Pawrt Ka *lahng* (UK Pawt...)

Portland, Australia; England; USA : *Pawrt* lund (UK *Pawt* lund)

Portlaoise, Ireland : Pawrt *lee* sha (UK Pawt *lee* sha)

Port Lavaca, USA : Pawrt La *vak* a (UK Pawt...)

Port Lincoln, Australia : Pawrt *Ling* kun (UK Pawt...)

Port Loko, Sierra Leone : Pawrt *Loh* koh (UK Pawt...)

Port Louis, Mauritius : Pawrt *Looh* us (UK Pawt *Looh* i)

Port-Louis, Guadeloupe : Pawr *Lwee*

Port Lyautey, Morocco : Pawr Lyoh *tay* (UK Paw...)

Port Macquarie, Australia : Pawrt Ma *kwah* ri (UK Pawt Ma *kwor* i)

Portmeirion, Wales : Pawrt *mer* i un (UK Pawt *mer* i un)

Port Moresby, Papua New Guinea : Pawrt *Mawrz* bi (UK Pawt *Mawz* bi)

Port Nicholson, New Zealand : Pawrt *Nik* ul sun (UK Pawt...)

Port Nolloth, South Africa : Pawrt *Nah* luth (UK Pawt *Nol* uth)

Porto, Portugal : *Pawr* toh (UK *Paw* toh) (Portuguese *Pohr* tooh)

Pôrto Alegre, Brazil : Pohr tooh Ah *lay* gree

Portobelo, Panama : Pawr toh *bel* oh (UK Paw toh *bel* oh)

Portofino, Italy : Pawr toh *fee* noh

Port of Spain, Trinidad and Tobago : Pawrt ahv *Spayn* ((UK Paw tuv...)

Portogruaro, Italy : Pawr toh grooh *ah* roh

Porto-Novo, Benin : Pawr toh *Noh* voh (UK Paw toh...)

Port Orange, USA : Pawrt *Aw* rinj (UK Pawt *Or* inj)

Porto-Vecchio, Corsica, France : Pawr toh *Vek* kyoh

Pôrto Velho, Brazil : Pohr tooh *Vel* yooh

Portoviejo, Ecuador : Pohr toh *vyay* hoh

Port Phillip (Bay), Australia : Pawrt *Fil* up (UK Pawt...)

Port Pirie, Australia : Pawrt *Pir* i (UK Pawt...)

Portreath, England : Pawr *treeth* (UK Paw *treeth*)

Portree, Scotland : Pawr *tree* (UK Paw *tree*)

Port Royal, USA : Pawrt *Roy* ul (UK Pawt...)

Portrush, Northern Ireland : Pawrt *rahsh* (UK Pawt *rahsh*)

Port Said, Egypt : Pawrt *Siyd* (UK Pawt...) [Ross, p. 144, rejects this pronunciation, preferring Pawt *Sayd*. But his recommendation is never heard today.]

Port St. Lucie, USA : Pawrt Saynt *Looh* si (UK Pawt Sunt...)

Portsea, England : *Pawrt* see (UK *Pawt* see)

Port Shepstone, South Africa : Pawrt *Shep* stun (UK Pawrt...)

Portslade, England : *Pawrt* slayd (UK *Pawt* slayd)

Portsmouth, England; USA : *Pawrts* muth (UK *Pawts* muth)

Port Stanley, Falkland Islands : Pawrt *Stan* li (UK Pawt...)

Port Stephens, Australia : Pawrt *Stee* vunz (UK Pawt...)

Port Sudan, Sudan : Pawrt Sooh *dan* (UK Pawt Sooh *dahn*)

Port Sunlight, England : Pawrt *Sahn* liyt (UK Pawt...)

Port Talbot, Wales : Pawrt *Tawl* but (UK Pawt...)

Port Taufiq, Egypt : Pawrt Tow *feek* (UK Pawt...)

Portugal, Europe : *Pawr* cha gul (UK *Paw* choo gul) (Portuguese Poohr tooh *gahl*)

Portugalete, Spain : Pohr tooh gah *lay* tay

Port-Vila, Vanuatu : Pawr Vee *lah*

Port Washington, USA : Pawrt *Waw* shing tun (UK Pawt *Wosh* ing tun)

Porvoo, Finland : *Pawr* vaw

Posadas, Argentina : Poh *sah* dhahs

Potchefstroom, South Africa : *Pah* chuf stroohm (UK *Poch* uf stroohm)

Potenza, Italy : Poh *tent* sah

Poti, Georgia : *Paw* tee

Potidaea, Greece : Pah ti *dee* a (UK Pot i *dee* a)

Potomac, USA : Pa *toh* muk (UK Pa *toh* mak)

Potosi, USA : Pa *toh* si

Potosí, Bolivia : Poh toh *see*

Potsdam, Germany; USA : *Pahts* dam (UK *Pots* dam) (German *Pawts* dahm)

Potters Bar, England : Pah turz *Bahr* (UK Pot uz *Bah*)

Pottstown, USA : *Pahts* town (UK *Pots* town)

Pottsville, USA : *Pahts* vil (UK *Pots* vil)

Poughkeepsie, USA : Pa *kip* si

Pouliguen, France : Pooh lee *gahn*

Poulton-le-Fylde, England : Pohl tun li *Fiyld*

Pouso Alegre, Brazil : Poh zooh A *lay* gree

Poway, USA : *Poh* way

Powhatan, USA : Pow a *tan*

Powys, Wales : *Pow* is [Ross, p. 144, claims that the correct pronunciation of the county's name is *Poh* is.]

Poynings, England : *Poy* ningz

Požarevac, Serbia : Poh *zhahr* a vahts

Poza Rica, Mexico : Poh sah *Ree* kah

Poznań, Poland : *Pohz* nahn (UK *Poz* nan) (Polish *Pawz* nahn)

Pozo Colorado, Paraguay : Poh soh Koh loh *rah* dhoh

Pozzallo, Italy : Pawt *zah* loh

Pozzuoli, Italy : Pawt *swaw* li

Praa Sands, England : Pray *Sandz*

Prague, Czech Republic : Prahg [English speakers formerly pronounced the Czech capital's name as Prayg, as in Edward Lear's 1846 limerick: "There was an Old Person of Prague, / Who was suddenly seized with the plague." Ross, p. 144, recounts the item below.]

The older pronunciation existed until the [nineteen] 'thirties, for there was the "joke"—in poor taste even then—*Don't be vague, ask for Prague*, in which *Prague* replaced *Haig* in the well-known whisky slogan. It was supposed to be said to Hitler before the occupation of Czecho-Slovakia.

Prahran, Australia : Pra *ran*

Praia, Cape Verde : *Priy* a

Prairie du Chien, USA : Prer i da *Sheen* (UK Pray a ri...)

Prato, Italy : *Prah* toh

Prattville, USA : *Prat* vil

Pravdinsk, Russia : *Prahv* deensk

Prenzlau, Germany : *Prents* low

Prescot, England : *Pres* kut

Prescott, USA : *Pres* kut

Preseli, Wales : Pri *sel* i

Presidente Prudente, Brazil : Pray see den tay Prooh *den* tay

Prešov, Slovakia : *Presh* ow

Presque Isle, USA : Pres *kiyl* [The Michigan county's name is usually pronounced Pres *keel*.]

Prestatyn, Wales : Pres *tat* in

Presteigne, Wales : Pres *teen*

Preston, Australia; Canada; England : *Pres* tun

Prestonpans, Scotland : Pres tun *panz*

Prestwich, England : *Prest* wich

Prestwick, Scotland : *Prest* wik

Pretoria, South Africa : Pri *taw* ri a

Pribilof (Islands), USA : *Prib* i lahf (UK *Prib* i lof)

Příbram, Czech Republic : *Prshee* brahm

Priene, Turkey : Priy *ee* nee

Prieska, South Africa : *Prees* ka

Prievidza, Slovakia : *Pre* vid zah

Prilep, Macedonia : *Pree* lep

Primorsk, Russia : Pree *mawrsk*

Prince Albert, Canada : Prins *Al* burt (UK ... *Al* but)

Prince Edward (Island), Canada : Prins *Ed* wurd (UK ... *Ed* wud)

Prince George, Canada : Prins *Jawrj* (UK ... *Jawj*)

Prince Rupert, Canada : Prins *Rooh* purt (UK ... *Rooh* put)

Princes Risborough, England : Prin siz *Riz* buhr oh (UK ... *Riz* bra)

Princess Astrid (Coast), Antarctica : Prin sus *As* trid (UK Prin ses...)

Princess Martha (Coast), Antarctica : Prin sus *Mahr* tha (UK Prin ses *Mah* tha)

Princess Ragnhild (Coast), Antarctica : Prin sus *Rahng* un hil (UK Prin ses...)

Princeton, USA : *Prin* stun

Princetown, England : *Prins* town

Príncipe (Island), São Tomé and Príncipe : *Prin* si pay

Priozersk, Russia : Pree a *zyawrsk*

Pripet (Marshes), Europe : *Pri* pet

Priština, Serbia : Preesh *tee* nah

Privas, France : Pree *vah*

Prizren, Serbia : *Preez* ren

Probolinggo, Indonesia : Proh boh *ling* goh

Prokopyevsk, Russia : Pra *kawp* yifsk

Prome, Myanmar : Prohm

Propriá, Brazil : Proh pree *ah*

Prostějov, Czech Republic : *Praws* tye yawf

Provence, France : Pra *vahns* (UK Pra vons) (French Praw *vahns*)

Providence, USA : *Prah* va duns (UK *Prov* i duns)

Provincetown, USA : *Prah* vins town (UK *Prov* ins town)

Provins, France : Praw *vahn*

Provo, USA : *Proh* voh

Prudentópolis, Brazil : Prooh den *taw* poo lees

Prudhoe, England : *Prah* doh [Locally

the Northumberland town is also
known as *Proo* doh.]

Prudhoe (Bay), USA : *Prooh* doh

Prudnik, Poland : *Proohd* nik

Prussia, Germany : *Prah* sha

Pruszków, Poland : *Proohsh* koohf

Przemyśl, Poland : *Pshe* mish ul

Przhevalsk, Kyrgyzstan : Pur zhi *vahlsk*

Pskov, Russia : Pskawf

Pszczyna, Poland : *Pshchi* nah

Puch'ŏn, South Korea : Pooh *chawn*

Puckeridge, England : *Pah* ka rij

Puddletown, England : *Pah* dul town

Pudsey, England : *Pahd* si

Puebla, Mexico : *Pweb* lah

Pueblo, USA : *Pweb* loh

Puente del Inca, Argentina : Pwen tay del *Ing* ka (Spanish Pwen tay dhel *Eeng* kah)

Puerto Ayacucho, Venezuela : Pwer toh Iy ah *kooh* choh

Puerto Barrios, Guatemala : Pwer toh *Bahr* ree ohs

Puerto Cabello, Venezuela : Pwer toh Kah *bay* yoh

Puerto Carreño, Colombia : Pwer toh Kahr *ray* nyoh

Puerto Castilla, Honduras : Pwer toh Kahs *tee* yah

Puerto Cortés, Honduras : Pwer toh Kawr *tes*

Puerto La Cruz, Venezuela : Pwer toh Lah *Kroohz*

Puerto Lempira, Honduras : Pwer toh Lem *pee* rah

Puerto Limón, Costa Rica : Pwer toh Lee *mohn*

Puertollano, Spain : Pwer toh *lyah* noh

Puerto Madryn, Argentina : Pwer toh Mah *dreen* (Spanish Pwer toh Mah *dhreen*)

Puerto Montt, Chile : Pwer toh *Mawnt*

Puerto Padre, Cuba : Pwer toh *Pah* dray

Puerto Plata, Dominican Republic : Pwer toh *Plah* tah

Puerto Princesa, Philippines : Pwer toh Prin *say* sah

Puerto Real, Spain : Pwer toh Ray *ahl*

Puerto Rico, West Indies : Pwer ta *Ree* koh (UK Pwuh toh...)

Puerto Vallarta, Mexico : Pwer toh Vah *yahr* tah

Pugachov, Russia : Pooh ga *chawf*

Puget (Sound), USA : *Pyooh* jut

Puglia, Italy : *Pooh* lyah

Pukë, Albania : *Pooh* ka

Pula, Croatia : *Pooh* lah

Pulaski, USA : Pa *las* ki

Puławy, Poland : Pooh *wah* vi

Pulborough, England : *Pool* buhr oh (UK *Pool* bra)

Pullman, USA : *Pool* mun

Pune, India : *Pooh* na

Punjab, India : Pahn *jahb* [The state and former province of British India is popularly referred to by English speakers as Poon *jahb*, a pronunciation perhaps influenced by that of **Poona**, a city familiar under British rule (although not located in the Punjab).]

Puno, Peru : *Pooh* noh

Punta Arenas, Chile : Poohn tah Ah *ray* nahs

Punta Gorda, Belize : Poohn tah *Gawr* dah

Puntarenas, Costa Rica : Poohn tah *ray* nahs

Punxsutawney, USA : Pahngk sa *taw* ni

Purbeck, England : *Puhr* bek (UK *Puh* bek)

Purfleet, England : *Puhr* fleet (UK *Puh* fleet)

Purgatoire, USA : Pur ga *twahr* [The name of the Colorado river is sometimes corrupted in writing to *Pick-etwire*, when it is pronounced *Pik* ut wiyr.]

Purley, England : *Puhr* li (UK *Puh* li)

Purmerend, Netherlands : Pur ma *rent*

Puruándiro, Mexico : Poohr *wahn* dee roh

Purwakata, Indonesia : Poor wa *kahr* ta (UK Poo a wa *kah* ta)

Purwokerto, Indonesia : Poor wa *ker* toh (UK Poo a wa *kuh* toh)

Pusan, South Korea : Pooh *sahn* (UK Pooh *san*)
Pusey, England : *Pyooh* zi
Pushkin, Russia : *Poosh* kin
Putney, England : *Paht* ni
Puttenham, England : *Paht* num
Putumayo, Colombia : Pooh tooh *mah* yoh
Puyallup, USA : Pyooh *a* lup
Puy-de-Dôme, France : Pweed *Dawm*
Puylaurens, France : Pwee law *rahns*
Puyo, Ecuador : *Pooh* yoh
Pwllheli, Wales : Pool *hel* i (Welsh Poohl *hel* i) [The hyphen in the Welsh transliteration of the coastal resort's name is exceptionally inserted to avoid a misleading *ooh*, normally used to denote a long vowel sound. Ross, p. 146, prefers Pool *thel* i for the town's name. Leaver, using his own simplified transcription system, renders the name *pooth-helly*. Desperate English attempts at the name include Pa *thel* i and Pooth *lel* i. The name itself is in fact a straightforward combination of Welsh *pwll*, "pool," and *heli*, "brine."]
  (1) PWLLHELI [pronounced] pool-thelly [Johnston, p. 408].
  (2) PWLLHELI (pronounced something like "Pootl-heli") [*The Rough Guide to Wales*, 1998].
  (3) Lively seaside Pwllheli (poolth-heh-lee) [*Lonely Planet Great Britain*, 2005].
Pyapon, Myanmar : Pyah *pohn*
Pyatigorsk, Russia : Pi tee *gawrsk*
Pydna, Greece : *Pid* na
Pyè, Myanmar : Pyay
P'yŏngyang, North Korea : Pyahng *yahng* (UK Pyong *yang*)
Pyrenees, Europe : *Pir* a neez (UK Pir a *neez*)
Pyrgos, Greece : *Pir* gaws (UK *Pi* a gos)
Pytchley, England : *Piych* li [The name of the Northamptonshire village is pronounced with an unexpected long vowel.]
Qaanaaq, Greenland : Kah *nahk*

Qalyûb, Egypt : Kahl *yoohb*
Qandahar, Afghanistan : Kan da *hahr* (UK Kan da *hah*)
Qaqortoq, Greenland : *Kah* kawr tawk
Qaraghandy, Kazakhstan : Kah rah *gahn* da
Qarshi, Uzbekistan : *Kahr* shee
Qatar, Asia : *Kah* tur (UK *Kat* ah)
Qazvin, Iran : Kaz *veen*
Qena, Egypt : *Kee* na
Qeqertarsuaq, Greenland : Ke ker tahr *sooh* ahk
Qingdao, China : Ching *dow*
Qinghai, China : Ching *hiy*
Qinhuangdao, China : Chin hwahng *dow*
Qiqihar, China : Chi chi *hahr*
Qom, Iran : Kohm
Qormi, Malta : *Kawr* mee
Qostanay, Kazakhstan : Koos ta *niy*
Quantock (Hills), England : *Kwahn* tahk (UK *Kwon* tuk)
Qu'Appelle, Canada : Kwah *pel*
Quarndon, England : *Kwawrn* dun (UK *Kwawn* dun)
Quatre Bornes, Mauritius : Kaht ra *Bawrn*
Queanbeyan, Australia : *Kween* bi un
Quebec, Canada : Kwi *bek*
Québec, Canada : Kay *bek*
Quedlinburg, Germany : *Kfayd* lun boork
Queenborough, England : *Kween* buhr oh (UK *Kween* bra)
Queen Charlotte (Islands), Canada : Kween *Shahr* lut (UK ... *Shah* lut)
Queen Mary (Land), Antarctica : Kween *Mer* i (UK ... *May* a ri)
Queen Maud (Land), Antarctica : Kween *Mawd*
Queens, USA : Kweenz
Queensferry, Wales : *Kweenz* fer i
Queensland, Australia : *Kweenz* lund [In Australia itself the state is usually referred to as *Kweenz* land, although in adjective use the pronunciation given is more common.]
Queenstown, Australia; South Africa : *Kweenz* town

Quelimane, Mozambique : Ka lee *maw* na

Queluz, Portugal : Ke *loohsh*

Quemado de Güines, Cuba : Kay mah dhoh dhay *Gwee* nays

Quemoy, Taiwan : Ki *moy*

Quenington, England : *Kwen* ing tun

Que Que, Zimbabwe : *Kway* Kway

Quercy, France : Ker *see*

Querétaro, Mexico : Kay *ray* tah roh

Quesnel, Canada : Ka *nel*

Questembert, France : Kay stahn *ber*

Quetta, Pakistan : *Kwet* a

Quetzaltenango, Guatemala : Ket sahl tay *nahng* goh

Quevedo, Ecuador : Kay *vay* dhoh

Quezon City, Philippines : Kay zahn *Si* ti (UK Kay zon...)

Qufu, China : Chooh *fooh*

Quibdó, Colombia : Keeb *doh*

Quiberon, France : Keeb *rohn*

Quillan, France : Kee *yahn*

Quillota, Chile : Kee *yoh* tah

Quilmes, Argentina : *Keel* mays

Quimper, France : Kahn *per*

Quimperlé, France : Kahn per *lay*

Quincy, USA : *Kwin* si [The name of Quincy, Massachusetts, is often pronounced *Kwin* zi.]

Quindío, Colombia : Keen *dee* oh

Qui Nhon, Vietnam : Kwee *Nyawn*

Quintana Roo, Mexico : Keen tah na *Roh*

Quissac, France : Kwee *sahk*

Quito, Ecuador : *Keeh* toh

Quixadá, Brazil : Kee sha *dah*

Quorn, England : Kwawrn (UK Kwawn)

Quornden, England : *Kwawrn* dun (UK *Kwawn* dun)

Quqon, Uzbekistan : Ka *kawn*

Qurghonteppa, Tajikistan : Koor gahn te *pah*

Qwaqwa, South Africa : *Kwah* kwah

Qyzylorda, Kazakhstan : Ka sil ur *dah*

Raalte, Netherlands : *Rahl* ta

Raasay, Scotland : *Rah* say

Rabastens, France : Rah bah *stahns*

Rabat, Morocco : Ra *baht*

Rabaul, Papua New Guinea : Ra *bowl*

Rach Gia, Vietnam : Raht *Zhah*

Racibórz, Poland : Rah *chee* boosh

Racine, USA : Ra *seen*

Rădăuţi, Romania : Ra da *oot* si

Radcliffe, England : *Rad* klif

Radebeul, Germany : *Rah* da boyl

Radford, USA : *Rad* furd (UK *Rad* fud)

Radlett, England : *Rad* lut

Radnor, USA; Wales : *Rad* nur (UK *Rad* na)

Radom, Poland : *Rah* dawm

Radomsko, Poland : Ra *dawm* skoh

Rafaela, Argentina : Rah fah *ay* lah

Raglan, Wales : *Rag* lun

Ragusa, Italy : Rah *gooh* sah

Rahway, USA : *Raw* way

Raiganj, India : *Riy* gunj

Rainford, England : *Rayn* furd (UK *Rayn* fud)

Rainham, England : *Ray* num

Rainhill, England : Rayn *hil*

Rainier, USA : Ra *nir* (UK *Ray* ni a) [The name of the Washington peak has the alternate US pronunciation Ray *nir*.]

Raipur, India : *Riy* poor

Raismes, France : Raym

Rajahmundry, India : Rah ja *moon* dree

Rajapalaiyam, India : Rah ja *pah* liy yum

Rajasthan, India : *Rah* ja stahn

Rajkot, India : *Rahj* koht

Rajputana, India : Rahj pa *tah* na

Rajshahi, Bangladesh : Rahj *shah* hee

Raleigh, USA : *Raw* li
  Raleigh, N.C., is *Rolly*, rhyming with *jolly* [Mencken, p. 541].

Ram Allah, West Bank : Rahm A *lah*

Ramat Gan, Israel : Ra *maht* Gahn

Rambervillers, France : Rahn ber vee *lay*

Rambouillet, France : Rahn booh *yay*

Ramillies, Belgium : *Ram* il eez (French Rah mee *yee*)

Ramla, Israel : *Rahm* la

Rampur, India : *Rahm* poor

Ramsbottom, England : *Ramz* bah tum (UK *Ramz* bot um)

Ramsey, England; USA : *Ram* zi
Ramsgate, England : *Ramz* gayt
Rancagua, Chile : Rahn *kah* gwah
Ranchi, India : *Rahn* chee
Rancho Cordova, USA : Ran choh *Kawr* da va
Rancho Cucamonga, USA : Ran choh Kooh ka *mahng* ga (UK ... Kooh ka *mong* ga)
Rancho Palos Verdes, USA : Ran choh Pal us *Vuhr* deez (UK ... *Vuh* deez)
Randalstown, Northern Ireland : *Ran* dulz town
Randburg, South Africa : *Rahnd* boorg
Randers, Denmark : *Rah* nurs
Randfontein, South Africa : *Rahnt* fahn tayn (UK *Rahnt* fon tayn)
Randwick, Australia : *Rand* wik
Rangiora, New Zealand : Rahng i *aw* ra
Rangoon, Myanmar : Rang *goohn*
Rangpur, Bangladesh : *Rahng* poor
Rannoch, Scotland : *Ran* ukh
Raon-l'Étape, France : Rah awn lay *tahp*
Rapallo, Italy : Rah *pah* loh
Rapidan, USA : Rap a *dan* (UK Rap i *dan*)
Rapid City, USA : Rap ud *Si* ti (UK Rap id...)
Rappahannock, USA : Rap a *han* uk
Rapu-Rapu, Philippines : Rah pooh *Rah* pooh
Raritan, USA : *Rar* a tun (UK *Rar* i tun)
Rarotonga, Cook Islands : Rar a *tahng* ga (UK Ray a ra *tong* ga)
Ra's al Khaymah, United Arab Emirates : Rahs al *Khiy* ma
Rasht, Iran : Rasht
Ras Tanura, Saudi Arabia : Rahs Ta *noor* a
Rastatt, Germany : *Rah* shtaht
Ratcliffe, England : *Rat* klif
Rathenow, Germany : *Rah* ta noh
Rathfarnham, Ireland : Rath *fahr* num (UK Rath *fah* num)
Rathlin, Northern Ireland : *Rath* lin
Ratingen, Germany : *Rah* ting un
Ratnagiri, India : Rut *nah* ga ree

Ratnapura, Sri Lanka : Rut na *poor* a
Raton (Pass), USA : Ra *tohn* [The name of the pass separating New Mexico from Colorado retains its Spanish pronunciation in New Mexico but is usually Ra *toohn* in Colorado.]
Rattray, Scotland : *Rat* ri
Rauma, Finland : *Row* mah
Raunds, England : Rawndz
Raurkela, India : Rawr *kay* la
Ravenglass, England : *Ray* vun glas (UK *Ray* vun glahs)
Ravenna, Italy : Ra *ven* a (Italian Rah *ven* nah)
Ravensbrück, Germany : *Ray* vunz brook (German *Rah* vuns breek)
Ravensburg, Germany : *Ray* vunz buhrg (UK *Ray* vunz buhg) (German *Rah* vuns boork)
Rawalpindi, Pakistan : Rah wul *pin* di (UK Rawl *pin* di)
Rawlins, USA : *Raw* lunz (UK *Raw* linz)
Rawmarsh, England : *Raw* mahrsh (UK *Raw* mahsh)
Rawson, Argentina : *Raw* sun
Rawtenstall, England : *Raw* tun stawl
Rayleigh, England : *Ray* li
Raz, France : Rah
Razgrad, Bulgaria : *Rahz* graht
Reading, England; USA : *Red* ing [The pronunciation is valid for most US places, although Reading, Michigan, is *Ree* ding.]
Rechytsa, Belarus : Ra *chit* sa
Recife, Brazil : Ri *see* fee
Recklinghausen, Germany : Rek ling *how* zun
Reculver, England : Ri *kahl* vur (UK Ri *kahl* va)
Redbridge, England : *Red* brij
Redcar, England : *Red* kahr (UK *Red* kah)
Redcliff, Zimbabwe : *Red* klif
Red Deer, Canada : *Red* Dir (UK *Red* Di a)
Redding, USA : *Red* ing
Redditch, England : *Red* ich

Redfield, USA : *Red* feeld
Redhill, England : Red *hil*
Redlands, USA : *Red* lundz
Redmond. USA : *Red* mund
Redondo Beach, USA : Ri dahn doh *Beech* (UK Ri don doh...)
Redruth, England : Red *roohth* [The name of the Cornish town means "red ford," with the first syllable representing Cornish *rys*, "ford," not English *red*.]
  [Early spellings] probably show that the name ... was pronounced "Red-*reeth*"; but the pronunciation "Red-*rooth*" has prevailed [O.J. Padel, *A Popular Dictionary of Cornish Place-Names*, 1988].
Redwood City, USA : Red wood *Si* ti
Reepham, England : *Ree* fum
Regensburg, Germany : *Ray* gunz buhrg (UK *Ray* gunz buhg) (German *Ray* gunz boork)
Reggio di Calabria, Italy : Red joh dee Kah *lah* bree ah
Reggio nell'Emilia, Italy : Red joh nel E *meel* yah
Reghin, Romania : *Ray* gin
Regina, Canada : Ri *jiy* na
Registan, Afghanistan : Ray gi *stahn*
Regla, Cuba : *Ray* glah
Rehoboth, Namibia; USA : Ri *hoh* buth
Rehovot, Israel : Ri *hoh* voht
Reichenau, Germany : *Riy* khun ow
Reichenbach, Germany : *Riy* khun bahkh
Reigate, England : *Riy* gut (UK *Riy* gayt)
Reims, France : Reemz (French Rahns)
Reinosa, Spain : Ray *noh* sah
Relizane, Algeria : Re lee *zahn*
Remagen, Germany : *Ray* mah gun
Rembang, Indonesia : *Rem* bahng
Remiremont, France : Ri meer *mawn*
Remscheid, Germany : *Rem* shiyt
Renaix, Belgium : Ri *nay*
Rendsburg, Germany : *Rents* boork
Renens, Switzerland : Ri *nawn*
Renfrew, Scotland : *Ren* frooh

Renishaw, England : *Ren* i shaw
Renkum, Netherlands : *Reng* kum
Rennes, France : Ren
Reno, USA : *Ree* noh
Rensselaer, USA : Ren sa *lir* (UK Ren sa *li* a)
Renton, Scotland; USA : *Ren* tun
Renwick, England : *Ren* ik
Repton, England : *Rep* tun
Resende, Brazil : Ri *zen* dee
Resistencia, Argentina : Ray sees *ten* syah
Reşiţa, Romania : *Re* sheet sah
Resolven, Wales : Ri *zahl* vun (UK Ri *zol* vun)
Retalhuleu, Guatemala : Ray tah looh *lay* ooh
Retallack, Canada : Ri *tal* uk
Retford, England : *Ret* furd (UK *Ret* fud)
Réunion, Indian Ocean : Ree *yoohn* yun (French Ray ee *nyohn*)
Reus, Spain : *Re* oohs
Reutlingen, Germany : *Royt* ling un
Revelstoke, Canada : *Rev* ul stohk
Revere, USA : Ri *vir* (UK Ri *vi* a)
[1]**Revillagigedo**, Pacific Ocean : Ray vee yah hee *hay* dhoh [A group of islands belonging to Mexico.]
[2]**Revillagigedo**, USA : Ri vi la ga *gee* doh [An island in the Alexander Archipelago, Alaska.]
Reykjavík, Iceland : *Ray* kyah veek
Reynoldsburg, USA : *Ren* uldz buhrg (UK *Ren* uldz buhg)
Reynosa, Mexico : Ray *noh* sah
Rezé, France : Ruh *zay*
Rhaetia, Europe : *Ree* sha
Rhayader, Wales : *Riy* a dur (UK *Riy* a da) [Welsh names beginning or containing *rh* often have these letters pronounced *hr* by the Welsh, although the *h* is frequently unsounded.]
Rheden, Netherlands : *Ray* dun
Rheidol, Wales : *Riy* dahl (UK *Riy* dol) (Welsh *Ray* dawl)
Rheims, France : Reemz
Rheine, Germany : *Riy* na

Rheydt, Germany : Riyt
Rhine, Europe : Riyn
Rhineland, Germany : *Riyn* land
Rhinog Fawr, Wales : Ree nahg *Vow* ur
(UK Ree nog *Vow* a) (Welsh Ree
nawg *Vowr*) [The twin peaks *Rhinog
Fawr* ("Big Rhinog") and *Rhinog Fach*
("Little Rhinog") are popularly
referred to by English visitors and
walkers as "the Rhinogs" (*Riy* nogz).]
Rhode Island, USA : Rohd *Iy* lund
(UK *Rohd* Iy lund)
Rhodes, Greece : Rohdz
Rhodesia, Africa : Roh *dee* zha (UK
Roh *dee* sha) [As the former country
was named for Cecil Rhodes, one
would have expected a pronunciation
Rohd zi a. Instead, there appears to
have been an influence from a name
such as **Magnesia**, perhaps aided by
the African name's classical appear-
ance (as if from **Rhodes**).]
Rhodope, Bulgaria : *Rah* da pi (UK *Rod*
a pi)
Rhondda, Wales : *Rahn* da (UK *Ron* da)
(Welsh *Rawn* dhah)
Rhône, France : Rohn (French Rawn)
Rhosllanerchrugog, Wales : Rohs la
nur *kree* gahg (UK Rohs la na *kree*
gog) (Welsh Raws hlah nerkh *ri*
gog)
Rhosneigr, Wales : Rohs *niy* gur (UK
Rohs *niy* ga) (Welsh Raws *naygr*)
Rhuddlan, Wales : *Ridh* lun (Welsh
Ridh lahn)
Rhuys, France : Rwees
Rhyl, Wales : Ril
Rhymney, Wales : *Rahm* ni
Rialto, Italy : Ri *al* toh
Riau, Indonesia : *Ree* ow
Ribe, Denmark : *Ree* ba
Ribeauvillé, France : Ree boh vee *lay*
Ribécourt-Dreslincourt, France : Ree
bay koohr Dray lahn *koohr*
Ribeira, Spain : Ree *bay* rah
Ribeirão Prêto, Brazil : Ree biy rown
Pray tooh
Riccarton, Scotland : *Rik* ur tun (UK
Rik a tun)

Richardson, USA : *Rich* urd son (UK
Rich ud sun)
Richelieu, France : Reesh *lyuh*
Richfield, USA : *Rich* feeld
Richmond, Australia; Canada; En-
gland; USA : *Rich* mund
Rickmansworth, England : *Rik* munz
wuhrth (UK *Rik* munz wuhth)
Ridderkerk, Netherlands : *Rid* ur kerk
Rideau (Canal), Canada : Ri *doh*
Ridgecrest, USA : *Rij* krest
Ridgefield, USA : *Rij* feeld
Ridgewood, USA : *Rij* wood
Ridley, USA : *Rid* li
Riedisheim, France : Ree di *saym*
Riemst, Belgium : Reemst
Riesa, Germany : *Ree* za
Rieti, Italy : Ree *ay* tee
Rievaulx, England : *Ree* voh [According
to Ross, p. 150, the name of the
North Yorkshire village, famous for
its medieval abbey remains, is pro-
nounced *Riv* ulz. But this is now ob-
solete, as are most other variants.]
Finally there is Rievaulx (pronounced
Reevo or *Rivvez*, take your choice)
[Ruth McKenney and Richard
Bransten, *Here's England*, 1955].
Riga, Latvia : *Ree* ga [English speakers
formerly knew the capital city as *Riy*
ga, as in the anonymous limerick:
"There was a young lady of Riga /
Who went for a ride on a tiger."]
Rijeka, Croatia : Ree *yek* a
Rijswijk, Netherlands : *Riys* viyk
Rimini, Italy : *Rim* a ni (Italian *Ree* mi
nee)
Rîmnicu Sărat, Romania : Rum nee
kooh Sa *raht*
Rîmnicu Vîlcea, Romania : Rum nee
kooh *Vul* cha
Rimouski, Canada : Ri *mooh* ski
Ringerike, Norway : *Ring* a ree ka
Ringkøbing, Denmark : *Ring* kuh beng
Ringwood, Australia; England; USA :
Ring wood
Riobamba, Ecuador : Ree oh *bahm* bah
Rio Branco, Brazil : Ree ooh *Brahng*
kooh

Río Bravo, Mexico : Ree oh *Brah* voh [The upper course of the river is in the USA, where it is known as the **Rio Grande**.]

Rio Claro, Brazil : Ree ooh *Klah* rooh

Rio Cuarto, Argentina : Ree oh *Kwahr* toh

Rio de Janeiro, Brazil : Ree oh day Zha *ner* oh (UK ... da Zha *ni* a roh) (Portuguese Ree ooh dee Zha *nay* rooh)

Río de Oro, Western Sahara : Ree oh day *Oh* roh

Rio Gallegos, Argentina : Ree oh Gah *yay* gohs

Rio Grande, Brazil : Ree ooh *Grahn* dee

Río Grande, Mexico; Puerto Rico; USA : Ree oh *Grand* (Spanish Ree oh *Grahn* day) [The English pronunciation is generally used for the river (known in Mexico as the **Río Bravo**), which rises in Colorado and forms the entire Texas-Mexico border.]

Ríohacha, Colombia : Ree oh *ah* chah

Riom, France : Ryawn

Río Negro, Argentina; Uruguay : Ree oh *Nay* groh

Rio Pardo, Brazil : Ree ooh *Pahr* dooh

Río Piedras, Puerto Rico : Ree oh *Pyay* dhrahs

Rio Rancho, USA : Ree oh *Ran* choh

Ripley, England : *Rip* li

Ripon, England : *Rip* un

Risaralda, Colombia : Ree sah *rahl* dah

Risca, Wales : *Ris* ka

Rishon le-Ziyyon, Israel : Ree shawn li Tsee *yohn*

Rishton, England : *Rish* tun

Rivas, Nicaragua : *Ree* vahs

Rive-de-Gier, France : Reevd *Zhyay*

Rivera, Uruguay : Ree *vay* rah

Riverina, Australia : Riv a *ree* na [An alternate stress *Riv* a ree na is preferred by some, while Riv a *riy* na also exists.]

Riverside, USA : *Riv* ur siyd (UK *Riv* a siyd)

Riverton, USA : *Riv* ur tun (UK *Riv* a tun)

Riviera, Europe : Ri vi *er* a (UK Ri vi *ay* a ra)

Riviera Beach, USA : Ri vir a *Beech*

Rivière-du-Loup, Canada : Ree vyer dee *Looh*

Rivne, Ukraine : *Riv* na

Rivoli, Italy : *Ree* voh lee

Riyadh, Saudi Arabia : Ree *yahd* (UK *Ree* ad)

Rize, Turkey : *Ree* ze

Roanne, France : Roh *ahn*

Roanoke, USA : *Roh* a nohk

Roatán, Honduras : Raw ah *tahn*

Robertsport, Liberia : *Rah* burts pawrt (UK *Rob* uts pawt)

Roberval, Canada : *Rah* bur vul (UK *Rob* a vul) (French Raw ber *val*)

Rocester, England : *Roh* stur (UK *Roh* sta)

Rocha, Uruguay : *Raw* chah

Rochdale, England : *Rahch* dayl (UK *Roch* dayl)

Rochefort, Belgium; France : Rawsh *fawr*

Rochester, England; USA : *Rah* cha stur (UK *Roch* is ta)

Rochford, England : *Rahch* furd (UK *Roch* fud)

Rockford, USA : *Rahk* furd (UK *Rok* fud)

Rockhampton, Australia : Rahk *hamp* tun (UK Rok *hamp* tun)

Rockingham, Australia; England; USA : *Rahk* ing um (UK *Rok* ing um)

Rockville, USA : *Rahk* vil (UK *Rok* vil)

Rocroi, France : Raw *krwah*

Rodez, France : Raw *dayz*

Rodings, England : *Roh* dingz [The area of Essex known as The Rodings takes its name from the eight villages with names in *Roding*, formerly pronounced *Rooh* dhing locally. Pointon, p. 208, comments on this alternate form (and names the villages).]

The second, the historical pronunciation, has gradually given way, although not entirely succumbed, to the former. The group of villages known as The Rodings includes Abbess Roding, Aythorpe Roding, Beauchamp Roding, Berners Roding,

High Roding, Leaden Roding, Margaret Roding, and White Roding or Roothing. Except in the last case, where Roothing has been retained in the name of the civil parish, it appears that Roding is now accepted as the standard spelling.

Rodriguez, Indian Ocean : Roh *dree* ges

Roebling, USA : *Roh* bling

Roehampton, England : Roh *hamp* tun

Roermond, Netherlands : Roohr *mawnt*

Roeselare, Belgium : Rooh sa *lah* ra

Rohnert Park, USA : Roh nurt *Pahrk* (UK Roh nut *Pahk*)

Rohrbach-lès-Bitche, France : Rawr bahk lay *Beech*

Rohtak, India : *Roh* tuk

Rolla, USA : *Raw* la (UK *Rol* a)

Rolleston, England : *Rohl* stun

Romagna, Italy : Roh *mahn* ya

Roman, Romania : Raw *mahn*

Romanèche-Thorins, France : Raw mah naysh Taw *rahn*

Romang, Indonesia : *Roh* mahng

Romania, Europe : Roo *may* ni a

Romans-sur-Isère, France : Raw mahn seer Ee *zer*

Rombas, France : Rawm *bah*

Rome, Italy; USA : Rohm [At one time English speakers referred to the Italian capital as Roohm. Hence Shakespeare's pun: "Now is it Rome indeed and room enough" (*Julius Caesar*, I. ii. 156, *c.* 1599).]

Romford, England : *Rahm* furd (UK *Rom* fud)

Romney (Marsh), England : *Rahm* ni (UK *Rom* ni)

Romsey, England : *Rahm* zi (UK *Rom* zi) [Ross, p. 151, gives the US pronunciation as the preferred UK one for the Hampshire town, branding *Rom* zi as incorrect.]

Romulus, USA : *Rahm* ya lus [UK *Rom* yoo lus)

Rona, Scotland : *Roh* na

Ronda, Spain : *Rawn* dah

Rondônia, Brazil : Rawn *doh* nya

Rønne, Denmark : *Ruh* na

Ronneby, Sweden : *Raw* na bi

Ronne (Ice Shelf), Antarctica : *Roh* na

Roodepoort, South Africa : *Roh* da pohrt

Roosevelt, USA : *Roh* za velt

Roraima, Brazil : Raw *riy* mah

Rosales, Philippines : Roh *sah* lays

Rosario, Argentina : Roh *sah* ree oh (UK Roh *zah* ri oh)

Roscommon, Ireland : Rahs *kah* mun (UK Ros *kom* un)

Roscrea, Ireland : Rahs *kray* (UK Ros *kray*)

Roseau, Dominica : Roh *zoh*

Roseburg, USA : *Rohz* buhrg (UK *Rohz* buhg)

Roselle, USA : Roh *zel*

Rosemead, USA : *Rohz* meed

Rosenheim, Germany : *Roh* zun hiym

Rosetta, Egypt : Roh *zet* a

Roskilde, Denmark : *Rahs* kil da (UK *Ros* kil da) (Danish *Raws* ki la)

Roslavl, Russia : *Raws* lah vul

Rosny-sous-Bois, France : Roh nee sooh *Bwah*

Rosporden, France : Raws pawr *dahn*

Ross, USA : Raws (UK Ros)

Rossano, Italy : Raw *sah* noh

Ross (Dependency), Antarctica : Raws (UK Ros)

Rossendale, England : *Raw* sun dayl (UK *Ros* un dayl)

Rosslare, Ireland : Rahs *ler* (UK Ros *lay* a)

Rosso, Mauritania : *Raw* soh (UK *Ros* o)

Ross-on-Wye, England : Raws ahn *Wiy* (UK Ros on...)

Rostock, Germany : *Rahs* tahk (UK *Ros* tok) (German *Raws* tawk)

Rostov, Russia : *Rahs* tahv (UK *Ros* tov) (Russian Rahs *tawf*)

Rostrenen, France : Raws tray *nahn*

Roswell, USA : *Rahz* wel (UK *Roz* wel)

Rosyth, Scotland : Raw *siyth*

Rothbury, England : *Rahth* bri (UK *Roth* bri)

Rothenburg, Germany : *Roh* tun boork

Rotherham, England : *Rah* dhur um (UK *Rodh* a rum)

Rotherhithe, England : *Rah* dhur hiyth (UK *Rodh* a hiydh)

Rothersthorpe, England : *Rah* dhurz thawrp (UK *Rodh* uz thawp) [The name of the Northamptonshire village has the alternate local pronunciation *Rodh* uz thrup.]

Rothes, Scotland : *Rah* thiz (UK *Roth* iz)

Rothesay, Scotland : *Rahth* si (UK *Roth* si)

Rothwell, England : *Rahth* wel (UK *Roth* wel) [There are two towns of this name. That in Northamptonshire is locally also known as *Roh* ul.]

Roti, Indonesia : *Raw* ti

Rotorua, New Zealand : Roh toh *rooh* a

Rotterdam, Netherlands : *Rah* tur dam (UK *Rot* a dam) (Dutch *Raw* tur dahm)

Rottingdean, England : *Rah* ting deen (UK *Rot* ing deen)

Rottweil, Germany : *Rawt* viyl

Rotuma, Fiji : Roh *tooh* ma

Roubaix, France : Rooh *bay*

Rouen, France : Roo *ahn* (UK *Rooh* awn) (French Rwahn)

Rouffach, France : Rooh *fahk*

Rough Tor, England : *Row* Tur

Rourkela, India : Rawr *kay* la

Rousay, Scotland : *Row* zay

Roussillon, France : Rooh see *yohn*

Rouyn-Noranda, Canada : Rooh un Naw *ran* da

Rovaniemi, Finland : Raw *vah* nye mee

Rovereto, Italy : Roh vay *ray* toh

Rovigo, Italy : Roh *vee* goh

Rovno, Ukraine : *Rawv* na

Rowlett, USA : *Row* lut

Rowley Regis, England : Row li *Ree* jis

Roxas, Philippines : *Roh* hahs

Roxburgh, Scotland : *Rahks* buhr oh (UK *Roks* bra)

Royan, France : Rwah *yahn*

Royat, France : Rwah *yah*

Royston, England : *Roy* stun

Royton, England : *Roy* tun

Rrëshen, Albania : *Rah* shun

Ruabon, Wales : Roo *ab* un

Rub' al Khali, Saudi Arabia : Roohb al *Khah* lee

Rubtsovsk, Russia : Roop *tsawfsk*

Ruda Śląska, Poland : Rooh da *Shlawn* ska

Rudny, Kazakhstan : *Roohd* ni

Rudolstadt, Germany : *Rooh* dul shtaht

Rudyard, England : *Rah* jurd (UK *Rah* jud)

Rueil-Malmaison, France : Rway Mahl may *zawn*

Rufiji, Tanzania : Rooh *fee* jee

Rufisque, Senegal : Rooh *feesk*

Rugby, England : *Rahg* bi

Rugeley, England : *Roohj* li

Rügen, Germany : *Ree* gun

Ruhr, Germany : Roor (UK *Roo* a)

Ruislip, England : *Riys* lip [Ross, p. 153, prefers the pronunciation *Riyz* lip for the name of the London district and former Middlesex village. But this is infrequent now.]

The local pronunciation of Ruislip is either "Rizelip" or "Ryeslip" [A.D. Mills, *A Dictionary of London Place Names*, 2001].

Ruitz, France : Rwee

Rum, Scotland : Rahm

Rumelia, Europe : Roo *mee* li a

Runcorn, England : *Rahng* kawrn (UK *Rahng* kawn)

Runnymede, England : *Rah* ni meed

Rupat, Indonesia : *Rooh* paht

Ruse, Bulgaria : *Rooh* say

Rushden, England : *Rahsh* dun

Rushmore, USA : *Rahsh* mawr (UK *Rahsh* maw)

Rusper, England : *Rahs* pur (UK *Rahs* pa)

Russell, New Zealand : *Rah* sul

Russellville, USA : *Rah* sul vil

Rüsselsheim, Germany : *Ree* suls hiym

Russia, Eurasia : *Rah* sha

Rustavi, Georgia : Roos *tah* vee

Rustenburg, South Africa : *Rahs* tun buhrg (UK *Rahs* tun buhg) (Afrikaans *Roos* tun boork)

Ruswarp, England : *Rah* surp (UK *Rah* sup)

Ruthenia, Ukraine : Roo *thee* ni a

Rutherford, Scotland; USA : *Rah* dhur furd (UK *Rah* dha fud)

Rutherglen, Scotland : *Rah* dhur glen (UK *Rah* dha glen) [The name of the town near Glasgow has a local pronunciation *Rah* dha glun.]

Ruthin, Wales : *Rith* in [The town is often referred to as *Rooh* thin by those unfamiliar with the name.]

¹Ruthven, Scotland (near Alyth) : *Riv* un

²Ruthven, Scotland (near Huntly) : *Rahth* vun

Rutland, England; USA : *Raht* lund

Ruwenzori, Africa : Rooh un *zaw* ri

Rwanda, Africa : Roo *ahn* da (UK Roo *an* da)

Ryazan, Russia : Ri *zahn*

Rybinsk, Russia : *Rib* unsk

Rybnik, Poland : *Rib* nik

Rydal, England : *Riy* dul

Ryde, Australia; England : Riyd

Rye, England : Riy

Ryton, England : *Riy* tun

Ryukyu (Islands), Japan : Ree *yooh* kyooh

Rzeszów, Poland : *Zhe* shoohf

Rzhev, Russia : Rzhef

Saalfeld, Germany : *Zahl* felt

Saar, Europe : Sahr (UK Sah) (German Zahr)

Saarbrücken, Germany : *Sahr* brook un (UK *Sah* brook un) (German *Zahr* bree kun)

Saaremaa, Estonia : *Sahr* a mah

Saarland, Germany : *Sahr* land (UK *Sah* land) (German *Zahr* lahnt)

Saarlouis, Germany : *Zahr* looh ee

Saas Fee, Switzerland : Sahs *Fay*

Saba, West Indies : *Say* ba [Some sources give the island's name the incorrect pronunciation *Sah* ba.]

Sabadell, Spain : Sah bah *dhel*

Sabah, Malaysia : *Sah* ba

Sabaneta, Dominican Republic : Sah bah *nay* tah

Sabang, Indonesia : Sah *bahng*

Sabine, USA : Sa *been*

Sabrina (Coast), Antarctica : Sa *briy* na

Sabzevar, Iran : Sab za *vahr*

Sacramento, USA : Sak ra *men* toh

Sá da Bandeira, Angola : Sah da Bahn *day* ra

Safaqis, Tunisia : Sa *fah* kis

Saffron Walden, England : Saf run *Wawl* dun

Safi, Morocco : *Sa* fee

Saga, Japan : *Sah* gah

Sagaing, Myanmar : Sa *giyng*

Sagamihara, Japan : Sah gah mee *hah* rah

Sagar, India : *Sah* gur

Saginaw, USA : *Sag* a naw (UK *Sag* i naw)

Saguache, USA : Sa *wahch*

Sagua la Grande, Cuba : Sah gway lah *Grahn* day

Saguenay, Canada : Sag a *nay*

Sagunto, Spain : Sah *goohn* toh

Sahara, Africa : Sa *har* a (UK Sa *hah* ra)

Saharanpur, India : Sa *hah* run poor

Sahel, Africa : Sah *hel*

Sahiwal, Pakistan : *Sah* hee wahl

Saida, Algeria : Siy *dah*

Saigon, Vietnam : Siy *gahn* (UK Siy *gon*)

Sains-en-Gogelle, France : Sahn ahn *Gwahl*

St. Abbs, England : Saynt *Abz* (UK Sunt...)

St. Agnes, England : Saynt *Ag* nis (UK Sunt...) [The pronunciation is valid both for the Cornish resort and the island in the Isles of Scilly.]

St. Albans, England; USA : Saynt *Awl* bunz (UK Sunt...)

St. Albert, Canada : Saynt *Al* burt (UK Sunt *Al* but)

St.-Amand-les-Eaux, France : Sahnt A mahn lay *zoh*

St.-Amand-Montrond, France : Sahnt A mahn Mawn *rawn*

St. Andrews, Scotland : Saynt *An* droohz (UK Sunt...) [The name of the university town is locally also pronounced Sin *tan* droohz.]

St. Asaph, Wales : Saynt *As* uf (UK Sunt...)

St. Athan, Wales : Saynt *Ath* un (UK Sunt...)

St. Augustine, USA : Saynt *Aw* ga steen (UK Sunt Aw *gahs* tin)

St. Austell, England : Saynt *Aw* stul (UK Sunt...) [Locally the name of the Cornish town is pronounced Sunt *Aw* sul, or according to Johnston, p. 427, "St. Ossles."]

St. Bees, England : Saynt *Beez* (UK Sunt...)

St. Boniface, Canada : Saynt *Bah* na fays (UK Sunt *Bon* i fays)

St. Breock, England : Saynt *Bree* uk (UK Sunt...)

St. Briavels, England : Saynt *Brev* ulz (UK Sunt...)

St.-Brieuc, France : Sahn Bree *uh*

St. Budeaux, England : Saynt *Byooh* doh (UK Sunt...)

St. Catherines, Canada : Saynt *Kath* rinz (UK Sunt...)

St.-Chamond, France : Sahn Shah *mawn*

St. Charles, USA : Saynt *Chahrlz* (UK Sunt *Chahlz*)

St.-Chély-d'Apcher, France : Sahn Chay lee dahp *shay*

St. Clair, Canada; USA : Saynt *Kler* (UK Sunt *Klay* a)

St. Cloud, USA : Saynt *Klowd* (UK Sunt...)

St.-Cloud, France : Sahn *Klooh*

St. Columb, England : Saynt *Kah* lum (UK Sunt *Kol* um) [This pronunciation is valid for the three Cornish villages *St. Columb Major*, *St. Columb Minor* (now a district of Newquay), and *St. Columb Road*, although the stress in these names will fall on the final word.]

St. Croix, USA : Saynt *Kroy* (UK Sunt...)

St. David's, Wales : Saynt *Day* vidz (UK Sunt...)

St.-Denis, France; Réunion : Sahnd *nee*

St.-Denis-du-Sig, Algeria : Sahnd nee di *Seeg*

St.-Dié, France : Sahn *Dyay*

St.-Dizier, France : Sahn Dee *zyay*

Ste.-Anne, Guadeloupe : Sahnt *An*

Ste.-Foy, Canada : Sahnt *Fwah*

Ste. Genevieve, USA : Saynt *Jen* a veev (UK Sunt...)

Ste.-Menehoud, France : Sahnt Muh *nooh*

St. Erth, England : Saynt *Uhrth* (UK Sunt *Uhth*)

Saintes, France : Sahnt

St.-Étienne, France : Sahnt Ay *tyen*

St.-Étienne-de-St.-Geoirs, France : Sahnt Ay tyend Sahn Zhwahr

St.-Eustache, Canada : Sahnt Uh *stahsh*

St. Fagans, Wales : Saynt *Fag* unz (UK Sunt...)

St.-Fons, France : Sahn *Fawn*

St. Gall, Switzerland : Saynt *Gawl* (UK Sunt...) [This is the anglicized form of the next name.]

St.-Gall, Switzerland : Sahn *Gal*

St.-Gaudens, France : Sahn Goh *dahns*

St.-Genier-d'Olt, France : Sahn Zhuh nyay *dawlt*

St. George, USA : Saynt *Jawrj* (UK Sunt *Jawj*)

St. George's, Grenada : Saynt *Jawrj* uz (UK Sunt *Jawj* iz)

St.-Germain, France : Sahn Zher *mahn*

St.-Gildas-de-Rhuys, France : Sahn Zheel dahd *Rwees*

St.-Girons, France : Sahn Zhee *rawn*

St. Gotthard, Switzerland : Saynt *Gah* turd (UK Sunt *Got* ud)

St. Govan's Head, Wales : Saynt Gah vunz *Hed* (UK Sunt...) [The local pronunciation of the headland's name is Sunt *Gov* unz.]

St.-Gratien, France : Sahn Grah *syahn*

St.-Guilhem-le-Désert, France : Sahn Gee yem luh Day *zer*

St. Helena, Atlantic Ocean : Saynt Hi *lee* na (UK Sunt...)

St. Helens, England : Saynt *Hel* unz (UK Sunt...)

St. Helier, Channel Islands, Europe : Saynt *Hel* yur (UK Sunt *Hel* i a)

St.-Hyacinthe, Canada : Saynt *Hiy* a

sinth (UK Sunt...) (French Sahnt Yah *sahnt*)

St. Ignace, USA : Saynt *Ig* nus (UK Sunt...)

St. Issey, England : Saynt *Iz* i (UK Sunt...) [The saint in the name of the Cornish village is the same as in the name of **Mevagissey**, but there usually pronounced *Is* i.]

St. Ive, England : Saynt *Eev* (UK Sunt...) [The saint in the name of the Cornish village is not the same as in **St. Ives**.]

St. Ives, England : Saynt *Iyvz* (UK Sunt...) [The pronunciation is valid for both the Cambridgeshire (formerly Huntingdonshire) town and the Cornish seaside resort.]

St.-Jean-de-Losne, France : Sahn Zhahnd *Lohn*

St.-Jean-de-Luz, France : Sahn Zhahnd *Leez*

St.-Jean-en-Royans, France : Sahn Zhahn ahn Rwah *yawn*

St.-Jean-sur-Richelieu, Canada : Sahn Zhahn seer Reesh *lyuh*

St.-Jeoire, France : Sahn *Zhwahr*

St.-Jérôme, Canada : Sahn Zhay *rohm*

Saint John, Canada : Saynt *Jahn* (UK ... *Jon*) [*Saint* in the name of the New Brunswick seaport city is properly written and spoken in full.]

St. John's, Antigua and Barbuda; Canada : Saynt *Jahnz* (UK Sunt *Jonz*)

St. Joseph, USA : Saynt *Joh* zuf (UK Sunt *Joh* zif)

St. Just, England : Saynt *Jahst* (UK Sunt...)

St. Keyne, England : Saynt *Kayn* (UK Sunt...)

St. Kilda, Australia; Scotland : Saynt *Kil* da (UK Sunt...)

St. Kitts, West Indies : Saynt *Kits* (UK Sunt...)

St.-Lambert, Canada : Saynt *Lam* burt (UK Sunt *Lam* but) (French Sahn Lahn *ber*)

St. Laurent, Canada : San Loh *rahn* (UK ... Lo *rong*)

St. Lawrence, Canada : Saynt *Law* runs (UK Sunt *Lor* uns)

St. Leonard, Canada : San Lay oh *nahr* [The pronunciation of the Quebec city's name represents that of its French spelling as *St.-Léonard*.]

St. Leonards, England : Saynt *Len* urdz (UK Sunt *Len* udz)

St.-Lô, France : Sahn *Loh*

St. Louis, USA : Saynt *Looh* us (UK Sunt *Looh* is) [*Cp.* **Louisville**.]
   St. Louis, to the people of the city, is *St. Lewis* [Mencken, p. 541].

St.-Louis, Réunion; Senegal : Sahn *Lwee*

St. Lucia, West Indies : Saynt *Looh* sha (UK Sunt...)

St.-Malo, France : Sahn Mah *loh* [The seaport city's name is sometimes given the anglicized British pronunciation Sunt *Mah* loh, as current during and after World War II.]

St.-Marc, Haiti : Saynt *Mahrk* (UK Sunt *Mahk*)

St. Maries, USA : Saynt Ma *reez* (UK Sunt...)

St.-Mars-la-Jaille, France : Sahn Mahr la *Zhiy*

St.-Martin-de-Seignanx, France : Sahn Mahr tahnd Sayn *yahns*

St.-Maur-des-Fossés, France : Sahn Mawr day Faw *say*

St. Mawes, England : Saynt *Mawz* (UK Sunt...)

St. Mawgan, England : Saynt *Maw* gun (UK Sunt...)

St.-Max, France : Sahn *Mah*

St.-Méen-le-Grand, France : Sahn May ahn luh *Grahn*

St.-Mihiel, France : Sahn Mee *yel*

St. Monance, Scotland : Saynt *Moh* nuns (UK Sunt...)

St. Moritz, Switzerland : Saynt *Maw* rits (UK Sunt *Mor* its)

St.-Nazaire, France : Sahn Nah *zer*

St. Neot, England : Saynt *Nee* ut (UK Sunt *Nee* ut)

St. Neots, England : Saynt *Nee* uts (UK Sunt...) [The name of the Cam-

bridgeshire (former Huntingdonshire) town is pronounced Sunt *Neets*
by some, and this is the form recommended by Lloyd James 1936 and
Ross, p. 154. Forster also lists it as the
primary pronunciation in the sources
he cites. But Sunt *Nee* uts is now the
regular spoken form.]

St. Ninians, Scotland : Saynt *Nin* yunz
(UK Sunt *Nin* i unz)

St.-Omer, France : Sahnt Aw *mer*

St. Osyth, England : Saynt *Oh* zuth
(UK Sunt *Oh* zith)

St.-Ouen, France : Sahnt *Wahn*

St. Pancras, England : Saynt *Pang* krus
(UK Sunt...)

St. Paul, USA : Saynt *Pawl* (UK
Sunt...)

St.-Paul, Réunion : Sahn *Pawl*

St.-Père-en-Retz, France : Sahn Per
ahn *Ray*

St. Peter Port, Channel Islands, Europe
: Saynt Pee tur *Pawrt* (UK Sunt Pee ta
Pawt)

St. Petersburg, Russia; USA : Saynt
Pee turz buhrg (UK Sunt *Pee* tuz
buhg)

St.-Pierre, Martinique; Réunion; St.-
Pierre and Miquelon : Saynt *Pir* (UK
Sunt *Pi* a) (French Sahn *Pyer*)

St.-Pierre-Montlimart, France : Sahn
Pyer Mawn lee *mahr*

St.-Pol-de-Léon, France : Sahn Pawld
Lay *awn*

St.-Pons-de-Thomières, France : Sahn
Pawnd Taw *myer*

St.-Priest, France : Sahn Pree *est*

St.-Quentin, France : Sahn Kahn *tahn*

St.-Raphaël, France : Sahn Rah fah *el*

St.-Saëns, France : Sahn *Sahns*

St.-Saulve, France : Sahn *Sawlv*

St.-Sever, France : Sahn Sa *vay*

St. Teath, England : Saynt *Teth* (UK
Sunt...)

St. Thomas, Canada : Saynt *Tah* mus
(UK Sunt *Tom* us)

St.-Tropez, France : Sahn Traw *pay*

St. Tudy, England : Saynt *Tooh* di (UK
Sunt *Tyooh* di)

St.-Vaast-la-Hougue, France : Sahn
Vah la *Oohg*

St. Vigeans, Scotland : Saynt *Vij* unz
(UK Sunt...)

St. Vincent, St. Vincent and the
Grenadines : Saynt *Vin* sunt (UK
Sunt...)

St.-Yrieix-la-Perche, France : Sahnt Ee
ryay la *Persh*

Saïs, Egypt : *Say* is

Saipan, Pacific Ocean : Siy *pan*

Sakai, Japan : Sah *kiy*

Sakha, Russia : *Sah* kha

Sakhalin, Russia : *Sak* a leen (Russian
Sa kha *leen*)

Sakon Nakhon, Thailand : Sa kawn Na
kawn

Salaberry de Valleyfield, Canada : Sal a
ber i di *Val* i feeld (French Sah la bay
reed Vah lay *feeld*)

Salamá, Guatemala : Sah lah *mah*

Salamanca, Mexico; Spain : Sal a *mang*
ka (Spanish Sah lah *mahng* kah)

Salamis, Cyprus; Greece : *Sal* a mis

Salatiga, Indonesia : Sah la *tee* ga

Salavat, Russia : Sa *lah* vaht

Salbris, France : Sal *bree*

Salcedo, Dominican Republic : Sahl *say*
dhoh

Salcombe, England : *Sawl* kum

Sale, Australia; England : Sayl

Salé, Morocco : Sa *lay*

Salekhard, Russia : Sa li *khahrt*

Salem, India; USA : *Say* lum

Salerno, Italy : Sa *ler* noh (UK Sa *luh*
noh)

Salers, France : Sah *lers*

Salford, England : *Sawl* furd (UK *Sawl*
fud) [The name of the city near
Manchester has a local alternate pronunciation *Sal* fud.]

Salgótarján, Hungary : *Shawl* goh tawr
yahn

Salida, USA : Sa *liy* da

Salies-de-Béarn, France : Sah lees duh
Bay *ahrn*

Salies-du-Salat, France : Sah lees di Sah
lah

¹Salina, Italy : Sah *lee* nah

²**Salina**, USA : Sa *liy* na

Salinas, USA : Sa *lee* nus

¹**Saline**, Scotland : *Sal* in

²**Saline**, USA : Sa *leen*

Salisbury, England; USA : *Sawlz* ber i (UK *Sawlz* bri)

Salonica, Greece : Sa *lah* ni ka (UK Sa *lon* i ka)

Salta, Argentina : *Sahl* tah

Saltaire, England : *Sawl* ter (UK *Sawl* tay a)

Saltash, England : *Sawl* tash

Saltburn, England : *Sawlt* buhrn (UK *Sawlt* buhn)

Saltcoats, Scotland : *Sawlt* kohts

Saltillo, Mexico : Sahl *tee* yoh

Salt Lake City, USA : Sawlt Layk *Si* ti

Salto, Argentina; Uruguay : *Sahl* toh

Salto del Guiará, Paraguay : Sahl toh dhel Gee ah *rah*

Salton Sea, USA : Sawl tun *See*

Salvador, Brazil : *Sal* va dawr (UK *Sal* va daw) (Portuguese Sahl vah *dohr*)

Salvatierra, Mexico : Sahl vah *tyay* rah

Salween, Asia : *Sal* ween

Salzburg, Austria : *Sawlz* buhrg (UK *Salts* buhg) (German *Zahlts* boork) [The name of the city and musical center has been handled variously by English speakers. "To use the German pronunciation would be slightly pedantic," says Ross, p. 154, while earlier Lloyd James 1937 recommended a compromise in the form of US *Zalts* buhrg, UK *Zalts* buhg.]

Salzgitter, Germany : *Zahlts* git ur

Salzwedel, Germany : *Zahlts* vay dul

Samaná, Dominican Republic : Sah mah *nah*

Samar, Philippines : *Sah* mahr (UK *Sah* mah)

Samara, Russia : Sa *mah* ra

Samaria, West Bank : Sa *mer* i a (UK Sa *may* a ri a)

Samarinda, Indonesia : Sa ma *rin* da

Samarkand, Uzbekistan : *Sam* ur kand (UK Sam ah *kand*) (Russian Sa mahr *kahnt*)

Samarra, Iraq : Sa *mah* ra

Samer, France : Sah *may*

Samlesbury, England : *Samz* ber i (UK *Samz* bri)

Samoa, Pacific Ocean : Sa *moh* a

Samoëns, France : Sah maw *ahns*

Samokov, Bulgaria : *Sah* ma kawf

Samos, Greece : *Say* mahs (UK *Say* mos)

Samosir, Indonesia : Sah moh *sir*

Samothrace, Greece : *Sam* a thrays (UK *Sam* oh thrays)

Samsun, Turkey : Sahm *soohn*

Samut Prakan, Thailand : Sah mooht Prah *kahn*

Samut Songkhram, Thailand : Sah mooht Sung *krahm*

Sanaa, Yemen : Sah *nah*

Sanandaj, Iran : Sah nun *dahj*

San Andreas (Fault), USA : San An *dray* us

San Andrés, Colombia : Sahn Ahn *drays*

San Andres Tuxtla, Mexico : Sahn Ahn drays *Toohs* tlah

San Angelo, USA : San *An* ja loh

San Antonio, USA : San An *toh* ni oh [A local elided pronunciation San *toh* ni oh also exists for the name of the Texas city, as described in the quote below.]

> San Antonio, Tex., is *Santonyo*, although the second *an* is often inserted by the fastidious [Mencken, p. 541].

San Antonio de los Baños, Cuba : Sahn Ahn toh nyoh dhay lohs *Bah* nyohs

San Bernardino, USA : San Buhr nur *dee* noh (UK ... Buh na *dee* noh) [The California city is locally also known as San Buhr *dooh* or even just Buhr *dooh*.]

San Bernardo, Chile : Sahn Ber *nahr* doh

San Bruno, USA : San *Brooh* noh

San Carlos, Nicaragua; Philippines; USA; Venezuela : San *Kahr* lus (UK ... *Kah* los) (Spanish Sahn *Kahr* lohs)

San Carlos de Bariloche, Argentina : San Kahr lus day Bah ri *loh* chay

(Spanish Sahn Kahr lohs dhay Bah ree *loh* chay)

Sancerre, France : Sahn *ser*

Sánchez Ramírez, Dominican Republic : Sahn chays Rah *mee* rays

San Clemente, USA : San Kla *men* ti

San Cristóbal, Cuba; Dominican Republic; Mexico; Venezuela : Sahn Krees *toh* bahl

Sancti Spíritus, Cuba : Sahnk tee *Spee* ree toohs

Sandakan, Malaysia : Sahn dah *kahn*

Sanday, Scotland : *San* day

Sandbach, England : *Sand* bach

Sandefjord, Norway : *Sah* na fyoohr

Sanderson, USA : *San* dur son (UK *San* da sun)

Sanderstead, England : *San* dur sted (UK *Sahn* da sted)

Sandhurst, England : *Sand* huhrst (UK *Sand* huhst)

San Diego, USA : San Di *ay* goh

Sandnes, Norway : *Sahn* nus

Sandomierz, Poland : Sahn *daw* myesh

Sandown, England : *San* down

Sandringham, Australia; England : *Sand* ring um

Sandusky, USA : San *dahs* ki

Sandviken, Sweden : *Sand* vee kun

Sandwich, England; USA : *Sand* wij

Sandy, England; USA : *San* di

San Felipe, Colombia; Venezuela : Sahn Fay *lee* pay

San Fernando, Argentina; Chile; Philippines; Trinidad and Tobago; USA; Venezuela : San Fur *nan* doh (UK ... Fa *nan* doh) (Spanish Sahn Fer *nahn* doh)

San Francisco, Argentina; USA : San Frun *sis* koh (Spanish Sahn Frahn *sees* koh)

San Francisco de Macorís, Dominican Republic : Sahn Frahn sees koh dhay Mah koh *rees*

San Gabriel, USA : San *Gay* bri ul

Sangerhausen, Germany : *Zahng* ur how zun

San Germán, Puerto Rico : Sahng Her *mahng*

Sangihe (Islands), Indonesia : Sahng *gee* a

San Gimignano, Italy : Sahn Jee mee *nyah* noh

Sangre de Cristo (Mountains), USA : Sang gri da *Kris* toh

San Ignacio, Belize; Paraguay : Sahn Eeg *nah* syoh

San Isidro, Argentina; Costa Rica : Sahn Ee *see* dhroh

¹**San Jacinto**, USA (California) : San Ya *sin* toh

²**San Jacinto**, USA (Texas) : San Ja *sin* toh

San Joaquin, USA : San Wah *keen*

San Jose, Philippines; USA : San Hoh zay (Spanish Sahng Hoh *say*)

San José, Costa Rica; Guatemala; Uruguay : Sahng Hoh *say*

San José de Buenavista, Philippines : Sahng Hoh say day Bway nah *vees* tah

San José de Guanipa, Venezuela : Sahng Hoh say dhay *Gwah* nee pah

San José de las Lajas, Cuba : Sahng Hoh say dhay lahs *Lah* hahs

San Juan, Argentina; Dominican Republic; Philippines; Puerto Rico; USA : San *Wahn* (Spanish Sahn *Hwahn*)

San Juan Bautista, Paraguay : Sahn Hwahn Bow *tees* tah

San Juan Capistrano, USA : San Hwahn Kap i *strah* noh

San Juan de la Maguana, Dominican Republic : Sahn Hwahn dhay lah Mah *gwah* nah

San Juan de los Morros, Venezuela : Sahn Hwahn dhay lohs *Mohr* rohs

San Juan del Río, Mexico : Sahn Hwahn dhel *Ree* oh

San Justo, Argentina : Sahn *Hoohs* toh

Sankt Gallen, Switzerland : Zahngtk *Gah* lun

Sankt Ingbert, Germany : Zahngkt *Ing* bert

Sankt Pöllten, Austria : Sankt *Puhl* tun (German Zahngkt *Puhl* tun)

San Leandro, USA : San Lee *an* droh

San Lorenzo, Argentina; Honduras;

Paraguay; Puerto Rico; USA : San La *ren* zoh (Spanish Sahn Loh *ren* zoh)

Sanlucar de Barrameda, Spain : Sahn Looh kahr dhay Bah rah *may* dhah

San Luis, Argentina; Cuba : Sahn *Lwees*

San Luis Obispo, USA : San Looh is A *bis* poh

San Luis Potosí, Mexico : Sahn Lwees Poh toh *see*

San Luis Río Colorado, Mexico : Sahn Lwees Ree oh Koh loh *rah* dhoh

San Marcos, Guatemala; USA : San *Mahr* kus (UK San *Mah* kus) (Spanish Sahn *Mahr* kohs)

San Marino, Europe : San Ma ree noh (Italian Sahn Mah *ree* noh)

San Martín, Argentina : Sahn Mahr *teen*

San Mateo, USA : San Ma *tay* oh

San Miguel, El Salvador; Philippines : Sahn Mi *gel*

San Miguel de Tucumán, Argentina : Sahn Mee gel dhay Tooh kooh *mahn*

San Nicolás de los Arroyos, Argentina : Sahn Nee kaw lahs dhay lohs Ahr *roh* yohs

San Pablo, Philippines : Sahn *Pah* bloh

[1]**San Pedro**, Argentina; Bolivia; Colombia; Costa Rica; Mexico : Sahn *Pay* dhroh

[2]**San Pedro**, USA : San *Pee* droh

San-Pédro, Côte d'Ivoire : Sahn *Pay* droh

San Pedro de Macorís, Dominican Republic : Sahn Pay dhroh dhay Mah koh *rees*

San Pedro Sula, Honduras : Sahn Pay dhroh *Sooh* lah

Sanquhar, Scotland : *Sang* kur (UK *Sang* ka)

[1]**San Rafael**, Argentina : Sahn Rah fah *el*

[2]**San Rafael**, USA : San Ra *fel*

San Remo, Italy : San *Ray* moh

San Salvador, El Salvador : San *Sal* va dawr (UK ... *Sal* va daw) (Spanish Sahn Sahl vah *dhawr*)

San Salvador de Jujuy, Argentina : Sahn Sahl vah dhawr dhay Hooh *hwee*

San Sebastián, Argentina; Puerto Rico : Sahn Say Bahs *tyahn*

Santa Ana, El Salvador; USA : San ta *An* a (UK Santur...) (Spanish Sahn tah *Ah* nah)

Santa Barbara, Philippines; USA : San ta *Bahr* bur a (UK ... *Bah* bra)

Santa Bárbara, Honduras : Sahn tah *Bahr* bah rah

Santa Catalina, USA : San ta Ka ta *lee* na

Santa Catarina, Brazil : Sahn tah Kah tah *ree* nah

Santa Clara, Cuba; USA : San ta *Klar* a (Spanish Sahn tah *Klah* rah)

Santa Cruz, Bolivia; Philippines; USA : *San* ta Kroohz (UK San ta *Kroohz*) (Spanish Sahn tah *Kroohs*) [Ross, p. 155, says that the various places of this name are "usually" pronounced San ta *Krahz*, but this is hardly the case today.]

Santa Cruz del Quiché, Guatemala : Sahn tah Kroohs dhel Kee *chay*

Santa Cruz del Sur, Cuba : Sahn tah Kroohs dhel *Soohr*

Santa Cruz de Tenerife, Canary Islands : Sahn tah Kroohs dhay Tay nay *ree* fay

Santa Fe, Argentina; USA : *San* ta Fay (UK San ta *Fay*) (Spanish Sahn tah *Fay*)

Santa Isabel, Equatorial Guinea : San ta *Iz* a bel (Spanish Sahn tah *Ee* sah bel)

Santa Maria, Brazil; USA : San ta Ma *ree* a (Portuguese Sahn ta Mah *ree* a)

Santa Marta, Colombia : Sahn tah *Mahr* tah

Santa Monica, USA : San ta *Mah* ni ka (UK ... *Mon* i ka)

Santana do Livramento, Brazil : Sahn tah na dooh Lee vra *men* tooh

Santander, Colombia; Spain : Sahn tahn *der* (UK San tun *day* a) [British speakers sometimes pronounce the Spanish seaport's name as San *tan* da.]

Santarém, Brazil; Portugal : Sahn ta *rem*

Santa Rita, Brazil : Sahn ta *Ree* ta

Santa Rosa, Argentina; Honduras; USA : San ta *Roh* za (Spanish Sahn tah *Roh* sah)

Santee, USA : San *tee*

Santiago, Brazil; Chile; Dominican Republic; Panama; Philippines; Spain : San ti *ah* goh (Spanish Sahn *tyah* goh)

Santiago de Compostela, Spain : Sahn tyah goh dhay Kawm poh *stay* lah

Santiago de Cuba, Cuba : Sahn tyah goh dhay *Kooh* bah

Santiago del Estero, Argentina : Sahn tyah goh dhel Es *tay* roh

Santiago de los Caballeros, Dominican Republic : Sahn tyah goh dhay laws Kah bah *yay* rohs

Santiago Rodríguez, Dominican Republic : Sahn tyah goh Raw *dree* gays

Santo Amaro, Brazil : San tooh A *mah* rooh

Santo André, Brazil : San tooh Ahn *dray*

Santo Ângelo, Brazil : San tooh *Ahn* zhay looh

Santo Antonio de Jesus, Brazil : San toh Ahn toh nyoh dhay *Hay* soohs

Santo Domingo, Dominican Republic : San ta Da *ming* goh (UK San toh...) (Spanish Sahn toh Dhoh *meeng* goh)

Santo Domingo de los Colorados, Ecuador : Sahn toh Dhoh meeng goh dhay lohs Koh loh *rah* dhohs

Santoríni, Greece : San ta *ree* ni

Santos, Brazil : *Sahn* toohsh

San Vicente, El Salvador : Sahn Vee *sen* tay

São Carlos, Brazil : Sown *Kahr* loohs

São Gonçalo, Brazil : Sown Gohn *sah* looh

São João del Rei, Brazil : Sown Zhwown del *Ray*

São João de Meriti, Brazil : Sown Zhwown dee Mi ree *tee*

São José do Rio Prêto, Brazil : Sown Zhoh zay dooh Ree ooh *Pray* tooh

São Leopoldo, Brazil : Sown Lyoh *pohl* dooh

São Lourenço, Brazil : Sown Loh *rayn* sooh

São Luís, Brazil : Sown *Lwees*

Saône, France : Sohn (French Sawn)

São Paolo, Brazil : Sowm *Pow* looh

São Tomé, São Tomé and Príncipe : Sown Ta *may*

São Vicente, Brazil : Sown Vee *sayn* tee

Sapele, Nigeria : Sah *pay* lay

Sapporo, Japan : Sah *poh* roh

Sapudi, Indonesia : Sa *pooh* di

Sara Buri, Thailand : Sah ra *Boor* ee

Saragossa, Spain : Sa ra *gah* sa (UK Sa ra *gos* a)

Sarajevo, Bosnia-Herzegovina : Sa ra *yay* voh (Serbo-Croat *Sah* rah ye vaw)

Saranac, USA : *Sar* a nak

Sarandë, Albania : Sa *rahn* da

Saransk, Russia : Sa *rahnsk*

Sarapul, Russia : Sa *rah* pool

Sarasota, USA : Sa ra *soh* ta

Saratoga, USA : Sa ra *toh* ga

Saratoga Springs, USA : Sa ra toh ga *Springz*

Saratov, Russia : Sa *rah* tahv (UK Sa *rah* tov) (Russian Sa *rah* tuf)

Sarawak, Malaysia : Sa *rah* wahk

Sardinia, Italy : Sahr *din* i a (UK Sah *din* i a)

Sardis, Turkey : *Sahr* dis (UK *Sah* dis)

Sargasso (Sea), Atlantic Ocean : Sahr *gas* oh (UK Sah *gas* oh)

Sarghoda, Pakistan : Sur *goh* da

Sarh, Chad : Sahr (UK Sah)

Sari, Iran : Sah *ree*

Sariwŏn, North Korea : Sah ree *wahn*

Sark, Channel Islands, Europe : Sahrk (UK Sahk)

Sarmatia, Europe : Sahr *may* sha (UK Sah *may* sha)

Sarnen, Switzerland : *Zahr* nun

Sarnia, Canada : *Sahr* ni a (UK *Sah* ni a)

Saronic (Gulf), Greece : Sa *rah* nik (UK Sa *ron* ik)

Saros (Gulf), Turkey : *Sar* ahs (UK *Sa* ros)

Sarpsborg, Norway : *Sahrps* bawr

Sarreguemines, France : Sahrg *meen*

Sarthe, France : Sahrt

Sasebo, Japan : *Sah* say boh

Saskatchewan, Canada : Sas *kach* a wahn (UK Sas *kach* a wun)

Saskatoon, Canada : Sas ka *toohn*

Sasolburg, South Africa : *Sah* sul buhrg (UK *Sah* sul buhg)

Sassandra, Côte d'Ivoire : Sa *san* dra

Sassari, Italy : *Sah* sah ree

Sátoraljaújhely, Hungary : *Shah* tohr oy jowj hay

Satterthwaite, England : *Sat* ur thwayt (UK *Sat* a thwayt)

Satu Mare, Romania : Sah tooh *Mah* ray

Saudi Arabia, Asia : Sow di A *ray* bi a

Saugus, USA : *Saw* gus

Sauk, USA : Sawk

Sault Ste. Marie, Canada; USA : Sooh Saynt Ma *ree* [As suggested by the passage quoted below, the pronunciation of *Sault* ("Falls") for the identically named cities, respectively in Michigan, USA, and Ontario, Canada, may have been influenced by *Sioux*.]
> In Northern Michigan the pronunciation of *Sault* in *Sault Ste. Marie* is commonly more or less correct; the Minneapolis, St. Paul & Sault Ste. Marie Railroad is called the *Soo*, and there is a *Soo* canal. This may be due to Canadian example, or to some confusion between *Sault* and *Sioux* [Mencken, p. 542].

Saumur, France : Soh *meer*

Saundersfoot, Wales : *Sawn* durz foot (UK *Sawn* duz foot)

Saunton, England : *Sawn* tun

Saurimo, Angola : Sow ree moh

Savai'i, Samoa : Sa *viy* ee

Savannah, USA : Sa *van* a

Savannakhet, Laos : Sa vah na *ket*

Savanna-la-Mar, Jamaica : Sa van a la *Mahr* (UK ... *Mah*)

Savernake, England : *Sav* ur nak (UK *Sav* a nak) [An alternate pronunciation *Sav* a nayk exists for Savernake Forest in Wiltshire.]

Savona, Italy : Sah *voh* nah

Savonlinna, Finland : *Sah* vawn leen nah

Savoy, France : Sa *voy*

Savu, Indonesia : *Sah* vooh

Sawatch (Range), USA : Sa *wahch* (UK Sa *woch*)

Sawbridgeworth, England : *Saw* brij wuhrth (UK *Saw* brij wuhth) [The name of the Hertfordshire town was also at one time locally pronounced *Saps* wuth or *Sap* sed, giving written forms *Sapsworth* and *Sapsed*, as noted in quotes (1) and (4) for **Daventry**.] *Sawbridgeworth* may have been *Sapsed* in the past, but it is to be *Sawbridgeworth* in the future [Lloyd James 1936, p. 9].

Sawston, England : *Saw* stun

Sawtry, England : *Saw* tri

Saxmundham, England : Saks *mahn* dum

Saxony, Germany : *Sak* sun i

Sayan (Mountains), Russia : Sa *yahn*

Sayreville, USA : *Say* ur vil (UK *Say* a vil)

Scafell (Pike), England : *Skaw* fel]

Scalpay, Scotland : *Skal* pay

Scandicci, Italy : Skahn *dee* chee

Scandinavia, Europe : Skan di *nay* vi a

Scapa Flow, Scotland : Skap a *Floh* (UK Skah pa...)

Scarborough, Canada; England : *Skahr* buhr oh (UK *Skah* bra)

Scarisbrick, England : *Skerz* brik (UK *Skay* uz brik)

Scarsdale, USA : *Skahrz* dayl (UK *Skahz* dayl)

Schaan, Liechtenstein : Shahn

Schaerbeek, Belgium : *Skhahr* bayk

Schaffhausen, Switzerland : Shahf *how* zun

Schaghticoke, USA : *Skat* i kook

Schaumburg, USA : *Shawm* buhrg (UK *Shawm* buhg)

Scheidegg, Switzerland : *Shiy* dek

Schelde, Europe : *Skhel* da

Scheldt, Europe : Shelt

Schenectady, USA : Ska *nek* ta di

Scheveningen, Netherlands : *Skay* va ning un (Dutch *Skhay* va ning a) [The *Sch-* that begins Dutch (and Belgian) names is pronounced *s* followed immediately by *kh*, unlike the *Sch-* of German names, which is *sh*.]

Schiedam, Netherlands : *Skee* dam (Dutch Skhee *dahm*)

Schiehallion, Scotland : Shee *hal* yun

Schilde, Belgium : Skild (Flemish *Skhil* da)

Schiphol, Netherlands : *Skip* ohl (UK *Skip* ol) (Dutch Skhip *hawl*)

Schleicher, USA : *Shliy* kur (UK *Shliy* ka)

Schleswig, Germany : *Shlez* vig (German *Shlays* vikh)

Schleswig-Holstein, Germany : Shlez vig *Hol* stiyn (German Shlays vikh *Hawl* shtiyn)

Schlucht, France : Shloort

Schmalkalden, Germany : *Shmahl* kahl dun

Schönebeck, Germany : *Shuh* na bek

Schoten, Belgium : *Skoh* tun (Flemish *Skhaw* ten)

Schouten (Island), Australia : *Shooh* tun

Schouten (Islands), Indonesia : *Skow* tun

Schuylerville, USA : *Skiy* lur vil (UK *Skiy* la vil)

Schuylkill, USA : *Skoohl* kil

Schwabach, Germany : *Shfah* bahkh

Schwäbisch Gmünd, Germany : Shfay bish *Gmeent*

Schwäbisch Hall, Germany : Shfay bish *Hahl*

Schwarzwald, Germany : *Shvahrts* vahld (UK *Shvahts* vald) (German *Shvahrts* vahlt) [The more usual English name for the mountainous region is *Black Forest*.]

Schwedt, Germany : Shvayt

Schweinfurt, Germany : *Shfiyn* foort

Schwerin, Germany : Shfay *reen*

Schwerte, Germany : *Shfer* ta

Schwyz, Switzerland : Shfeets

Scilly (Isles), England : *Si* li

Scionzier, France : Syawn *zyay*

Scioto, USA : Siy *oh* toh

Scituate, USA : *Si* choo ayt

Scone, Australia; Scotland : Skoohn

[The name of the Australian town is also Skohn.]

Scoresby (Sound), Greenland : *Skawrz* bi (UK *Skawz* bi)

Scotia (Sea), Antarctica : *Skoh* sha

Scotland, Europe : *Skaht* lund (UK *Skot* lund)

Scotstoun, Scotland : *Skahts* tun (UK *Skots* tun)

Scottsbluff, USA : *Skahts* bluf (UK *Skots* blahf)

Scottsdale, USA : *Skahts* dayl (UK *Skots* dayl)

Scranton, USA : *Skran* tun

Scrooby, England : *Skrooh* bi

Scunthorpe, England : *Skahn* thawrp (UK *Skahn* thawp)

Scuppernong, USA : *Skah* pur nahng (UK *Skah* pa nong)

Scutari, Albania; Turkey : *Skooh* ta ri

Scythia, Eurasia : *Sith* i a (UK *Sidh* i a)

Seaford, England; USA : *See* furd (UK *See* fud) [The name of the town and resort in East Sussex, England, is alternately pronounced *See* fawd or See *fawd*. Ross, p. 156, approves the first of these, rejecting the now regular form *See* fud.]

Seaham, England : *See* um

Searcy, USA : *Suhr* si (UK *Suh* si)

Seascale, England : *See* skayl

Seaside, USA : *See* siyd

Seaton, England : *See* tun

Seaton Delaval, England : See tun *Del* a vul

Seattle, USA : See *at* ul

Sebastopol, Ukraine : Sa *bas* ta pohl (UK Sa *bas* ta pol)

Sebeş, Romania : *Say* besh

Sebha, Libya : *Seb* hah

Sebring, USA : *See* bring

Secaucus, USA : Si *kaw* kus

Secunderabad, India : Si *kahn* da ra bad

Sedalia, USA : Si *day* lya

Sedan, France; USA : Si *dan* (French Suh *dahn*)

Sedbergh, England : *Sed* buhrg (UK *Sed* ba) [An alternate UK pronunciation

Sed buhg exists for the Cumbria town, and was formerly also used for the public school here.]

Sedgefield, England : *Sej* feeld

Sedgemoor, England : *Sej* moor (UK *Sej* maw)

Sedlescombe, England : *Sed* ulz kum

Seekonk, USA : *See* kahngk (UK *See* kongk)

Ségou, Mali : Say *gooh*

Segovia, Spain : Si *goh* vi a (Spanish Say *goh* vyah)

Seguin, USA : Sa *geen*

Seinäjoki, Finland : *Say* na yaw kee

Seine, France : Sayn (French Sen)

Sekondi-Takoradi, Ghana : Sek un dee Tah ka *rah* day

Selangor, Malaysia : Sa *lang* oor (UK Sa *lang* a)

Selayar, Indonesia : Sa *lah* yur (UK Sa *lah* ya)

Selborne, England : *Sel* bawrn (UK *Sel* bawn)

Selby, England : *Sel* bi

Seldovia, USA : Sel *doh* vi a

Selebi-Phikwe, Botswana : Se lay bee *Pee* kway

Selenga, Asia : Si ling *gah*

Sélestat, France : Say les *tah*

Seleucia, Turkey : Sa *looh* sha (UK Sa *looh* si a)

Selkirk, Canada; Scotland : *Sel* kuhrk (UK *Sel* kuhk)

Selma, USA : *Sel* ma

Selsey, England : *Sel* si

Selukwe, Zimbabwe : Se *looh* kway

Semarang, Indonesia : Sa *mah* rahng

Semer Water, England : *Sem* ur Waw tur (UK *Sem* a Waw ta)

Semey, Kazakhstan : Se *may*

Semipalatinsk, Kazakhstan : Si mi pa *lah* tinsk

Semnan, Iran : Sem *nahn*

Semur-en-Auxois, France : Suh meer ahn Aw *swah*

Sendai, Japan : Sen *diy*

Seneca, USA : *Sen* i ka

Senegal, Africa : Sen i *gawl*

Senegambia, Africa : Sen i *gam* bi a

Senftenberg, Germany : *Zenf* tun berk

Senghenydd, Wales : Seng *hen* idh

Senigallia, Italy : Say ni *gah* lya

Senlis, France : Sahn *lees*

Senneterre, Canada : Sen *ter* (UK Sen *tay* a)

Sens, France : Sahns

Sensuntepeque, El Salvador : Sen soohn te *pay* kay

Seoul, South Korea : Sohl

Sept-Îles, Canada : Se *teel*

Seraing, Belgium : Sa *rahn*

Serang, Indonesia : *Say* rahng

Serbia, Europe : *Suhr* bi a (UK *Suh* bi a) [In the late 19th and early 20th centuries Serbia was known to English speakers as *Servia*, US *Suhr* vi a, UK *Suh* vi a.]

Serekunda, Gambia : Se re *koohn* dah

Seremban, Malaysia : Sa *rem* bun

Serengeti, Tanzania : Ser un *get* ee

Sergipe, Brazil : Ser *zhee* pee

Sergiyev Posad, Russia : *Syer* gi yif Pa saht

Seringapatam, India : Sa ring ga pa *tahm*

Serov, Russia : *Ser* uf

Serowe, Botswana : Sa *roh* way

Serpukhov, Russia : *Syer* pooh khuf

Serra do Mar, Brazil : Ser ra dooh *Mahr*

Sérrai, Greece : *Se* re

Seshego, South Africa : Se *shay* goh

Sessa Aurunca, Italy : Se sah Ow *roohng* kah

Sestao, Spain : Say *stow*

Sesto Fiorentino, Italy : Ses toh Fyawr en *tee* noh

Sestri Levante, Italy : Ses tree Lay *vahn* tay

Sète, France : Set

Sete Lagoas, Brazil : Se tee La *goh* us

Sétif, Algeria : Say *teef*

Settat, Morocco : Set *taht*

Setúbal, Portugal : Sa *tooh* bul

Sevastopol, Ukraine : Sa *vas* ta pohl (UK Sa *vas* ta pol) (Russian Si vas *taw* pul)

Sevenoaks, England : *Sev* nohks [A former pronunciation of the Kent town's name is on record as Snoohks, popularly regarded as the origin of the surname *Snooks*.]

Lower, followed by Bardsley and Weekley, derives this surname from the old pronunciation of Sevenoaks and states that Sussex deeds relating to a family of Snooks give all the modes of spelling from *Sevenoakes* down to *S'nokes* [P.H. Reaney and R.M. Wilson, *A Dictionary of English Surnames*, 3d ed., 1991].

Severn, England : *Sev* urn (UK *Sev* un)

Severnaya Zemlya, Russia : Sye vir na ya Zim *lyah*

Severodonetsk, Ukraine : Sye vi ra da *nyetsk*

Severodvinsk, Russia : Sye vi ra *dvinsk*

Severomorsk, Russia : Sye vi ra *mawrsk*

Sevilla, Colombia : Say *vee* yah

Seville, Spain : Sa *vil* [Lloyd James 1937 favored a pronunciation *Sev* il for the English form of the city's name, as now generally used for Seville oranges.]

For the Spanish city, stress second syllable. For the type of bitter orange and the marmalade made with it, stress first [Kingsley Amis, *The King's English*, 1997].

Sèvres, France : Sevr

Seychelles, Indian Ocean : Say *shelz*

Seymour, USA : *See* mawr (UK *See* maw)

Sfax, Tunisia : Sfaks

Sfîntu Gheorghe, Romania : Sfin tooh *Gyawr* ge

Shaanxi, China : Shahn *shee*

Shaba, Democratic Republic of the Congo : *Shah* ba

Shabani, Zimbabwe : Shah *bah* nay

Shackleton (Ice Shelf), Antarctica : *Shak* ul tun

Shaftesbury, England : *Shafs* ber i (UK *Shahfs* bri)

Shagamu, Nigeria : Shah *gah* mooh

Shah Alam, Malaysia : Shah *Ah* lum

Shahjahanpur, India : Shah ja *hahn* poor

Shahr-e Kord, Iran : Shahr ee *Kohrd*

Shakhrisabz, Uzbekistan : Sha khri *syahps*

Shakhtersk, Ukraine : Shahkh *tyawrsk*

Shakhty, Russia : *Shahkh* ti

Shaki, Nigeria : *Shah* ki

Shaldon, England : *Shawl* dun

Shalford, England : *Shal* furd (UK *Shal* fud)

Shan, Myanmar : Shahn

Shandong, China : Shahn *doong* (UK Shan *dong*)

Shanghai, China : Shahng *hiy* (UK Shang *hiy*)

Shanklin, England : *Shang* klin

Shannon, Ireland : *Shan* un

Shantou, China : Shahn *toh* (UK Shan *toh*)

Shantung, China : Shahn *tahng* (UK Shan *tahng*)

Shanxi, China : Shahn *shee* (UK Shan *shee*)

Shaoxing, China : Show *shing*

Shaoyang, China : Show *yahng*

Shap, England : Shap

Sharjah, United Arab Emirates : *Shahr* jah (UK *Shah* jah)

Sharm al-Sheikh, Egypt : Shahrm ahl *Sheek*

¹Sharon, Israel : *Shah* run (UK *Shay* a run)

²Sharon, USA : *Shar* un

Sharpsburg, USA : *Shahrps* buhrg (UK *Shahps* buhg)

Shashi, China : Shah *shee*

Shasta, USA : *Shas* ta

Shatt al Arab, Asia : Shat al *A* rub

Shawangunk (Mountains), USA : *Shahng* gum [The quote below refers to the US essayist Richard G. White (1821–1885).]

White said that in his youth the name of the *Shawangunk* mountains, in New York, was pronounced *Shongo*, but that the custom of pronouncing it as spelled had arisen during his manhood [Mencken, p. 540]. (A footnote adds: "This spelling pronunciation seems to have disappeared. The local pronunciation today is *Shongum*.")

Shawinigan, Canada : Sha *win* i gun
Shawnee, USA : Shaw *nee*
Shchelkovo, Russia : *Shchawl* ka va
Shchuchinsk, Kazakhstan : *Shchooh* chinsk
Sheba, Arabia : *Shee* ba
Sheboygan, USA : Shi *boy* gun
Sheerness, England : Shir *nes* (UK Shi a *nes*)
Sheffield, England; USA : *Shef* eeld [A local pronunciation *Shef* ild also exists for the English city's name.]
Shefford, England : *Shef* urd (UK *Shef* ud)
Shelburne, Canada : *Shel* buhrn (UK *Shel* bun)
Shelby, USA : *Shel* bi
Shelbyville, USA : *Shel* bi vil
Shelton, USA : *Shel* tun
Shemakha, Azerbaijan : Shem a *khah*
Shenandoah, USA : Shen un *doh* a
Shenyang, China : Shen *yahng* (UK Shen *yang*)
Shenzhen, China : Shen *jen*
Shepherdswell, England : *Shep* urdz wel (UK *Shep* udz wel) [The name of the Kent village was originally *Sibertswold*, but this gradually acquired the present pronunciation and a spelling to match (*Shepardysweld* as early as the 16th century.) When the East Kent Railway opened a station here in 1916 the current name was endorsed, although *Sibertswold* is given as an alternate in some present-day gazetteers and atlases, so that "Shepherdswell or Sibertswold" appears in the index to *Kent* (2001) in the Automobile Association's "Street by Street" series.]
Shepparton, Australia : *Shep* ur tun (UK *Shep* a tun)
Sheppey, England : *Shep* i
Shepreth, England : *Shep* ruth
Shepshed, England : *Shep* shed
Shepton Mallet, England : Shep tun *Mal* it
Sherborne, England : *Shuhr* bawrn (UK *Shuh* bun)

Sherbro (Island), Sierra Leone : *Shuhr* broh (UK *Shuh* broh)
Sherbrooke, Canada : *Shuhr* brook (UK *Shuh* brook)
Shere, England : Shir (UK *Shi* a)
Sheridan, USA : *Sher* a dun (UK *Sher* i dun)
Sheringham, England : *Sher* ing um
Sherman, USA : *Shuhr* mun (UK *Shuh* man)
's Hertogenbosch, Netherlands : Ser toh khun *baws*
Sherwood (Forest), England : *Shuhr* wood (UK *Shuh* wood)
Shetland, Scotland : *Shet* lund
Shibin al-Kawm, Egypt : Shi been al *Kawm*
Shifnal, England : *Shif* nul
Shijiazhuang, China : Shi ji a joo *ahng* (UK Shi ji a joo *ang*)
Shikoku, Japan : Shee *koh* kooh
Shillong, India : Shi *lawng*
Shiloh, West Bank : *Shiy* loh
Shimizu, Japan : Shee *mee* zooh
Shimonoseki, Japan : Shee moh noh *se* kee
Shinyanga, Tanzania : Shee *nyahng* gah
Shipka (Pass), Bulgaria : *Ship* ka
Shipley, England : *Ship* li
Shipston on Stour, England : Ship stun ahn *Stow* ur (UK ... on *Stow* a)
Shiraz, Iran : Shee *rahz*
Shire, Malawi : *Shir* ay (UK *Shi* a ray)
Shirley, England : *Shuhr* li (UK *Shuh* li)
Shirvan, Azerbaijan : Shir *vahn*
Shishaldin, USA : Shi *shal* dun
Shizuoka, Japan : Shee zoo *woh* ka
Shkodër, Albania : *Shkoh* dur
Shoalhaven, Australia : Shohl *hay* vun
Shoeburyness, England : Shooh bri *nes*
Sholapur, India : *Shoh* la poor
Shoreham-by-Sea, England : Shaw rum biy *See*
Shoshone, USA : Sha *shoh* ni
Shotton, Wales : *Shah* tun (UK *Shot* un)
Show Low, USA : *Shoh* Loh
Shreveport, USA : *Shreev* pawrt (UK *Shreev* pawt)

¹Shrewsbury, England : *Shrohz* ber i (UK *Shrohz* bri) [The name of the Shropshire town is locally also pronounced as for **²Shrewsbury**, and this is equally the form used by those unfamiliar with the place. The "correct" pronunciation is thus mostly associated with "county" (landed) families or by members of Shrewsbury School, one of the nation's leading public schools. The pronunciation came about because words such as *shrew* and *shrewd* were formerly pronounced to rhyme with *show* and *showed*, as seen in the lines from Shakespeare quoted below (in which *shrew* has its variant spelling of *shrow*.) An occasional local pronunciation *Shoohz* bri, omitting the *r*, is also sometimes heard.]

> *Rosaline.* O, that your face were not so full of O's!
> *Katharine.* A pox of that jest! and beshrew all shrows! [*Love's Labour's Lost*, II. ii. 45, 1598].

²Shrewsbury, USA : *Shroohz* ber i (UK *Shroohz* bri)

Shrivenham, England : *Shriv* num

Shropshire, England : *Shrahp* shur (UK *Shrop* sha)

Shubra al-Khaymah, Egypt : Shooh brah el *Khay* ma

Shumagin (Islands), USA : *Shooh* ma geen

Shumen, Bulgaria : *Shooh* men

Shurugwi, Zimbabwe : Shooh *rooh* gwi

Shuswap, Canada : *Shoos* wahp (UK *Shoos* wop)

Shuya, Russia : *Shooh* ya

Shweba, Myanmar : *Shway* boh

Shymkent, Kazakhstan : Shim *kent*

Sialkot, Pakistan : *Syahl* koht

Siam, Asia : Siy *am*

Šiauliai, Lithuania : *Show* lay

Šibenik, Croatia : Shee *ben* ik

Siberia, Russia : Siy *bir* i a (UK Siy *bi* a ri a)

Siberut, Indonesia : See ba *rooht*

Sibiu, Romania : See *bee* ooh

Sible Hedingham, England : Sib ul *Hed* ing um

Sibolga, Indonesia : Si *bol* ga

Sichuan, China : Sich *wahn*

Sicily, Italy : *Sis* a li

Sidcup, England : *Sid* kahp

Sidi Barrani, Egypt : See dee Ba *rah* nee

Sidi Bel Abbès, Algeria : See dee Bel A *bes*

Sidi Kacem, Morocco : See dee *Kah* sum

Sidlaw (Hills), Scotland : *Sid* law

Sidmouth, England : *Sid* muth

Sidney, Canada; USA : *Sid* ni

Sidoarjo, Indonesia : See doh *ahr* joh

Sidon, Lebanon : *Siy* dun

Siedlce, Poland : *Shed* ul tse

Siegen, Germany : *Zee* gun

Siemianowice Śląskie, Poland : She myah naw *veet* se Shlawn skee a

Siem Reap, Cambodia : See um *Ree* up

Siena, Italy : See *en* ah

Sieradz, Poland : *Sher* ahts

Sierra Leone, Africa : See er a Lee *ohn*

Sierra Madre, Mexico; Philippines : See er a *Mah* dray (Spanish Syer rah *Mah* dhray)

Sierra Morena, Spain : Syer rah Moh *ray* nah

¹Sierra Nevada, Spain : Syer rah Nay *vah* dhah

²Sierra Nevada, USA : See er a Na *vad* a (UK ... Ni *vah* da)

Sierra Vista, USA : See er a *Vis* ta

Sig, Algeria : Seeg

Sighet Marmaţiei, Romania : See get Mahr mah *tyay*

Sighişoara, Romania : See gee *shwah* rah

Siglufjördhur, Iceland : *Sig* lee fyuhr dheer

Siguiri, Guinea : Si *gee* ri

Siirt, Turkey : Si *yirt*

Sikasso, Mali : Si *kah* soh

Sikhote Alin (Range), Russia : See kha tay A *leen*

Sikkim, India : *Sik* im

Silbury (Hill), England : *Sil* ber i (UK *Sil* bri)

Silchar, India : Sil *chahr*
Silchester, England : *Sil* chis tur (UK *Sil* chis ta)
Silesia, Europe : Siy *lee* zha (UK Siy *lee* zi a)
Silistra, Bulgaria : Si *lis* tra
Silloth, England : *Sil* uth
Silverstone, England : *Sil* vur stohn (UK *Sil* va stohn)
Silves, Portugal : *Seel* vish
Simanggang, Malaysia : See *mahng* gahng
Simbirsk, Russia : Sim *birsk*
Simcoe, Canada : *Sim* koh
Simeulue, Indonesia : See ma *looh* a
Simferopol, Ukraine : Sim fi *raw* pul
Simla, India : *Sim* la
Simonsbath, England : *Sim* unz bath (UK *Sim* unz bahht)
Simonstown, South Africa : *Siy* munz town
Simplon (Pass), Switzerland : *Sam* plahn (UK *Sam* plon) (French Sahm *plawn*)
Simpson (Desert), Australia : *Simp* sun
Simsbury, USA : *Simz* ber i (UK *Simz* bri)
Sinai, Egypt : *Siy* niy
Sincelejo, Colombia : Sin say *lay* hoh
Sind, Pakistan : Sind
Sindelfingen, Germany : *Zin* dul fing un
Singapore, Asia : Sing ga *pawr* (UK Sing a *paw*) [The UK pronunciation of the republic's name formerly sounded the *g*.]
Singaraja, Indonesia : Sing ga *rah* ja
Singen, Germany : *Zing* un
Singida, Tanzania : Sing *gee* dah
Singkawang, Indonesia : Sing *kah* wahng
Singkep, Indonesia : *Sing* kep
Singleton, Australia : *Sing* gul tun
Sinkiang Uighur, China : Shin jyahng Wee *goor*
Sinop, Turkey : Si *nawp*
Sint-Niklaas, Belgium : Sint *Nee* klahs
Sint-Truiden, Belgium : Sint *Troy* dun
Sinŭiju, North Korea : Seen wee *jooh*

Sion, Switzerland : Syohn
Sioux City, USA : Sooh *Si* ti
Sioux Falls, USA : Sooh *Fawlz*
Siping, China : Sa *ping*
Siracusa, Italy : See rah *kooh* zah
Sirajganj, Bangladesh : Si *rahj* gunj
Sirte, Libya : *Sir* tay (UK *Si* a tay)
Sisak, Croatia : *See* sahk
Sisimiut, Greenland : Si *see* myooht
Sisophon, Cambodia : *Sis* a pahn
Sissinghurst, England : *Sis* ing huhrst (UK *Sis* ing huhst)
Sitka, USA : *Sit* ka
Sittingbourne, England : *Sit* ing bawrn (UK *Sit* ing bawn)
Sittwe, Myanmar : *Sit* wee
Situbondo, Indonesia : See tooh *bon* doh
Sivas, Turkey : See *vahs*
Siwalik (Range), Nepal : Si *wah* lik
Sizewell, England : *Siyz* wul
Sjælland, Denmark : *She* lahn
Skagerrak, Denmark : *Skag* a rak (Danish *Sgah* ga rahk)
Skagway, USA : *Skag* way
Skåne, Sweden : *Skoh* na
Skara Brae, Scotland : Ska ra *Bray*
Skedsmo, Norway : *Shedz* moh
Skegness, England : Skeg *nes*
Skellefteå, Sweden : She *lef* tay oh
Skelmersdale, England : *Skel* murz dayl (UK *Skel* muz dayl) [The name of the Lancashire town is locally also pronounced *Skem* uz dayl, giving its local nickname *Skem*.]
Skibbereen, Ireland : Skib a *reen*
Skiddaw, England : *Skid* aw
Skien, Norway : *Shay* un
Skierniewice, Poland : Skyer nye *veet* sa
Skikda, Algeria : *Skeek* da
Skipton, England : *Skip* tun
Skokholm, Wales : *Skahk* hohm (UK *Skok* hohm)
Skokie, USA : *Skoh* ki
Skomer, Wales : *Skoh* mur (UK *Skoh* ma)
Skopje, Macedonia : *Skaw* pye [This is the Macedonian form of the capital city's name.]

Skoplje, Macedonia : *Skaw* plye [This is the Serbian form of the capital city's name.]

Skövde, Sweden : *Shuhv* da

Skrapar, Albania : Skrah *pahr*

Skye, Scotland : Skiy

Skyros, Greece : *Skiy* rahs (UK *Skiy* ros)

Sla, Morocco : Slah

Slaithwaite, England : *Slath* wayt [An alternate local pronunciation of the Yorkshire town's name is *Slow* it, and it was long claimed that this was the sole "correct" form. As often elsewhere, however, the spelling pronunciation prevailed.]

    Slaithwaite must take heart of grace and face adversity with all the courage that her famous county breeds. So long as she looks like *Slaithwaite* she must be content to be called something like it, and *Slowit* will be a term of endearment restricted to her nearest and dearest [Lloyd James 1936, p. 8].

Slatina, Romania : *Slah* tee nah

Slaugham, England : *Slaf* um

Slavgorod, Russia : *Slahv* ga rut

Slavkov, Czech Republic : *Slahf* kawf

Slavonia, Croatia : Sla *voh* ni a

Slavonski Brod, Croatia : *Slah* vawn ski Brawt

Slavyansk, Ukraine : Slah *vyahnsk*

Sleaford, England : *Slee* furd (UK *Slee* fud)

Sliedrecht, Netherlands : *Slee* drekht

Slieve Donard, Northern Ireland : Sleev *Dah* nurd (UK ... *Don* ud)

Sligo, Ireland : *Sliy* goh

Slimbridge, England : *Slim* brij

Sliven, Bulgaria : *Slee* ven

Slobozia, Romania : Sloh *baw* zya

Slough, England : Slow

Slovakia, Europe : Sloh *vak* i a

Slovenia, Europe : Sloh *veen* i a

Słupsk, Poland : Swoohpsk

Slutsk, Belarus : Sloohtsk

Smallingerland, Netherlands : *Smah* ling ur lahnt

Smarden, England : *Smahr* dun (UK *Smah* dun)

Smederovo, Serbia : *Sme* de re vaw

Smethwick, England : *Smedh* ik

Smithfield, USA : *Smith* feeld

Smolensk, Russia : Smoh *lensk* (Russian Sma *lyensk*)

Smolyan, Bulgaria : Smoh *lyahn*

Smyrna, Turkey; USA : *Smuhr* na (UK *Smuh* na)

Snaefell, Isle of Man, British Isles : Snay *fel*

Snake, USA : Snayk

Snape, England : Snayp

Sneek, Netherlands : Snayk

Śniardwy, Poland : *Shnyahrd* vi

Snowdon, Wales : *Snoh* dun

Snowy Mountains, Australia : Snoh i *Mown* tinz

Snyder, USA : *Sniy* dur (UK *Sniy* da)

Soay, Scotland : *Soh* ay

Sobral, Brazil : Sooh *brahl*

Sochaczew, Poland : Saw *khah* chef

Sochi, Russia : *Saw* chi

Socorro, USA : Sa *kaw* roh (UK Sa *kor* oh)

Socotra, Yemen : Soh *koh* tra (UK Sa *koh* tra)

Söderhamn, Sweden : *Suh* dur hah mun

¹Soest, Germany : Zohst

²Soest, Netherlands : Soohst

Sofia, Bulgaria : *Soh* fee a

Sogamoso, Colombia : Soh goh *moh* soh

Sogdiana, Asia : Sahg di *an* a (UK Sog di *ah* na)

Sogne Fjord, Norway : *Sawng* nya Fyawrd

Sohâg, Egypt : *Soh* hahg

Soham, England : *Soh* um

Soignies, Belgium : Swah *nyee*

Soissons, France : Swah *sohn*

Sokodé, Togo : Soh *koh* day

Sokolov, Czech Republic : *Saw* ka luf

Sokoto, Nigeria : Soh *koh* toh

Soledad, Colombia : Soh lay *dhahdh*

Solent, England : *Soh* lunt

Solesmes, France : Soh *lem*

Soligorsk, Belarus : Sul i *gawrsk*

Solihull, England : Soh li *hahl*

Solikamsk, Russia : Sul i *kahmsk*

Sol-Iletsk, Russia : Sawl I *lyetsk*
Solingen, Germany : *Zoh* ling un
Sollentuna, Sweden : *Sooh* lun tee na
Sololá, Guatemala : Soh loh *lah*
Solomon (Islands), Pacific Ocean : *Sah* la mun (UK *Sol* a mun)
Solor, Indonesia : *Soh* lawr
Solothurn, Switzerland : *Zoh* la toorn
Solway (Firth), Scotland : *Sahl* way (UK *Sol* way)
Somalia, Africa : Soh *mah* li a (UK Sa *mah* li a)
Sombor, Serbia : *Sohm* bohr
Sombrerete, Mexico : Sawm bray *ray* tay
Somerleyton, England : *Sah* mur lay tun (UK *Sah* ma lay tun)
Somerset, England; USA : *Sah* mur set (UK *Sah* ma set)
Somers Town, England : *Sah* murz Town (UK *Sah* muz Town)
Somerton, England : *Sah* mur tun (UK *Sah* ma tun)
Somerville, USA : *Sah* mur vil (UK *Sah* ma vil)
Somme, France : Sahm (UK Som) (French Sawm)
Somoto, Nicaragua : Soh *moh* toh
Sompting, Sompting : *Sahmp* ting (UK *Somp* ting)
Sønderborg, Denmark : *Suhn* dur bawr
Sønderjylland, Denmark : *Suh* nur yee lahn
Sondershausen, Germany : *Zawn* durs how zun
Sondrio, Italy : *Sawn* dree oh
Songea, Tanzania : Song *gay* ah
Songkhla, Thailand : Sawng *klah*
Songnam, South Korea : Song *nahm*
Sonipat, India : *Soh* na put
Sonneberg, Germany : *Zaw* na berk
Sonning, England : *Sah* ning (UK *Son* ing)
Sonoma, USA : Sa *noh* ma
Sonora, USA : Sa *naw* ra
Sonsonate, El Salvador : Sawn soh *nah* tay
Sonyea, USA : Sawn yi *ay*
Sopot, Poland : *Saw* pawt

Sopron, Hungary : *Shoh* prohn
Sorel, Canada : Saw *rel*
Soria, Spain : *Soh* ree yah
Sorocaba, Brazil : Saw roh *kah* ba
Sorong, Indonesia : Saw *rohng*
Sorrento, Italy : Saw *ren* toh
Sortavala, Russia : *Sawr* tah vah lah
Sosnowiec, Poland : Saw *snoh* vyets
Soufrière, West Indies : Soo *fri* ur (UK Soo *fri* a)
Souk-Ahras, Algeria : Soohk *Ar* ahs
Soultz-Haut-Rhin, France : Soohlts Oh *Rahn*
Sousse, Tunisia : Soohs
South : For names prefixed with this word and not given below, as *South Carolina, South Georgia*, see the main name. (*South* is rarely stressed as a separate word.)
Southall, England : Sow thawl
Southam, England : Sow dhum
Southampton, England; USA : Sowth *hamp* tun [The pronunciation of the English seaport city's name is true to its etymology, which is "South Hampton." But Sow *thamp* tun is also heard, and the *p* sound is often omitted in both. *Cp.* **Northampton**.]
Southborough, England : *Sowth* buhr oh (UK *Sowth* bra)
Southend, England : Sow *thend*
Southfield, USA : *Sowth* feeld
South Island, New Zealand : *Sowth* Iy lund
Southport, England : *Sowth* pawrt (UK *Sowth* pawt)
Southsea, England : *Sowth* see
South Shields, England : Sowth *Sheeldz*
South Uist, Scotland : Sowth *Yooh* ist
Southwark, England : *Sah* dhurk (UK *Sah* dhuk) [In the source of the first quote below, the American coauthor shows how he voices an instinctive *r* when saying the name of the London borough, even when otherwise adopting its British pronunciation. The "local" UK pronunciation referred to by the author of the second quote is in fact generally current.]

(1) I say "suhthurrk" for *Southwark*, ... not "suhthuk" [Eric Partridge and John W. Clark, *British and American English Since 1900*, 1951].
(2) The local pronunciation of [the name] Southwark is "Sutherk" with a short vowel and with the *w* unsounded, in spite of its conservative spelling [A.D. Mills, *A Dictionary of London Place Names*, 2001].

Southwell, England : *Sah* dhul [The name of the Nottinghamshire town is also pronounced *Sowth* wul, as noted by the author of the quote below.]
Southwell ... is still Suthl to everyone in the county, though the porters at the [railroad] station call out South Well for the information of the unenlightened foreigner [Ernest Weekley, *Adjectives—And Other Words*, 1930].

Southwick, England : *Sowth* wik [There are half-a-dozen places of this name in England, with the Hampshire and Northamptonshire villages alternately known as *Sah* dhik.]

Southwold, England : *Sowth* wohld

Sovetsk, Russia : Sa *vyetsk*

Sovetskaya Gavan, Russia : Sa vyet ska ya *Gah* vun

Sowerby, England : *Soh* ur bi (UK *Soh* a bi] [The name of the West Yorkshire village is also pronounced *Sow* a bi, as is that of the nearby town of *Sowerby Bridge*, and this is also the usual pronunciation for the identically named North Yorkshire village adjacent to Thirsk.]

Soweto, South Africa : Sa *way* toh

Spa, Belgium : Spah

Spain, Europe : Spayn

Spalding, England : *Spawl* ding

Spandau, Germany : *Span* dow (German *Shpahn* dow)

Spanish Town, Jamaica : *Span* ish Town

Sparks, USA : Spahrks (UK Spahks)

Sparta, Greece; USA : *Spahr* ta (UK *Spah* ta)

Spartanburg, USA : *Spahr* tun buhrg (UK *Spah* tun buhg)

Spearfish, USA : *Spir* fish (UK *Spi* a fish)

Speightstown, Barbados : *Spiyts* town

Spencer, USA : *Spen* sur (UK *Spen* sa)

Spennymoor, England : *Spen* i moor (UK *Spen* i maw)

Speyer, Germany : *Shpiy* ur

Spijkenisse, Netherlands : *Spiy* ka nis a

Spilsby, England : *Spilz* bi

Spion Kop, South Africa : Spiy un Kahp (UK ... *Kop*)

Spišska Nová Ves, Slovakia : Spish skah *Naw* vah Ves

Spithead, England : Spit *hed*

Spitsbergen, Arctic Ocean : *Spits* buhrg un (UK *Spits* buhg un)

Split, Croatia : Split

Spofforth, England : *Spah* furth (UK *Spof* uth)

Spokane, USA : Spoh *kan* [The official pronunciation of the Washington city's Native American name has preserved the local one, much as **Arkansas** came to be *Ahr* kan saw.]
All good citizens religiously *write* Spokane, and just as carefully *say* Spokán [George R. Stewart, *Names on the Land*, 1967].

Spoleto, Italy : Spoh *lay* toh

Sporades, Greece : *Spawr* a deez (UK *Spor* a deez)

Spotsylvania, USA : Spaht sil *vayn* ya (UK Spot sil *vayn* i a)

Spratly (Islands), South China Sea : *Sprat* li

Spree, Germany : Shpray

Spremberg, Germany : *Shprem* berk

Springdale, Canada; USA : *Spring* dayl

Springfield, England; USA : *Spring* feeld

Springs, South Africa : Springz

Springville, USA : *Spring* vil

Sproughton, England : *Spraw* tun

Spurn Head, England : Spuhrn *Hed* (UK Spuhn...)

Spuyten Duyvil (Creek), USA : *Spiy* tun Diy vul

Squillace, Italy : Skwee *lah* chay

Sragen, Indonesia : *Srah* gun

Srebrenica, Bosnia-Herzegovina : Sreb ra *neet* sa

Sremska Mitrovica, Serbia : Srem skah
Meet roh veet sah
Sremski Karlovci, Serbia : Srem skee
Kahr lohv tsee
Sri Lanka, Asia : Sree *Lahng* ka (UK
Shree *Lang* ka) [Sources are divided
regarding the pronunciation of the
honorific prefix that is the first word
of the island republic's name. The
passage quoted below considers the
dilemma.]
  "Shree" or "Sri"? During a radio in-
terview a Sri Lankan diplomat consis-
tently said "Sri," whereas his English
interviewer persisted in "Shree." I
asked, in a letter to *Radio Times*, how
we should say it. A correspondence
ensued, from which it emerged that
both are "correct" and that variations
occur in the country itself [Fritz
Spiegl, *MediaSpeak*, 1989].
Srinagar, India : Sree *nah* gur
Srirangam, India : Sree *rahng* gum
Staaten, Australia : *Stat* un
Stade, Germany : *Shtah* da
Stadskanaal, Netherlands : Stahts ka
nahl
Staffa, Scotland : *Staf* a
Stafford, England; USA : *Staf* urd (UK
Staf ud)
Stagira, Greece : Sta *jiy* ra
Staines, England : Staynz
Stainforth, England : *Stayn* fawrth (UK
Stayn fawth)
Stains, France : Stahn
Staithes, England : Staydhz
Stakhanov, Ukraine : Sta *khah* nuf
Stalingrad, Russia : *Stah* lin grad
Stalowa Wola, Poland : Stah loh va *Vaw*
lah
Stalybridge, England : *Stay* li brij
Stamboul, Turkey : Stam *boohl*
Stamford, England; USA : *Stam* furd
(UK *Stam* fud)
Stamfordham, England : *Stam* furd um
(UK *Stam* fud um) [The Northum-
berland village has a name recorded
in the alternate local pronunciation
Stan a tun, so that A.J. Ellis, in *On
Early English Pronunciation* (1889),

describes it as "formerly called and
still known to the peasantry as Stan-
nerton."]
Stanford le Hope, England : Stan furd
li *Hohp* (UK Stan fud...)
Stanhope, England : *Stan* up
Stanley, England : *Stan* li
Stanmore, England : *Stan* mawr (UK
Stan maw)
Stans, Switzerland : Shtahns
Stansted, England : *Stan* sted
Stanthorpe, Australia : *Stan* thawrp
(UK *Stan* thawp)
Stanton, USA : *Stan* tun
Stanwell, England : *Stan* wel
Stapleford, England : *Stay* pul furd (UK
Stay pul fud) [The pronunciation is
valid for most places of the name but
Stapleford, Leicestershire, is UK *Stap*
ul fud.]
Staplehurst, England : *Stay* pul huhrst
(UK *Stay* pul huhst)
Starachowice, Poland : Stah rah khaw
veet se
Staraya Russa, Russia : Stah ra ya *Rooh*
sa
Stara Zagora, Bulgaria : Stah ra Za *gaw*
ra
Stargard Szczeciński, Poland : Stahr
gahrt Shche *cheen* ski
Stary Oskol, Russia : Stah ri Ahs *kohl*
Stassfurt, Germany : *Shtahs* foort
Staten Island, USA : Stat un *Iy* lund
¹**Staunton**, England; USA (Illinois) :
Stawn tun
²**Staunton**, USA (Virginia) : *Stan* tun
Stavanger, Norway : Stah *vahng* ur
Staveley, England : *Stayv* li
Staverton, England : *Stav* ur tun (UK
Stav a tun)
Stavropol, Russia : *Stahv* ra pul
Stavrós, Greece : Stah *vraws*
Stawell, Australia; England : Stawl
Stębark, Poland : *Stem* bahrk
Stechford, England : *Stech* furd (UK
Stech fud)
Steenvoorde, France : Stahn *vawrd*
Steenwijk, Netherlands : *Stayn* viyk
Steinkjer, Norway : *Stayn* khar

Stellenbosch, South Africa : *Stel* un baws

Stendal, Germany : *Shten* dahl

Stenhousemuir, Scotland : Sten hows *myoor* (UK Sten hows *myoo* a)

Stepney, England : *Step* ni

Sterling, USA : *Stuhr* ling (UK *Stuh* ling)

Sterlitamak, Russia : Stir li ta *mahk*

Steubenville, USA : *Stooh* bun vil (UK *Styooh* bun vil)

Stevenage, England : *Stee* vun ij

Steventon, England : *Stee* vun tun

Stewart (Island), New Zealand : *Stooh* urt (UK *Styooh* ut)

Steyning, England : *Sten* ing

Steyr, Austria : Shtiyr

Stiffkey, England : *Stif* ki [The name of the Norfolk village was formerly pronounced *Styooh* ki or *Stooh* ki, but as Pointon notes, p. 230, "the two latter are rarely heard today."]
   Whether it is pronounced as it is spelled, or as is often said, "Stewkey," is still a subject for argument [John Hadfield, ed., *The New Shell Guide to England*, 1981].

Stillwater, USA : *Stil* waw tur (UK *Stil* waw ta)

Stilton, England : *Stil* tun

Stirling, Australia; Scotland : *Stuhr* ling (UK *Stuh* ling)

Stockbridge, England : *Stahk* brij (UK *Stok* brij)

Stockholm, Sweden : *Stahk* hohm (UK *Stok* hohm) (Swedish *Stawk* hawlm)

Stockport, England : *Stahk* pawrt (UK *Stok* pawt)

Stocksbridge, England : *Stahks* brij (UK *Stoks* brij)

Stockton, USA : *Stahk* tun (UK *Stok* tun)

Stockton-on-Tees, England : Stahk tun ahn *Teez* (UK Stok tun on...)

Stoke d'Abernon, England : Stohk *dab* ur nun (UK ... *dab* un un)

Stokeinteignhead, England : Stohk in *tin* hed

Stoke Mandeville, England : Stohk *Man* da vil

Stoke-on-Trent, England : Stohk ahn *Trent* (UK ... on...)

Stoke Poges, England : Stohk *Poh* jus (UK ... *Poh* jiz)

Stolberg, Germany : *Shtawl* berk

Stone, England : Stohn

Stonehaven, Scotland : Stohn *hay* vun [The name of the fishing port near Aberdeen is also locally pronounced Stayn *hiy*.]

Stonehenge, England : *Stohn* henj (UK Stohn *henj*)

Stonehouse, England : *Stohn* hows

Stonor, England : *Stahn* ur (UK *Ston* a)

Stony Brook, USA : *Stoh* ni Brook

Stony Point, USA : Stoh ni *Poynt*

Stony Stratford, England : Stoh ni *Strat* furd (UK ... *Strat* fud)

Stornoway, Scotland : *Stawrn* a way (UK *Stawn* a way)

Storrington, England : *Staw* ring tun (UK *Stor* ing tun)

Storstrøm, Denmark : *Stawr* struhm

¹Stoughton, England (Leicestershire, West Sussex); USA : *Stoh* tun

²Stoughton, England (Somerset) : *Staw* tun

³Stoughton, England (Surrey) : *Stow* tun

Stour, England : *Stow* ur (UK *Stow* a) [There are several rivers of this name in England. In the east and southeast, the pronunciation is usually *Stoo* a, as for the Stour that forms the border between Suffolk and Essex and that is depicted in many of Constable's paintings (as *View on the Stour near Dedham*). However, the two forms are often interchangeable.]

Stourbridge, England : *Stow* ur brij (UK *Stow* a brij)

Stourhead, England : *Stow* ur hed (UK *Stow* a hed)

Stourmouth, England : *Stow* ur mowth (UK *Stow* a mowth) [As its name implies, the Kent village, with name also pronounced *Stoo* a mowth, stands near the point where the Great Stour joins the Little Stour to form the

Stour. As Pointon notes, p. 231, the first pronunciation is more usual for the village, but the river here is often known as the *Stoo* a.]

Stourpaine, England : *Stow* ur payn (UK *Stow* a payn)

Stourport-on-Severn, England : Stow ur pawrt ahn *Sev* urn (UK Stow a pawt on *Sev* un)

Stourton, England : *Stuhr* tun (UK *Stuh* tun) [This is the usual pronunciation of the Wiltshire village's name, although US *Stawr* tun, UK *Staw* tun is also heard, and is more common for other places of the same name.]

Stow cum Quy, England : Stoh kum *Kwiy*

Stowmarket, England : *Stoh* mahr kut (UK *Stoh* mah kit)

Stow-on-the-Wold, England : Stoh ahn dha *Wohld* (UK ... on...)

Strabane, Northern Ireland : Stra *ban*

Strakonice, Czech Republic : *Strah* kaw nyeet se

Stralsund, Germany : *Shtrahl* zunt

Strangford (Lough), Northern Ireland : *Strang* furd (UK *Strang* fud)

Stranraer, Scotland : Stran *rahr* (UK Stran *rah*)

Strasbourg, France : *Strahs* buhrg (UK *Straz* buhg) (French Strahz *boohr*)

Stratford, Canada; England; New Zealand; USA : *Strat* furd (UK *Strat* fud)

Stratford-upon-Avon, England : Strat furd a pahn *Ay* vahn (UK Strat fud a pon *Ay* vun)

Strathaven, Scotland : *Stray* vun

Strathclyde, Scotland : Strath *kliyd*

Strathcona, Canada : Strath *koh* na

Strathfield, Australia : *Strath* feeld

Strathmore, Scotland : Strath *mawr* (UK Strath *maw*)

Strathpeffer, Scotland : Strath *pef* ur (UK Strath *pef* a)

Strathroy, Canada : Strath *roy*

Stratton, England : *Strat* un

Straubing, Germany : *Shtrow* bing

Strausberg, Germany : *Shtrows* berk

Streatham, England : *Stret* um [The name of the London district means literally "street homestead," referring to its location by a Roman road.] Streatham is pronounced "Strettem" (with a short vowel); in spite of the current spelling ... this has probably been the local pronunciation since medieval times [A.D. Mills, *A Dictionary of London Place Names*, 2001].

¹Streatley, England (Bedfordshire) : *Stret* li

²Streatley, England (Berkshire) : *Street* li

Streator, USA : *Stree* tur (UK *Stree* ta)

Street, England : Street

Stresa, Italy : *Stray* zah

Stretford, England : *Stret* furd (UK *Stret* fud)

Stretton, England : *Stret* un

Stromboli, Italy : *Strahm* ba li (UK *Strom* ba li)

Stromness, Scotland : *Strahm* nes (UK *Strom* nes)

Stronsay, Scotland : *Strahn* zay (UK *Stron* zay)

Strood, England : Stroohd

Stroud, England : Strowd

Strumica, Macedonia : *Strooh* meet sah

Strzelce Opolskie, Poland : Schelt se Aw *pawl* skye

Strzelin, Poland : *Sche* leen

Sturminster Newton, England : Stuhr min stur *Nooh* tun (UK Stuh min sta *Nyooh* tun)

¹Stuttgart, Germany : *Shtoot* gahrt

²Stuttgart, USA : *Staht* gahrt (UK *Staht* gaht)

Styal, England : Stiyl

Styria, Austria : *Stir* i a

Subang, Indonesia : *Sooh* bahng

Subiaco, Australia : Sooh bi *ak* oh

Subic, Philippines : *Sooh* bik

Subotica, Serbia : *Sooh* baw teet sah

Succoth, Egypt; Jordan : Sa *kahth* (UK Sa *koth*)

Suceava, Romania : Sooh *chyah* vah

Sucre, Bolivia : *Sooh* kray

Sucumbíos, Ecuador : Sooh koohm *bee* ohs

Sudan, Africa : Sooh *dan* (UK Sooh *dahn*)

Sudbury, Canada; England; USA : *Sahd* ber i (UK *Sahd* bri)

Sudetenland, Europe : Soo *day* tun land

Sueca, Spain : Soo *ay* kah

Suez, Egypt : Sooh *ez* (UK *Sooh* iz)

Suffern, USA : *Sah* furn (UK *Sah* fun)

Suffield, USA : *Sah* feeld

Suffolk, England; USA : *Sah* fuk

Suhl, Germany : Zoohl

Suita, Japan : Sooh *ee* tah

Sukabumi, Indonesia : Sooh ka *booh* mi

Sukhumi, Georgia : Soo *khoo* mi

Sukkur, Pakistan : *Soo* kur (UK *Soo* ka)

Sula (Islands), Indonesia : *Sooh* la

Sulawesi, Indonesia : Sooh la *way* si

Sulgrave, England : *Sahl* grayv

Sullana, Peru : Sooh *yah* nah

Sullom Voe, Scotland : Sooh lum *Voh*

Sulmona, Italy : Soohl *mohn* nah

Sultanpur, India : Sool *tahn* poor

Sulu (Sea), Philippines : *Sooh* looh

Sulzbach, Germany : *Zoolts* bahkh

Sumatra, Indonesia : Soo *mah* tra

Sumba, Indonesia : *Soohm* ba

Sumbawa, Indonesia : Soohm *bah* wa

Sumbawanga, Tanzania : Soohm bah *wahng* gah

Sumbe, Angola : *Soom* bay

Sumburgh, Scotland : *Sahm* bra

Sumedang, Indonesia : *Sooh* ma dahng

Sumenep, Indonesia : *Sooh* ma nep

Sumer, Iran : *Sooh* mur (UK *Sooh* ma)

Sumgait, Azerbaijan : Soom *giy* it

Summerside, Canada : *Sah* mur siyd (UK *Sah* ma siyd)

Summerville, USA : *Sah* mur vil (UK *Sah* ma vil)

Sumoto, Japan : Sooh *moh* toh

Sumpango, Guatemala : Soohm *pahng* goh

Sumqayit, Azerbaijan : Soom *kiy* it

Sumter, USA : *Sahm* tur (UK *Sahm* ta)

Sumy, Ukraine : *Sooh* mi

Sunbury, Australia; England; USA : *Sahn* ber i (UK *Sahn* bri)

Sunch'ŏn, South Korea : Soohn *chahn*

Sunda (Isles), Indonesia : *Sahn* da

Sundbyberg, Sweden : Soond bee *ber*

Sunderland, England : *Sahn* dur lund (UK *Sahn* da lund)

Sundsvall, Sweden : *Soonds* vahl

Sunningdale, England : *Sah* ning dayl

Sunnyvale, USA : *Sah* ni vayl

Sunrise, USA : *Sahn* riyz

Sunyani, Ghana : Soon *yah* ni

Superior, USA : Soo *pir* i ur (UK Soo *pi* a ri a)

Surabaya, Indonesia : Soor a *biy* a (UK Soo a ra *biy* a)

Surakarta, Indonesia : Soor a *kahr* ta (UK Soo a ra *kah* ta)

Surat, India : *Soor* ut

Surbiton, England : *Suhr* ba tun (UK *Suh* bi tun)

Suresnes, France : See *rayn*

Surgut, Russia : Soor *gooht*

Surin, Thailand : Soo *rin*

Suriname, South America : Soor a *nahm* (UK Soo a ri *nam*) (Dutch See ri *nah* ma)

Surrey, Canada; England : *Suh* ri (UK *Sah* ri)

Surt, Libya : Surt (UK Suht)

Surtsey, Iceland : *Suhrt* si (UK *Suht* si) (Icelandic *Seerts* ay)

Susa, Iran; Tunisia : *Sooh* za

Susquehanna, USA : Sahs kwa *han* a (UK Sahs kwi *han* a)

Sussex, Canada; England; USA : *Sah* siks

Sutherland, Scotland : *Sah* dhur lund (UK *Sah* dha lund)

Sutlej, Asia : *Saht* lij

Sutton, England : *Sah* tun

Sutton Coldfield, England : Sah tun *Kohld* feeld

Sutton in Ashfield, England : Sah tun in *Ash* feeld

Suva, Fiji : *Sooh* vah

Suwałki, Poland : Sooh *vow* kee

Suwannee, USA : Sa *wah* ni (UK Sa *won* i)

Suwŏn, South Korea : Sooh *wuhn*

Suzdal, Russia : *Soohz* dul

Suzhou, China : Sooh *joh*
Svalbard, Arctic Ocean : *Sfahl* bahr
Svealand, Sweden : *Svay* a lahnd
Svendborg, Denmark : *Sfen* bawr
Sverdlovsk, Russia : Svird *lawfsk*
Sverdrup (Islands), Canada : *Sfer* drup
Svetlogorsk, Belarus : Svit la *gawrsk*
Svishtov, Bulgaria : Svish *tawf*
Svobodnyy, Russia : Sfa *bawd* ni
Swabia, Germany : *Sway* bi a
Swadlincote, England : *Swahd* lun koht (UK *Swod* lin koht)
Swaffham, England : *Swah* fum (UK *Swof* um)
Swakopmund, Namibia : *Sfah* kawp munt
Swanage, England : *Swah* nij (UK *Swon* ij)
Swanley, England : *Swahn* li (UK *Swon* li)
Swanscombe, England : *Swahnz* kum (UK *Swonz* kum)
¹**Swansea**, Australia : *Swahn* see (UK *Swon* si)
²**Swansea**, USA; Wales : *Swahn* zee (UK *Swon* zi)
Swanwick, England : *Swah* nik (UK *Swon* ik)
Swarkestone, England : *Swawrk* stun (UK *Swawk* stun)
Swavesey, England : *Swayv* zi
Sway, England : *Sway*
Swaziland, Africa : *Swah* zi land
Sweden, Europe : *Swee* dun
Sweetwater, USA : *Sweet* waw tur (UK *Sweet* waw ta)
Swellendam, South Africa : *Swel* un dam
Swettenham, England : *Swet* num
Świdnica, Poland : Shfeed *neet* sa
Swindon, England : *Swin* dun
Świnoujście, Poland : Shfee naw *ooh* eesh che
Swinton, England : *Swin* tun
Switzerland, Europe : *Swit* sur lund (UK *Swit* sa lund)
Swords, Ireland : Sawrdz (UK Sawdz)
Sydenham, England : *Sid* num
Sydney, Australia; Canada : *Sid* ni

Syktyvkar, Russia : Sik tif *kahr*
Sylhet, Bangladesh : Sil *het*
Symonds Yat, England : Sim undz *Yat*
Syracuse, Italy; USA : *Sir* a kyoohs (UK *Siy* ra kyoohz)
Syr Darya, Asia : Sir Dur *yah*
Syria, Asia : *Sir* i a
Syros, Greece : *Siy* rahs (UK *Siy* ros)
Syston, England : *Siy* stun
Syzran, Russia : *Siz* run
Szczecin, Poland : *Shchet* sheen
Szczecinek, Poland : Shche *chee* nek
Szczytno, Poland : *Shchit* naw
Szechuan, China : Sech *wahn*
Szeged, Hungary : *Seg* ed
Székesfehérvár, Hungary : *Say* kesh fe hayr vahr
Szekszárd, Hungary : *Sek* sahrd
Szentendre, Hungary : *Sen* ten dre
Szentes, Hungary : *Sen* tesh
Szolnok, Hungary : *Sohl* nohk
Szombathely, Hungary : *Sohm* bawt hay
Szprotawa, Poland : Shpraw *tah* vah
Taal, Philippines : Tah *ahl*
Tabaco, Philippines : Tah *bah* koh
Tabor, Israel : *Tay* bur (UK *Tay* ba)
Tábor, Czech Republic : *Tah* bawr
Tabora, Tanzania : Tah *boh* rah
Tabriz, Iran : Ta *breez*
Tabuaeran, Kiribati : Ta booh a *er* un
Tacámbaro, Mexico : Tah *kahm* bah roh
Tacaná, Guatemala : Tah kah *nah*
Tacloban, Philippines : Tah *kloh* bahn
Tacna, Peru : *Tahk* nah
Tacolneston, England : *Tak* ul stun
Tacoma, USA : Ta *koh* ma
Tacuarembó, Uruguay : Tah kwah rem *boh*
Tadcaster, England : *Tad* kas tur (UK *Tad* kas ta)
Tadjoura, Djibouti : Tah *jooh* rah
Taegu, South Korea : Tay *gooh*
Taejŏn, South Korea : Tay *jawn*
Tafí Viejo, Argentina : Tah fee *Vyay* hoh
Taganrog, Russia : Ta gan *rawk*
Tagum, Philippines : *Tah* goohm
Tagus, Europe : *Tay* gus

Tahiti, Pacific Ocean : Ta *hee* ti
Tahoe, USA : *Tah* hoh
Tahoua, Niger : *Tow* ah
Taichung, Taiwan : Tiy *choong*
Taif, Saudi Arabia : *Tah* if
Taimyr (Peninsula), Russia : Tiy *mir*
Tainan, Taiwan : Tiy *nahn*
Taipei, Taiwan : Tiy *pay*
Taiping, Malaysia : Tiy *ping*
Taishan, China : Tiy *shan*
Taiwan, Asia : Tiy *wahn*
Taiyuan, China : Tiy yoo *ahn*
Ta'izz, Yemen : Tah *eez*
Tajikistan, Asia : Tah jee ki *stahn*
Takamatsu, Japan : Tah kah *maht* sooh
Takaoka, Japan : Tah *kow* kah
Takapuna, New Zealand : Tah ka *pooh* na
Takarazuka, Japan : Tah kah rah *zuh* kah
Takasaki, Japan : Tah kah *sah* kee
Takatsuki, Japan : Tah *kahts* kee
Takla Makan, China : Tah kla Ma *kahn*
Takoradi, Ghana : Tah ka *rah* di
Talara, Peru : Tah *lah* rah
Talas, Kyrgyzstan : Tah *lahs*
Talaud (Islands), Indonesia : Ta *lowd*
Talavera, Philippines : Tah lah *vay* rah
Talavera de la Reina, Spain : Tah lah vay rah thay lah *Ray* nah
Talca, Chile : *Tahl* kah
Talcahuano, Chile : Tahl kah *wah* noh
Taldy-Kurgan, Kazakhstan : Tal dee Koor *gahn*
Talence, France : Tah *lahns*
Talgarth, Wales : *Tal* gahrth (UK *Tal* gahth)
Taliqan, Afghanistan : Tah li *kahn*
Tallahassee, USA : Tal a *has* i
Tallinn, Estonia : *Tah* lin (UK *Tal* in)
Tallmadge, USA : *Tal* mij
Talybont, Wales : Tal i *bahnt* (UK Tal i *bont*) (Welsh Tahl a *bawnt*)
Tal-y-llyn, Wales : Tal i *lin* (Welsh Tahl a *hlin*)
Tamale, Ghana : Tah *mah* lay
Tamanrasset, Algeria : Tam un *ras* ut
Tamar, England : *Tay* mur (UK *Tay* mah) [A local pronunciation *Tay* ma

exists for the name of the river that for much of its course forms the boundary between Devon and Cornwall.]
Tamazunchale, Mexico : Tah mah soohn *chah* lay
Tambacounda, Senegal : Tahm bah *koohn* dah
Tambov, Russia : Tahm *bawf*
Tamil Nadu, India : Tam ul *Nah* dooh
Tampa, USA : *Tam* pa
Tampere, Finland : *Tahm* pe ray
Tampico, Mexico : Tahm *pee* koh
Tamworth, Australia; England : *Tam* wuhrth (UK *Tam* wuhth)
Tanagra, Greece : *Tan* a gra
Tanauan, Philippines : Tah *nah* wahn
Tandil, Argentina : Tahn *deel*
Tanga, Tanzania : *Tahng* gah
Tanganyika, Africa : Tang gun *yee* ka
Tangier, Morocco : Tan *jir* (UK Tan *ji* a)
Tangmere, England : *Tang* mir (UK *Tang* mi a)
Tangshan, China : Tahn *shahng* (UK Tang *shang*)
Tanimbar (Islands), Indonesia : Ta *nim* bahr
Tanjungbalai, Indonesia : Tahn joohng *bah* liy
Tanjungkarang, Indonesia : Tahn joohng *kah* rahng
Tanjungpinang, Indonesia : Tahn joohng *pee* nahng
Tanta, Egypt : *Tahn* ta
Tantoyuca, Mexico : Tahn toh *yooh* kah
Tanzania, Africa : Tan za *nee* a
Taormina, Italy : Towr *mee* nah
Taos, USA : Tows
Taoudenni, Mali : Tow de *nee*
Tapachula, Mexico : Tah pah *chooh* lah
Taplow, England : *Tap* loh
Tara, Ireland : *Tah* ra
Tarakan, Indonesia : Tah ra *kahn*
Taranaki, New Zealand : Tar a *nak* i
Taranto, Italy : Ta *ran* toh (Italian *Tah* rahn toh)
Tarapacá, Chile : Tah rah pah *kah*
Tarascon, France : Tah rah *skawn*

Tarawa, Kiribati : Ta *rah* wa
Taraz, Kazakhstan : Tah *rahz*
Tarbert, Scotland : *Tahr* burt (UK *Tah* but)
Tarbes, France : Tahrb
Tarbet, Scotland : *Tahr* but (UK *Tah* bit)
Taree, Australia : Ta *ree*
Tarfaya, Morocco : Tahr *fiy* a (UK Tah *fiy* a)
Tarifa, Spain : Ta *ree* fa
Tarija, Bolivia : Tah *ree* hah
Tarkwa, Ghana : Tahr *kwah* (UK Tah *kwah*)
Tarlac, Philippines : *Tahr* lahk
Tarleton, England : *Tahrl* tun (UK *Tahl* tun)
Tarma, Peru : *Tahr* mah
Tarn, France : Tahrn
Tarnobrzeg, Poland : Tahr *nawb* zhek
Tarnów, Poland : *Tahr* noohf
Tarnowskie Góry, Poland : Tahr nawf skye *Goor* ee
Tarouddant, Morocco : Tah rooh *dahn*
Tarporley, England : *Tahr* pur li (UK *Tah* pli)
Tarquinia, Italy : Tahr *kwee* nyah
Tarragona, Spain : Tar a *goh* na (Spanish Tahr rah *goh* nah)
Tarrasa, Spain : Tahr *rah* sah
Tarrytown, USA : *Tar* i town
Tarsus, Turkey : *Tahr* sus (UK *Tah* sus)
Tartu, Estonia : *Tahr* tooh (UK *Tah* tooh)
Tartus, Syria : Tahr *toohs*
Tarvin, England : *Tahr* vun (UK *Tah* vin)
Tashauz, Turkmenistan : Ta *showz* (Russian Tuh sha *oohs*)
Tashkent, Uzbekistan : Tash *kent* (Russian Tahsh *kyent*)
Tasikmalaya, Indonesia : Tah sik ma *liy* a
Tasmania, Australia : Taz *may* ni a
Tatabánya, Hungary : *Taw* taw bahn yaw
Tatarstan, Russia : Ta tur *stan* (UK Tah ta *stahn*)
Tatra (Mountains), Slovakia : *Tah* tra

Taubaté, Brazil : Tow ba *tay*
Taumarunui, New Zealand : Tow ma roo *nooh* i
Taunggyi, Myanmar : Town *jee*
Taunton, England; USA : *Tawn* tun [The name of the English town is also locally pronounced *Tahn* tun. This represents a West-Country trait in which an *aw* sound becomes *ah*, so that the personal name *George* (normally spoken *Jawj*) is pronounced *Jahrj*. According to Mencken, p. 541, some Americans pronounce the Massachusetts city's name as *Tawrn* tun, with an inorganic *r* sound.]
Taunus, Germany : *Tow* nus
Taupo, New Zealand : *Tow* poh
Taurage, Lithuania : Tow rah *gay*
Tauranga, New Zealand : Tow *rahng* a
Taurida, Ukraine : *Tawr* a da (UK *Taw* ri da)
Taurus (Mountains), Turkey : *Taw* rus
Tavira, Portugal : Tah *vir* a
Tavistock, England : *Tav* i stahk (UK *Tav* i stok)
Tavoy, Myanmar : Ta *voy*
Taxco, Mexico : *Tahs* koh
Tay, Scotland : Tay
Taylor, USA : *Tay* lur
Tayport, Scotland : *Tay* pawrt (UK *Tay* pawt)
Tayside, Scotland : *Tay* siyd
Taza, Morocco : *Tah* za
Tbilisi, Georgia : Tbi *lee* si
Tchibanga, Gabon : Chee *bahng* gah
Tczew, Poland : Chef
Te Anau, New Zealand : Tay *Ah* now
Te Aroa, New Zealand : Tay *Ah* roh a
Tebay, England : *Tee* bay [A local pronunciation of the Cumbria village's name is *Tee* bi.]
Tébessa, Algeria : Ti *bes* a
Tebingtinggi, Indonesia : Ti bing *ting* gi
Tecomán, Mexico : Tay koh *mahn*
Tecumseh, USA : Ta *kahm* sa
Teddington, England : *Ted* ing tun
Tedzhen, Turkmenistan : Te *jen*
Tees, England : Teez

Teesdale, England : *Teez* dayl
Teesside, England : *Teez* siyd
Tegal, Indonesia : Tay *gahl*
Tegelen, Netherlands : *Tay* ga lun
Tegucigalpa, Honduras : Tay gooh see *gahl* pah
Tehran, Iran : Tay a *ran* (UK Tay a *rahn*)
Tehuacán, Mexico : Tay wah *kahn*
Tehuantepec, Mexico : Tay *wahn* tah pek
Teignmouth, England : *Tin* muth [The name of the Devon resort is also locally pronounced *Ting* muth. As its name implies, the town is at the mouth of the *Teign*, pronounced Teen.]
Teixeira Pinto, Guinea-Bissau : Tay shay ra *Peen* tooh
Tekirdağ, Turkey : Te *kir* dahg
Tel Aviv, Israel : Tel A *veev*
Telde, Canary Islands : *Tel* day
Telford, England : *Tel* furd (UK *Tel* fud)
Télimélé, Guinea : Tay li may *lay*
Tellicherry, India : Tel a *cher* i
Teloloapan, Mexico : Tay lohl *wah* pahn
Telscombe, England : *Tels* kum
Tema, Ghana : *Tay* mah
Temecula, USA : Ti *mek* yoo la
Temirtau, Kazakhstan : *Tay* mir tow
¹**Tempe**, Greece : *Tem* pi
²**Tempe**, USA : Tem *pee*
Temuco, Chile : Tay *mooh* koh
Tena, Ecuador : *Tay* nah
Tenafly, USA : *Ten* a fliy
Tenali, India : Tay *nah* lee
Tenbury Wells, England : Ten bri *Welz*
Tenby, Wales : *Ten* bi
Tenerife, Canary Islands : Ten a *reef* (Spanish Tay nay *ree* fay)
Tennessee, USA : Ten a *see* [Locally the state's name is also pronounced *Ten* a see.]

"Far as I'm concerned, we got it all in *Tinnessay*," says a man pumping gas at a highway gas station near Memphis [*Lonely Planet USA*, 2004].

Tenterden, England : *Ten* tur dun (UK *Ten* ta dun)
Teófilo Otoni, Brazil : Tee aw fee looh Oh *toh* nee
Teotihuacán, Mexico : Tay oh tee wah *kahn*
Tepelenë, Albania : Tay pa *lay* na
Tepic, Mexico : Tay *peek*
Teplice, Czech Republic : Te *pleet* se
Teramo, Italy : *Ter* ah moh
Terengganu, Malaysia : Te reng *gah* nooh
Teresina, Brazil : Tay ray *zee* na
Teresópolis, Brazil : Tay ray *zaw* pooh lees
Termez, Uzbekistan : Ter *mez*
Termini Imerese, Italy : Ter mee nee Ee may *ray* zay
Ternate, Indonesia : Tur *nah* ti
Terneuzen, Netherlands : Ter *nuh* za
Terni, Italy : *Ter* nee
Ternopol, Ukraine : Ter *noh* pul
Terracina, Italy : Ter rah *chee* nah
Terre Haute, USA : Ter a *Hoht*
Teruel, Spain : *Tayr* wel
Teslin, Canada : *Tez* lin
Tetbury, England : *Tet* ber i (UK *Tet* bri)
Tete, Mozambique : *Tay* ta
Teton, USA : *Tee* tahn (UK *Tee* tun)
Tétouan, Morocco : Tay *twahn*
Tetovo, Macedonia : *Te* taw vaw
Tettenhall, England : *Tet* un hawl
Teutoburg (Forest), Germany : *Tooh* ta buhrg (UK *Tyooh* ta buhg)
Teversham, England : *Tev* ur shum (UK *Tev* a shum)
Teviot, Scotland : *Tee* vi ut
Tewkesbury, England : *Toohks* ber i (UK *Tyoohks* bri)
Tewksbury, USA : *Toohks* ber i (UK *Tyoohks* bri)
Texarkana, USA : Tek sahr *kan* a (UK Tek sah *kan* a)
Texas, USA : *Tek* sus
Texel, Netherlands : *Te* sul
Teyateyaneng, Lesotho : Tay yah tay *yah* neng
Teziutlán, Mexico : Tay syooht *lahn*

Thabana Ntlenyana, Lesotho : Tah bah nahnt len *yah* nah

Thabazimbi, South Africa : Tah bah *zim* bi

Thailand, Asia : *Tiy* land

Thame, England : Taym

¹**Thames**, Canada; England; New Zealand : Temz

²**Thames**, USA : Thaymz

Thane, India : *Tah* na

Thanet, England : *Than* it

Thanh Hoa, Vietnam : Tahn *Hwah*

Thanjavur, India : Tahn ja *voor*

Thaon-les-Vosges, France : Tahn lay *Vohzh*

Thapsus, Tunisia : *Thap* sus

Thasos, Greece : *Thay* sahs (UK *Thay* sos)

Thatcham, England : *Thach* um

Thaxted, England : *Thaks* tid

Thayetmyo, Myanmar : Tha *yet* myoh

The : for names beginning thus, as *The Dalles*, *The Hague*, see the next word.

Theale, England : Theel

Thebes, Egypt; Greece : Theebz

Thermopolis, USA : Thur *mah* pa lis (UK Tha *mop* a lis)

Thermopylae, Greece : Thur *mah* pa li (UK Tha *mop* a li)

Thessalonica, Greece : Thes a *lah* ni ka (UK Thes a *lon* ik a)

Thessaly, Greece : *Thes* a li

Thetford, England : *Thet* furd (UK *Thet* fud)

Thetford Mines, Canada : Thet furd *Miynz* (UK Thet fud...)

Theydon Bois, England : Thay dun *Boyz*

Thibodaux, USA : *Tib* a doh

Thiès, Senegal : Tyes

Thika, Kenya : *Tee* kah

Thimphu, Bhutan : Thim *pooh*

Thionville, France : Tyawn *veel*

Thirlmere, England : *Thuhrl* mir (UK *Thuhl* mi a)

Thirsk, England : Thuhrsk (UK Thuhsk)

Thisted, Denmark : *Tees* tedh

Thohoyandou, South Africa : Toh hoy *ahn* dooh

Thompson, Canada : *Tahmp* sun (UK *Tomp* sun)

Thonburi, Thailand : Tawn boo *ree*

Thonon-les-Bains, France : Toh nawn lay *Bahn*

Thorley, England : *Thawr* li (UK *Thaw* li)

Thornaby-on-Tees, England : Thawrn a bi ahn *Teez* (UK Thawn a bi on...)

Thornton Heath, England : Thawrn tun *Heeth* (UK Thawn tun...)

Thorold, Canada : *Thaw* ruld (UK *Thor* uld)

Thorpeness, England : *Thawrp* nes (UK *Thawp* nes)

Thouars, France : Twahr

Thrace, Turkey : Thrays

Threlkeld, England : *Threl* keld

Thuin, Belgium : Twahn

Thule, Greenland : *Thooh* li (UK *Tooh* li)

Thun, Switzerland : Toohn

Thunder Bay, Canada : Thahn dur *Bay* (UK Thahn da...)

Thurgarton, England : *Thuhr* gur tun (UK *Thuh* ga tun)

Thurgau, Switzerland : *Toohr* gow

Thuringia, Germany : Thoo *rinj* i a (UK Thyoo *rinj* i a)

Thurleigh, England : Thuhr *liy* (UK Thuh *liy*)

Thurles, Ireland : *Thuhr* lus (UK *Thuh* lis)

Thurlestone, England : *Thuhrl* stun (UK *Thuhl* stun)

Thurrock, England : *Thuhr* uk (UK *Thah* ruk)

Thurso, Scotland : *Thuhr* soh (UK *Thuh* soh)

Tianjin, China : Ti ahn *jin* (UK Ti an *jin*)

Tian Shan, Asia : Tyen *Shahn*

Tiaret, Algeria : Tee a *ret*

Tibenham, England : *Tib* num

Tiber, Italy : *Tiy* bur (UK *Tiy* ba)

Tiberias, Israel : Tiy *bir* i us (UK Tiy *bi* a ri as)

Tibesti (Mountains), Chad : Ti *bes* ti
Tibet, China : Ti *bet*
Ticao, Philippines : Tee *kow*
Ticehurst, England : *Tiys* huhrst (UK *Tiys* huhst)
Tichborne, England : *Tich* bawrn (UK *Tich* bawn)
Ticino, Italy; Switzerland : Tee *chee* noh
Ticonderoga, USA : Tiy kahn da *roh* ga (UK Tiy kon da *roh* ga)
Tideford, England : *Tid* i furd (UK *Tid* i fud) [The name of the Cornish village means "ford over the *Tiddy* River," not "tide ford," as reflected in the pronunciation.]
By coincidence, the river is tidal up to the bridge. That fact, and the misleading modern spelling, have led to the misconception that the name is English "tidal ford"; but the constant *i* in early spellings ... and the pronunciation "Tiddyford" show the correct derivation [O.J. Patel, *A Popular Dictionary of Cornish Place-Names*, 1988].
Tidenham, England : *Tid* num
Tideswell, England : *Tiydz* wel [The name of the Derbyshire town has the alternate local pronunciation *Tid* zul.]
Tidore, Indonesia : Ti *doh* ray
Tiel, Netherlands : Teel
Tielt, Belgium : Teelt
Tierra Blanca, Mexico : Tyer rah *Blahng* kah
Tierra del Fuego, Argentina : Ti er a del *Fway* goh (UK Ti ay ra...) (Spanish Tyer rah dhel *Fway* goh)
Tietjerksteradeel, Netherlands : Teet *yerk* stur a dayl
Tiflis, Georgia : *Tif* lis
Tifton, USA : *Tif* tun
Tighina, Moldova : Ti *gee* na
Tigray, Ethiopia : Tee *gray* (UK *Tig* ray)
Tigre, Argentina : *Tee* gray
Tigris, Asia : *Tiy* grus (UK *Tiy* gris)
Tijuana, Mexico : Ti a *wah* na (UK Ti *wah* na) (Spanish Tee *hwah* nah)
Tikal, Guatemala : Tee *kahl*
Tikhoretsk, Russia : Tee kha *ryetsk*
Tikhvin, Russia : *Tikh* vin

Tilburg, Netherlands : *Til* buhrg (UK *Til* buhg) (Dutch *Til* beerkh)
Tilbury, England : *Til* ber i (UK *Til* bri)
Tilehurst, England : *Tiyl* huhrst (UK *Tiyl* huhst)
Tillamook, USA : *Til* a mook
Tillicoultry, Scotland : Til i *kooh* tri
Tilsit, Russia : *Til* sit
Timaru, New Zealand : *Tim* a rooh
Timbuktu, Mali : Tim bahk *tooh*
Timişoara, Romania : Tee mee *shwah* rah
Timmins, Canada : *Tim* unz (UK *Tim* inz)
Timor, Indonesia : *Tee* mawr (UK *Tee* maw)
Tingewick, England : *Tinj* wik
Tingwall, Scotland : *Ting* wul
Tintagel, England : Tin *taj* ul
Tintern (Abbey), Wales : *Tin* turn (UK *Tin* tun)
Tippecanoe, USA : Tip i ka *nooh*
Tipperary, Ireland : Tip a *rer* i (UK Tip a *ray* a ri)
Tiptree, England : *Tip* tree
Tirana, Albania : Ti *rah* na
Tiraspol, Moldova : Ti *ras* pul
Tiree, Scotland : Tiy *ree*
Tîrgovişte, Romania : Tur *goh* veesh te
Tîrgu Jiu, Romania : Tur gooh *Zhee* ooh
Tîrgu Mureş, Romania : Tur gooh *Moor* esh
Tîrgu Neamţ, Romania : Tur gooh *Nyahmts*
Tirich Mir, Pakistan : Tir ich *Mir*
Tirol, Austria : Ti *rohl*
Tiruchchirappalli, India : Tir a cha *rah* pa lee (UK Tir a chi *rah* pa li)
Tirruppur, India : *Tir* a poor
Tisbury, England : *Tiz* ber i (UK *Tiz* bri)
Titicaca, South America : Tee tee *kah* kah
Titovo Užice, Serbia : *Tee* taw va Ooh zhit se
Titov Veles, Macedonia : *Tee* tawv Ve les

Tittensor, England : *Tit* un sur (UK *Tit* un sa)

Titusville, USA : *Tiy* tus vil

Tiverton, England; USA : *Tiv* ur tun (UK *Tiv* a tun)

Tivoli, Italy : *Tiv* a li (Italian *Tee* voh lee)

Tizi-Ouzou, Algeria : Tee zee Ooh *zooh*

Tkibuli, Georgia : Tkee *booh* li

Tkvarcheli, Georgia : Tkvahr *che* li

Tlalnepantla, Mexico : Tlahl nay *pahnt* lah

Tlalpán, Mexico : Tlahl *pahn*

Tlaquepaque, Mexico : Tlah kay *pah* kay

Tlaxcala, Mexico : Tlahs *kah* lah

Tlemcen, Algeria : Tlem *sen*

Toa Baja, Puerto Rico : Toh ah *Bah* hah

Toamasina, Madagascar : Toh a ma *see* na

Tobago, Trinidad and Tobago : Ta *bay* goh

Tobermory, Scotland : Toh bur *maw* ri (UK Toh ba *maw* ri)

Tobolsk, Russia : Ta *bawlsk*

Tobruk, Libya : Toh *brook*

Tocantins, Brazil : Toh kahn *teens*

Tocopilla, Chile : Toh koh *pee* yah

Todmorden, England : *Tahd* mawr dun (UK *Tod* ma dun)

Togo, Africa : *Toh* goh

Tokelau, Pacific Ocean : *Toh* ka low

Tokmak, Kyrgyzstan : Tawk *mahk*

Tokushima, Japan : Toh kooh *shee* mah

Tokuyama, Japan : Toh kooh *yah* mah

Tokyngton, England : *Toh* king tun

Tokyo, Japan : *Toh* ki oh

Tolago (Bay), New Zealand : Ta *lah* go

¹**Toledo**, Spain : Ta *lay* doh (Spanish Toh *lay* dhoh)

²**Toledo**, USA : Ta *lee* doh

Toliara, Madagascar : *Toh* lee ar a

Tolima, Colombia : Toh *lee* mah

Tolleshunt d'Arcy, England : Tohlz hahnt *dahr* si (UK ... *dah* si)

Tolpuddle, England : *Tahl* pah dul (UK *Tol* pah dul) [The Dorset village is also locally known as *Tol* pid ul. The

river here, the Piddle, gave the regular name in altered form.]

Toluca, Mexico : Toh *looh* kah

Tolworth, England : *Tahl* wuhrth (UK *Tol* wuth)

Tolyatti, Russia : Tawl *yah* ti

Tomaszów Mazowiecki, Poland : Taw mah shoohf Mah zaw *vyet* ski

Tomato, USA : Ta *mat* oh ["You say tomato and I say to-mah-to," but residents of the Arkansas community say something in between.]

Tombouktou, Mali : Tohn boohk *tooh*

Tombstone, USA : *Toohm* stohn

Tomé, Chile : Toh *may*

Tomelloso, Spain : Toh mel *yoh* soh

Tomintoul, Scotland : Tah min *towl* (UK Tom in *towl*)

Tomsk, Russia : Tawmsk (UK Tomsk)

Tonbridge, England : *Tahn* brij [The Kent town was earlier *Tunbridge*, but then reverted to its old spelling for distinction from nearby **Tunbridge Wells**, to which it gave its name.]

Tonga, Pacific Ocean : *Tahng* ga (UK *Tong* ga)

Tongatapu, Tonga : Tahng gah *tah* pooh

Tonkin, Vietnam : Tahn *kin* (UK Ton *kin*)

Tonle Sap, Cambodia : Tohn lay *Sahp*

Tonneins, France : Taw *nahns*

Tonopah, USA : *Toh* na pah

Tønsberg, Norway : *Tuhns* bar

Tonypandy, Wales : Tah na *pan* di (UK Ton a *pan* di) (Welsh Tawn a *pahn* di) [The name of the Rhondda Valley town comprises Welsh *ton*, "grassland," *y*, "of the," and *pandy*, "fulling mill."]

Tonyrefail, Wales : Tah ni *rev* iyl (UK Ton i *rev* iyl) (Welsh Tawn ur *ev* iyl) [The village near **Tonypandy** has a name comprising Welsh *ton*, "grassland," *yr*, "of the," and *gefail*, "smithy."]

Tooele, USA : Too *el* a

Tooting, England : *Tooh* ting

Toowoomba, Australia : Ta *woom* ba

Topeka, USA : Ta *pee* ka (UK Toh *pee* ka)

Topsham, England : *Tahp* sum (UK *Top* sum)

Torbay, England : Tawr *bay* (UK Taw *bay*)

Torcross, England : Tawr *kraws* (UK Taw *kros*)

Torez, Ukraine : Ta *res*

Torfaen, Wales : Tawr *viyn* (UK Taw *viyn*)

Torgau, Germany : *Tawr* gow

Torino, Italy : Toh *ree* noh

Tornio, Finland : *Tawr* nee oh

Törökszentmiklós, Hungary : *Tuh* ruhk sent mee klohsh [The town's name resolves into the Hungarian personal name *Török* ("Turkish"), *szent*, "saint," and *Miklós*, "Nicholas."]

Toronto, Canada : Ta *rahn* toh (UK Ta *ron* toh)

Torpenhow, England : *Tawr* pun how (UK *Taw* pun how) [A local alternate pronunciation of the Cumbria village's name is Tri *pen* a.]

Torpoint, England : Tawr *poynt* (UK Taw *poynt*)

Torquay, England : Tawr *kee* (UK Taw *kee*)

Torrance, USA : *Tawr* uns (UK *Tor* uns)

Torremolinos, Spain : Tawr a ma *lee* nohs (UK Tor i ma *leen* os) (Spanish Tawr ray moh *lee* nohs)

Torrens, Australia : *Tawr* unz (UK *Tor* unz)

Torreón, Mexico : Tawr ray *ohn*

Torres (Strait), Australia : *Taw* riz (UK *Tor* iz)

Torres Vedras, Portugal : Tawr riz *Ved* rush

Torrington, England; USA : *Tawr* ing tun (UK *Tor* ing tun)

Tórshavn, Faeroe Islands : *Tawrs* hown

Tortola, British Virgin Islands : Tawr *toh* la (UK Taw *toh* la)

Tortosa, Spain : Tawr *toh* sah

Toruń, Poland : *Taw* roohn

Toshkent, Uzbekistan : Tawsh *kent*

Totnes, England : *Taht* nis (UK *Tot* nis)

Totonicapán, Guatemala : Toh toh nee kah *pahn*

Tottenham, England : *Tah* tun um (UK *Tot* num)

Totteridge, England : *Tah* ta rij (UK *Tot* a rij)

Tottington, England : *Tah* ting tun (UK *Tot* ing tun)

Totton, England : *Tah* tun (UK *Tot* un)

Tottori, Japan : Toh *toh* ree

Toubkal, Morocco : *Toohb* kal

Touggourt, Algeria : Too *goort*

Toul, France : Toohl

Toulon, France : Tooh *lawn*

Toulouse, France : Tooh *loohz*

Toungoo, Myanmar : *Towng* gooh

Touraine, France : Tooh *rayn*

Tourcoing, France : Toohr *kwahn*

Tournai, Belgium : Toohr *nay*

Tournus, France : Toohr *nee*

Tours, France : Toohr [English speakers formerly knew the city as US Toorz, UK *Too* uz.]

Toussus-le-Noble, France : Tooh seel *Nawbl*

Towcester, England : *Toh* stur (UK *Toh* sta)

Tow Law, England : Tow *Law*

Townsville, Australia : *Townz* vil

Towy, Wales : *Tow* i

Towyn, Wales : *Tow* in

Toyama, Japan : Toh *yah* mah

Toyanaka, Japan : Toh yoh *nah* kah

Toyohashi, Japan : Toh yoh *hah* shee

Toyota, Japan : Toh *yoh* tah

Tozeur, Tunisia : Toh *zuhr*

Trabzon, Turkey : Trab *zahn* (UK Trab *zon*)

Tracy, Canada; USA : *Tray* si

Trafalgar, Spain : Tra *fal* gur (UK Tra *fal* ga) (Spanish Trah fahl *gahr*) [The name of the Spanish cape, the scene of Admiral Nelson's victory over the French and Spanish in 1805, was formerly also familiar to English speakers in the pronunciation *Traf* ul gah(r), still found for *Trafalgar*

House, near Salisbury, Wiltshire, but now only rarely for London's *Trafalgar* Square. The first two quotes below contain the Spanish accentuation, while the third whimsically comments on it.]

(1) And [Nelson] launch'd that thunderbolt of war
On Egypt, Hafnia, Trafalgar [Sir Walter Scott, *Marmion*, 1808].

(2) When Nelson sailed for Trafalgar With all his country's best,
He held them dear as brothers are,
But one beyond the rest [Henry Newbolt, "Northumberland," *Collected Poems*, 1897–1907].

(3) The day of Trafalgar is Spanish in name
And the Spaniards refuse to pronounce it the same [G.K. Chesterton, "Songs of Education: II Geography," 1922].

Trafford, England : *Traf* urd (UK *Traf* ud)
Trail, Canada : Trayl
Tralee, Ireland : Tra *lee*
Tranent, Scotland : Tra *nent*
Trang, Thailand : Trahng
Trani, Italy : *Trah* nee
Tranquebar, India : *Trang* kwa bahr
Transkei, South Africa : Trans *kiy*
Transvaal, South Africa : Trans *vahl* (UK Tranz *vahl*) [The name of the former province was at one time also locally pronounced Tranz *fahl*.]
Transylvania, Romania : Tran sul *vay* nya (UK Tran sil *vay* ni a)
Trapani, Italy : *Trah* pah nee
Traralgon, Australia : Tra *ral* gun
Traun, Austria : Trown
Travancore, India : *Trav* un kawr (UK Trav un *kaw*)
Travnik, Bosnia-Herzegovina : *Trahv* neek
Trawsfynydd, Wales : Trows *vah* nidh
Třebíč, Czech Republic : Tur *zhe* beech
Trebizond, Turkey : *Treb* a zahnd (UK *Treb* i zond)
Treblinka, Poland : Tre *bling* kah

Tredegar, Wales : Tri *dee* gur (UK Tri *dee* ga)
Tregaron, Wales : Tri *gar* un
Treharris, Wales : Tri *har* is
Treinta y Tres, Uruguay : Trayn tah ee *Trays*
Trelew, Argentina : Tray *lay* oo
Trelleborg, Sweden : *Tre* la bawr
Trenčín, Slovakia : Tren *cheen*
Trent, England; Italy : Trent
Trento, Italy : *Tren* toh
Trenton, Canada; USA : *Tren* tun
Treorchy, Wales : Tri *awr* ki (UK Tri *aw* ki)
Tres Arroyos, Argentina : Trays Ahr *roy* ohs
Tresco, England : *Tres* koh
Tresillian, England : Tri *sil* i un
Três Rios, Brazil : Trays *Ree* oohs
Trets, France : Tray
Treviso, Italy : Tray *vee* zoh
Tribeca, USA : Triy *bek* a
Trichinopoly, India : Trich a *nah* pa li (UK Trich i *nop* a li)
Trier, Germany : Trir (UK *Tri* a) (German Treer) [The city was formerly known in English as *Treves*, pronounced Treevz, from its French name *Trèves*. Cp. *Cleves* for **Kleve**.]
Trieste, Italy : Tri *est* (Italian Tree *es* tay)
Trim, Ireland : Trim
Trincomalee, Sri Lanka : Tring ka ma *lee* (UK Tring koh ma *lee*)
Třinec, Czech Republic : Tur *zhee* nets
Tring, England : Tring
Trinidad, Bolivia; Cuba; Trinidad and Tobago; Uruguay : *Trin* i dad
Tripoli, Lebanon; Libya : *Trip* a li
Tripolis, Greece : *Trip* a lus (UK *Trip* a lis)
Tripolitania, Africa : Trip a li *tayn* i a
Tripura, India : *Trip* a ra
Tristan da Cunha, Atlantic Ocean : Tris tun da *Kooh* nya
Trith-St.-Léger, France : Tree Sahn Lay *zhay*
Trivandrum, India : Tra *van* drum (UK Tri *van* drum)
Trnava, Slovakia : *Tur* na va

Troas, Turkey : *Troh* as
Trobriand (Islands), Pacific Ocean : *Troh* bri und
Trogir, Croatia : *Troh* gir
Trois-Rivières, Canada; Guadeloupe : Trwah Ree *vyer*
Troitsk, Russia : *Traw* itsk
Trollhättan, Sweden : *Trawl* het tun
Tromsø, Norway : *Troohm* suh
Trondheim, Norway : *Trahn* hiym (UK *Trond* hiym) (Norwegian *Trawn* haym)
Troon, Scotland : Troohn
Tropojë, Albania : Tro *paw* ya
Trossachs, Scotland : *Trah* saks (UK *Tros* uks)
Trottiscliffe, England : *Trahz* li (UK *Troz* li)
One of a number of unhelpful Kentish spellings; the name of this village is pronounced "Trosley" [John Hadfield, ed., *The Shell Guide to England*, 1970].
Troutbeck, England : *Trowt* bek
Trouville, France : *Trooh* vil (French Trooh *veel*)
Trowbridge, England : *Troh* brij
Troy, Turkey; USA : Troy
Troyes, France : Trwah
Truckee, USA : *Trah* ki
Trujillo, Honduras; Peru; Venezuela : Trooh *hee* yoh
Truro, Canada; England : *Troor* oh (UK *Troo* a roh)
Truskavets, Ukraine : Troohs ka *vyets*
Trutnov, Czech Republic : *Troot* nawf
Tryfan, Wales : *Triv* un (Welsh *Truh* vahn)
Tsavo, Kenya : *Tsah* voh
Tsévié, Togo : *Tsay* vyay
Tshwane, South Africa : *Tshwah* nay
Tskhinvali, Georgia : Tskhin *vah* li
Tsu, Japan : Tsooh
Tsugaru (Strait), Japan : Tsooh *gah* rooh
Tsumeb, Namibia : *Tsooh* meb
Tsushima, Japan : Tsooh *shee* mah
Tuam, Ireland : *Tooh* um
Tuamotu (Archipelago), Pacific Ocean : Tooh a *moh* tooh

Tuapse, Russia : Too ahp *se*
Tuban, Indonesia : *Tooh* bahn
Tubarão, Brazil : Tooh ba *rown*
Tubbergen, Netherlands : *Tooh* bur kha
Tübingen, Germany : *Tooh* bing un (UK *Tyooh* bing un) (German *Tee* bing un)
Tuckahoe, USA : *Tah* ka hoh
Tucson, USA : *Tooh* sahn (UK *Tooh* son) [The Arizona city's name has an alternate local stress as Tooh *sahn*. Ross, p. 169, gives the sole pronunciation Tooh *sawn*. The name itself, of Native American origin, gained its pronunciation under Spanish influence.]
The local pronunciation of *Tucson*, according to the Tucson Sunshine-Climate Club, is *Tu-sahn*, with the accent on the second syllable, but most Americans make it *Too-s'n*, with the accent on the first syllable [Mencken, p. 541].
Tucumán, Argentina : Tooh kooh *mahn*
Tucupita, Venezuela : Tooh kooh *pee* tah
Tudela, Spain : Tooh *dhay* la
Tugela, South Africa : Tooh *gay* la
Tukangbesi (Islands), Indonesia : Tooh kahng *bay* si
¹Tula, Mexico : *Tooh* lah
²Tula, Russia : *Tooh* la
Tulancingo, Mexico : Tooh *lahn* sing goh
Tulare, USA : Tooh *lar* i
Tulcán, Ecuador : Toohl *kahn*
Tulcea, Romania : *Toohl* chah
Tullahoma, USA : Tah la *hoh* ma
Tullamore, Ireland : *Tah* la mawr (UK *Tah* la maw)
Tulle, France : Teel
Tullins, France : Tee *lahns*
Tulsa, USA : *Tahl* sa
Tuluá, Colombia : Tooh loo *ah*
Tulungagung, Indonesia : Tooh loong *ah* goong
Tumaco, Colombia : Tooh *mah* koh
Tumbes, Peru : *Toohm* bays
Tunbridge Wells, England : Tahn brij

Wells [The Kent town and former spa, officially *Royal Tunbridge Wells*, takes its name from nearby **Tonbridge**, which was earlier *Tunbridge* but then reverted to its original spelling for distinction from the newer town.]

Tungurahua, Ecuador : Toong gooh *rah* wah

Tunguska, Russia : Toon *goohs* ka

Tunis, Tunisia : *Tooh* nus (UK *Tyooh* nis)

Tunisia, Africa : Tooh *nee* zha (UK Tyoo *niz* i a)

Tunja, Colombia : *Toon* jah

Tunstall, England : *Tahn* stul

Tuolumne, USA : Too *ahl* a mi (UK Too *ol* a mi)

Tupã, Brazil : Tooh *pawn*

Tupelo, USA : *Tooh* pa loh (UK *Tyooh* pa loh)

Tura, Russia : Too *rah*

Turda, Romania : *Toor* da

Turfan, China : Toor *fahn*

Turin, Italy : *Toor* un (UK Tyoo a *rin*)

Turkana, Kenya : Tur *kan* a (UK Tuh *kah* na)

Turkestan, Kazakhstan : Toor ki *stahn*

Turkey, Eurasia : *Tuhr* ki (UK *Tuh* ki)

Turkistan, Asia : Tuhr ki *stahn* (UK Tuh ki *stahn*)

Turkmenabat, Turkmenistan : Toork men ah *baht*

Turkmenbashi, Turkmenistan : Toork men bah *shee*

Turkmenistan, Asia : Tuhrk men i *stahn* (UK Tuhk men i *stahn*)

Turks (Islands), West Indies : Tuhrks (UK Tuhks)

Turku, Finland : *Toor* kooh (UK *Too* a kooh)

Turlock, USA : *Tuhr* lahk (UK *Tuh* lok)

Turnberry, Scotland : *Tuhrn* ber i (UK *Tuhn* bri)

Turnhouse, Scotland : *Tuhrn* hows (UK *Tuhn* hows)

Turnhout, Belgium : *Toorn* howt

Turnov, Czech Republic : *Toor* nawf

Turnu Măgurele, Romania : Toor nooh Ma gooh *re* le

Turriff, Scotland : *Tuhr* if (UK *Tah* rif)

Tuscaloosa, USA : Tahs ka *looh* sa

Tuscany, Italy : *Tahs* ka ni

Tuscarora, USA : Tahs ka *raw* ra

Tuskegee, USA : Ta *skee* gee

Tustin, USA : *Tahs* tun (UK *Tahs* tin)

Tutbury, England : *Taht* bri

Tuticorin, India : Tooh ti ka *rin*

Tuttlingen, Germany : *Toot* ling un

Tutuila, American Samoa : Tooh tooh *wee* lah

Tuva, Russia : *Tooh* va

Tuvalu, Pacific Ocean : Too *vah* looh

Tuxford, England : *Tahks* furd (UK *Tahks* fud)

Tuxpan, Mexico : *Toohs* pahn

Tuxtla, Mexico : *Toohst* lah

Tuzla, Bosnia-Herzegovina : *Toohz* lah

Tver, Russia : Tver

Tweed, Scotland : Tweed

Tweeddale, Scotland : *Tweed* dayl

Twickenham, England : *Twik* num
[The name of the former Middlesex village and present district of London was earlier pronounced *Twit* num, with written forms to match.]

(1) Where silver Thames round Twit'-nam meads

His winding current sweetly leads;

Twit'nam the Muses' fav'rite seat,

Twit'nam the Graces' loved retreat [Horace Walpole, "The Parish Register of Twickenham," 1760].

(2) Twit'nam! so dearly loved, so often sung,

Theme of each raptured heart and glowing tongue [Thomas Maurice, "Richmond Hall, a Poem," 1807].

(3) *Twittenham* survived down almost to the present generation in popular usage, and in the last century it was a customary form among the best-educated inhabitants [James Thorne, *Handbook to the Environs of London*, 1876].

Twyford, England : *Twiy* furd (UK *Twiy* fud)

Tychy, Poland : *Tee* khee

Tyldesley, England : *Tildz* li
Tyler, USA : *Tiy* lur (UK *Tiy* la)
Tynda, Russia : *Tin* da
Tyne, England : Tiyn
Tynemouth, England : *Tiyn* mowth
[The name of the town and resort at
the mouth of the Tyne was earlier
pronounced *Tin* muth, given as the
primary form in Lloyd James 1936.
As such, it risked confusion with
Teignmouth, another resort town,
albeit a southern one.]
Tyneside, England : *Tiyn* siyd
Tyre, Lebanon : Tiyr (UK *Tiy* a)
Tyrol, Austria : Ti *rohl*
¹**Tyrone**, Northern Ireland : Ti *rohn*
[The county's name is alternately
pronounced Tiy *rohn*.]
²**Tyrone**, USA (Georgia, New Mexico) :
Tiy *rohn*
³**Tyrone**, USA (Pennsylvania) : *Tiy* rohn
Tyrrhenian (Sea), Mediterranean Sea :
Ti *ree* ni un
Tyumen, Russia : Tyooh *men*
Tywyn, Wales : *Tow* in (Welsh *Tuh* win)
Ubangi, Africa : Ooh *bang* ee
Ube, Japan : *Ooh* bee
Ubeda, Spain : *Ooh* bay dhah
Uberaba, Brazil : Ooh be *rah* ba
Uberlândia, Brazil : Ooh bur *lahn* dee a
Ubon Ratchathani, Thailand : Oo bun
Rah cha *tah* nee
Uckfield, England : *Ahk* feeld
Udagamandalam, India : Ooh da ga
mun *dah* lum
Udaipur, India : Ooh *diy* poor
Uddevalla, Sweden : *Oo* da vah la
Udimore, England : *Yooh* di mawr (UK
Yooh di maw)
Udine, Italy : *Ooh* dee nay
Udmurtia, Russia : Ood *moor* sha (UK
Ood *moo* a ti a)
Udon Thani, Thailand : Oo dawn *Tah*
nee
Uelzen, Germany : *Eel* tsun
Ufa, Russia : Ooh *fah*
Uganda, Africa : Yoo *gan* da
Uglegorsk, Russia : Oog li *gawrsk*
Ugley, England : *Ahg* li

Uig, Scotland : *Ooh* ig
Uíge, Angola : *Wee* zhay
Uinta (Mountains) USA : Yoo *in* ta
Uist, Scotland : *Yooh* ist
Uitenhage, South Africa : *Yooh* tun
hayg (Afrikaans *Oy* tun hah kha)
Ujiji, Tanzania : Ooh *jee* jee
Ujjain, India : Ooh *jiyn*
Ujung Pandang, Indonesia : Ooh joong
Pahn dahng
Ukiah, USA : Yoo *kiy* a
Ukhta, Russia : Ookh *tah*
Ukraine, Europe : Yoo *krayn*
Ulaanbaatar, Mongolia : Ooh lahn *bah*
tawr
Ulan Bator, Mongolia : Ooh lahn *Bah*
tawr
Ulan-Ude, Russia : Ooh lahn Oo *day*
Ulcinj, Montenegro : *Oohlt* seen ya
Uliastay, Mongolia : *Oohl* yah stiy
Ullapool, Scotland : *Ahl* a poohl
Ullswater, England : *Ahlz* waw tur (UK
Ahlz waw ta)
Ulm, Germany : Oolm
Ulsan, South Korea : Oohl *sahn*
Ulster, Northern Ireland : *Ahl* stur (UK
Ahl sta)
Ulundi, South Africa : Ooh *loohn* dee
Uluru, Australia : Ooh la *rooh*
Ulverston, England : *Ahl* vur stun (UK
Ahl va stun)
Uman, Ukraine : Ooh *mahn*
Umbria, Italy : *Ahm* bri a (Italian *Oohm*
bree ah)
Umeå, Sweden : *Ooh* may oh
Umlazi, South Africa : Oohm *lah* zee
Umnak, USA : *Oohm* nak
Umtali, Zimbabwe : Oom *tah* li
Umtata, South Africa : Oohm *tah* tah
Umuahia, Nigeria : Oom *wah* hee ah
Umuarama, Brazil : Oom wa *rah* ma
Unalaska, USA : Ahn a *las* ka
Ungava, Canada : Ahng *gah* va
Unggi, North Korea : *Oohn* gee
União dos Palmares, Brazil : Ooh
nyown doohs Pahl *mah* rees
Unimak, USA : *Yooh* na mak
Union, USA : *Yoohn* yun
Uniondale, USA : *Yoohn* yun dayl

Unión de Reyes, Cuba : Ooh nyawn dhay *Ray* yes
Unley, Australia : *Ahn* li
Unna, Germany : *Oon* a
Unst, Scotland : Ahnst
Unterwalden, Switzerland : *Oon* tur vahl dun
Unzen, Japan : *Oon* zen
Upington, South Africa : *Ahp* ing tun
Upland, USA : *Ahp* lund
Upminster, England : *Ahp* min stur (UK *Ahp* min sta)
Upolu, Samoa : Ooh *poh* looh
Uppingham, England : *Ahp* ing um
Uppsala, Sweden : Oop *sah* lah (Swedish *Oop* sah lah)
Ur, Iraq : Uhr (UK Uh)
Ural (Mountains), Eurasia : *Yoor* ul (UK *Yoo* a rul) (Russian Oo *rahl*)
Uralsk, Kazakhstan : Ooh *rahlsk*
Urartu, Asia : Oo *rahr* tooh
Ura-Tyube, Tajikistan : Ooh rah Tyooh *bay*
Urbana, USA : Uhr *ban* a (UK Uh *ban* a)
Urbandale, USA : *Uhr* bun dayl (UK *Uh* bun dayl)
Urbino, Italy : Oor *bee* noh
Urfa, Turkey : *Oohr* fah
Urgench, Uzbekistan : Oor *gyench*
Uri, Switzerland : *Ooh* ree
Urmia, Iran : *Oor* mee a
Urmston, England : *Uhrm* stun (UK *Uhm* stun)
Uroteppa, Tajikistan : Oor a te *pah*
Uruapan, Mexico : Oohr *wah* pahn
Uruguaiana, Brazil : Ooh rooh gwa *ya* na
Uruguay, South America : *Yoor* a gwiy (UK *Yoo* a ra gwiy) (Spanish Ooh rooh *gwiy*)
Uruk, Iraq : *Ooh* rook
Urumchi, China : Oo *room* chee
Ürümqi, China : Ee reem *chee*
Uşak, Turkey : *Ooh* shahk
Ushant, France : *Ah* shunt
Ushuaia, Argentina : Ooh *swah* yah
Usk, Wales : Ahsk
Üsküdar, Turkey : Ees kee *dahr*

Usolye-Sibirskoye, Russia : Ooh sawl ye Si *bir* ska ya
Ussuriysk, Russia : Ooh soo *reesk*
Ustaritz, France : Ee stah *reets*
Ust-Ilimsk, Russia : Oohst I *leemsk*
Ústí nad Labem, Czech Republic : Ooh styee *nahd* Lah bem
Ust-Kamenogorsk, Kazakhstan : Oohst Ka min a *gawrsk*
Ust-Kut, Russia : Oohst *Kooht*
Ust-Ordynskiy, Russia : Oohst Ar *din* ski
Ustyurt, Kazakhstan : Ooh *styoort*
Usulafter, El Salvador : Ooh sooh looh *tahn*
Utah, USA : *Yooh* tah [Ross, p. 170, prefers the pronunciations US *Yooh* taw, UK *Yooh* ta.]
Utica, Tunisia; USA : *Yooh* ti ka
Utrecht, Netherlands; South Africa : *Yooh* trekt (Dutch *Ee* trekht)
Utrera, Spain : Ooh *tray* rah
Utsunomiyah, Japan : Ooht soo *noh* mee yah
Uttar Pradesh, India : Oot ur Pra *daysh*
Uttoxeter, England : Yoo *tahk* sa tur (UK Yoo *tok* si ta) [An alternate pronunciation of the Staffordshire town's name is *Ahk* si ta, although this is (or was) mostly current among "county" families and members of Denstone College, the local public school. Lloyd James 1936 gives no less than five possible pronunciations: Ah *tok* si ta, Yooh *tok* si ta, *Ahk* si ta, *Ahk* sta, and *Ah* ch ita. The last three of these are now rare, despite the quote below.]
> The strangest thing about this small market town is its name. Today it is often called "Ucheter" or "Uxeter" and in the past it has been spelled in a variety of ways [John Hadfield, ed., *The New Shell Guide to England*, 1981].

Uusikaupunki, Finland : *Ooh* see kow poong kee
Uvalde, USA : Yoo *val* di
Uyo, Nigeria : *Ooh* yoh

Uxbridge, Canada; England; USA : *Ahks* brij

Uxmal, Mexico : Oohz *mahl*

Uzbekistan, Asia : Ooz *bek* a stan (UK Ooz bek i *stahn*)

Uzhgorod, Ukraine : *Oohzh* ga rut

Uzhhorod, Ukraine : *Oohzh* ha rod

Užice, Serbia : *Ooh* zheet se

Uzlovaya, Russia : Oohz la *vah* ya

Vaasa, Finland : *Vah* sah

Vács, Hungary : Vahts

Vacaville, USA : *Vak* a vil

Vacoas-Phoenix, Mauritius : Va koh us *Fee* niks

Vadodara, India : Va *doh* da rah

Vaduz, Liechtenstein : Vah *doohts* (German Fah *doohts*)

Vagarshapat, Armenia : Vah gahr shah *paht*

Vaigach, Russia : Viy *gahch*

Valais, Switzerland : Va *lay*

Valdai (Hills), Russia : Vahl *diy*

Valdepeñas, Spain : Vahl day *pay* nyahs

Valdez, USA : Val *deez*

Valdivia, Chile : Vahl *dee* vyah

Val-d'Or, Canada : Val *dawr* (UK Val *daw*)

Valdosta, USA : Val *dah* sta (UK Val *dos* ta)

Valença, Brazil : Va *layn* sa

Valence, France : Va *lahns*

¹Valencia, Ireland : Va *len* shi a [The island's Spanish-seeming name is actually a corruption of Irish *Béal Inse*, "mouth of the island," the name of a nearby sound. Its real name is *Dairbhre*, "place of oaks."]

²Valencia, Spain; Venezuela : Va *len* shi a (Spanish Vah *len* thee ah)

Valenciennes, France : Va len si *enz* (UK Va len si *en*) (French Va lahn *syen*)

Valera, Venezuela : Vah *lay* rah

Valkenswaard, Netherlands : *Vahl* kuns vahrt

Valladolid, Spain : Va la da *lid* (UK Va la doh *lid*) (Spanish Vahl yah dhoh *leedh*)

Vallauris, France : Va law *rees*

Valle de la Pascua, Venezuela : Vah yay dhay lah *Pahs* kwah

Valle de Santiago, Mexico : Vah yay dhay Sahn tee *ah* goh

Valledupar, Colombia : Vah yay dooh *pahr*

Vallejo, USA : Va *lay* oh

Valletta, Malta : Va *let* a

Valleyfield, Canada : *Val* i feeld

Valois, France : Vahl *wah*

¹Valparaiso, USA (Florida) : Val pa *riy* zoh

²Valparaiso, USA (Indiana) : Val pa *ray* zoh

Valparaíso, Chile : Vahl pah rah *ee* soh [When spelled without the accent as Valparaiso the seaport's name is pronounced as either **¹Valparaiso** or **²Valparaiso**.]

Valréas, France : Vahl ray *ahs*

Valverde, Dominican Republic : Vahl *ver* dhay

Van, Turkey : Van

Vanadzor, Armenia : Va *nahd* zawr

Vancouver, Canada : Van *kooh* vur (UK Van *kooh* va)

Vandalia, USA : Van *day* lya (UK Van *day* li a)

Vanderbijlpark, South Africa : *Van* dur biyl pahrk (UK *Van* da biyl pahk)

Van Diemen (Gulf), Australia : Van *Dee* mun

Vänersborg, Sweden : Va nurs *bawrg*

Vannes, France : Vahn

Vantaa, Finland : *Vahn* tah

Vanua Levu, Fiji : Vahn wah *Lay* vooh

Vanuatu, Pacific Ocean : Van *wah* tooh

Var, France : Vahr

Varanasi, India : Va *rah* na see

Varanger (Fjord), Norway : Vah *rahng* ur

Varaždin, Croatia : Vah *rahzh* deen

Varberg, Sweden : *Vahr* ber i

Vardø, Norway : *Vahr* duh

Varennes, France : Vah *ren*

Varese, Italy : Vah *ray* see

Varginha, Brazil : Vahr *zheen* ya

Varilhes, France : Vah *ree*

Varna, Bulgaria : *Vahr* na

Vaslui, Romania : Vahs *looh* ee
Västerås, Sweden : Ves tur *ohs*
Västervik, Sweden : *Ves* tur veek
Vatersay, Scotland : *Vat* ur say (UK *Vat* a say)
Vatican (City), Europe : *Vat* i kun
Vatnajökull, Iceland : *Vaht* nah yuh koohtl
Vättern, Sweden : *Vet* urn
Vaucluse, France : Voh *kloohz* (French Voh *kleez*)
Vaud, Switzerland : Voh
Vaughan, Canada : Vawn
Vaulx-en-Velin, France : Voh ahn Vuh *lahn*
Vaupés, Colombia : Vow *pays*
Vauxhall, England : *Vahk* sawl (UK *Vok* sawl) [Ross, p. 171, prefers a pronunciation *Voks* hawl for the London district, sounding the *h*, although Willey, p. 517, gives both "voxhall" and "voxall."]
Växjö, Sweden : *Vek* shuh
Vechte, Germany : *Fekh* ta
Veendam, Netherlands : Vayn *dahm*
Veenendaal, Netherlands : *Vay* nun dahl
Vega Alta, Puerto Rico : Vay gah *Ahl* tah
Vejle, Denmark : *Viy* la
Veldhoven, Netherlands : *Velt* hoh va
Velenje, Slovenia : Ve *len* ya
Vélez-Málaga, Spain : Vay lays *Mah* lah gah
Velia, Italy : *Vee* li a
Velikiye Luki, Russia : Vi lee kee ya *Looh* ki
Velikiy Ustyug, Russia : Vi lee kee *Ooh* styook
Veliko Tŭrnovo, Bulgaria : Ve li kaw *Toor* na voh
Velindre, Wales : Va *lin* dray
Velingrad, Bulgaria : *Ve* ling graht
Velletri, Italy : Ve *lay* tree
Vellore, India : Va *lohr*
Velsen, Netherlands : *Vel* sa
Venado Tuerto, Argentina : Vay nah doh *Twer* toh (Spanish Vay nah dhoh *Twer* toh)
Venda, South Africa : *Ven* da

Vendée, France : Vahn *day*
Vendôme, France : Vahn *dohm*
Venetia, Italy : Vi *nee* shi a
Venezuela, South America : Ven a *zway* la (Spanish Vay nay *sway* lah)
Venice, Italy : *Ven* us (UK *Ven* is)
Vénissieux, France : Vay nee *syuh*
Venlo, Netherlands : *Ven* loh
Venray, Netherlands : *Ven* riy
Ventimiglia, Italy : Ven tee *meel* yah
Ventnor, England : *Vent* nur (UK *Vent* na)
Ventspils, Latvia : *Vent* spils
Ventura, USA : Ven *toor* a (UK Ven *tyoo* ra)
Veracruz, Mexico : Ver a *kroohz* (UK Vi a ra *kroohz*) (Spanish Vay rah *kroohs*)
Vercelli, Italy : Ver *chel* lee
Verde, USA : *Vuhr* di (UK *Vuh* di)
Verden, Germany : *Fer* dun
¹**Verdun**, Canada : *Vuhr* dun (UK *Vuh* dun)
²**Verdun**, France : Vuhr *dahn* (UK Vuh *dahn*) (French Ver *dahn*)
Vereeniging, South Africa : Va *ray* na khing
Vergennes, USA : Vur *jenz*
Verkhoyansk, Russia : Vyer kha *yahnsk*
Vermont, USA : Vur *mahnt* (UK Va *mont*)
Vernal, USA : *Vuhr* nul (UK *Vuh* nul)
¹**Vernon**, Canada; USA : *Vuhr* nun (UK *Vuh* nun)
²**Vernon**, France : Ver *nohn*
Vero Beach, USA : Vir oh *Beech*
Verona, Italy : Va *roh* na (Italian Vay *roh* nah)
¹**Versailles**, France : Ver *siy*
²**Versailles**, USA : Vur *saylz*
Vertus, France : Ver *tee*
Verviers, Belgium : Ver *vyay*
Verwood, England : *Vuhr* wood (UK *Vuh* wood)
Veryan, England : *Ver* i un
Vesoul, France : Va *zoohl*
Vesterålen, Norway : *Ves* tur oh lun
Vestsjælland, Denmark : Vest *she* lahn
Vesuvius, Italy : Va *sooh* vi us
Veszprém, Hungary : *Ves* praym

Veurne, Belgium : *Vuhr* na
Vevey, Switzerland : Va *vay*
Viana do Castelo, Portugal : Vyah na dooh Kash *tel* ooh
Viareggio, Italy : Vee ah *red* joh
Viborg, Denmark : *Vee* bawr
Vibraye, France : Vee *bray*
Vicente López, Argentina : Vee sen tay *Loh* pes
Vicenza, Italy : Vee *chen* sah
Vich, Spain : Veek
Vichada, Colombia : Vee *chah* dah (Spanish Vee *chah* dhah)
Vichy, France : *Vee* shi (French Vee *shee*)
Vicksburg, USA : *Viks* buhrg (UK *Viks* buhg)
Viçosa, Brazil : Vi *saw* za
Victoria, Africa; Argentina; Australia; Canada; Malaysia; Seychelles; USA : Vik *taw* ri a (Spanish Veek *toh* ryah)
Victoria de la Tunas, Cuba : Veek toh ryah dhay las *Tooh* nahs
Victoriaville, Canada : Vik *toh* ri a vil
Victorville, USA : *Vik* tur vil (UK *Vik* ta vil)
Vidin, Bulgaria : *Vee* din
Viedma, Argentina : *Vyayd* mah
¹**Vienna**, Austria; USA (Virginia, West Virginia) : Vi *en* a
²**Vienna**, USA (Georgia, Illinois) : Viy *en* a
Vienne, France : Vyen
Vientiane, Laos : Vyen *tyahn*
Viersen, Germany : *Fir* zun
Vierzon, France : Vyer *zohn*
Vietnam, Asia : Vyet *nahm* (UK Vyet *nam*)
Vieux Carré, USA : Vooh Kah *ray*
Vieux Fort, Guadeloupe; St. Lucia : Vyuh *Fawr* (UK ... *Faw*)
Vigevano, Italy : Vee *je* vah noh
Vigia, Brazil : Vi *zhee* a
Vigo, Spain : *Vee* goh [English speakers often use the pronunciation *Viy* goh for the seaport where the French and Spanish were defeated by the English and Dutch in 1702, and this applies to any transferred use of the name, as for *Vigo Village*, Kent, England.]

Vihiers, France : Vee *yay*
Vijayawada, India : Vi ja ya *wah* da
Vila da Manhiça, Mozambique : Vee la da Mun *yee* sa
Vila Nova de Gaia, Portugal : Vee la Naw va dee *Giy* a
Vila Real, Portugal : Vee la *Ree* ul
Vila Velha, Brazil : Vee la *Vel* ya
Villa Alemana, Chile : Vee yah Ah le *mah* nah
Villach, Austria : Fi *lahkh*
Villa Clara, Cuba : Vee yah *Klah* rah
Villa Dolores, Argentina : Vee yah Dhoh *loh* rays
Villa Flores, Mexico : Vee yah *Floh* rays
Villaguay, Argentina : Vee yah *gwiy*
Villahermosa, Mexico : Vee yah er *moh* sah
Villajoyosa, Spain : Vee lyah hoh *yoh* sah
Villa María, Argentina : Vee yah Mah *ree* yah
Villard-de-Lans, France : Vee yahrd *Lahns*
Villarreal, Spain : Veel yahr ray *ahl*
Villarrica, Paraguay : Vee yah *ree* kah
Villavicencio, Colombia : Vee yah vee *sen* syoh
Villecresnes, France : Veel *krayn*
Villefranche, France : Veel *frahnsh*
Villejuif, France : Veel *zhweef*
Villeneuve, France : Veel *nuhv*
Villers-Bocage, France : Vee ler Baw *kahzh*
Villerupt, France : Veel *ree*
Villeurbanne, France : Vee luhr *bahn*
Villingen-Schwenningen, Germany : Fil ing un *Shven* ing un
Vilnius, Lithuania : *Vil* nee us
Vilvoorde, Belgium : *Vil* vawr da
Vimy, France : *Vee* mi (French Vee *mee*)
Viña del Mar, Chile : Veen ya del *Mahr*
¹**Vincennes**, France : Vahn *sen*
²**Vincennes**, USA : Vin *senz*
Vindhya (Range), India : *Vin* dya
Vineland, USA : *Viyn* lund
Vinh, Vietnam : Vin
Vinkovci, Croatia : *Ving* kawft see
Vinnitsa, Ukraine : *Vin* nit sya

Vinnytsya, Ukraine : *Vin* nit sya
Virden, Canada; USA : *Vuhr* dun (UK *Vuh* dun)
Virginia, South Africa; USA : Vur *jin* ya (UK Va *jin* i a)
Virginia Beach, USA : Vur jin ya *Beech* (UK Va jin ia...)
Virgin (Islands), West Indies : *Vuhr* jun (UK *Vuh* jin)
Virovitica, Croatia : Vee *raw* vee teet sah
Virunga, Africa : Vee *roohng* gah
Visalia, USA : Vi *say* lya
Visby, Sweden : *Viz* bee
Visé, Belgium : Vee *zay*
Viseu, Portugal : Vi *zay* ooh
Vishakhapatnam, India : Vi sha ka *paht* num
Vista, USA : *Vis* ta
Vistula, Poland : *Vis* choo la (UK *Vis* tyoo la)
Vitebsk, Belarus : *Vee* tipsk
Viterbo, Italy : Vee *ter* boh
Viti Levu, Fiji : Vee tee *Lay* vooh
Vitoria, Spain : Vee *toh* ree ah
Vitória, Brazil : Vee *toh* rya
Vitória da Conquista, Brazil : Vee toh rya da Kawn *kee* sta
Vitória de Santo Antão, Brazil : Vee toh rya dee Sahn tooh Ahn *town*
Vitsyebsk, Belarus : *Veet* syipsk
Vittorio Veneto, Italy : Vee toh ree oh Ve *nay* toh
Vizianagaram, India : Vi zee a *nah* grum
Vlaardingen, Netherlands : *Vlahr* ding un
Vladikavkaz, Russia : Vla di kaf *kahs*
Vladimir, Russia : *Vlad* a mir (UK *Vlad* i mi a) (Russian Vla *dee* mir)
Vladimir-Volynskiy, Ukraine : Vla dee mir Va *lin* ski
Vladivostok, Russia : Vla da *vahs* tahk (UK Vlad i *vos* tok) (Russian Vla di vas *tawk*)
Vlissingen, Netherlands : *Vlis* ing a
Vlorë, Albania : *Vloh* ra
Vltava, Czech Republic : *Vool* tah vah
Voghera, Italy : Voh *gay* rah

Voi, Kenya : Voy
Vojvodina, Serbia : Voy va *dee* na (Serbo-Croat *Voy* vaw dee nah)
Volga, Russia : *Vahl* ga (UK *Vol* ga) (Russian *Vawl* ga)
Volgograd, Russia : *Vahl* ga grad (UK *Vol* ga grad) (Russian Vul ga *graht*)
Volhynia, Europe : Vahl *hin* i a (UK Vol *hin* i a)
Volkhov, Russia : *Vawl* khuf
Völklingen, Germany : *Fuhlk* ling un
Volodymyr-Volynskyy, Ukraine : Va la di mir Va *lin* ski
Vologda, Russia : *Vaw* lug da
Volokolamsk, Russia : Vaw la ka *lahmsk*
Volta, Ghana : *Vohl* ta (UK *Vol* ta)
Volta Redonda, Brazil : Vohl ta Re *dohn* da
Volyn, Ukraine : Va *lin*
Volzhsk, Russia : *Vawlshsk*
Volzhskiy, Russia : *Vawlsh* ski
Voorburg, Netherlands : *Vohr* boorkh
Voorst, Netherlands : Vohrst
Vorarlberg, Austria : Fohr *ahrl* buhrg
Vordingborg, Denmark : Vawr ding *bawr*
Vorkuta, Russia : Vawr kooh *tah*
Voronezh, Russia : Va *raw* nish
Vosges, France : Vohzh
Voskresensk, Russia : Vus kri *syensk*
Voss, Norway : Vaws
Votkinsk, Russia : *Vawt* kinsk
Vratsa, Bulgaria : *Vraht* sa
Vryburg, South Africa : *Friy* buhrg (UK *Friy* buhg)
Vryheid, South Africa : *Friy* hayt
Vught, Netherlands : Veekht
Vukovar, Croatia : *Vooh* ka vahr (UK *Vooh* ka vah) (Serbo-Croat Vooh *koh* vahr)
Vyatka, Russia : *Vyaht* ka
Vyazma, Russia : *Vyahz* ma
Vyborg, Russia : *Vee* bawrg (UK *Viy* bawg) (Russian *Vwi* boork)
Vychegda, Russia : *Vwi* chik da
Vyrnwy, Wales : *Vuhrn* wi (UK *Vuhn* wi)
Vyshniy Volochek, Russia : Vwish ni Vul a *chawk*

Wa, Ghana : Wah
Wabash, USA : *Waw* bash
Waco, USA : *Way* koh
Waddesdon, England : *Wahdz* dun (UK *Wodz* dun)
Waddington, Canada; England : *Wah* ding tun (UK *Wod* ing tun)
Wadebridge, England : *Wayd* brij
Wadhurst, England : *Wahd* huhrst (UK *Wod* huhst)
Wadi Halfa, Sudan : Wah dee *Hal* fa
Wad Medani, Sudan : Wahd *Med* a ni
Waes, Belgium : Wahs
Wageningen, Netherlands : *Vah* kha ning un
Wagga Wagga, Australia : *Wah* ga Wah ga (UK *Wog* a Wog a)
Wah, Pakistan : Wah
Wahiawa, USA : Wah hee a *wah*
Wahpeton, USA : *Waw* pa tun
Waianae, USA : Wiy ah *niy*
Waiblingen, Germany : *Viy* bling un
Waigeo, Indonesia : Wiy *gay* oh
Waihi, New Zealand : Wiy *hee*
Waikato, New Zealand : Wiy *kah* toh (UK Wiy *kat* oh)
Waikiki, USA : Wiy ka *kee*
Wailuku, USA : Wiy *looh* kooh
Waimea, USA : Wiy *may* ah
Wainwright, Canada : *Wayn* riyt
Waipahu, USA : Wiy *pah* hooh
Wairoa, New Zealand : Wiy *roh* a
Waitangi, New Zealand : Wiy *tang* i
Waitara, New Zealand : *Wiy* ta ra
Wakayama, Japan : Wah kah *yah* mah
Wakefield, England; USA : *Wayk* feeld
Wake (Island), Pacific Ocean : Wayk
Walachia, Romania : Wah *lay* ki a (UK Wa *lay* ki a)
Walberswick, England : *Wawl* burz wik (UK *Wawl* buz wik)
Wałbrzych, Poland : *Vahlb* zhik
Walcheren, Netherlands : *Vahl* kha run
Wałcz, Poland : Vowch
Wales, Europe : Waylz
Wallaceburg, Canada : *Wah* lus buhrg (UK *Wol* is buhg)
Wallachia, Romania : Wah *lay* ki a (UK Wa *lay* ki a)

Wallasey, England : *Wah* la si (UK *Wol* a si)
Walla Walla, USA : Wah la *Wah* la (UK Wol a *Wol* a)
Wallerawang, Australia : Wa *ler* a wang (UK Wa *lay* a ra wang)
Wallingford, England ; USA : *Wah* ling furd (UK *Wol* ing fud)
Wallis (Islands), Pacific Ocean : *Wah* lus (UK *Wol* is)
Wallonia, Belgium : Wah *loh* ni a (UK Wa *loh* ni a)
Wallsend, England : *Wawlz* end
Walmer, England : *Wawl* mur (UK *Wawl* ma)
Walney (Island), England : *Wawl* ni
Walnut, USA : *Wawl* nut (UK *Wawl* naht)
Walpole, USA : *Wawl* pohl
Walsall, England : *Wawl* sawl [The name of the town near Birmingham has an alternate local pronunciation *Waw* sul.]
Walsingham, England : *Wawlz* ing um [The name of the Norfolk village, famous as a medieval place of pilgrimage, is pronounced *Wawl* sing um by many.]
Waltham, USA : *Wawl* thum [The usual local pronunciation of the Massachusetts city's name is *Wawl* tham.]
Waltham, England : *Wawl* thum [This pronunciation applies for the Essex town of *Waltham Abbey* and villages of *Great Waltham* and *Little Waltham* as well as for the London borough of *Waltham Forest* and district of *Waltham Cross* in Cheshunt, Hertfordshire. Forster, p. 245, quotes the passage below from the 1974 edition of Jones (substituting the present book's phonetic transcription for his standard IPA forms).]
    Note.— The traditional local pronunciation at Great Waltham and Little Waltham in Essex is *Wawl* tum, and this is the pronunciation used by those who have lived there

for a long time. Some new residents pronounce *Wawl* thum. In telephoning to these places from a distance it is advisable to pronounce *Wawl* thum; otherwise the caller is liable to be given Walton(-on-the-Naze), which is in the same county.

Walthamstow, England : *Wawl* thum stoh [The name of the town in the London borough of Waltham Forest was formerly pronounced *Wawl* tum stoh. *Cp.* **Waltham**.]

Walton-le-Dale, England : Wawl tun li *Dayl*

Walton on Thames, England : Wawl tun ahn *Temz* (UK ... on...)

Walton on the Naze, England : Wawl tun ahn dha *Nayz* (UK ... on...)

Walvis Bay, Namibia : Wawl vis *Bay*

Walworth, England : *Wawl* wurth (UK *Wawl* wuth)

Wanaka, New Zealand : *Wah* na ka (UK *Won* a ka)

Wandsworth, England : *Wahndz* wurth (UK *Wondz* wuth)

Wanganui, New Zealand : Wahng ga *nooh* i (UK *Wong* a nooh i) [According to Jones, p. 586, the UK pronunciation, not voicing the *g*, is "the form always used by those of Polynesian descent."]

Wangaratta, Australia : Wang ga *rat* a

Wankie, Zimbabwe : *Wahng* ki

Wansbeck, England : *Wahnz* bek (UK *Wonz* bek)

Wanstead, England : *Wahn* stid (UK *Won* stid)

Wantage, England : *Wahn* tij (UK *Won* tij)

Wapping, England : *Wah* ping (UK *Wop* ing)

The name is pronounced "Wopping," already in use for several centuries as suggested by the 17th-century spelling [*Woppin*] [A.D. Mills, *A Dictionary of London Place Names*, 2001].

Wappingers Falls, USA : Wah pun jurz *Fawlz* (UK Wop in juz...)

Warangal, India : *Waw* rung gul

Warboys, England : *Wawr* boyz (UK *Waw* boyz)

Warburton, England : *Wawr* buhr tun (UK *Waw* ba tun)

Wardha, India : *Wawr* da

Ware, England : *Way* ur (UK *Way* a)

Waregem, Belgium : *Wah* ra khem

Wareham, England; USA : *Wer* um (UK *Way* a rum)

Waremme, Belgium : Wah *raym*

Waren, Germany : *Vah* run

Warkworth, England : *Wawrk* wurth (UK *Wawk* wuth)

Warley, England : *Wawr* li (UK *Waw* li)

Warlingham, England : *Wawr* ling um (UK *Waw* ling um)

Warminster, England; USA : *Wawr* min stur (UK *Waw* min sta)

Warner Robins, USA : Wawr nur *Rah* bunz (UK Waw na *Rob* inz)

Warninglid, England : *Wawr* ning lid (UK *Waw* ning lid)

Warren, USA : *Waw* run (UK *Wor* un)

Warri, Nigeria : *Waw* ri

Warrington, England : *Waw* ring tun (UK *Wor* ing tun)

Warrnambool, Australia : *Wawr* num boohl (UK *Waw* num boohl)

Warsaw, Poland; USA : *Wawr* saw (UK *Waw* saw)

Warsop, England : *Wawr* sahp (UK *Waw* sop)

¹**Warwick**, Australia; England : *Waw* rik (UK *Wor* ik)

²**Warwick**, Canada; USA : *Wawr* wik (UK *Waw* wik)

Wasatch (Range), USA : *Waw* sach

Washington, England; USA : *Wah* shing tun (UK *Wosh* ing tun)

Washita, USA : *Wah* sha taw (UK *Wosh* i taw)

Washoe, USA : *Wah* shoh (UK *Wosh* oh)

Wasquehal, France : Wahs *kahl*

Wassenaar, Netherlands : *Vah* sa nahr

Wast Water, England : *Wahst* Waw tur (UK *Wost* Waw ta)

Watauga, USA : Wah *taw* ga

Watchet, England : *Wah* chut (UK *Woch* it)

Waterbury, USA : *Waw* tur ber i (UK *Waw* ta bri)

Waterford, Ireland; USA : *Waw* tur furd (UK *Waw* ta fud)

Waterloo, Belgium; Canada; USA : Waw tur *looh* (UK Waw ta *looh*) (Flemish *Vah* tur loh, French Wah ter *loh*)

Waterlooville, England : Waw tur looh *vil* (UK Waw ta looh *vil*)

Watermael-Boitsfort, Belgium : Vah tur mahl Bwah *fawr* (French Wah ter mal...)

Watertown, USA : *Waw* tur town (UK *Waw* ta town)

Waterville, USA : *Waw* tur vil (UK *Waw* ta vil)

Watford, England : *Waht* furd (UK *Wot* fud)

Wath upon Dearne, England : Wahth a pahn *Duhrn* (UK Woth a pon *Duhn*)

Watsonville, USA : *Waht* sun vil (UK *Wot* sun vil)

Wattignies, France : Wah teen *yee*

Wattrelos, France : Wah tur *loh*

Watts, USA : Wahts (UK Wots)

Wauchope (Forest), Scotland : *Waw* kup

Waukegan, USA : Waw *kee* gun

Waukesha, USA : *Waw* ki shaw

Waupun, USA : Waw *pahn*

Wauwatosa, USA : Waw wa *toh* sa

Waveney, England : *Wayv* ni

Waverley, Australia; England : *Way* vur li (UK *Way* va li)

Waverly, USA : *Way* vur li (UK *Way* va li)

Wavertree, England: *Way* va tri [The district of Liverpool has a local pronunciation *Waw* tree.]

Wavre, Belgium : Wahvr

Wawona, USA : Waw *woh* na

Waxahachie, USA : Wawk sa *hach* i

Waycross, USA : *Way* kraws (UK *Way* kros)

Wayland, USA : *Way* lund

Wayne, USA : Wayn

Waynesboro, USA : *Waynz* buhr oh (UK *Waynz* bra)

Wayzata, USA : Wiy *zet* a

Wazirabad, Pakistan : Wa *zir* a bahd

Waziristan, Pakistan : Wa zir i *stan* (UK Wa *zi* a ri stahn)

Weald, England : Weeld [The region of southeastern England between the North and South Downs has a name with a local pronunciation Wild, especially in Sussex.]
The Weald of Sussex is always spoken of as The Wild by people who live in the Downs [W.D. Parish, *A Dictionary of the Sussex Dialect*, 1875].

Wealden, England : *Weel* dun

Wealdstone, England : *Weeld* stohn

Wearmouth, England : *Wir* mowth (UK *Wi* a mowth)

Weatherford, USA : *Wedh* ur furd (UK *Wedh* a fud)

Webster, USA : *Web* stur (UK *Web* sta)

Weddell (Sea), Antarctica : *Wed* ul

Wedel, Germany : *Vay* dul

Wednesbury, England : *Wenz* bri [At one time the name of the former Staffordshire town, now a district of West Bromwich, had the alternate local pronunciation *Wej* bri, written *Wedgebury*.]

Wednesfield, England : *Wens* feeld [The name of the former Staffordshire town, now a district of Wolverhampton, was at one time also locally pronounced *Wej* feeld, written *Wedgefield*.]

Weehawken, USA : Wee *haw* kun

Weenen, South Africa : *Vee* nun

Weert, Netherlands : Vert

Weesp, Netherlands : Vaysp

Węgorzewo, Poland : Ven gaw *zhe* vaw

Weiden, Germany : *Viy* dun

Weifang, China : Way *fahng*

Weihaiwei, China : Way hiy *way*

Weimar, Germany : *Viy* mahr

Weinheim, Germany : *Viyn* hiym

Weirton, USA : *Wir* tun (UK *Wi* a tun)

Weiser, USA : *Wee* sur (UK *Wee* sa)

Weissenburg, Germany : *Viy* sun boork

Weissenfels, Germany : *Viy* sun fels

Weisswasser, Germany : *Viys* vah sur

Wejherowo, Poland : Vay he *raw* vaw
Welkom, South Africa : *Vel* kum
Welland, Canada; England : *Wel* und
Wellesley, USA : *Welz* li
Wellingborough, England : *Wel* ing buhr oh (UK *Wel* ing bra)
Wellington, England; New Zealand; South Africa; USA : *Wel* ing tun [The New Zealand capital's name is locally often pronounced *Wal* ing ton.]
Wells, England; USA : Welz
Wels, Austria : Vels
Welshpool, Wales : *Welsh* poohl
Welwyn, England : *Wel* in
Welwyn Garden City, England : Wel in Gahr dun *Si* ti (UK ... Gah dun...)
Wem, England : Wem
Wembley, England : *Wem* bli
Wenatchee, USA : Wa *nach* i
Wendover, England : *Wen* doh vur (UK *Wen* doh va)
Wengen, Switzerland : *Veng* un
Wenlock Edge, England : Wen lahk *Ej* (UK Wen lok...)
Wensleydale, England : *Wenz* li dayl
Wentworth, England : *Went* wuhrth (UK *Went* wuth)
Wenzhou, China : Wen *joh*
Weobley, England : *Web* li [The spelling of the Herefordshire village's name, with its unpronounced *o*, was probably influenced by that of the nearby town of **Leominster**.]
Werdau, Germany : *Ver* dow
Wermelskirchen, Germany : *Ver* muls kir khun
Wernigerode, Germany : Ver ni ga *roh* da
Werribee, Australia : *Wer* a bee
Werwik, Belgium : Ver *veek*
Wesel, Germany : *Vay* zul
Weser, Germany : *Vay* zur (UK *Vay* za) [In Browning's poem "The Pied Piper of Hamelin" (1842), the river name is pronounced US *Wee* zur, UK *Wee* za, rhyming with "Caesar."]
Weslaco, USA : *Wes* la koh
Wesseling, Germany : *Ves* a ling
Wessex, England : *Wes* iks

West : For names prefixed with this word and not given below, as *West Bengal*, *West Virginia*, see the main name. (*West* is rarely stressed as a separate word.)
West Allis, USA : West *A* lus (UK ... *A* lis)
West Bridgford, England : West *Brij* furd (UK ... *Brij* fud)
West Bromwich, England : West *Brah* mich (UK ... *Brom* ich)
Westbury, England; USA : *West* ber i (UK *West* bri)
Westbury-on-Trym, England : West ber i ahn *Trim* (UK West bri on...)
Westchester, USA : *West* ches tur (UK *West* ches ta)
West Country, England : *West* Kahn tri
West Covina, USA : West Koh *vee* nah
Westerham, England : *West* rum
Westerlo, Belgium : Ves ter *loh*
Westerly, USA : *Wes* tur li (UK *Wes* ta li)
Western Isles, Scotland : Wes turn *Iylz* (UK Wes tun...)
Westerville, USA : *Wes* tur vil (UK *Wes* ta vil)
Westfield, USA : *West* feeld
Westford, USA : *West* furd (UK *West* fud)
Westhoughton, England : West *haw* tun
Westland, New Zealand; USA : *West* lund
West Malling, England : West *Maw* ling [The main name of the Kent village is sometimes popularly pronounced *Mal* ing.]
Westmeath, Ireland : West *meedh*
Westminster, England; USA : *Wes* min stur (UK *Wes* min sta) [Ross, p. 174, cautions against a middle stress Wes *min* sta for the name of the London, England, borough, yet Jones give this as the prime pronunciation. A UK mispronunciation Wes *min* i sta is sometimes heard, presumably by association with "minister."]
To speak of Mersey*side* or West*min*-

ster is to reveal a misunderstanding of what such place-names denote and how they came into being [Fritz Spiegl, *MediaSpeak*, 1989].

Westmoreland, USA : West *mawr* lund (UK West *maw* lund) [The name of Westmoreland, Virginia, is usually pronounced as for **Westmorland**.]

Westmorland, England : *West* mur lund (UK *West* ma lund)

Westmount, Canada : *West* mownt

Weston, England; USA : *Wes* tun

Weston-super-Mare, England : Wes tun sooh pur *Mer* (UK ... sooh pa *May* a) [A UK middle stress, Wes tun *sooh* pa May a, is sometimes heard for the name of the former Somerset resort, and Pointon, p. 258, records a rendering of the Latin *super-Mare* ("on-Sea") suffix as a now dated syooh pa *May* a ri.]

Westphalia, Germany : West *fay* li a

West Point, USA : *West* Poynt

Westport, Ireland; New Zealand; USA : *West* pawrt (UK *West* pawt)

Westray, Scotland : *Wes* tray

Weststellingwerf, Netherlands : Vest stel ing *verf*

Westward Ho!, England : West wurd *Hoh* (UK West wud...)

Westwego, USA : West *wee* goh

Westwood, USA : *West* wood

Wetar, Indonesia : *Wet* ahr

Wetaskiwin, Canada : Wi *tas* ka win

Wete, Tanzania : *Way* tee

Wetherby, England : *Wedh* ur bi (UK *Wedh* a bi)

Wethersfield, USA : *Wedh* urz feeld (UK *Wedh* uz feeld)

Wetteren, Belgium : *Way* tur un (Flemish *Vay* tur un)

Wettingen, Switzerland : *Vet* ing un

Wetzikon, Switzerland : *Vet* si kawn

Wetzlar, Germany : *Vets* lahr

Wevelgem, Belgium : *Way* vul gaym (Flemish *Vay* vul khum)

Wewak, Papua New Guinea : *Way* wahk

Wexford, Ireland : *Weks* furd (UK *Weks* fud)

Weybridge, England : *Way* brij

Weyburn, Canada : *Way* burn (UK *Way* bun)

Weymouth, England; USA : *Way* muth

Whakatane, New Zealand : Wah ka *tah* nee

Whalley, England : *Waw* li [Names beginning *Wh-* are often pronounced with an initial *Hw-* in the USA and by Scottish and Irish speakers in the UK, so that, e.g., **Whitby** is *Hwit* bi. This pronunciation largely has its origin in the Old English forms of many *wh-* words, such as *hwǣte*, "wheat," and *hwīt*, "white."]

Whangarei, New Zealand : Wahng ga *ray* (UK Wong ga *ray*)

Wharfe, England : Wawrf (UK Wawf)

Wheathampstead, England : *Weet* um sted

Wheaton, USA : *Wee* tun

Wheaton-Glenmont, USA : Wee tun *Glen* mahnt (UK ... *Glen* mont)

Wheeling, USA : *Wee* ling

Whickham, England : *Wik* um

Whipsnade, England : *Wip* snayd

Whitby, Canada; England : *Wit* bi

¹Whitchurch, England : *Wit* chuhrch (UK *Wit* chuhch)

²Whitchurch, Wales : *Wi* chuhch

Whitechapel, England : *Wiyt* chap ul

Whitefield, England : *Wiyt* feeld

Whitehall, USA : *Wiyt* hawl

Whitehaven, England : *Wiyt* hay vun

Whitehorse, Canada : *Wiyt* hawrs (UK *Wiyt* haws)

Whitewater, USA : *Wiyt* waw tur (UK *Wiyt* waw ta)

Whithorn, Scotland : *Wit* hawrn (UK *Wit* hawn)

Whitley Bay, England : Wit li *Bay*

Whitney, USA : *Wit* nee

Whitstable, England : *Wit* sta bul

Whittier, USA : *Wit* i ur (UK *Wit* i a)

Whittlesea, Australia : *Wit* ul see

Whittlesey, England : *Wit* ul see

Whitworth, England : *Wit* wuhrth (UK *Wit* wuhth)

Whyalla, Australia : Wiy *al* a [An alternate stress *Wiy* a la is also heard for the South Australia town.]

Whyteleafe, England : *Wiyt* leef

Wibsey, England : *Wib* si [The district of Bradford, West Yorkshire, is also known locally as *Wip* si.]

Wichita, USA : *Wich* i taw

Wick, Scotland : Wik

Wickford, England : *Wik* furd (UK *Wik* fud)

Wickham, England : *Wik* um

Wicklow, Ireland : *Wik* loh

Widecombe in the Moor, England : Wid i kum in dha *Moor* (UK ... *Moo* a)

Widemouth Bay, England : Wid muth *Bay*

Widnes, England : *Wid* nus (UK *Wid* nis)

Wieluń, Poland : *Vye* loohn

Wiener Neustadt, Austria : Vee nur *Noy* shtaht

Wierden, Netherlands : *Veer* da

Wieringen, Netherlands : *Veer* ing a

Wiesbaden, Germany : *Vees* bah dun

Wigan, England : *Wig* un

Wight *see* **Isle of Wight**

Wigston, England : *Wig* stun

Wigton, England : *Wig* tun

Wigtown, Scotland : *Wig* town [Some Scots prefer a pronunciation *Wig* tun for the town.]

Wil, Switzerland : Veel

Wilbraham, USA : *Wil* bra ham (UK *Wil* bra hum)

Wilhelmshaven, Germany : Vil helmz *hah* fun

Wilkes-Barre, USA : *Wilks* Bar a

Wilkinsburg, USA : *Wil* kunz buhrg (UK *Wil* kinz buhg)

Willamette, USA : Wi *lam* ut (UK Wi *lam* it) [As a reminder that the name of the Oregon river is stressed on the second syllable, the story is told that when the explorers Meriwether Lewis and William Clark were leading an expedition to the Pacific coast, Lewis turned to Clark and supposedly said, "Will, am it a river?"]

Willebroek, Belgium : *Wee* la brook (Flemish *Vee* la brook)

Willemstad, Netherlands Antilles : *Vil* um staht

Willenhall, England : *Wil* un hawl

Willesden, England : *Wilz* dun

Williamsburg, USA : *Wil* yumz buhrg (UK *Wil* yumz buhg)

Williamsport, USA : *Wil* yumz pawrt (UK *Wil* yumz pawt)

Williamstown, Australia; USA : *Wil* yumz town

Willimantic, USA : Wi la *man* tik (UK Wi li *man* tik)

Willingboro, USA : *Wil* ing bur oh (UK *Wil* ing bra)

Williston, USA : *Wil* a stun (UK *Wil* is tun)

Willmar, USA : *Wil* mahr (UK *Wil* mah)

Willoughby, USA : *Wil* a bi

Wilmette, USA : Wil *met*

Wilmington, England; USA : *Wil* ming tun

Wilmslow, England : *Wilmz* loh

Wilson, USA : *Wil* sun

Wilton, England; USA : *Wil* tun

Wiltshire, England : *Wilt* shir (UK *Wilt* sha)

Wimbledon, England : *Wim* bul dun

Wimborne, England : *Wim* bawrn (UK *Wim* bawn)

Wimmera, Australia : *Wim* a ra

Wincanton, England : Win *kan* tun

Winchelsea, England : *Win* chul see

Winchester, England; USA : *Win* ches tur (UK *Win* chis ta)

Windermere, England : *Win* dur mir (UK *Win* da mi a)

Windham, USA : *Win* dum

Windhoek, Namibia : *Vint* hook

Windlesham, England : *Win* dul shum

Windsor, Canada; England; USA : *Win* zur (UK *Win* za)

Windward (Islands), West Indies : *Wind* wurd (UK *Wind* wud)

Winfield, USA : *Win* feeld

Wingles, France : Wahngl

Winlaton, England : Win *lay* tun

Winneba, Ghana : Wi *nay* ba
Winnebago, USA : Win a *bay* goh (UK Win i *bay* goh)
Winnemucca, USA : Win a *mah* ka (UK Win i *mah* ka)
Winnipeg, Canada : *Win* a peg (UK *Win* i peg)
Winnipegosis, Canada : Win a pa *goh* sus (UK Win i pi *goh* sis)
Winnipesaukee, USA : Win a pa *saw* ki (UK Win i pa *saw* ki)
Winona, USA : Wa *noh* na (UK Wi *noh* na)
Winschoten, Netherlands : *Vin* skhoh ta
Winsford, England : *Winz* furd (UK *Winz* fud)
Winslow, England; USA : *Winz* loh
Winston-Salem, USA : Win stun *Say* lum
Winterswijk, Netherlands : *Vin* turs viyk
Winterthur, Switzerland : *Vin* tur toor (UK *Vin* ta too a) (German *Vin* tur toohr)
Winterton, England : *Win* tur tun (UK *Win* ta tun)
Winthrop, USA : *Win* thrup (UK *Win* throp)
Winwick, England : *Win* ik
Wirksworth, England : *Wuhrks* wuhrth (UK *Wuhks* wuth)
Wirral, England : *Wuhr* ul (UK *Wir* ul)
Wisbech, England : *Wiz* beech
Wisch, Netherlands : Vis
Wisconsin, USA : Wis *kahn* sun (UK Wis *kon* sin)
Wishaw, Scotland : *Wish* aw
Wismar, Germany : *Vis* mahr
Wissant, France : Wee *sahn*
Wissembourg, France : Vee sahn *boohr*
Witbank, South Africa : *Wit* bank
¹**Witham**, England (Essex town) : *Wit* um
²**Witham**, England (Lincolnshire river) : *Widh* um
Withernsea, England : *Widh* urn see (UK *Widh* un see)
Withycombe, England : *Widh* i kum

Witney, England : *Wit* ni
Witten, Germany : *Vit* un
Wittenberg, Germany : *Vit* un berk
Wittenberge, Germany : Vit un *ber* ga
Witwatersrand, South Africa : *Wit* waw turz rand (UK Wit *waw* tuz rand)
Wiveliscombe, England : *Wiv* a lis kum [The name of the Somerset town is also locally pronounced *Wils* kum.]
Wivelsfield, England : *Wiv* ulz feeld
Wivenhoe, England : *Wiv* un hoh
Włocławek, Poland : Vwawt *swah* vek
¹**Woburn**, England : *Woh* buhrn (UK *Woh* buhn) [The name of the Bedfordshire village is also pronounced as ²**Woburn**. Pointon, p. 263, argues that since the latter pronunciation is used by the family of the Duke of Bedford, it is correct for his ancestral home of Woburn Abbey nearby and thus also for Woburn Safari Park there. But *Woh* buhn predominates.]
²**Woburn**, USA : *Wooh* buhrn
Wodzisław Śląski, Poland : Vaw jee swahf *Shlawn* ski
Woerden, Netherlands : *Voohr* da
Woëvre, France : Vwahvr
Woking, England : *Woh* king
Wokingham, England : *Woh* king um
Woldingham, England : *Wohl* ding um
Wolds, England : Wohldz
Wolfen, Germany : *Vawl* fun
Wolfenbüttel, Germany : *Vawl* fun bee tul
Wolfsburg, Germany : *Vawlfs* boork
Wollaston, Canada : *Wool* us tun
Wollondilly, Australia : *Wool* un dil i
Wollongong, Australia : *Wool* un gahng (UK *Wool* un gong)
Wołomin, Poland : Vaw *waw* meen
Woluwe-St.-Lambert, Belgium : Waw li way Sahn Lahm *ber*
Wolverhampton, England : Wool vur *hamp* tun (UK Wool va *hamp* tun)
Wolverton, England : *Wool* vur tun (UK *Wool* va tun)
Wombourne, England : *Wahm* bawrn (UK *Wom* bawn)
Wombwell, England : *Woom* wel

Wonersh, England : *Wahn* uhrsh (UK *Won* uhsh)

Wŏnju, South Korea : Wun *jooh*

Wŏnsan, North Korea : Wun *sahn*

Wonthaggi, Australia : Wahn *thag* i (UK Won *thag* i)

Woodbridge, England; USA : *Wood* brij

Woodbury, USA : *Wood* ber i (UK *Wood* bri)

Woodland, USA : *Wood* lund

Woodstock, Canada; England; USA : *Wood* stahk (UK *Wood* stok)

Wookey, England : *Wook* i

Woolacombe, England : *Wool* a kum

Woolfardisworthy, England : Wool *fahr* dus wuhr dhi (UK Wool *fah* dis wuh dhi) [The name of the Devon village is also often pronounced *Wool* zur i, written *Woolsery* as an alternate form of the longer name. There are actually two villages of this name in the county. The alternate name usually applies to the larger and more westerly.]

Woolloomooloo, Australia : Wool a ma *looh* [The name of the Sydney suburb is alternately stressed *Wool* a ma looh.]

Woolwich, England : *Wool* ij [As for **Greenwich**, the -*wich* of the London district's name gives an alternate pronunciation *Wool* ich.

The name Woolwich is pronounced "Wullitch" or "Wullidge" [A.D. Mills, *A Dictionary of London Place Names*, 2001].

Woomera, Australia : *Woom* a ra

Woonsocket, USA : Woohn *sah* kut (UK Woohn *sok* it)

Wooster, USA : *Woos* tur (UK *Woos* ta)

Wootton Bassett, England : Woo tun *Bas* it

Worcester, England; South Africa; USA : *Woos* tur (UK *Woos* ta)

In *Worcester* county, Maryland, the name is usually pronounced *Wooster*, but on the Western Shore of the State one hears *Worcest'r* [i.e. *Wawr* ses tur] [Mencken, p. 540].

Workington, England : *Wuhrk* ing tun (UK *Wuhk* ing tun)

Worksop, England : *Wuhrk* sahp (UK *Wuhk* sop)

Worlingham, England : *Wuhr* ling um (UK *Wuhr* ling um)

Worms, Germany : Wuhrmz (UK Vuhmz) (German Vawrms) [In its historical context as the seat of the Diet of Worms (1521), the city's name is often pronounced US Wuhrmz, UK Wuhmz by English speakers, evoking a surreal "diet of worms." Lloyd James 1937 favors a compromise pronunciation US Vawrmz, UK Vawmz.]

Worplesdon, England : *Wawr* pulz dun (UK *Waw* pulz dun)

Worsley, England : *Wuhrs* li (UK *Wuhs* li)

Worthing, England : *Wuhr* dhing (UK *Wuh* dhing)

Worthington, USA : *Wuhr* dhing tun (UK *Wuh* dhing tun)

Wotton-under-Edge, England : Woot un ahn dur *Ej* [The name of the Gloucestershire town is also locally pronounced Woot un *ahnd* rij, omitting the fourth syllable.]

Wrangel (Island), Russia : *Rang* gul

Wrangell, USA : *Rang* gul

Wraysbury, England : *Rayz* bri [The name of the former Buckinghamshire village was earlier spelled *Wyrardisbury*, pronounced as now.]

Wreay, England : *Ree* a

Wrekin, England : *Ree* kin

Wrexham, Wales : *Rek* sum

Wrocław, Poland : *Vrawt* swahf

Wrotham, England : *Rooh* tum

Wroughton, England : *Raw* tun

Wroxeter, England : *Rahks* a tur (UK *Roks* it a)

Wrzesnia, Poland : *Vshesh* nyah

Wuhan, China : Wooh *hahn* (UK Wooh *han*)

Wuhu, China : Wooh *hooh*

Wülfrath, Germany : *Veelf* raht

Wuppertal, Germany : *Voop* ur tahl (UK *Voop* a tahl) (German *Voopr* tahl)

Württemberg, Germany : *Wuhr* tum

buhrg (UK *Vuh* tum buhg) (German *Veer* tum berk)

Würzburg, Germany : *Wuhrts* buhrg (UK *Vuhts* buhg) (German *Veerts* boork)

Wuxi, China : Wooh *shee*

Wyandotte, USA : *Wiy* un daht (UK *Wiy* un dot)

Wye, England; Wales : Wiy

Wylye, England : *Wiy* li

¹Wymondham, England (Leicestershire) : *Wiy* mund um

²Wymondham, England (Norfolk) : *Wim* un dum [The town's name has a traditional local pronunciation *Win* dum.]

> Go to Norfolk and enquire for "WYMONDHAM" and the chances are that you won't find anyone who has ever heard of it, the reason being that for so long it has been merely "Windham" [H.G. Stokes, *English Place-Names*, 1948].

Wyndham, Australia : *Win* dum

Wynyard, Australia : *Win* yurd (UK *Win* yud)

Wyoming, USA : Wiy *ohm* ing

Wyre, England : *Wiy* ur (UK *Wiy* a)

Wyszków, Poland : *Vish* koohf

Xaafuun, Somalia : Kah *foohn*

Xai-Xai, Mozambique : *Shiy* Shiy

Xankändi, Azerbaijan : Zahn *kan* dee

Xánthi, Greece : *Ksahn* thee

Xenia, USA : *Zee* nya

Xiamen, China : Shah *mahn*

Xi'an, China : Shee *ahn*

Xingu, Brazil : Shing *gooh*

Xining, China : Shee *ning*

Xinjiang, China : Shin *jyahng*

Xinxiang, China : Shin *shyahn*

Xochimilco, Mexico : Soh chee *meel* koh

Xuzhou, China : Shee *joh*

Yabucoa, Puerto Rico : Yah booh *koh* ah

Yacuiba, Bolivia : Yah *kwee* bah

Yafo, Israel : *Yah* foh

Yakima, USA : *Yak* i maw (UK *Yak* i mah)

Yakutsk, Russia : Ya *koohtsk* (UK Ya *kootsk*)

Yalding, England : *Yawl* ding

Yalta, Ukraine : *Yawl* ta (UK *Yal* ta)

Yalutorovsk, Russia : Ya *looh* ta rufsk

Yamagata, Japan : *Yah* mah gah tah

Yamal, Russia : Ya *mahl*

Yamato, Japan : Yah *mah* toh

Yambol, Bulgaria : *Yahm* bohl

Yamoussoukro, Côte d'Ivoire : Yah mooh *sooh* kroh

Yan'an, China : Ya *nahn*

Yancheng, China : Yan *cheng*

Yangon, Myanmar : Yahng *gohn*

Yangquan, China : Yahng *chwen*

Yangton, USA : *Yangk* tun

Yangtze, China : *Yahng* tsi

Yangzhou, China : Yahng *joh* (UK Yang *joh*)

Yantai, China : Yan *tiy*

Yao, Japan : *Yah* oh

Yaoundé, Cameroon : Yown *day* (UK Yah *oon* day)

Yap, Pacific Ocean : Yahp (UK Yap)

Yapen, Indonesia : *Yah* pun

Yaqui, USA : *Yah* ki

Yarkand, China : Yahr *kahnd*

Yarmouth, Canada; England; USA : *Yahr* muth (UK *Yah* muth)

Yaroslavl, Russia : Yah ra *slah* vul

Yass, Australia : Yas

Yasuj, Iran : Yaw *soohj*

Yauco, Puerto Rico : *Yow* koh

Yautepec, Mexico : Yow tay *pek*

Yazd, Iran : Yazd

Yazoo, USA : Ya *zooh*

Yeading, England : *Yed* ing [The pronunciation of the London district's name corresponds to earlier spellings, such as *Yeddings* in 1325.]

> In spite of the unhistorical modern spelling, the pronunciation of the name is "Yedding" [A.D. Mills, *A Dictionary of London Place Names*, 2001].

¹Yeadon, England : *Yee* dun

²Yeadon, USA : *Yay* dun

Yealmpton, England : *Yamp* tun

Yegoryevsk, Russia : Yi *gawr* yifsk

Yekaterinburg, Russia : Yi *kat* ur in buhrg (UK Yi *kat* a rin buhg) (Russian Yi ka ti reem *boork*)

Yekepa, Liberia : Ye *kay* pa

Yelets, Russia : Yi *lyets*

Yell, Scotland : Yel

Yellowknife, Canada : *Yel* oh niyf

Yellowstone, USA : *Yel* oh stohn

Yelverton, England : *Yel* vur tun (UK *Yel* va tun) [The name of the Devon town is recorded in 1765 as *Elverton*, and a nearby farm is still *Elfordtown*. Local dialect pronunciation produced the present spelling with *Y*, which was adopted by the Great Western Railway when they built a station here in 1859.]

Yemen, Asia : *Yem* en

Yenangyaung, Myanmar : Ye nahn *jown*

Yendi, Ghana : *Yen* di

Yenisey, Russia : Yen i *say* (Russian Yi ni *syay*)

Yeniseysk, Russia : Yi ni *syaysk*

Yeovil, England : *Yoh* vil

Yerba Buena (Island), USA : Yer ba *Bway* na (UK Yay a ba...)

Yerevan, Armenia : Yer a *vahn* (UK Yer a *van*) (Russian Yi ri *vahn*)

Yessentuki, Russia : Yus un too *kee*

Yevpatoriya, Ukraine : Yif pa *toh* ri ya

Yeysk, Russia : Yaysk

Yibin, China : Ee *bin*

Yichang, China : Ee *chahng*

Yichun, China : Ee *choon*

Yiewsley, England : *Yoohz* li [The spelling of the London district's name was earlier *Wewesley*, which could have given a modern pronunciation *Woohz* li.]

The development of the modern pronunciation and spelling ... is to be noted [A.D. Mills, *A Dictionary of London Place Names*, 2001].

Yinchuan, China : Yin *chwahn*

Yingkou, China : Ying *koh*

Yogyakarta, Indonesia : Yahg ya *kahr* ta (UK Yog ya *kah* ta)

Yokkaichi, Japan : Yoh *kiy* chee

Yokohama, Japan : Yoh koh *hah* mah

Yokosuka, Japan : Yoh *koh* sa kah

Yola, Nigeria : *Yoh* lah

Yonezawa, Japan : Yoh *nay* zah wah

Yonkers, USA : *Yahng* kurz (UK *Yong* kuz)

Yonne, France : Yawn

Yopal, Colombia : Yoh *pahl*

Yorba Linda, USA : Yawr ba *Lin* da (UK Yaw ba...)

York, Canada; England; USA : Yawrk (UK Yawk)

Yorkton, Canada : *Yawrk* tun (UK *Yawk* tun)

Yorktown, USA : *Yawrk* town (UK *Yawk* town)

Yoro, Honduras : *Yoh* roh

Yosemite (Falls), USA : Yoh *sem* a ti

Yoshkar-Ola, Russia : Yush kahr A *lah*

Youghal, Ireland : Yawl

Youghiogheny, USA : Yah ka *gay* ni

Youngstown, USA : *Yahngz* town

Youssoufia, Morocco : Yoo *sooh* fi a

Yozgat, Turkey : Yawz *gaht*

Ypres, Belgium : *Eep* ra (French Eepr) [A World War I army rendering of the town's name as *Wiy* puz is legendary, featuring in written form as *Wipers* in popular literature.]

Ypsilanti, USA : Ip sa *lan* ti

Yreka, USA : Wiy *ree* ka

Ystad, Sweden : *Ee* stahd

Ystalyfera, Wales : Ahs ta la *ver* a

Ystradgynlais, Wales : Ahs trud *gahn* liys

Yuba, USA : *Yooh* ba

Yucaipa, USA : Yooh *kiy* pa

Yucatán, Mexico : Yooh ka *tan* (UK Yoo ka *tahn*) (Spanish Yooh kah *tahn*)

Yugoslavia, Europe : Yooh goh *slah* vi a

Yukon, Canada : *Yooh* kahn (UK *Yooh* kon)

Yuma, USA : *Yooh* ma

Yumen, China : Yee *men*

Yundum, Gambia : *Yoohn* doohm

Yunnan, China : Yee *nahn*

Yuriria, Mexico : Yooh *ree* ree ah

Yuscarán, Honduras : Yooh skah *rahn*

Yuzhno-Sakhalinsk, Russia : Yoohzh na Sa kha *linsk*

Yvelines, France : Eev *leen*
Yverdon-les-Bains, Switzerland : Ee ver dohn lay *Bahn*
Zaandam, Netherlands : Zahn *dahm*
Zaanstad, Netherlands : *Zahn* staht
Zabol, Iran : Zah *bohl*
Zabrze, Poland : *Zahb* zhe
Zacapa, Guatemala : Sah *kah* pah
Zacapu, Mexico : Sah *kah* pooh
Zacatecas, Mexico : Sah kah *tay* kahs
Zacatecoluca, El Salvador : Sah kah tay koh *looh* kah
Zacatlán, Mexico : Sah kaht *lahn*
Zadar, Croatia : *Zah* dahr
Zagazig, Egypt : Za *gah* zig
Zaghouan, Tunisia : Zah *gwahn*
Zagreb, Croatia : *Zah* greb
Zahedan, Iran : Zah hi *dahn*
Zahlah, Lebanon : *Zah* la
Zaire, Africa : Zah *i* ur (UK Ziy *i* a)
Zákinthos, Greece : *Zah* ken thaws
Zakopane, Poland : Zah kaw *pah* ne
Zalaegerszeg, Hungary : *Zaw* law eg er seg
Zalău, Romania : Za *low*
Zama, Tunisia : *Zay* ma
Zambezi, Africa : Zam *bee* zi
Zambia, Africa : *Zam* bi a
Zamboanga, Philippines : Zahm boh *ahng* gah
Zamora, Spain : Sah *moh* rah
Zamość, Poland : *Zah* mawshch
Zandvoort, Netherlands : *Zahnt* vohrt
Zanesville, USA : *Zaynz* vil
Zanjan, Iran : Zan *jahn*
Zante, Greece : *Zan* ti (Greek *Dzahn* tay)
Zanzibar, Tanzania : Zan zi *bahr* (UK Zan zi *bah*)
Zapopan, Mexico : Sah poh *pahn*
Zaporizhzhya, Ukraine : Za pa *reezh* zhya
Zaporozhye, Ukraine : Za pa *roh* zha
Zárate, Argentina : *Zah* rah tay
Zaria, Ethiopia; Nigeria : *Zah* ri a
Zarqa, Jordan : *Zahr* ka (UK *Zah* ka)
Żary, Poland : *Zhah* ri
Zawia, Libya : *Zah* wi a
Zduńska Wola, Poland : Zdoohn skah *Vaw* lah

Zeebrugge, Belgium : Zay *broog* a (Flemish *Zay* bree kha) [English speakers formerly favored a pronunciation Zee *broog* a for the town. The name itself denotes a seaport (Flemish *zee*, "sea") for *Brugge*, the Flemish form of **Bruges**.]
Zeeland, Netherlands : *Zee* lund (Dutch *Zay* lahnt)
Zefat, Israel : *Tse* faht
Zeist, Netherlands : Ziyst
Zeitz, Germany : Tsiyts
Zele, Belgium : Zay la
Zelenodolsk, Russia : Zi lyaw na *dawlsk*
Zenica, Bosnia-Herzegovina : Ze *neet* sah
Zenjan, Iran : Zen *jahn*
Zennor, England : *Zen* ur (UK *Zen* a)
Zerbst, Germany : Tserpst
Zermatt, Switzerland : Tser *maht* (UK *Zuh* mat) (German Tser *maht*)
Zetland, Scotland : *Zet* lund
Zevenaar, Netherlands : Zay va *nahr*
Zgierz, Poland : Zgyesh
Zhambyl, Kazakhstan : Zhahm *bil*
Zhangjiakou, China : Jahng jyah *koh*
Zhejiang, China : Juh *jyahng*
Zheleznogorsk, Russia : Zhi liz na *gawrsk*
Zhengzhou, China : Jeng *joh*
Zhezqazghan, Kazakhstan : Zhez kuz *gahn*
Zhigulevsk, Russia : Zhi gul *yawfsk*
Zhitomir, Ukraine : Zhi *taw* mir
Zhlobin, Belarus : Zhloh *byin*
Zhuhai, China : Jooh *hiy*
Zhukovskiy, Russia : Zhooh *kawf* ski
Zhuzhou, China : Jooh *joh*
Zhytomyr, Ukraine : Zhi *taw* mir
Zibo, China : Zi *boh*
Zielona Góra, Poland : Zhe law nah *Gooh* rah
Ziguinchor, Senegal : Zee gahn *shawr*
Zile, Turkey : Zi *lay*
Žilina, Slovakia : *Zhee* lee nah
Zimbabwe, Africa : Zim *bahb* wi
Zinder, Niger : *Zin* dur (UK *Zin* da)
Zion, Israel; USA : *Ziy* un
Zitácuaro, Mexico : Zi *tah* kwah roh

Zittau, Germany : *Tsit* ow
Zlatoust, Russia : Zlah ta *oohst*
Zlín, Czech Republic : Zleen
Znojmo, Czech Republic : *Znoy* maw
Zoersel, Belgium : *Zoor* sel
Zoetermeer, Netherlands : Zooh tur *mahr*
Zomba, Malawi : *Zohm* bah
Zonguldak, Turkey : Zawn gool *dahk*
Zonhoven, Belgium : *Zawn* hoh vun (French Zaw no *vayn*)
Zouirat, Mauritania : Zwee *raht*
Zrenjanin, Serbia : *Zren* ya nin
Zug, Switzerland : Tsoohk
Zugspitze, Germany : *Tsoohk* shpit sa
Zuider Zee, Netherlands : Ziy dur *Zee* (UK Ziy da...) (Dutch Ziy dur *Zay*)
Zululand, South Africa : *Zooh* looh land

Zürich, Switzerland : *Zoor* ik (UK *Zoo* a rik) (German *Tsee* rikh) [An alternate English pronunciation of the city's name is *Zyoo* a rik.]
Zutphen, Netherlands : *Zeet* fa
Zvishavane, Zimbabwe : Zvee shah *vah* nay
Zweibrücken, Germany : Tsfiy *bree* kun
Zwelitsha, South Africa : *Zway* lit shah
Zwickau, Germany : *Tsfik* ow
Zwijndrecht, Belgium : *Zviyn* drekht
Zwolle, Netherlands : *Zvaw* la
Żyrardów, Poland : Zhi *rahr* doohf
Zyryanovsk, Kazakhstan : Zur *yah* nufsk
Żywiec, Poland : *Zhi* vets

Appendix:
The Pronunciation
of Native Names

The three listings below give the pronunciations of the native names of well-known countries, regions (including islands), and cities where they differ from the English, or where the English has come to differ from the native. The difference may be total, as for **Suomi**, or simply the matter of a single letter or accent, as **Roma** and **Cádiz**. Where the names are absolutely identical, as **France**, **Liguria**, or **Oslo**, the indigenous pronunciation is given in the main entry. The English name follows the native in parentheses, as **Deutschland** (Germany). The actual locations of the named places (country in continent, region or city in country) can be found, as necessary, in the main entries or in any atlas or gazetteer. However, the name of the language that follows the transcription in parentheses will itself serve as an indication of the location, as Kah tah *looh* nyah (Spanish) for **Cataluña** (Catalonia). It should be borne in mind, even so, that some countries have a native language that is primarily associated with another country. In Austria, for example, the official language is

German, while in Belgium it is French or Flemish (Dutch). In Mexico and Brazil it is respectively Spanish and Portuguese, as a consequence of those countries' colonial history.

Names of places that now generally appear in their indigenous form (or a transcription thereof) rather than in an English or other rendering, as **Guangzhou** for formerly familiar **Canton**, do not appear here, but in the main part of the dictionary, where both forms appear. This means that the English or non-native names below are by and large still in regular English usage, appearing as the primary form in gazetteers and encyclopedias. The London *Times* of June 22, 2006, thus carried news reports from **Athens**, **Moscow**, and **Prague**, not **Athínai**, **Moskva**, and **Praha**. (Even so, as recently as 2003 *The Times Style and Usage Guide* recommended the use of **Gothenburg** rather than Swedish **Göteborg**. However, it drew the line at **Leghorn** for **Livorno**, while its sole comment on **Nuremberg** was a note to spell the name with *-berg*, not *-burg*, assuming its standard use for German **Nürnberg**.)

219

Where a historical region is now located in more than one country, as Savoy in France (**Savoie**) and Italy (**Savoia**), it appears under the respective native names. Conversely, a single country or region may be known by more than one native name, as Switzerland, which is respectively Romansh **Helvetica**, German **Schweiz**, French **Suisse**, and Italian **Svizzera**. By definition, a non–English name for a non-native place, as Italian *Parigi* for Paris, France, will not appear here. At the end of each listing, an English index refers the English names to the indigenous, as Japan : Nihon.

Countries

België (Belgium) : *Bel* khee a (Flemish)
Belgique (Belgium) : Bel *zheek* (French)
Bharat (India) : *Buh* rut (Sanskrit)
Brasil (Brazil) : Brah *zeel* (Portuguese)
Bŭlgariya (Bulgaria) : Bool *gah* ree yah (Bulgarian)
Crna Gora (Montenegro) : Tsur na *Goh* ra (Serbo-Croat)
Danmark (Denmark) : *Dahn* mahrk (Danish)
Deutschland (Germany) : *Doych* lahnt (German)
Eesti (Estonia) : *Ay* stee (Estonia)
Éire (Ireland) : *Er* a (Irish)
Ellás (Greece) : E *lahs* (Greek)
España (Spain) : Ay *spah* nyah (Spanish)
Hayasdan (Armenia) : Hah yus *dahn* (Armenian)
Helvetica (Switzerland) : Hel *vay* tee ka (Romansh)
Hrvatska (Croatia) : Hur *vaht* skah (Croatian)
Island (Iceland) : *Ees* lahn (Icelandic)
Italia (Italy) : Ee *tah* lyah (Italian)
Kibris (Cyprus) : *Kee* bris (Turkish)
Kypros (Cyprus) : *Kee* praws (Greek)
Latvija (Latvia) : *Laht* vee yah (Latvian)

Lietuva (Lithuania) : Lye *tooh* vah (Lithuanian)
Magyarország (Hungary) : *Maw* jawr awr sahg (Hungarian)
Makedonija (Macedonia) : Mah ke *daw* ni ya (Macedonian)
Méjico (Mexico) : *Me* hee koh (Spanish)
Mişr (Egypt) : Misr (Arabic)
Nederland (Netherlands) : *Nay* dur lahnt (Dutch)
Nihon (Japan) : Nee *hawn* (Japanese)
Norge (Norway) : *Nawr* ga (Norwegian)
Österreich (Austria) : *Uhs* tur riykh (German)
Panamá (Panama) : Pah nah *mah* (Spanish)
Perú (Peru) : Pay *rooh* (Spanish)
Polska (Poland) : *Pawl* skah (Polish)
România (Romania) : Roh *mah* nyah (Romanian)
Rossiya (Russia) : Ra *see* ya (Russian)
Sakartvelo (Georgia) : Sah *kahrt* ve loh (Georgian)
Schweiz (Switzerland) : Shviyts (German)
Shqipëri (Albania) : Shkyee pa *ree* (Albanian)
Slovenija (Slovenia) : Slaw *vay* nee yah (Slovene)
Slovensko (Slovakia) : Slaw *ven* skaw (Slovak)
Srbija (Serbia) : *Sur* bee yah (Serbian)
Suisse (Switzerland) : Swees (French)
Suomi (Finland) : *Swaw* mee (Finnish)
Sverige (Sweden) : *Svar* ya (Swedish)
Svizzera (Switzerland) : *Zveet* say rah (Italian)
Türkiye (Turkey) : Teer kee *ye* (Turkish)
Ukrayina (Ukraine) : Ooh krah *ee* nah (Ukrainian)

Cyprus : (1) Kibris; (2) Kypros
Denmark : Danmark
Egypt : Mişr
Estonia : Eesti
Finland : Suomi
Georgia : Sakartvelo
Germany : Deutschland
Greece : Ellás
Hungary : Magyarország
Iceland : Island
India : Bharat
Ireland : Éire
Italy : Italia
Japan : Nihon
Latvia : Latvija
Lithuania : Lietuva
Macedonia : Makedonija
Mexico : Méjico
Montenegro : Crna Gora
Netherlands : Nederland
Norway : Norge
Panama : Panamá
Peru : Perú
Poland : Polska
Romania : România
Russia : Rossiya
Serbia : Srbija
Slovakia : Slovensko
Slovenia : Slovenija
Spain : España
Sweden : Sverige
Switzerland : (1) Helvetica; (2) Schweiz;
(3) Suisse; (4) Svizzera
Turkey : Türkiye
Ukraine : Ukrayina

Regions

Açores (Azores) : A *soh* rish (Portuguese)
Aitolía (Aetolia) : E toh *lee* ah (Greek)
Akhaïa (Achaea) : A *khiy* a (Greek)
Almería (Almeria) : Ahl may *ree* ah (Spanish)
Anadolu (Anatolia) : Ah nah doh *looh* (Turkish)
Andalucía (Andalusia) : Ahn dhah looh *thee* ah (Spanish)
Aragón (Aragon) : Ah rah *gohn* (Spanish)

Arkadhía (Arcadia) : Ahr kah *dhee* ah (Greek)
Attikí (Attica) : Ah tee *kee* (Greek)
Baleares (Balearic Islands) : Bah lay *ah* rays (Spanish)
Bayern (Bavaria) : *Biy* yuhrn (German)
Berner Oberland (Bernese Oberland) : Ber nuhr *Oh* buhr lahnt (German)
Böhmen (Bohemia) : *Buh* mun (German)
Bosna (Bosnia) : *Baws* nah (Serbo-Croat)
Bourgogne (Burgundy) : Boohr *goyn* (French)
Braunschweig (Brunswick) : *Brown* shfiyk (German)
Bretagne (Brittany) : Bre *tiyn* (French)
Canarias (Canary Islands) : Kah *nahr* yahs (Spanish)
Castilla (Castile) : Kah *stee* lyah (Spanish)
Cataluña (Catalonia) : Kah tah *looh* nyah (Spanish)
Catalunya (Catalonia) : Kah tah *looh* nyah (Catalan)
Corse (Corsica) : Kawrs (French)
Dalmacija (Dalmatia) : Dahl *maht* see yah (Serbo-Croat)
Dhodhekánisos (Dodecanese) : Dhoh dhe *kah* nee saws (Greek)
Erdély (Transylvania) : Er *day* (Hungarian)
Évvoia (Euboea) : *E* vee ah (Greek)
Færøerne (Faeroe Islands) : Fa *roh* uhr na (Danish)
Flandre (Flanders) : Flahndr (French)
Franken (Franconia) : *Frahng* kun (German)
Gascogne (Gascony) : Gahs *koyn* (French)
Halicz (Galicia) : *Hah* lich (Polish)
Hessen (Hesse) : *Hes* un (German)
Itháki (Ithaca) : Ee *thah* kee (Greek)
Jylland (Jutland) : *Yee* lawn (Danish)
Kalaallit Nunaat (Greenland) : Kah laht leet Noo *naht* (Greenlandic)
Kärnten (Carinthia) : *Kern* tun (German)
Kefallinía (Cephalonia) : Ke fah lee *nee* ah (Greek)

Kérkyra (Corfu) : Ker kee rah (Greek)
Kikládhes (Cyclades) : Kee klah dhes (Greek)
Kórinthos (Corinth) : Kaw reen thaws (Greek)
Krain (Carniola) : Kriyn (German)
Kríti (Crete) : Kree tee (Greek)
Krym (Crimea) : Krim (Russian)
Lakonía (Laconia) : Lah koh nee ah (Greek)
Lappi (Lapland) : Lahp pee (Finnish)
Lappland (Lapland) : Lahp land (Swedish)
Limbourg (Limburg) : Lahm boohr (French)
Lombardia (Lombardy) : Lawm bahr dee ah (Italian)
Luzern (Lucerne) : Looh tsern (German)
Magnisía (Magnesia) : Mahg nee see ah (Greek)
Mähren (Moravia) : May run (German)
Makedonia (Macedonia) : Mah ke dhoh nee ah (Greek)
Mallorca (Majorca) : Mah lyawr kah (Spanish)
Menorca (Minorca) : May nawr kah (Spanish)
Messínia (Messenia) : Me see nyah (Greek)
Morava (Moravia) : Maw rah vah (Czech)
Navarra (Navarre) : Nah vahr rah (Spanish)
Normandie (Normandy) : Nawr mahn dee (French)
Picardie (Picardy) : Pee kahr dee (French)
Piemonte (Piedmont) : Pyay mawn tay (Italian)
Pommern (Pomerania) : Pawm uhrn (German)
Preussen (Prussia) : Proy sun (German)
Rheinland (Rhineland) : Riyn lahnt (German)
Sachsen (Saxony) : Zahk sun (German)
Sardegna (Sardinia) : Sahr dayn yah (Italian)
Savoia (Savoy) : Sah vaw yah (Italian)
Savoie (Savoy) : Sah vwah (French)

Schlesien (Silesia) : Shlay zee un (German)
Schwaben (Swabia) : Shvah bun (German)
Sibir' (Siberia) : Si bir (Russian)
Sicilia (Sicily) : See chee lyah (Italian)
Siebenbürgen (Transylvania) : Zee bun beer gun (German)
Slavonija (Slavonia) : Slah vaw nee yah (Serbian)
Sporádhes (Sporades) : Spaw rah dhes (Greek)
Thessalía (Thessaly) : Thay sah lee ah (Greek)
Steiermark (Styria) : Shtiy ur mahrk (German)
(Greek)
Thráki (Thrace) : Thrah kee (Greek)
Thüringen (Thuringia) : Tee ring un (German)
Toscana (Tuscany) : Toh skah nah (Italian)
Transilvania (Transylvania) : Trahn seel vahn yah (Romanian)
Venezia (Venetia) : Vay net syah (Italian)
Vlaanderen (Flanders) : Vlahn da run (Flemish)
Voiotía (Boeotia) : Vyaw tee a (Greek)
Wallonie (Wallonia) : Wah law nee (French)
Westfalen (Westphalia) : Vest fah lun (German)
Xianggang (Hong Kong) : Shyahng gahng (Chinese)

Achaea : Akhaïa
Aetolia : Aitolía
Almeria : Almería
Anatolia : Anadolu
Andalusia : Andalucía
Aragon : Aragón
Arcadia : Arkadhía
Attica : Attikí
Azores : Açores
Balearic Islands : Baleares
Bavaria : Bayern
Boeotia : Voiotía
Bohemia : Böhmen
Bosnia : Bosna

Brittany : Bretagne
Brunswick : Braunschweig
Burgundy : Bourgogne
Bernese Oberland : Berner Oberland
Canary Islands : Canarias
Carinthia : Kärnten
Carniola : Krain
Castile : Castilla
Catalonia : (1) Cataluña, (2) Catalunya
Cephalonia : Kefallinía
Corfu : Kérkyra
Corinth : Kórinthos
Corsica : Corse
Crete : Kríti
Crimea : Krim
Cyclades : Kikládhes
Dalmatia : Dalmacija
Dodecanese : Dhodhekánisos
Euboea : Évvoia
Faeroe Islands : Færøerne
Flanders : (1) Flandre; (2) Vlaanderen
Franconia : Franken
Galicia : Halicz
Gascony : Gascogne
Greenland : Kalaallit Nunaat
Hesse : Hessen
Hong Kong : Xianggang
Ithaca : Itháki
Jutland : Jylland
Laconia : Lakonía
Lapland : (1) Lappi; (2) Lappland
Limburg : Limbourg
Lombardy : Lombardia
Lucerne : Luzern
Macedonia : Makedonia
Magnesia : Magnisía
Majorca : Mallorca
Minorca : Menorca
Moravia : (1) Mähren, (2) Morava
Navarre : Navarra
Normandy : Normandie
Picardy : Picardie
Piedmont : Piemonte
Pomerania : Pommern
Prussia : Preussen
Rhineland : Rheinland
Sardinia : Sardegna
Savoy : (1) Savoia, (2) Savoie
Saxony : Sachsen

Siberia : Sibir'
Sicily : Sicilia
Silesia : Schlesien
Slavonia : Slavonija
Sporades : Sporádhes
Styria : Steiermark
Swabia : Schwaben
Thessaly : Thessalía
Thrace : Thráki
Thuringia : Thüringen
Transylvania : (1) Erdély; (2) Siebenbür-
   gen; (3) Transilvania
Tuscany : Toscana
Venetia : Venezia
Wallonia : Wallonie
Westphalia : Westfalen

Cities

'Akko (Acre) : *Ah* koh (Hebrew)
Al Iskandariyah (Alexandria) : Al Is
   jahn dah *ree* ya (Arabic)
Al Jaza'ir (Algiers) : Al Ja *zah* ir (Arabic)
Al Quds (Jerusalem) : Al *Koohts* (Arabic)
Antwerpen (Antwerp) : *Ahnt* wer pun
   (Flemish)
Anvers (Antwerp) : Ahn *ver* (French)
Athínai (Athens) : Ah *thee* ne (Greek)
Baile Átha Cliath (Dublin) : Blah *klee* a
   (Irish)
Béal Feirste (Belfast) : Bee ul *Fersh* chi
   (Irish)
Beograd (Belgrade) : Bay *aw* grahd
   (Serbo-Croat)
Braunschweig (Brunswick) : *Brown*
   shfiyk (German)
Brugge (Bruges) : *Bree* kha (Flemish)
   [*See also* **Zeebrugge** in Dictionary.]
Brussel (Brussels) : *Bree* sel (Flemish)
Bruxelles (Brussels) : Bree *sel* (French)
Bucureşti (Bucharest) : Booh kooh *resht*
   (Romanian)
Cádiz (Cadiz) : *Kah* dheeth (Spanish)
Caerdydd (Cardiff) : *Kiyr* didh (Welsh)
Dar el Beida (Casablanca) : Dahr el *Biy*
   dah (Arabic)
Den Haag (The Hague) : Dun *Hahkh*
   (Dutch)
Dhelfoí (Delphi) : Dhel *fee* (Greek)

Dimashq (Damascus) : Di *mahshk* (Arabic)

Dumyat (Damietta) : Doom *yaht* (Arabic)

Dunkerque (Dunkirk) : Duhn *kerk* (French)

El Qâhira (Cairo) : El *Kah* hee ra (Arabic)

Firenze (Florence) : Fee *rent* say (Italian)

Gand (Ghent) : Gahn (French)

Genève (Geneva) : Zhe *nayv* (French)

Genf (Geneva) : Genf (German)

Genova (Genoa) : *Jen* oh vah (Italian)

Gent (Ghent) : Khent (Flemish)

Ginevra (Geneva) : Jee *nay* vrah (Italian)

Haleb (Aleppo) : *Ha* lab (Arabic)

Hannover (Hanover) : *Hah* noh vur (German)

Hoek van Holland (Hook of Holland) : Hoohk vahn *Haw* lahnt (Dutch)

Iráklion (Heraklion) : Ee *rahk* lee ohn (Greek)

København (Copenhagen) : Kuh bun *hown* (Danish)

Köln (Cologne) : Kuhln (German)

Kórinthos (Corinth) : *Kaw* reen thaws (Greek)

La Habana (Havana) : Lah Ah *bah* nah (Spanish)

Lisboa (Lisbon) : Leezh *voh* a (Portuguese)

Luzern (Lucerne) : Looh *tsern* (German)

Makkah (Mecca) : *Mah* ka (Arabic)

Malines (Mechlin) : Mah *leen* (French)

Mantova (Mantua) : *Mahn* toh vah (Italian)

Mechelen (Mechlin) : *May* kha lun (Flemish)

Milano (Milan) : Mee *lah* noh (Italian)

Moskva (Moscow) : Mahsk *vah* (Russian)

München (Munich) : *Meen* khun (German) [See also note on **Munich** in Dictionary.]

Napoli (Naples) : *Nah* poh lee (Italian)

Oostende (Ostend) : Oh *sten* da (Flemish)

Ostende (Ostend) : Aw *stahnd* (French)

Padova (Padua) : *Pah* doh vah (Italian)

Praha (Prague) : *Prah* hah (Czech)

Rashid (Rosetta) : Rah *sheed* (Arabic)

Roma (Rome) : *Roh* mah (Italian)

Sankt-Peterburg (St. Petersburg) : Sahnkt Pi tir *boork* (Russian)

Sevilla (Seville) : Say *veel* yah (Spanish)

's Gravenhage (The Hague) : Skhrah vun *hah* kha (Dutch)

Sofiya (Sofia) : *Saw* fee yah (Bulgarian)

Thessaloníki (Thessalonica or Salonica) : Thes ah loh *nee* kee (Greek)

Thívai (Thebes) : *Thee* ve (Greek)

Tiranë (Tirana) : Ti *rah* na (Albanian)

Torino (Turin) : Toh *ree* noh (Italian)

Venezia (Venice) : Vay *net* syah (Italian)

Warszawa (Warsaw) : Vahr *shah* vah (Polish)

Wien (Vienna) : Veen (German)

Yerushalayim (Jerusalem) : Ye rooh shah *liy* im (Hebrew)

Zaragoza (Saragossa) : Thah rah *goh* thah (Spanish)

Acre : 'Akko

Aleppo : Haleb

Alexandria : Al Iskandariyah

Algiers : Al Jaza'ir

Antwerp : (1) Antwerpen, (2) Anvers

Athens : Athínai

Belfast : Béal Feirste

Belgrade : Beograd

Bruges : Brugge

Brunswick : Braunschweig

Brussels : (1) Brussel, (2) Bruxelles

Bucharest : Bucureşti

Cadiz : Cádiz

Cairo : El Qâhira

Cardiff : Caerdydd

Casablanca : Dar el Beida

Cologne : Köln

Copenhagen : København

Corinth : Kórinthos

Damascus : Dimashq

Damietta : Dumyat

Delphi : Dhelfoí

Dublin : Baila Átha Cliath

Dunkirk : Dunkerque

Florence : Firenze

Geneva : (1) Genève, (2) Genf, (3) Ginevra
Genoa : Genova
Ghent : (1) Gand, (2) Gent
Hague, The : (1) Den Haag; (2) 's Gravenhage
Hanover : Hannover
Havana : La Habana
Heraklion : Iráklion
Hook of Holland : Hoek van Holland
Jerusalem : (1) Al Quds, (2) Yerushalayim
Lisbon : Lisboa
Lucerne : Luzern
Mantua : Mantova
Mecca : Makkah
Mechlin : (1) Malines; (2) Mechelen
Milan : Milano
Moscow : Moskva
Munich : München

Naples : Napoli
Ostend : (1) Oostende, (2) Ostende
Padua : Padova
Prague : Praha
Rome : Roma
Rosetta : Rashid
St. Petersburg : Sankt-Peterburg
Salonica : Thessaloníki
Saragossa : Zaragoza
Seville : Sevilla
Sofia : Sofiya
Thebes : Thívai
The Hague *see* Hague, The
Thessalonica : Thessaloníki
Tirana : Tiranë
Turin : Torino
Venice : Venezia
Vienna : Wien
Warsaw : Warszawa

Select Bibliography

For purposes of placename pronunciations worldwide, the key works in the list below are Cohen and *Merriam-Webster*. Unfortunately, Cohen is neither reliable nor consistent. The pronunciation of many placenames is omitted, and in some instances simply incorrect. Thus, to take only Volume 1 (A to G), and with random reference to some well-known British names, *Bacup* does not rhyme with *back up* but with *bake up*, *Brechin* has a first syllable rhyming with *beak*, not *beck*, *Calne* rhymes with *calm*, not *corn*, *Carnoustie* and *Dumfries* are stressed on the second syllable, not the first, *Dalbeattie* has a second syllable *beet* not *bate*, and the first syllable of *Gourock* rhymes with *coo*, not *cow*. Elsewhere, the name of the French city of *Reims* is not pronounced (to use the work's own notation) "RAIM" any more than that of the German city of *Ziegen* is "SEE-gen." Such errors tarnish the trustworthiness of an otherwise impressively detailed reference work.

Merriam-Webster must thus be the prime resource for pronunciations, although its 48,000 entries cannot compete with Cohen, which has 40,000 entries for the United States alone.

Forster is good on English (rather than British) placenames, with local and archaic variant pronunciations, while Pointon, although embracing personal names as well as placenames, is a reliable resource, with pronunciations in both the International Phonetic Alphabet and a system devised for the general reader (essentially the difference between coded and clear). Wells has many proper names, including placenames, among its 135,000 pronunciations, which are specifically based on the preferences of both American and British speakers. The same goes for Jones, with over 80,000 entries. (Jones himself died in 1967, but the noted phonetician's name is preserved as author of the successive revised editions of his seminal *An English Pronouncing Dictionary*, first published in 1917.) Neither Wells nor Jones gives locational information in placename entries and there is no differentiation between placenames and personal or family names, so that *Gorringe*, say, could well be either. Pointon does distinguish, however, with placenames located by county or region and family names marked "*f.n.*" On the other hand, Wells and Jones do indicate locations for identically spelled placenames, as *Hobart*, Australia, and *Hobart*, Indiana, USA, in Wells, and *Aden*

in Jones, where the pronunciations are respectively for places "in the [*sic*] Yemen" and "in Grampian region." (The latter Aden, a country park near Aberdeen, is hardly a major name. For sake of completeness, however, it can be indicated here that its name is pronounced *A* dun.) Jones also has several "information panels," one of which, "Names of people and places," cites the five English placenames *Alnwick, Cirencester, Lympne, Woolfardisworthy,* and *Worcester* (as well as the two Welsh names *Llanrwst* and *Penmaenmawr*) as being "a few of the most interesting."

Willey does not give pronunciations for all of its London entries, only "whenever there may be doubt." Any transcriptions from Willey, which uses standard English characters with the sole exception of the inverted "e" symbol to denote an indeterminate vowel sound (known phonetically as "schwa"), are adjusted to accord with the present book's system.

Johnston is included purely for its pronunciations, rendered in "free phonetic" form.

Some of the trickier French pronunciations, including those of relatively minor places, were based on those in the 1998 edition of *Le Petit Larousse Illustré,* not listed below.

The dictionary's placename spellings were primarily checked in *Merriam-Webster.* Names not in that work were checked in the three world atlases and the national gazetteer listed last below.

Aurousseau, M. *The Rendering of Geographical Names.* London: Hutchinson University Library, 1957.

Chisholm, George G. *A Pronouncing Vocabulary of Modern Geographical Names.* London: Blackie, n.d. [1885].

Cohen, Saul B., ed. *The Columbia Gazetteer of the World.* New York: Columbia University Press, 1998. 3 vols.

Forster, Klaus. *A Pronouncing Dictionary of English Place-Names.* London: Routledge & Kegan Paul, 1981.

Johnston, James B. *The Place-Names of England and Wales.* London: John Murray, 1914.

Jones, Daniel. *Cambridge English Pronouncing Dictionary,* ed. by Peter Roach, James Hartman, and Jane Setter. 16th ed. Cambridge: Cambridge University Press, 2003.

Leaver, Tony: *Pronouncing Welsh Placenames.* Llanrwst: Carreg Gwalch, 1998.

Lloyd James, A. *Broadcast English II: Recommendations to Announcers Regarding the Pronunciation of Some English Place-Names.* London: British Broadcasting Corporation, 1936.

_____. *Broadcast English VI: Recommendations to Announcers Regarding the Pronunciation of Some Foreign Place-Names* London: British Broadcasting Corporation, 1937.

Longley, Elias. *A Pronouncing Vocabulary of Geographical and Personal Names* (Michigan Historical Reprint Series). Ann Arbor: University of Michigan Library, 2005.

Mencken, H.L. *The American Language.* 4th ed. New York: Alfred A. Knopf, 1943.

Merriam-Webster's Geographical Dictionary. 3d ed. Springfield, MA: Merriam-Webster, 1998.

Pointon, G.E., ed. and transcriber. *BBC Pronouncing Dictionary of British Names.* 2d ed. Oxford: Oxford University Press, 1983.

Ross, Alan S.C. *How to Pronounce It.* London: Hamish Hamilton, 1970.

Wells, J.C. *Longman Pronunciation Dictionary.* 2d ed. Harlow: Pearson Education, 2000.

Willey, Russ. *London Gazetteer.* Edinburgh: Chambers Harrap, 2006.